E. Mellow

ENJOYING NATURE WITH YOUR FAMILY

ENJOYING NATURE WITH YOUR FAMILY

MICHAEL CHINERY

LOOK, LEARN, COLLECT,
CONSERVE. EXPLORE THE WILD LIFE OF
TOWN AND COUNTRY IN FASCINATING
PROJECTS AND EXPERIMENTS.

CROWN PUBLISHERS, INC./NEW YORK

Copyright© Roxby Press Productions Limited 1977
First published in USA 1977
by Crown Publishers, Inc.

Library of Congress Cataloging in Publication Data

Chinery, Michael.
  Enjoying nature with your family.

  Bibliography: p.
  Includes index.
  1. Nature study.   2. Biology—Field work.
3. Biology—Experiments. I. Title.
QH51.C55   574´.028   77-5789
ISBN 0-517-53007-4

Made by Roxby Press Productions,
98 Clapham Common Northside,
London, SW4 9SG

Editorial Director Michael Leitch
Art Director David Pocknell
Design Assistants Michael Cavers, Alan Docherty
Production Reynolds Clark Associates Limited
Phototypeset by SX Composing Limited, Leigh-on-Sea
Reproduction by Interlitho Limited, London
Printed and bound in Spain by TONSA, San Sebastian
and RONER, S. A., Madrid D.L. SS -599/1977

CONTENTS

ACKNOWLEDGMENTS

Many of the projects included in the book have been devised and improved over the years by a number of teachers and naturalists, and the author and publishers would like to thank them for their pioneering work. They also wish to thank The Royal Society for the Protection of Birds for helping with the section on Bird Casualties and several other pages; Mr Ray Goodwin, who contributed the section on Wildlife Sound Recording; Dougal Dixon, for his help with the geological projects; Christine Moat and Carol Barfoot, for much useful advice and help with the chapter on Trees; Cathy Kilpatrick, for her versatile assistance and comments, and Barbara Neill for her advice and contributions on American flora and fauna. The photographs appearing in the book were provided by the author and by Biofotos (Heather Angel), to whom grateful thanks are extended. Finally, the important contribution of the artists must be acknowledged. The consistency and excellence of their illustrations have given the book much of its distinctive character. They are: Ann Winterbotham, who did the colour illustrations, Ken Stott, Richard Draper, Brian Delf, Maggie Raynor, and Alun Hood.

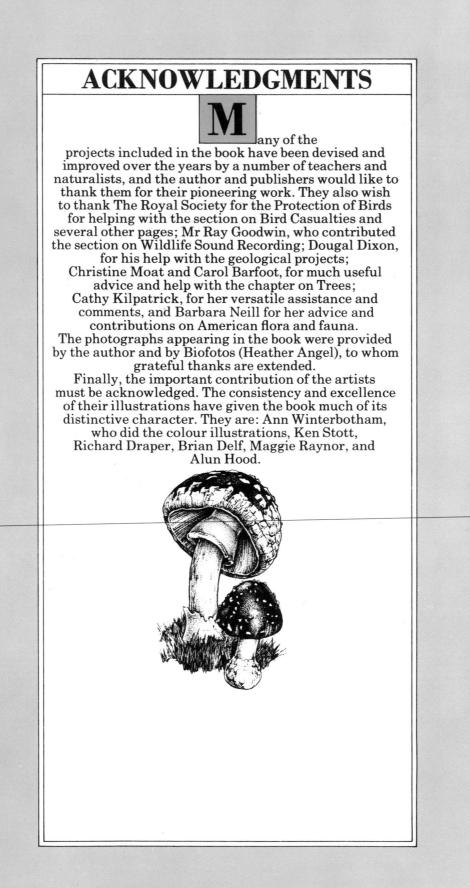

FOREWORD

Nature (if we may combine a billion interlocking miracles into one word) is the ultimate teacher. Never for a single moment are we out from under her influence. From the moment of our birth until our planet reclaims us we are locked into a web of incredible happenings. Our breathing is a miraculous (and extremely complicated) natural event, and so is every sound we hear, every flash of colour our eyes relay to our brains. In every touch, be it soft or rough or hard or smooth, our bodies in their every part are receivers of information – and nature is always the sender.

There is no real place for any of us unless we at least begin to understand that we belong to something larger than ourselves – the cosmos. There is no real peace for any of us unless we at least know that we can fit in. The greatest hope any of us can have for getting along with each other is to know that we are part of one design. That design is nature, the natural systems that control everything around us. For a child to understand that a leaf changing color in the fall or a bud unfolding in the spring is a part of his or her own life is the road to serenity for that child. No lesson is greater than this – we are a part of it all.

Michael Chinery has done something very important in *Enjoying Nature With Your Family*. He has given us a series of projects that both define the natural world and cement us to it. By walking with him and accepting his infectious sense of awe, we move through the natural world in easy stages. Best yet, we are exposed to the whole wonderful world in this series of projects that are more like games than lessons.

It is not a new idea, certainly, that the best way to learn is to do. Michael Chinery shows us how to do and thereby prepares us for the classroom that a good life can be. This book is a project book, but it is also much, much more than that.

Sociologists, psychiatrists, and good old-fashioned common sense tell us that families that share common interests are usually far healthier than those who do not. When the members of a family have things that they enjoy doing together they enjoy each other's company far more. Need anyone say more on that subject? In an age of alienation, dissociation, and drugs, what better way can there be than to return to some proven old values?

When our grandparents were young they pressed flowers, looked for mineral specimens, and collected shells. They drew mammals, insects and birds while recording their comings and goings in meticulously kept nature diaries. Young people knew the names of the flowers beside the road and the lane. They knew the names of the birds and cared where the rabbit had its hole. A visit to an antique shop that features the relics of the so-called Victorian era reveals the activities that have all but vanished from most homes today. First, there was music. People played music, not on high-fi, stereo, 8-track, superphonic, 10-speaker eardrum destroyers but on instruments. Then there was life. People lived life by observing life, instead of seeing it drift before them (between commercials) on 23-inch diagonal, lifelike, colored, stereophonic, self-adjusting, remote-control television sets. It is true, of course, that the youngsters in 1890 could not see a lion hunt an antelope on Sunday afternoon by flicking a switch. They could, however, watch a wren drive a crow away from its nest – outside, in the sunlight – by walking down a lane.

Michael Chinery has capitalized on some old values and truths. He has, in a very real sense, taken us back where we belong. We are, in that often referred-to final analysis, totally dependent on the land and the sky and water. Mr Chinery has linked us to that sky, earth and water by setting up projects that involve them. Every time we look up and see a cloud and understand it, we are closer to understanding ourselves. When we pick up a rock and admire it instead of heaving it at something, we are closer to some ultimate truth. When we hear a bird and stop for the sheer pleasure of that sound, we are far nearer to real life than we were before. When we acknowledge beauty, we benefit from it most. When we feel the texture of the world around us, we are closer to accepting with grace the best it can offer us.

The wise readers of this book will let Mr Chinery (in Chapter 1) take them through the amazing world of weather, show them how to observe and collect small artifacts and mementos of the natural world and make them into things of abiding interest and beauty. They will go with him (in Chapter 2) to visit the amazing life of the pond and the shore. They will beachcomb, and in each succeeding chapter study birds, their feathers and nests, and furred mammals, their tracks and behaviour; insects also are targets of this book's inherent curiosity, as well as trees, leaves and cones, seeds and fruits, flowers, grasses, mosses and ferns, and fossils. The microscope, sound recording and photography too are all fair game for the curious who will let Michael Chinery lead them.

Two suggestions. Don't do all of this alone. If you can, identify someone with whom you would like a closer relationship and do these things together. Miracles will occur. And go in peace. Do not unduly disturb, do not let the urge to collect and to possess outweigh your desire to belong as a non-belligerent. If you bring peace you will reap peace. If you are quiet you will hear. If you are attentive you will see. And if you are loving you will be loved.

Michael Chinery has done something not only worthwhile but vital. The degree to which you benefit depends on you. You can take away far more than you bring with you. *Enjoying Nature With Your Family* can be a most profitable venture.

Roger Caras

The study of the natural world around us must surely be one of the most satisfying of all pastimes. Wherever you live, be it in the middle of a city or deep in the country, you will always be within easy reach of nature: in fact, in most places you are positively surrounded by it and you cannot get away from it even if you try. But why try? We are a part of nature, and we depend upon the other components of the natural system for our very existence. Think what would happen if any part of our natural surroundings were to disappear.

To take a simple, but very important example, consider what would happen if all the world's grasses disappeared overnight. There would be no food for our cattle or for a great many other animals. We would have no cereals to eat, and we would have no lawns or grassy playing fields. Much of the land would become desert, for the grasses play a vital role in binding the soil particles together and preventing them from blowing about. Every component of the living world has its part to play as provider or consumer, or more often as both, and we are inextricably bound up in this system. It is therefore essential that we understand the natural world and respect it, but this should certainly be no chore. The never-ending cycle of natural events provides unlimited fascination for all who care to study it, and with well over a million different kinds of animals and perhaps half a million kinds of plants, there is abundant scope for study.

Nature and the countryside provide a most important 'safety valve' for those people whose lives are centred mainly on built-up areas, and we must not lose sight of this fact when considering future land use.

On the opposite page you can see a picture of nature at work in the spring. It is nature modified to some extent by human activity, in that there are buildings and cultivated fields, but this only serves to increase the diversity of the environment and therefore increases the subjects available for study by the naturalist. The picture also illustrates the various planes or levels on which you can pursue your nature study. You can veer to the geological side of nature (see page 152) and study the whole landscape and its relationship to the underlying rocks; you can relate the various plant communities to the different rocks and soils; you can zoom in close and make a study of one particular kind of plant (in this instance the blackthorn or sloe), and the associated animals; or you can zoom in even closer and study the biology of a flower or an insect in great detail. Another approach would be to study the changes that occur in the habitat during a complete year or over an even longer period. The natural world is a dynamic system, or, more correctly, a collection of dynamic systems, and there is a continuous turnover of life forms for you to observe.

Colonization and the Balance of Nature

In 1883 the island of Krakatoa in Indonesia was blown up and virtually destroyed by a violent volcanic eruption. Men landed on the remains of the island two months after the incident and reported that the blanket of ash and pumice was still hot. It is most unlikely that even the toughest burrowing animal could have survived, and the island was declared lifeless. But within nine months life was returning to the devastated land: a few blades of grass and a solitary spider were found. Sporadic visits were made to the island during the next few years and we know that a monster lizard had arrived, together with many insects, by 1889. A few birds were known to be present by 1896, and by 1908, 25 years after the eruption, the island was once again completely clothed with vegetation. No large-scale investigation was undertaken until 1933, but by comparison with the natural flora and fauna of neighbouring lands it was concluded that some 60 per cent of the animals and nearly all the original plant species had returned.

The island of Surtsey, which rose out of the sea off the coast of Iceland in 1963, carried no terrestrial life when it was born, but only six months later a fly was collected there, and fragments of coastal plants were found on the shore, although none had started to grow. The island now supports a thriving community of plants and animals.

Krakatoa and Surtsey are not commonplace examples, but there are many other situations in which you can study land colonization. Abandoned gravel pits provide expanses of bare rock, and the ever-increasing number of disused railway lines, or remote country roads, provide even more extensive areas of bare ground. Study of such areas over a number of years would be most rewarding because, although the general principles of colonization are known, there is still much to be learned about the detailed interactions between the colonists and the detailed pattern of succession in various habitats.

Colonization of new habitats takes place because animals and plants are continually reaching out, not consciously of course, for new areas. You will see on page 136 how many seeds are carried on air currents or on the backs and legs of various animals. Small animals can also be carried on the backs of larger ones, and some even hitch lifts on floating logs, but these external agencies are not the only ones at work. Internal forces sometimes urge animals to emigrate: well-known examples include the lemmings and the locusts. Most of the animals and plants that reach out in this way fail to survive because they fail to reach suitable places, but such is the power and productivity of nature that at least some usually manage to get through and establish themselves in the new habitats.

New habitats obviously draw most of their plants and animals from nearby areas. A disused railway line or a quarry, for example, will receive abundant seeds from the surrounding vegetation, and in time will become indistinguishable from the surrounding areas. But what about islands, cut off from neighbouring lands by stretches of water? Krakatoa took 50 years to get back 60 per cent of its animal life and it probably never will get back all the

CHAPTER 1

LOOKING AT NATURE

An introduction to the natural world about us, its delicately interlocking systems, and how best to appreciate them lost species, and Surtsey is unlikely ever to get a full complement of Icelandic animals. These islands are not far removed from neighbouring lands and, in time, they will approach the faunal composition of those lands, but time is not the only factor. Most important is the ability of the animals to cross salt water. If a species can survive a sea crossing, then there is a chance that it will reach an island. If a species is physically unable to cross salt water, then there is no chance of its colonizing an island, however much time it is allowed.

The longer the sea crossing, the less chance of success, and so we find that oceanic islands have very poor faunas when compared with off-shore islands. The few animals arriving on oceanic islands find most of the ecological niches unoccupied and they proceed to radiate or branch out along several different lines, each line adapted to a different ecological niche. This means that each develops its own specific feeding habits and occupies slightly different micro-habitats. Not every niche becomes filled on oceanic islands, however, and this is why oceanic faunas are so vulnerable to invasion when man brings along new creatures. Dozens of alien species have become established in New Zealand, where there were almost no native mammals before man arrived.

The Food Chain

Nothing lives alone. Every living organism depends on another for its food. Plants make their own food from simple materials, but they still depend on bacteria to release vital minerals from decaying matter. During the millions of years of evolution our plants and animals have become so adapted that, between them, they fill every possible niche on earth – from the bottoms of the oceans to the mountain tops and the polar ice-caps. Every food-source has been exploited.

Because nothing lives alone, all the plants and animals in a community or a

given area are intricately connected in what may be called the 'web of life'. Food is the major connection between the organisms and, within a community, we can recognize several food chains. Grass – vole – owl is a simple three-link chain, while a typical four-link chain might be leaf – caterpillar – bird – cat. Unless one includes parasites and hyper-parasites (parasites of parasites) in these chains, there are rarely more than four links, but there are, of course, many side links joining one simple chain to another. The two chains given above are linked by the cat, which will eat the vole as well as the bird. If we

take the chains even further – to the death of the final or top predator – we see that they actually come full circle: the dead animal decays and simple substances are released for the plants to absorb and start the cycle all over again.

The food chains might also be called energy chains, because food is concerned very largely with providing energy. Almost all the energy on the earth comes from the sun in the form of heat and light, but it has to be converted into chemical energy before it can be used by animals. This conversion is carried out by plants during the process of

photosynthesis (see page 132) and we therefore find a green plant at the beginning of every food chain. Work out a few food chains for yourself, and you will very soon find that you get back to a green plant or at least its remains. Earthworms, for example, do not at first appear to depend on green plants, but they do actually feed largely on decaying plant matter.

The energy-rich foods made by the plants are passed on to the animals that eat them, and then to other members of the food chain. A great deal of energy is lost at each stage, however, and vast amounts of plant material are necessary to produce just

one animal at the other end of the food chain. For example, it has been calculated that 10,000 tons of planktonic plants must be eaten to produce 1,000 tons of planktonic animals, and that these 1,000 tons of planktonic animals would produce only 100 tons of whale – one blue whale, in other words. This enormous loss of energy at each stage of the food chain is the main reason why food chains rarely have more than four links.

Food is not the only link between the members of a community. Plants, especially the larger ones, have a great effect on their

surroundings by casting shade, withdrawing water from the soil, and so on.

Keeping the food cycle in mind, we come back to the colonization of bare land, such as would be produced in nature by a landslide. The same processes can be observed in man-made situations such as quarries and road cuttings, or disused railway lines. The rate of colonization depends initially on the type of rock exposed: a soft, sandy rock will be covered more quickly than a hard granite. But the process will be rather slow in any event and it will be some years before all the plant and animal species arrive from even just a few metres away. Remembering that nothing lives alone, we see that an animal cannot colonize an area before its food plant is established, any more than an earthworm can invade bare rock. So, although huge numbers of plant seeds and small animals will be carried to the freshly exposed rock, they cannot live there until conditions are suitable. Only lichens (see page 144) and a few hardy mosses can gain a foothold on the bare rock, and these are the pioneer plants. They trap particles of the crumbling rock which, together with the dead plant fragments, form a primitive soil. Other mosses, and perhaps a few small grasses, can grow in this thin layer and they take the process further. As the rock weathers and the soil builds up, the pioneer species are replaced by other plants in a process known as succession and, as more plants establish themselves, more animals are able to come in and fill the niches provided. Eventually, assuming that the rock exposed by the initial landslide or quarrying operation is the same as that on the original surface, the community will return to its original state and will be just like that of the surrounding areas.

Climax Communities

The final nature of the community depends primarily on the climate. It is known as the climax community. It may be rain forest, grassland, deciduous

Copy
pages
10 & 11

Michael Chinery
England.
Enjoying Nature With
Your Family.

forest, or coniferous forest. These are the four great worldwide belts of vegetation. The nature of the plant community will naturally affect the animal community, but the climax community will have all the available niches filled with one species or another. A climax community is therefore a very complex community, and the complexity makes for great stability. No community could be more stable than the tropical rain forests, with up to 3,000 species of trees and shrubs to the square mile. Once it is established, the climax community will survive indefinitely. Only large-scale climatic changes, such as an impending Ice Age, or human intervention, can really upset a climax community.

There is great competition within a community for both food and shelter, and 'survival of the fittest' applies both within and between species. The application of this rule within a species plays some part in population control, and its application between species has led to specialization. No two species in a community can occupy *exactly* the same niche for long – one will always be better adapted, however slightly, and it will gradually replace the other – and so no two species in a community have exactly the same requirements. Even closely related species living together have evolved slightly different feeding habits or nesting habits and fill slightly different niches. The swallow and the house martin are good examples. Both capture their insect food on the wing, but the martins tend to fly a little higher than the swallows, and direct competition is therefore avoided.

With every niche filled, the community settles down to a stable existence and it is said to be 'in balance'. Each species becomes ideally suited to its own niche, and numbers are kept in check by food supplies, predators and other factors. But this does not mean that a balanced climax community is a static one: cyclical changes are going on all the while, with the continuous replacement of the old by the young and, in many communities, a very noticeable seasonal variation. You might not be able to study a full succession from bare land to forest, but you can certainly study the annual cycle in a forest without much difficulty.

The Woodland Cycle

Deciduous forests are widespread in North America and Europe, and also in Eastern Asia. Because most of the trees drop their leaves every autumn, the annual cycle of events is very clear, and you can get a great deal of

enjoyment from simply wandering through the woodlands at different times of the year and seeing the changes. You do not have to know the names of all the plants and animals that you see, although it adds to your enjoyment if you can identify some of them.

The North American forests are usually rather mixed, with a lot of tree species contributing to the community even in a small area. The trees include maples, hickories, buckeyes (horse chestnuts), tulip trees, oaks, birches, and many others. The European woodlands are quite poor in comparison, largely as a result of the effects of the Ice Age, and many of the woodlands are composed of just one or two dominant species. We thus find oak woods, beech woods, ash woods, and so on. Slight climatic differences may determine the types of trees that grow, and the nature of the underlying rock also has some effect. A few evergreen trees, such as yews and hollies, live in the deciduous forests. They are able to withstand the winter cold by virtue of their tough, waxy leaves. Compare the textures of some of these evergreen leaves with those of the deciduous leaves in the summer.

The trees are obviously the dominant components of the woodland community, because they overshadow and affect everything else, but, as we have already seen, the woodland community is an extremely complex one. In a typical deciduous woodland you can usually recognize several distinct layers of strata in addition to the main tree layer. There may be a secondary tree layer, composed of young trees awaiting their chance to break into the top canopy, or one of mature specimens of smaller trees, and below this there is usually a shrub layer. Below the shrubs there is a field layer of herbaceous plants including grasses, ferns and other familiar plants such as wood anemones, wood sorrel and bluebells. This field layer may be extremely dense: it has been estimated that one hectare (about 2½ acres) of old English oak wood may support about 28 million bluebell plants.

Examine the density of the field layer in different woodlands: does it vary according to the type of trees growing overhead? Below the field layer there is a fifth layer of vegetation – the ground layer, composed of mosses and lichens – and then, of course, there is the soil itself with its mass of roots and the ubiquitous fungal threads. Add to these layers the myriads of insects and other animals that inhabit them, and you will realize just how complex the community is.

In order to look at some of the changes that take place, let's break into the woodland cycle in what is known as the 'light phase', which begins when the leaves fall in the autumn. Not much activity is apparent during the winter because the conditions are too cold, but if you examine the leaf litter carefully (see page 80) you will find numerous mites and other tiny animals going about their business of breaking down the dead leaves and returning much of the goodness to the soil ready for the plant roots to absorb it. Fungal threads are also busy absorbing food from the dead leaves. As spring comes along and the days lengthen and temperatures rise, the field layer bursts into life. This is when the greatest amount of light reaches the woodland floor, and the herbaceous plants make the most of it covering the ground with sheets of flowers before the tree leaves expand overhead and cut off most of the light.

Many of the herbaceous plants die down in the summer, having made enough food for the year during the light phase, but some herbs continue to grow during the dark phase by increasing the size of their leaves and also by increasing the amount of chlorophyll in them and becoming a darker green. Both features enable the plants to absorb more of the available light. Compare the size and colour of primrose or wood anemone leaves in early spring and summer. The extent of the ground and field layers does, however, depend very much on the nature of the dominant trees. Oaks, ashes, birches, and others let quite a lot of light through, as you can see by looking up through the branches, but look up at a beech tree and you will see very little light in the summer. This is why so few herbaceous plants grow under the beech trees. The trees themselves generally flower early before their leaves are fully open, so that the insects or the wind-blown pollen can get through to the flowers without much hindrance.

Many insects and other animals are active throughout the summer dark phase, and if you visit the woodlands regularly you will be able to see how the leaf litter on the forest floor gradually disappears as the fungi and other organisms gradually consume the dead leaves. You can also watch the gradual development of the tree fruits, and later their dispersal by wind or by birds and other animals (see page 136).

The woodland cycle is precisely tuned so that the leaf litter is just about used up by the time the next lot of leaves are ready to fall. The fall is an extremely attractive time to walk in the woods because of the beautiful red and gold colours produced in many of the leaves just before they drop. The colours are the result of complex chemical changes associated with the re-absorption of much of the food material from the leaves. Many colourful toadstools also spring up, nourished by the underground threads that have been breaking down the previous season's dead leaves.

As well as watching the annual cycle in the deciduous woodlands, you can usually see something of the replacement cycle. Old trees eventually die and often fall, and there is then intense competition among other plants to take their

place. A fallen tree leaves a space where light can reach the woodland floor unhindered. Large numbers of grasses, ferns and other herbaceous plants quickly invade, together with a number of tree seedlings. For several years they all struggle on together, but if you watch over a longer period you will see the young trees starting to get the better of things and the smaller plants dying out. One tree will eventually shade out its weaker competitors and replace the original, with perhaps a few shade-tolerant plants beneath it. But in a mature woodland. of course, another tree will have died or fallen in the meantime, and there

will be another opportunity for the smaller woodland herbs to show themselves. Compare the cycles in the deciduous forest with those in a coniferous forest. Because most of the conifers keep their leaves all the year round, the cycles are much less obvious, but they are there for the observant naturalist.

Artificial Habitats

Man has destroyed the natural forests over large parts of the globe, especially in the deciduous forest belt where conditions are particularly favourable for human activity as well as for trees, and replaced them

with towns, cities, and agricultural land. These artificial habitats are easy to recognize as such, but don't think they are barren of wildlife. Many plants and animals have managed to take advantage of our activities and are, in fact, more often found in association with man than away from human habitation. How often do you see groundsel and house-sparrows away from buildings and gardens? There is plenty to see in the way of nature in such places, and it is interesting to note just how the creatures have altered their habits in order to fit in with the changed environment. Starlings, for example, roost on buildings instead of trees in many urban areas. Human activity maintains these habitats in their artificial state, but as soon as it stops, nature takes over and the processes of succession begin to restore the environment to its natural state again, as we have already seen with the quarry and the old railway line.

The rolling downs and the mountain sheepwalks of the British Isles may look natural, but they are not. These areas were once covered with trees, but they were cleared by man and his grazing animals during the last few thousand years, and under the grazing pressure

they became converted into grasslands of various kinds, according to the nature of the underlying rocks and soils. The grasslands are maintained only so long as grazing continues: if it stops, the process of succession takes up again. The coarser grasses and other herbs can then grow, and tree seedlings become established. The hillsides soon become dotted with hawthorns and other shrubs, and woodland eventually takes over. You can study these processes on many hillsides that were once grazed by innumerable rabbits but which started to return to woodland after outbreaks of myxomatosis killed off large numbers of the rabbits. Similar successional processes can be seen in Britain on some heathlands and moorlands which are also no more than semi-natural habitats. Many upland moors are regularly burned to encourage new heather growth for the benefit of grouse: without this burning, the land would return to woodland. These processes can also be seen in many areas of the United States, especially in the Northeast.

Aquatic Habitats

A great deal of plant and animal life lives in the water, both fresh and salt, and this aquatic life provides ample opportunity for the naturalist to look at some more of nature's ever-changing aspects. A single river, studied from its source to its mouth, can provide endless material for study, both geological and biological. The typical river has five major regions or reaches, each with its own special features, and you can learn a lot simply by looking at these reaches and their associated wild life.

The uppermost reach is the headstream, which is often no more than a trickle of water flowing down a 'ditch' on the hillside, although it may be moving quite fast. The soil is all washed away, but there is not enough volume of water to move the large stones or boulders. These are often covered with moss, and small insects, such as mayfly and stonefly nymphs, may cling to them. Farther down, the stream gathers more water, from surface run-off or other headstreams, and it becomes more powerful. This is the troutbeck. The stones are bowled rapidly along the bottom, and the stream bed is of solid rock or large boulders with little or no vegetation. A few flattened, crawling insects exist on the bottom, feeding on debris brought down from the headstream, and a few muscular fishes, such as trout, swim in the fast-flowing water.

Below the troutbeck the gradient flattens out to some extent and the stream widens into a true river. Stones are deposited on the bottom and often form banks in the middle. Plants grow along the sides and on the shingle banks. This is the minnow or grayling reach, so named because either or both of these fishes live here. Below it comes the cyprinoid reach, a slow-moving and relatively deep stretch with a muddy bottom and abundant waterside vegetation. Carp, bream, tench and many other fishes live here, feeding on the abundant insect life and other small creatures on the mud. Finally, as the river approaches the sea, there is the estuarine reach, where the water becomes brackish and tidal and there is an almost complete change of vegetation. It can be both interesting and rewarding to make a study of the distribution of the fishes, the plants, and other groups of organisms along the length of a river.

Lakes and ponds, although containing still water, support much the same kinds of life as the muddy, cyprinoid reach of a river, but lakes and ponds are not permanent features in the geological sense. They occupy hollows on the surface, and the natural processes of succession work to fill up these hollows and convert the watery environment into land. The complete succession takes a long time, but you can study it quite easily in a small pond or lake. It is basically a process of silting up, beginning at the edges, where plants trap the mud, and gradually spreading

right across the pond. As the mud and silt accumulate, the reeds can spread further out into the pond, and then they trap even mud and silt accumulate, Eventually, the silt and mud build up to the water level, and the original pond becomes a reed swamp or, in certain circumstances, a peat bog. The latter may remain for an indefinite period, but a reed swamp will gradually become converted into damp woodland, and then, eventually, it turns into high forest. You will not be able to watch all of this process, of course, but you can look at the various stages in an existing habitat and measure the water depths at which

the various colonizing plants grow. Try digging down into the soil at the edge of a pond or lake, especially one with trees and shrubs growing right up to the edge. See whether you find the remains of old water plants in peaty deposits; this will show that the ground was once under water. Remember, though, to respect the life of the pond, and take care not to trample down the edges of the pond when investigating the aquatic life.

A Code to Protect Wildlife

In the following pages of this book you will find numerous simple projects and suggestions for observing aspects of nature. A certain amount of collecting may be necessary for some projects, and instructions are given for making simple plant and insect collections. Sensible collecting does not in general harm wildlife, but never take more than you really need for your study. The following code of country behaviour has been drawn up by British conservationists under the auspices of the Society for the Promotion of Nature Conservation.

Follow the code and you will enjoy the countryside yourself as well as allowing others to enjoy it after you.

1 **Leave Wild Places as You Find Them**
Even trampling vegetation or removing logs and stones may destroy the homes of animals.
2 **Leave Wildlife in the Wild**
Wild plants and animals thrive best in their natural homes. Never dig up wild plants for your garden (this is already illegal in some countries).
3 **Disturbance May Mean Death**
Do not disturb birds or other animals. A frightened animal may desert its young, leaving them at the mercy of predators.

4 **Take Notes and Photographs, not Specimens**
Some collecting is necessary when you are studying very small creatures or making a detailed study of plants, but never take more than you actually need.
5 **Leave Wild Flowers for Others to Enjoy**
Picking wild flowers prevents them from seeding and may lead to the decline of the species.
6 **Observe Bye-Laws and Codes of Behaviour**
Nature reserves and similar places may have special regulations to protect wildlife. Observe the photographer's code (see page 170), and other codes drawn up by naturalists for the benefit of all. A more general code, focusing on the costly mistakes that unwary visitors to the countryside can make, appears in Chapter 10 (Information Guide).

MAKING A NATURE NOTEBOOK

The advantages of recording your observations in words and pictures in a notebook that you can refer to later

If you are seriously interested in studying plants and animals in their natural surroundings or habitats, you will no doubt want to keep a nature notebook or diary of everything you observe. This is a most rewarding thing to do because as the months pass and you build up an accurate record of your findings and observations, you will be compiling a reference book about the area that is most familiar to you.

The best way to keep records is to take a notebook with you on your outings or expeditions and keep a large diary at home in which your notes can be written up neatly at your leisure, together with any drawings, photographs or maps that you make. Your notebook will often get soil, dirt or rain on it, so it is a good idea to choose a notebook with a good binding so that it does not fall apart. A spirally bound type is recommended. When not in use, keep your notebook in a self-sealing plastic bag so that it does not get wet or soiled more than necessary.

It might seem obvious to suggest that you attach a pencil or pen to your notebook, but people who don't can waste valuable time searching the ground where they 'just put it down for a second', or rummaging through their pockets for it.

Always make sure you record sufficient information to be able to write up a full account later. Write the location of your observation or project and the date before you do anything else. Noting the time of day can also be quite important, and will help you to recall the occasion when referring to your records at a later date. Many mammals are most active at night (see page 60), especially just after sunset and before sunrise; these animals, which include hedgehogs, badgers, foxes, and bats, are rarely seen at other times, and so the moment of sighting is of special interest. The weather is another factor, especially if you are observing birds, mammals, reptiles, and certain insects, since their behaviour is closely connected with whether it is warm, sunny, cloudy, rainy, windy, etc. Snakes and lizards, for example, are most often sighted on warm days, either while sunbathing to warm their bodies, or while moving about once they have been sufficiently warmed.

A nature notebook need not be restricted to words. No matter how unskilled you may think you are at illustrating plants and animals, drawings, sketches and diagrams can add a great deal of information to your records of nature. Elsewhere in this book are descriptions of how to make leaf prints (see page 128), press flowers (see page 146), take prints in plaster (see page 72 for animals, and page 118 for plants), and photographs (see page 170). At the same time it is very satisfying to make realistic sketches taken in the animal's or plant's habitat. The illustrations on these pages are intended to give some idea of what can be done by learning and practising the basic shapes of a particular group.

The plant world is, of course, much easier to illustrate because your subjects will not run away. And while you can usually take a leaf, flower or fruit home with you – as long as you are sure it is not a rare specimen – it is extremely useful and instructive to make an on-the-spot record of the growing plant, noting its colour, size, number of flower heads, leaves, etc., also the type of soil in which the plant is growing. In the course of making your sketches you may find yourself recording a plant that has not been found in that particular area for years or even a plant that is on the verge of extinction.

Although the shape of an animal is important, identifications are often made from quick sketches, and notes of movements and any other feature that may strike you when you first see the animal. This is expecially true of birds, when all you might see is a quick flash of plumage. By recording the colours, bars, identification marks, etc., and sketching the way the bird flies (its flight-path) you can be more sure of identifying it later.

When drawing a tree make sure you put the main branches in the correct positions, and remember to record the date of your drawing, since the shape of the tree may well change during the year. Take a leaf and draw this on the same page of your notebook, either in outline (see page 128) or as a complete study. Draw a flower if the tree has them, and make sure you note the number of petals and the arrangement of the various flower parts.

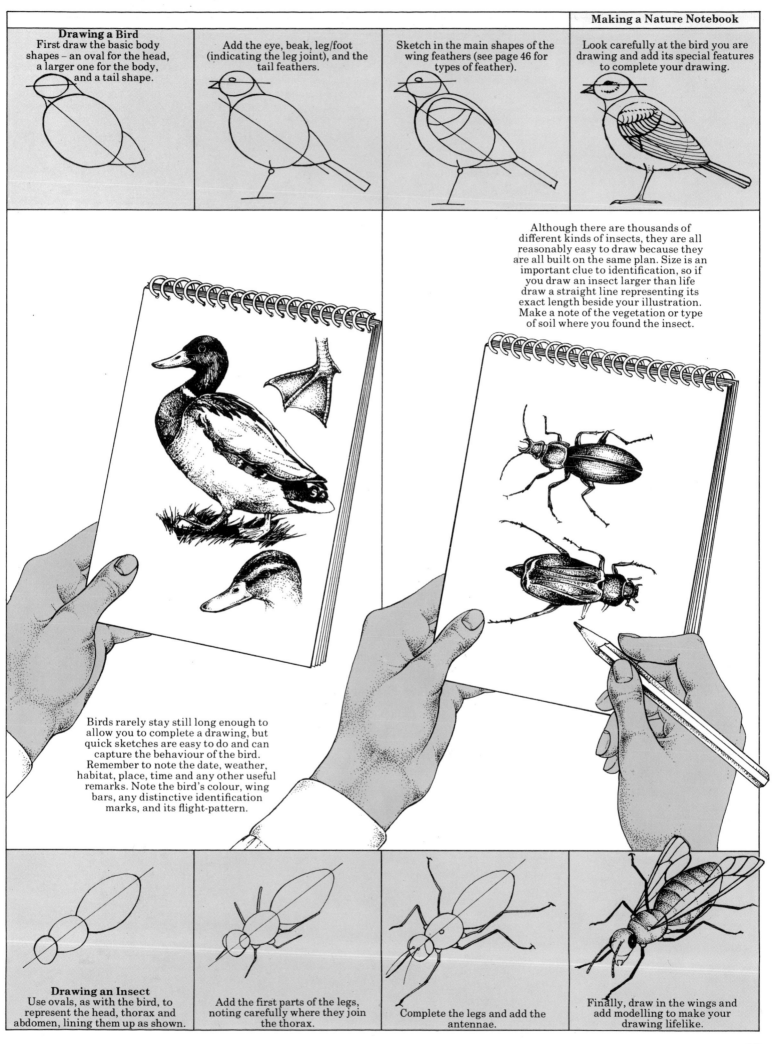

Making a Nature Notebook

Drawing a Bird
First draw the basic body shapes – an oval for the head, a larger one for the body, and a tail shape.

Add the eye, beak, leg/foot (indicating the leg joint), and the tail feathers.

Sketch in the main shapes of the wing feathers (see page 46 for types of feather).

Look carefully at the bird you are drawing and add its special features to complete your drawing.

Although there are thousands of different kinds of insects, they are all reasonably easy to draw because they are all built on the same plan. Size is an important clue to identification, so if you draw an insect larger than life draw a straight line representing its exact length beside your illustration. Make a note of the vegetation or type of soil where you found the insect.

Birds rarely stay still long enough to allow you to complete a drawing, but quick sketches are easy to do and can capture the behaviour of the bird. Remember to note the date, weather, habitat, place, time and any other useful remarks. Note the bird's colour, wing bars, any distinctive identification marks, and its flight-pattern.

Drawing an Insect
Use ovals, as with the bird, to represent the head, thorax and abdomen, lining them up as shown.

Add the first parts of the legs, noting carefully where they join the thorax.

Complete the legs and add the antennae.

Finally, draw in the wings and add modelling to make your drawing lifelike.

15

LEARNING ABOUT THE WEATHER

Some knowledge of the changing weather patterns can be a great help to the naturalist in the field

Formation of a Cyclone
The different temperatures at the earth's surface produce a series of global convection currents in the atmosphere giving rise to the prevailing wind systems of the world. The turning of the globe diverts these winds from their theoretical north-south directions so that they blow from the north-east or the south-west. The global pattern is such that the prevailing winds at the North Pole blow from the north-east while those in the temperate regions blow from the south-west. Between these regions, where the two winds approach one another, lies an area of very unstable weather. Another complex pattern of circulating air takes place in the upper atmosphere, where the air from converging masses rises and is distributed over the globe.

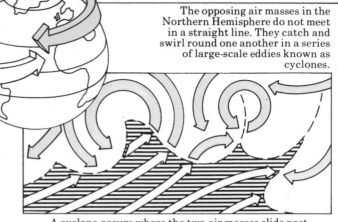

The opposing air masses in the Northern Hemisphere do not meet in a straight line. They catch and swirl round one another in a series of large-scale eddies known as cyclones.

A cyclone occurs where the two air masses slide past one another. The friction between the two causes the more southerly air mass to swing north and that in the north to swing south. The warmer air in the south has a lower density and so it tends to rise over the cold northern mass when they meet. The whole cyclone moves to the north-east and the moving boundaries between the warm air and the cold are known as warm and cold fronts.

It has been said that the difference between climate and weather is that climate is what we are supposed to get while weather is what we actually get. This is a bit over-simplified, but it brings out the basic distinction between the two. Climate is an average of atmospheric conditions, temperature, rainfall, humidity, etc., over a number of years and so is regarded as a fairly stable thing. Weather, on the other hand, is the day-to-day change in conditions at any particular place. Over large tracts of the earth's surface there is little difference between the two – for example in stable areas like deserts and equatorial rain forests – and it is possible that in past geological periods the climatic conditions were far more stable than they are today.

The great variations in day-to-day weather that we experience in the mid-latitudes of the Northern Hemisphere arise mainly because we live near the junction of the westward-moving mass of cold air at the Pole and the eastward-moving mass of warmer air in more temperate latitudes. The boundary between the two is very unstable and moves north and south, causing the air-masses to interact and swirl about each other in eddies that build up over a period of days and give weather conditions that are variable in the extreme.

Changes in the weather can be observed with the help of one or two very basic

As the cyclone continues to develop, a low-pressure area forms at the centre of the eddy and the winds blow into it in an anti-clockwise direction.

The movement of the cold front behind the tongue of warm air tends to be faster than that of the warm front before it, and so it catches up with it, wedging up the warm air off the ground. The two fronts are then combined into a single front called an occluded front.

Eventually the complicated system of air masses and pressures in an occluded front even themselves out and the whole formation dissipates. The occluded front itself vanishes and the mass of warm air forced up over the cold air is left as a pool that leaks away. The boundary between the polar air mass and the temperate air mass straightens out once more. Not for long, however, as the continuing movement of the globe sets up the frictional forces again and another cyclone is born.

instruments. A simple weather vane or windsock will show wind direction, and you can measure humidity by hanging up a piece of seaweed or a fir cone: in a humid atmosphere the seaweed becomes limp and the fir cone closes its scales. When the air grows dry the seaweed becomes crisp and the fir cone opens its scales.

Rainfall can be measured with a simple rain gauge. This can consist of a simple straight-sided receptacle, but if it is narrower at the neck than at the base, the catchment area will be different from the measurement area and

you will get false readings. To avoid this, place a funnel in the top of the receptacle which has the same diameter as that of the main body of the receptacle. Place your rain gauge out in the open and once a day or week measure the depth of rainwater that has collected in the gauge.

Temperature can be measured by setting up a thermometer in the open. If you have a thermometer of the maximum-minimum type, this will record the highest and the lowest temperatures during any period.

You can also count the hours of sunshine over

similar periods, and assess the density of cloud cover. This is usually expressed in terms of the number of eighths of the sky that are covered at a particular time. Cloud types vary according to altitude; some of the more common ones are featured opposite.

To understand the changing weather patterns in our latitudes it is important to understand the formation and features of a cyclone (see illustrations). The passage of a cyclone and its attendant fronts can be observed by watching wind direction and the different cloud formations.

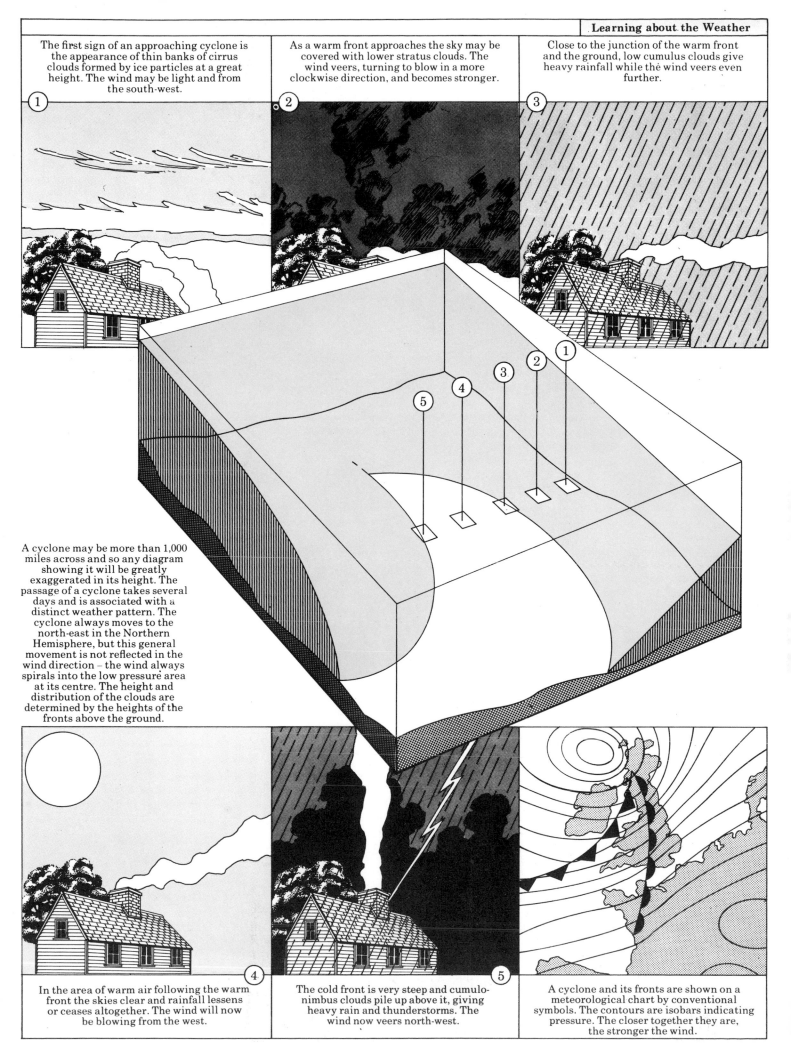

The first sign of an approaching cyclone is the appearance of thin banks of cirrus clouds formed by ice particles at a great height. The wind may be light and from the south-west.

As a warm front approaches the sky may be covered with lower stratus clouds. The wind veers, turning to blow in a more clockwise direction, and becomes stronger.

Close to the junction of the warm front and the ground, low cumulus clouds give heavy rainfall while the wind veers even further.

A cyclone may be more than 1,000 miles across and so any diagram showing it will be greatly exaggerated in its height. The passage of a cyclone takes several days and is associated with a distinct weather pattern. The cyclone always moves to the north-east in the Northern Hemisphere, but this general movement is not reflected in the wind direction – the wind always spirals into the low pressure area at its centre. The height and distribution of the clouds are determined by the heights of the fronts above the ground.

In the area of warm air following the warm front the skies clear and rainfall lessens or ceases altogether. The wind will now be blowing from the west.

The cold front is very steep and cumulo-nimbus clouds pile up above it, giving heavy rain and thunderstorms. The wind now veers north-west.

A cyclone and its fronts are shown on a meteorological chart by conventional symbols. The contours are isobars indicating pressure. The closer together they are, the stronger the wind.

THE HAND LENS

**An indispensable aid
for the inquiring
eye of the naturalist**

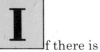

If there is any one piece of equipment that is indispensable to all keen naturalists, it is a simple hand lens. It is essential for the entomologist puzzling over the number of segments in a bee's antenna and for the botanist counting the stamens in a small flower, and it is just as important for almost all other naturalists, although bird watchers probably use their binoculars more than their hand lenses. Field identification of small creatures is impossible without a lens to magnify the important features, while for those with less scientific minds the lens can reveal some really wonderful patterns and textures on plants and animals and other everyday objects. Try looking at the stamens of a flower to see the tiny pollen grains, or else look at the dust in your pocket. You will be surprised how many different kinds of fibres you can see. In addition, the lens has some more basic uses, such as helping you to find and extract those irritating small thorns which you always seem to collect, without knowing it, on a nature ramble.

There are several different kinds of hand lens, each with its own particular uses and advantages. The large round reading glass or magnifying glass has a magnification of only two or three times and it is not powerful enough to reveal detailed structures on small creatures. Its wide field of view, however, makes it ideal for scanning tree trunks and other surfaces when looking for insects at rest. You can also use it for examining leaf litter on the table (see page 81) and for watching large insects, such as bumble bees and butterflies, feeding at flowers. The reading glass type can also be attached to a flexible 'stalk'. This arrangement allows you to have both hands free to manipulate a specimen and to make sketches at the same time.

The watchmaker's lens, which, with a bit of practice, can be held comfortably in one eye, also allows you to have both hands free and it is quite useful for bench work on specimens which you have brought home. For field use, however, most naturalists prefer the type of hand lens shown in the middle of the opposite page. You can buy this type of lens quite cheaply. Magnifications vary from × 5 to × 20, but a magnification of less than eight times is not of great use to the naturalist. Specialists dealing with very small insects and other animals might need a × 15 lens, but for general natural history a × 10 lens is the most practical. It gives a useful degree of magnification while still retaining a fairly wide field of view and a reasonable working distance. More

The illustrations at the top of the opposite page show some of the fascinating objects that are revealed by the hand lens. There are many other things you can investigate, such as the eye of a fly, and if you want to delve even further into detailed structures you might consider turning to the microscope (see page 168).

powerful lenses must be held much closer to the object and they magnify just a very small section. It is not easy for the non-specialist to relate this section to the whole object. The magnification should always be stamped on the side of the lens. Check this when you buy it: look for one marked × 10 – the most convenient kind for the family naturalist.

As for maintenance, there is very little to do. Keep your lens clean by wiping it occasionally with a *clean* handkerchief or a lens tissue, and *keep it with you.* A lens is no use if you have left it at home, or, worse still, left it somewhere in the woods. Absent-minded naturalists are recommended to put the lens on a string round the neck.

The reading glass or magnifying glass does not reveal much fine structure, but it is very useful for watching feeding insects without eye-strain.

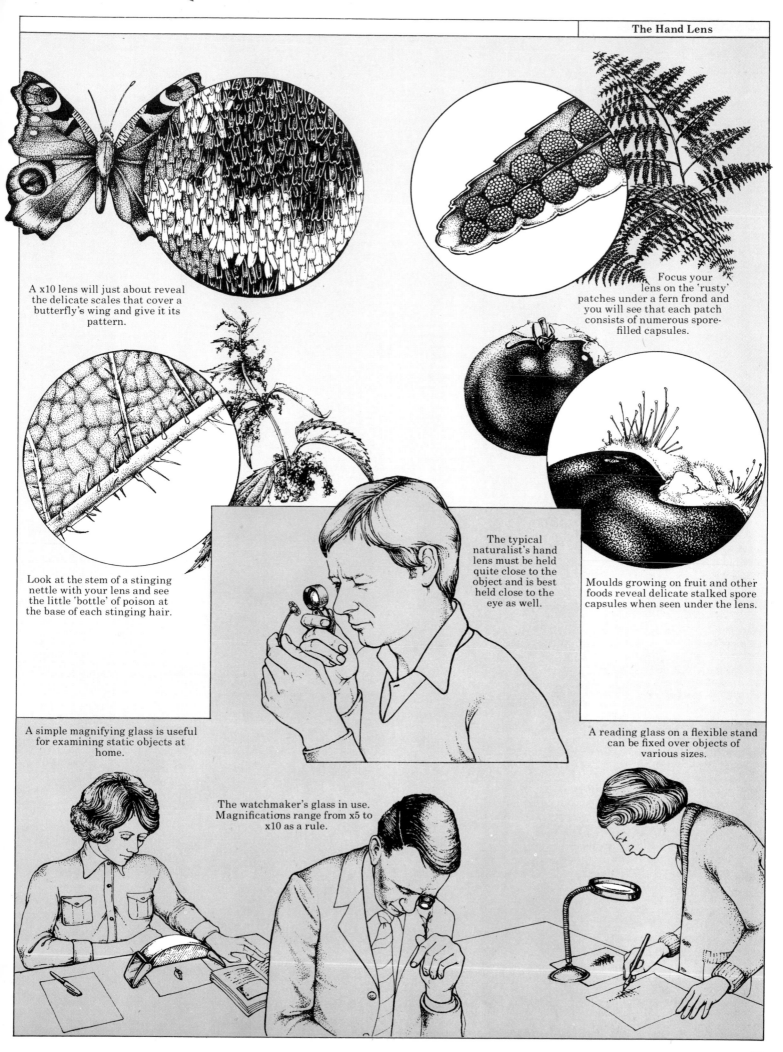

A x10 lens will just about reveal the delicate scales that cover a butterfly's wing and give it its pattern.

Focus your lens on the 'rusty' patches under a fern frond and you will see that each patch consists of numerous spore-filled capsules.

Look at the stem of a stinging nettle with your lens and see the little 'bottle' of poison at the base of each stinging hair.

The typical naturalist's hand lens must be held quite close to the object and is best held close to the eye as well.

Moulds growing on fruit and other foods reveal delicate stalked spore capsules when seen under the lens.

A simple magnifying glass is useful for examining static objects at home.

A reading glass on a flexible stand can be fixed over objects of various sizes.

The watchmaker's glass in use. Magnifications range from x5 to x10 as a rule.

THE NATURE TABLE

Setting up a display area for natural objects picked up during country walks

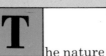

The nature table is an ever-changing exhibit which can involve the whole family throughout the year, for it consists of a display of natural items found during walks, drives, or other excursions. Country areas will clearly yield more material for the table than urban surroundings, but sharp eyes and inquiring minds will find a surprising amount of presentable items even in a town.

Although usually referred to as the nature table, the display does not actually have to be on a table: a sheet of peg-board or some such material on a wall, or even a convenient window sill, will suffice. Items put on show are there for the whole family to see and discuss in their own time. In effect they can form a kind of visual calendar of the natural world that you live amongst or have recently visited. Try to get everyone in the family to participate: each person has his or her own preferences, and the more contributors you have, the greater will be the variety of objects on display.

The ever-changing and seasonal nature of the 'table' means that there is always something new to be seen. Flowering grasses, for example, can be displayed in early summer, while autumn leaves can obviously be shown only during the autumn or fall. You can set a regular date, say once a month, for clearing and re-stocking the nature table if you wish, but interesting objects tend to be found at irregular intervals, and it is better to add new things as they are discovered and make room for them by removing some of the older exhibits. Withered flowers will obviously be discarded, but some of the items can be transferred to a permanent collection.

Rocks, fossils, bones, bird pellets, feathers, leaves, plant galls and many other things all have their place on the nature table. All must be labelled if they are to mean anything to other members of the family or to visitors—or even to the collector a few days later: it is very difficult to remember all the details of exactly when and where an object was found, and all such information should be written down in the notebook *at the time of discovery*. Labels can then be prepared from the notes, and the notebook itself can be kept on the table when it is not in use in the field.

Animal bones can be cleaned if necessary (see page 68), but most dry objects can be placed directly on the table without fear of creating smell and decay. A large magnifying glass, especially one on a flexible stand, will help to show up some of the details of the smaller exhibits, and the family microscope (see page 168) can also be kept on the table if there is enough light for you to be able to use it there.

Although most of the nature-table exhibits are of a temporary kind, you can include some more permanent items. Seeds or bulbs planted in the spring can be fed and watered throughout the year, with a record being kept of their progress and flowering. Try some simple hydroponics, which means growing plants in nutrient solutions instead of in soil (see page 140). But remember that you can grow plants successfully only if you have plenty of light on your table. A wormery (see page 84), a formicarium (page 98) or an aquarium (page 30) can also be placed on the table if space allows, and various caterpillars can be housed there. You can watch the caterpillars grow up (see page 96) and, if you are lucky, you will be able to watch the adult butterflies or moths dragging themselves out of their pupae at a later date and spreading their wings before they fly away.

One very useful addition to the nature table is some kind of storage bin—it can be simply a plastic bag hung under the table—in which you can keep all the little tubes and boxes that are so useful for putting specimens in while you are out for a walk. Get into the habit of taking a pocketful of small containers every time you go out, and when you empty them on to the table on your return wash them if necessary and put them straight back into the storage bin: you will then know where they are next time you need them.

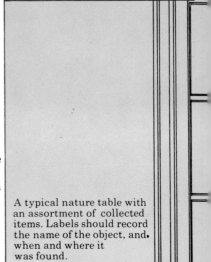

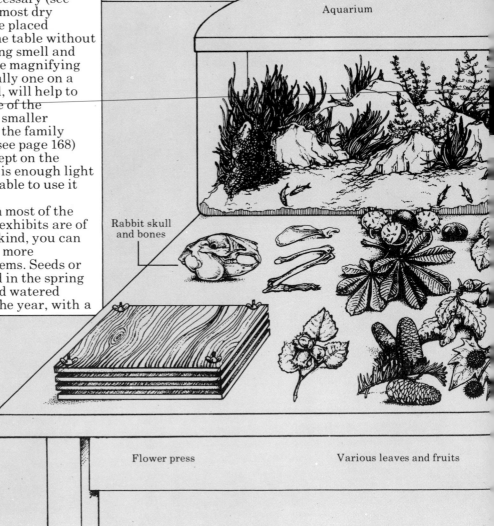

A typical nature table with an assortment of collected items. Labels should record the name of the object, and when and where it was found.

Aquarium

Rabbit skull and bones

Flower press

Various leaves and fruits

If space is a problem hang your nature table on the wall. Use a sheet of peg-board, criss-crossing some of it with tapes to take feathers, grasses, and other bulkier finds.

Seedlings growing on window sill

Grasses drying in jar without water

Magnifying glass

Hyacinth growing in water

Fossils

Seal skull

Galls

Plaster casts

Jar with butterfly pupae

Bag of assorted containers

Beetle

Feathers

Specimen tube with insects

Shells and other beach debris

Notebook

THE NATURE TRAIL

A guided tour of some of the many plants and animals that can be seen on a short walk

walk in the countryside with an experienced naturalist can be an eye-opener for beginners. The naturalist knows the signs to look for and he knows just the right places in which to look, and he will usually pick out far more animals and plants than the average person. A simple walk can thus be turned into a real journey of exploration and discovery. Many organizations lay out nature trails for this very purpose. A personal guide is not necessary on an organized trail because the necessary information is given either on sign-posts along the route or in a special handbook.

If you have some suitable land – either your own or that of a neighbour or friendly farmer – you might like to lay out your own nature trail. This could be of great interest to schools as well as to your family and friends.

The most interesting trails are those that take in several different kinds of habitat – grasslands, hedgerows, woodlands, and perhaps a pond or a stream – but such variation is not essential. An interesting trail can be made up in half a mile of hedgerow, or even in a single meadow if you know what to look for. Some of the features which you can point out on your nature trail are shown in the illustration, but there are many more possibilities. Do not ignore animal signs (see page 70) that can be found on the trail: point out squirrel feeding-places, identified by the broken nut

shells, and any regular tracks used by animals. If a fox regularly crosses the nature trail, suggest a good sniff at the appropriate place. This is the only way to teach someone what a fox smells like, and the smell will not be forgotten.

Your trail can be permanent, in the sense that visitors follow the same route throughout the year, but most of the 'stations' will be in use only at certain seasons: visitors are unlikely to want to look at a patch of ground where orchids grow unless they can see the plants in flower, and there is no point in stopping to look at 'Butterfly caterpillars' after they have turned into butterflies and flown away. It is worth varying the route slightly to take in seasonal features.

On private land, you can erect permanent signs which show visitors the way round. A sign-post at each station can give details about the plants or animals seen there, or else you can merely put a number on each post and make up a trail book to give the relevant information for each numbered station. If you use a loose-leaf book you can easily insert or remove details of seasonal stations. Alternatively, you can write in the relevant season immediately after the number and leave the page permanently in the booklet. You can also make up a perfectly satisfactory trail without posts or numbers, simply by giving detailed directions in your book. This is the only practical method for use on public land where sign-posts are likely to be damaged or removed. Use prominent trees, ditches, and so on as reference points, and give instructions in plenty of time: it is no good guiding someone right up to a branch overhanging a stream and saying, 'You can sometimes see a kingfisher on this branch.' Tell your visitors to look for the branch from farther away, and then they really might see the kingfisher. The same thing applies if you are using sign-posts: put the sign farther back and direct the eye to the branch.

Woodpecker at nest hole

A badger set

Rabbit droppings deposited regularly on a 'latrine'

Permanent signs can be erected on private land, one sign at each station. The sign gives information on the subject and points towards the next station.

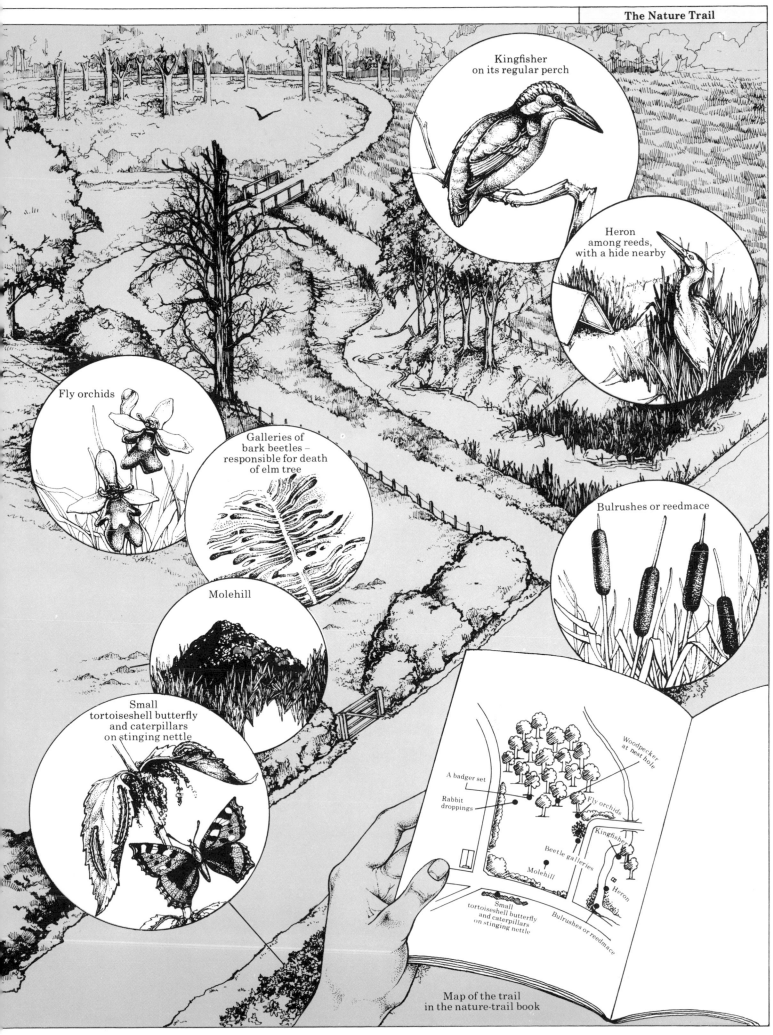

Kingfisher
on its regular perch

Heron
among reeds,
with a hide nearby

Fly orchids

Galleries of
bark beetles –
responsible for death
of elm tree

Bulrushes or reedmace

Molehill

Small
tortoiseshell butterfly
and caterpillars
on stinging nettle

A badger set

Rabbit
droppings

Woodpecker
at nest hole

Fly orchids

Kingfisher

Beetle galleries

Molehill

Heron

Small
tortoiseshell butterfly
and caterpillars
on stinging nettle

Bulrushes or reedmace

Map of the trail
in the nature-trail book

Life began in the seas something like 3,500 million years ago, when tiny organisms, perhaps very similar to some of today's bacteria, first acquired that vital spark of life which scientists are still trying to understand. For many millions of years life remained confined to the water, and it is clear that water contains everything needed for life – minerals and carbon dioxide for the plants, which in turn yield abundant food and oxygen for the animals. If you take a look into a pond or a rock pool such as that shown on the left you will see for yourself just how much is living there. Among other things, the rock pool contains barnacles, limpets, a starfish, a sunstar, a sea anemone, a crab, a prawn, and some gobies.

During the millions of years of evolution, most of the major animal groups have acquired freshwater and terrestrial representatives, but a few groups, notably the echinoderms – the starfishes and their relatives – have remained marine animals throughout their existence. Many more groups have remained aquatic, although inhabiting both fresh and salt water. The fishes and the coelenterates – the sea anemones and their relatives – are two well known examples, although the fishes did, of course, give rise to the land-living vertebrates in the distant past.

The pull of the aquatic environment has always been very strong, however, and many essentially terrestrial groups contain members which have gone back to the water: whales, turtles, and water beetles are but three examples which have reverted to an aquatic existence. Even people are strongly attracted to water, as can be seen by the vast numbers who go to the seaside or who spend hours fishing in ponds and streams. Aquatic life is clearly of great interest to divers and fishermen, but it is not just they who are interested in

what lives beneath the surface. Fishes, tadpoles, and sea shells all have a very wide appeal, and one of the most appealing things is perhaps the fact that many can be brought into the home for close study.

It is probably easier to set up an artificial aquatic environment than a terrestrial one. A sea-water aquarium is more difficult to set up and maintain than a freshwater one, but the formula given on page 176 will help you to get somewhere near the correct sea-water composition if you are not able to collect fresh sea water for yourself.

Plants have followed the same sort of route from water to land as the animals, although perhaps we should say that the animals have followed the plants, because animals cannot invade until after the food-providing plants have pioneered the way. Some of the algae – the seaweeds – have remained marine, while most others are still aquatic. Some of the aquatic green algae gave rise to the line which produced the fantastic array of land plants, but the wheel has turned full circle and many of the higher plants, such as the pondweeds and the duckweeds, have re-adopted an aquatic existence.

Let us now have a look at some of the aquatic animals and see how they are adapted for life in the water. All animals have to breathe oxygen, but this is no great problem because oxygen dissolves quite readily in water and the animals can absorb it. The smaller species merely absorb oxygen through their general body surfaces, but larger and more active creatures cannot get enough oxygen by this method and they employ special breathing organs called gills to absorb it for them.

The best known gills are those of the fishes. These gills are delicate, blood-filled filaments housed in pouches behind the fishes' mouths. The pouches open both into the throat and to the outside. A fish breathes by taking a mouthful of water, shutting its mouth, and forcing the water through the gill pouches. The blood contains the red pigment called haemoglobin, which acts like a magnet for the oxygen in the water, and much of this oxygen passes into the blood flowing through the gill filaments. The blood then distributes it to all parts of the body. The gills of the larger crustaceans, such as crabs and lobsters, act in much the same way, although they contain a

different oxygen-attracting pigment.

Aquatic insects are basically animals which have returned to the water, and the adult insects nearly all retain their air-breathing habits. Most of the water beetles and water bugs use the space under their tough wing covers as an air reservoir, and they come to the surface every now and then to replenish the supply. Some of the young stages also get their oxygen from the surface. The rat-tailed maggot, for example, which is the larva of a hover-fly, has a telescopic 'tail' which it can push up to the surface from various depths.

Other young insects have developed various kinds of gills projecting from the body surface. As the gills wave about they bring fresh water currents and the oxygen passes from the water into the air-passages (tracheae) inside the gills. The tracheae spread right through the body, keeping every part supplied with oxygen. The gills of dragonfly nymphs are actually inside the hind end of the body. The insect sucks water into the gill chamber and then squirts it out again, often with enough force to send the whole animal shooting forward.

Jet propulsion is a regular method of moving for the squids and their relatives, and these also squirt the water out of their gill chambers. Swimming in fishes is normally accomplished by means of a powerful tail which forces the animal through the water as it beats, while various fins on the sides and top and bottom of the animal assist with steering and the maintenance of stability. Backswimmers 'row' themselves through the water in an upside-down position with their long, hair-fringed legs, while pond-skaters actually row themselves across the water surface. Many small crustaceans, such as shrimps, use broad limbs near the hind end of the body to paddle themselves through the water, while many other aquatic animals merely crawl over the sea or river bed or burrow in the mud.

CHAPTER 2

AQUATIC LIFE

Life evolved in the water, and many groups of plants and animals still live there

POND DIPPING

A look at the fascinating world of pond life

Even a small pond contains a whole world of tiny animals that can be collected and studied.

All you really need for pond dipping is some kind of net and a few jars or dishes. Some other useful equipment is shown on this page, while the illustrations on the opposite page show some of the animals you can expect to catch. You will find that the animals fall into five fairly distinct groups, according to where they live in the pond.

The first group are the surface-dwellers, which skim rapidly about on the surface film in search of small flies and other insects that settle on the water. These surface-dwellers are very hard to catch because they detect the ripples caused by the approaching net long before it gets near them. Another group of creatures, typified by the mosquito larvae and their comma-shaped pupae, spend much of their time hanging from the surface layer. Water beetles and various water bugs also come to the surface periodically to renew their air supplies. Hordes of animals, ranging from tiny waterfleas to large fishes, swim freely in the water and can be caught with an ordinary net. Many animals crawl on water weeds, and the members of another group stay on the bottom of the pond.

You can collect these pond animals at any time of the year, but be careful not to trample the banks too much and damage the plants.

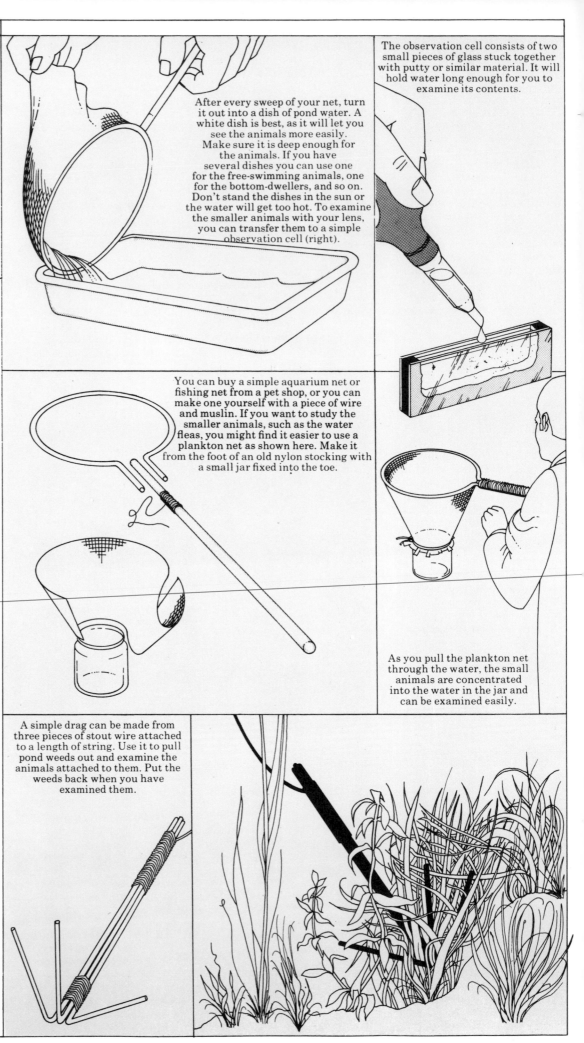

After every sweep of your net, turn it out into a dish of pond water. A white dish is best, as it will let you see the animals more easily. Make sure it is deep enough for the animals. If you have several dishes you can use one for the free-swimming animals, one for the bottom-dwellers, and so on. Don't stand the dishes in the sun or the water will get too hot. To examine the smaller animals with your lens, you can transfer them to a simple observation cell (right).

The observation cell consists of two small pieces of glass stuck together with putty or similar material. It will hold water long enough for you to examine its contents.

You can buy a simple aquarium net or fishing net from a pet shop, or you can make one yourself with a piece of wire and muslin. If you want to study the smaller animals, such as the water fleas, you might find it easier to use a plankton net as shown here. Make it from the foot of an old nylon stocking with a small jar fixed into the toe.

As you pull the plankton net through the water, the small animals are concentrated into the water in the jar and can be examined easily.

A simple drag can be made from three pieces of stout wire attached to a length of string. Use it to pull pond weeds out and examine the animals attached to them. Put the weeds back when you have examined them.

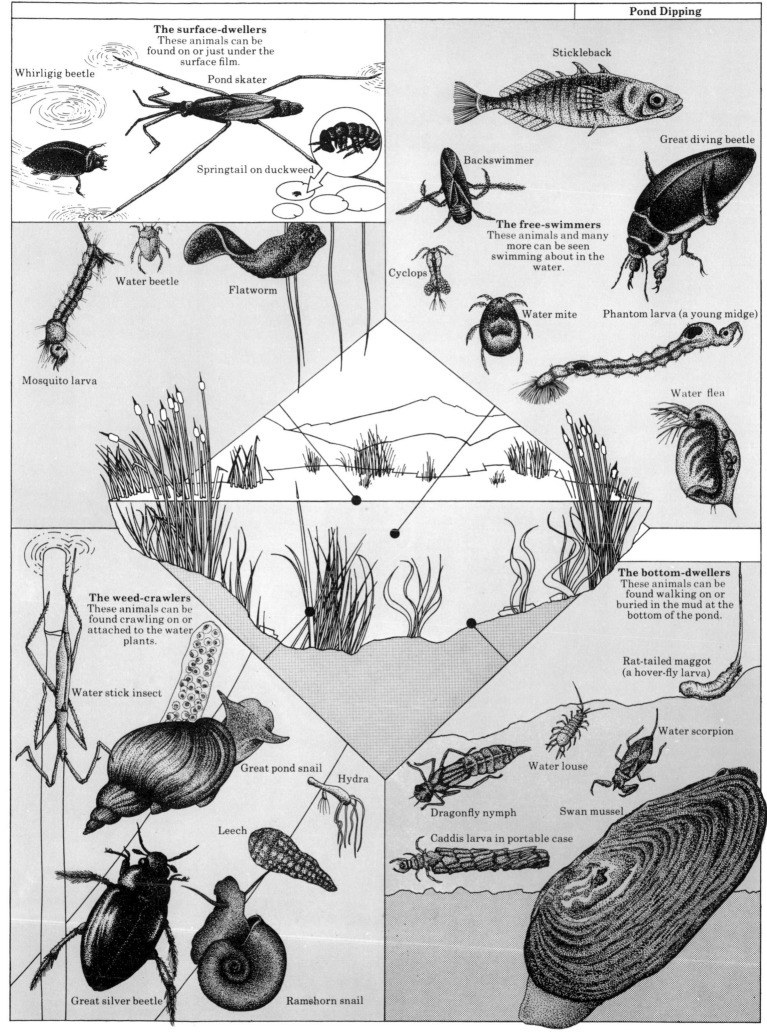

The surface-dwellers
These animals can be found on or just under the surface film.

Whirligig beetle

Pond skater

Springtail on duckweed

Stickleback

Backswimmer

Great diving beetle

The free-swimmers
These animals and many more can be seen swimming about in the water.

Cyclops

Water mite

Phantom larva (a young midge)

Water flea

Water beetle

Flatworm

Mosquito larva

The weed-crawlers
These animals can be found crawling on or attached to the water plants.

Water stick insect

Great pond snail

Hydra

Leech

Great silver beetle

Ramshorn snail

The bottom-dwellers
These animals can be found walking on or buried in the mud at the bottom of the pond.

Rat-tailed maggot (a hover-fly larva)

Water scorpion

Water louse

Dragonfly nymph

Swan mussel

Caddis larva in portable case

A GARDEN POND

How to make and stock a small pond in your garden

any of the animals that you collect during a pond-dipping excursion can be brought home and put into a garden pond for future study. If you have no garden pond it would be a good idea to install one: it will repay you handsomely in pleasure and relaxation, and at a time when farm and village ponds are fast disappearing a garden pond can play an important part in the conservation of frogs, newts, and other small water-loving animals.

Your garden pond can be any size you like from about 1 metre (40 in) square upwards, but it must be at least 40 cm (16 in) deep in the centre. Shallower water may freeze solid in a cold winter and kill the animals.

There are three main methods of installing a pond, the simplest being to buy an 'instant pond' made of fibreglass. You can buy these in a wide variety of formal and informal shapes and sizes, and all you have to do is to dig a hole and drop the pond in. The edge of the fibreglass can be covered with concrete or paving stones for a formal finish, or you can lay turf around it to produce a 'natural' pond.

Another simple way of making a pond is to use a pond liner. This is a waterproof sheet made of butyl rubber or thick black plastic. The latter is much cheaper, but possibly less durable. You dig a hole to the required shape and ensure that it has sloping sides to reduce the risk of caving-in. It is a good plan to build in at least two levels, so that you can accommodate different kinds of plants. Having dug the hole to the right shape and depth, you must cover the bottom with fine sand or peat, or with a layer of old newspaper. This ensures that no unseen sharp stones can pierce the liner.

When all is ready you lay the liner over the hole and hold down the edges with paving stones, rockery stones, or turf. Pour in the water, and the liner will mould itself to the shape of the hole.

A concrete pond is harder work, but you can make it any shape you like. Although a liner will mould itself to the shape of the pond, liners do come in fixed rectangular sizes and they are not suitable for long, narrow ponds snaking their way through rock gardens. Don't make the concrete too wet when mixing it, or you will be unable to shape it. The concrete should be at least 10 cm (4 in) thick, and preferably 15 cm (6 in) for a large pond. It is particularly important to ensure that you maintain this thickness over the edges of the shelves, for this is where cracks are likely to occur. Wire netting can be incorporated into the concrete for extra strength. A well-made concrete pond should be waterproof, but it is a wise plan to coat the concrete with a plastic paint made for this very purpose. You can then stock the pond as soon as the paint is dry.

You can put a wide variety of plants into your pond, but you must take care to plant them at the right depths. You can buy plants from a dealer or, with the permission of the owner, you can collect a few from a local pond. Fishes can also be bought or collected. Some suitable species are shown on the opposite page.

Pond snails and mussels, water beetles and other animals can all be brought in from natural ponds, but many creatures will find their own way to your new pond and help to create a natural, balanced community. A well-balanced pond with plenty of plants should not cause many maintenance problems, but if your pond is near some trees you will do well to cover it with wire netting during leaf-fall.

When digging out your concrete pond remember to slope the sides and to dig down far enough to accommodate at least 10 cm (4 in) of concrete and 40 cm (16 in) of water. Fresh concrete harms plants and animals, so it is best to coat the finished pond with plastic paint.

A typical ready-made fibreglass pond: this can be finished off with an edging of turf or 'crazy' paving to make an attractive addition to the garden.

If you are using a liner, the hole must first be lined with sand or old newspapers (see inset). Black plastic deteriorates in sunlight, so cover the edges with turf or paving stones and keep the pond full.

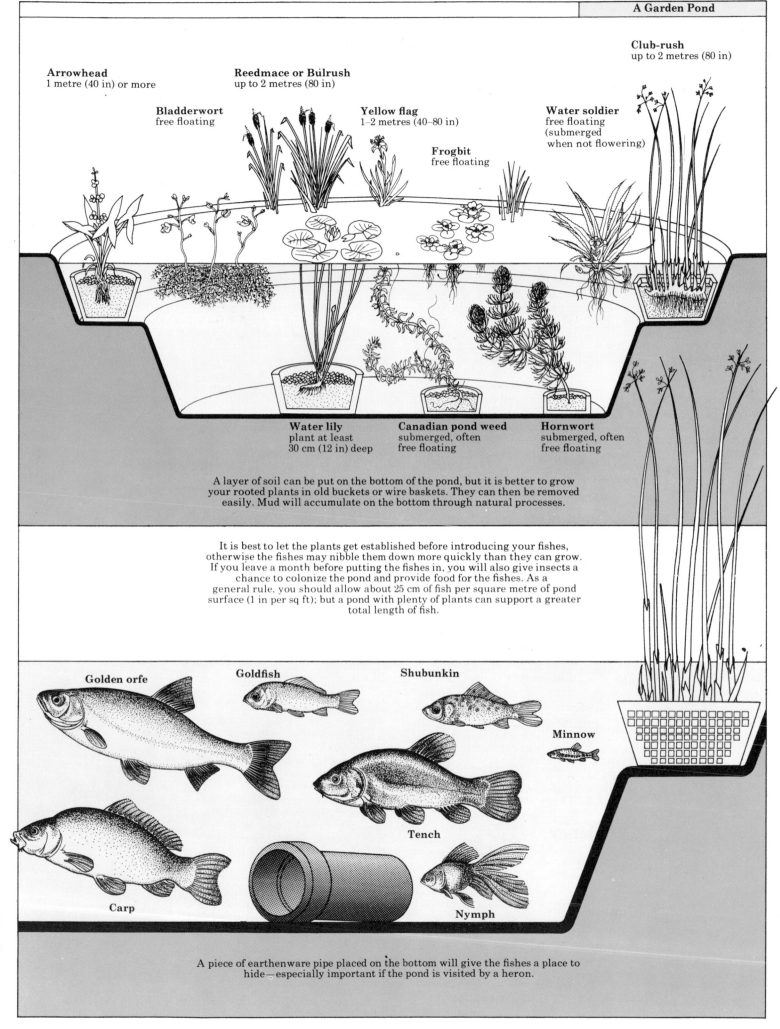

Club-rush
up to 2 metres (80 in)

Arrowhead
1 metre (40 in) or more

Reedmace or Bulrush
up to 2 metres (80 in)

Bladderwort
free floating

Yellow flag
1–2 metres (40–80 in)

Water soldier
free floating
(submerged
when not flowering)

Frogbit
free floating

Water lily
plant at least
30 cm (12 in) deep

Canadian pond weed
submerged, often
free floating

Hornwort
submerged, often
free floating

A layer of soil can be put on the bottom of the pond, but it is better to grow your rooted plants in old buckets or wire baskets. They can then be removed easily. Mud will accumulate on the bottom through natural processes.

It is best to let the plants get established before introducing your fishes, otherwise the fishes may nibble them down more quickly than they can grow. If you leave a month before putting the fishes in, you will also give insects a chance to colonize the pond and provide food for the fishes. As a general rule, you should allow about 25 cm of fish per square metre of pond surface (1 in per sq ft); but a pond with plenty of plants can support a greater total length of fish.

Golden orfe

Goldfish

Shubunkin

Minnow

Tench

Carp

Nymph

A piece of earthenware pipe placed on the bottom will give the fishes a place to hide—especially important if the pond is visited by a heron.

THE FRESH-WATER AQUARIUM

A miniature pond to keep on your table or beside a window

Many different kinds of pond animals will be discovered by dipping a net into the pond (see page 26), and most of them are quite easy to keep and watch at home in a simple aquarium. An old bowl or tin bath with some mud at the bottom will keep lots of pond animals happy, but such a container is not very attractive and most people prefer to set up a conventional glass-sided tank in which to keep their aquatic creatures. This enables you to see the animals more clearly and, if a few simple rules are obeyed, your aquarium should support a variety of pond animals for a considerable time with a minimum of attention.

First of all, the tank must be thoroughly cleaned and any dead algae coating the sides must be removed by scrubbing or scraping with a suitable tool: wet newspaper folded to form a 'sponge' will remove quite a lot of dirt from the glass. Next get some gravel. This can be spread over the bottom of the tank. The gravel can be bought from a pet shop, or it can be collected from a pollution-free stream if you have one in your neighbourhood. You will usually need more than you think, and, whether it comes from shop or stream, you must wash it thoroughly in running water until the water runs away crystal clear. Garden soil or beach sand is not suitable for an indoor aquarium. The washed gravel is spread on the floor of the tank in a layer about 25 mm (1 in) deep at the front and sloping gently up to the back. This ensures that debris collects at the front, where it can be seen.

Any rocks placed in the tank must be chosen carefully and they should be free from large cracks in which dirt can become lodged. Boil them in water and then scrub them thoroughly before placing them in the tank.

Sandstones, granites and several other kinds of rock are usually quite safe, but do not use limestones because they slowly dissolve in water and may change the chemical balance of your aquarium enough to kill the animals.

Plants can be added, with only the damp gravel to support them, as soon as the rocks are in position. They can be bought from dealers, or they can be collected from local ponds and streams if you obtain the owner's permission. Canadian pondweed (*Elodea*), water milfoil, and hornwort are particularly useful species which give off plenty of the oxygen that the animals need. Needle spike-rush (*Eleocharis acicularis*) and some of the smaller arrowhead species are useful, and the fascinating bladderwort is also worth including if you can get it. This plant carries small purse-like bladders which suck in water fleas and other small animals. The trapped animals die and decay and help to nourish the plant.

Plants collected from the wild should be washed to remove excess dirt and checked to see if they have any duckweed attached to them. Duckweed is not good for the aquarium, for it reproduces so quickly that it soon covers the surface and cuts off the light from the plants growing beneath it. Make sure also that the plants do not carry too many jelly-like batches of water-snail eggs: a few water snails are useful, but too many will destroy your plants. Remove all dead and damaged leaves from the plants and push the roots or bases of their stems into the gravel.

When you are satisfied with the arrangement of the plants, take two or three sheets of clean newspaper and fold them to fit neatly, but loosely, inside the tank. Lay them gently over the rocks and plants and then pour on your clean water. Tapwater will be suitable, but strained or filtered pond water is better. The newspaper will rise with the water in the tank without disturbing the plants beneath it. Any plants that do float to the surface can be replanted with a slender stick or a pickle fork.

Animals are best not introduced until a week or so after the tank has been filled. This will allow the plants to get established before animals start to nudge and nibble them. All kinds of pond and stream animals can be installed, but species from very fast streams will probably need additional aeration. A small aeration motor can be bought quite cheaply from a pet shop. Carnivores such as dragonfly nymphs and diving beetles should not be introduced because they will eat the other animals. Include a few snails, preferably the dark red flattened forms known as ramshorns, to keep down the growth of algae on the glass sides. A regular addition of live water fleas and mosquito larvae from the pond will keep any small fishes happy.

Excessive dirt can be siphoned out periodically, but a well-balanced tank should not present much of a problem because the small scavenging creatures such as water lice and various water beetles feed on the detritus and keep it under control. One freshwater mussel in the tank will also help to keep the water clear because it continuously filters the water through its body to extract small food particles.

Never stand your aquarium in the full sun, for this will cause the water to overheat and some of the animals may die. The water will also become green, due to excessive algal growth. A cover is not essential, but you may lose some water beetles if you do not stop them from flying away.

The stickleback is one of the best fishes for the cold-water aquarium.

Aquarium gravel must be thoroughly cleaned before use. This is best done in running water. Do not put too much gravel in the bucket at one time, and stir it continuously with a stick until the water runs clear.

Cut away dead and damaged leaves with a sharp knife or a pair of scissors before putting the plants in the tank. Vigorous plants may need trimming from time to time while in the tank: you can do this with scissors.

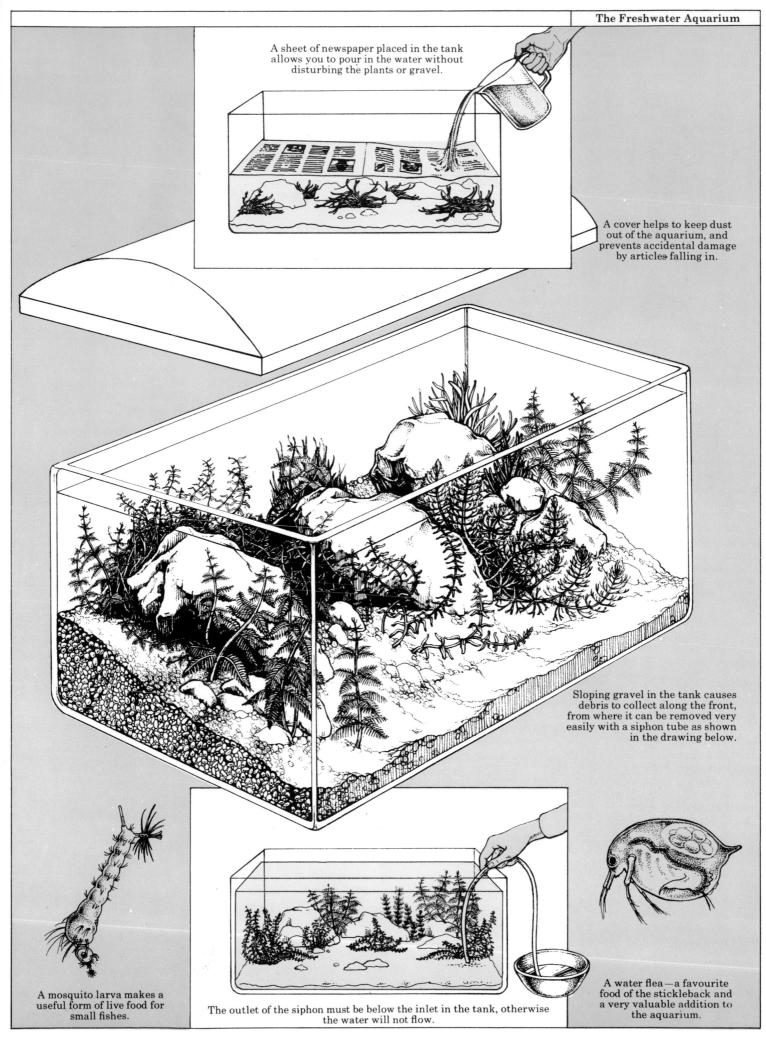

A sheet of newspaper placed in the tank allows you to pour in the water without disturbing the plants or gravel.

A cover helps to keep dust out of the aquarium, and prevents accidental damage by articles falling in.

Sloping gravel in the tank causes debris to collect along the front, from where it can be removed very easily with a siphon tube as shown in the drawing below.

A mosquito larva makes a useful form of live food for small fishes.

The outlet of the siphon must be below the inlet in the tank, otherwise the water will not flow.

A water flea—a favourite food of the stickleback and a very valuable addition to the aquarium.

REARING TADPOLES

The fascinating changes that take place during the first three months in the life of a frog or a toad

As soon as the weather starts to warm up in the spring the male frogs and toads make their way to their breeding ponds and set up the familiar croaky chorus. The noise attracts the females, and before long the edges of the ponds are thick with gelatinous masses of spawn. This gives the naturalist an excellent opportunity to study the fascinating development of these animals over a period of about three months. The only essential equipment is a watertight dish or bowl.

A handful of spawn scooped up from the pond and put into the dish will provide more than enough eggs. Put in sufficient pond water to keep the spawn off the bottom of the dish, and add a few pieces of water weed as well. Stand the dish in any convenient place that is not exposed to the full sun, and cover it with a piece of chicken wire if you have an inquisitive cat around the house. Daily observation is the rule from now on.

By using two containers you can compare growth rates under different conditions. Divide your original spawn into two lots and keep one in the house and one in the garden. See how much more quickly the indoor batch develops. If you have a thermometer you can make your observations more scientific by taking the temperature of the water daily—if possible, always at the same time of day.

Within a few days you will see the little black eggs changing into comma-shaped bodies. Write down

the age of the spawn when you first notice this change, and record with it the *average* daily temperature since you began your observations. Don't be surprised if some eggs turn grey and fail to change shape: there will be some infertile eggs in each batch.

The developing tadpoles soon acquire distinct heads and tails and start to wriggle about in the jelly. By the time the spawn is ten days old, most of the tadpoles will have wriggled right out of the jelly and you will see them clinging to the surface of the spawn or else to the neighbouring water weeds. Record the day on which the bulk of the tadpoles leave the jelly, and again note down the average daily temperature since the beginning of the project.

The tadpoles have no mouths when they first leave the jelly and they exist on the remains of the yolk from their eggs. They breathe by means of feathery gills fanning out from the sides of the body. After a day or two, their mouths open and they begin to feed on the minute water plants, called algae, that clothe the leaves of the larger plants.

The next obvious change comes when the tadpoles lose their external gills and start to breathe with internal gills like those of the fishes. Note down how many days they take to lose their external gills, and record the average daily temperature as before. The tadpoles are still largely vegetarian and they will be quite happy with a regular supply of pond plants which they can scrape with their horny jaws. You can also

give them dried fish food, but do not put too much in at once or you will pollute the water.

Your tadpoles will start to acquire legs when they are perhaps six or seven weeks old. The back legs appear first, as little buds at the base of the tail, and they grow quite large before the front legs make their appearance. Record the ages at which back and front legs appear, not forgetting the average daily temperature in each case. Try to record the average length of the tadpoles when the front legs appear. At this stage the animals are largely carnivorous and they will appreciate some finely chopped meat.

Soon after the front legs appear the tadpole's tail starts to shrink and the animal begins to come to the surface to gulp air into its newly-formed lungs. Record the age at which your tadpoles first start gulping air. You will then notice that the tadpoles' bodies are becoming distinctly frog-like. You must then give them a landing stage—a brick or a piece of turf in the dish—but make sure that they cannot jump out. It is necessary to release the little frogs as soon as they

start hopping out of the water regularly, for it is almost impossible to provide the regular supply of minute insects that they need. Put them into the pond where you found the spawn, or else into your garden pond. As well as learning how they grow, you will be helping with the conservation of these animals.

In addition to monitoring the effect of temperature, you can also investigate the action of iodine on the rate of development. Iodine is necessary for the production of the hormones controlling the change from tadpole to frog or toad, and if you add a few drops of iodine to the water when the hind legs start to appear you can speed up the change and produce miniature froglets or toadlets.

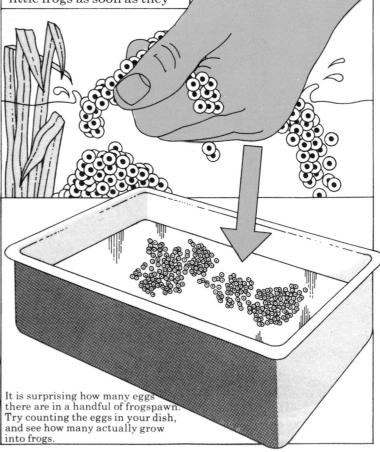

Collect your spawn as soon as you notice it. It will probably be only a day old if you have been watching the pond regularly.

It is surprising how many eggs there are in a handful of frogspawn. Try counting the eggs in your dish, and see how many actually grow into frogs.

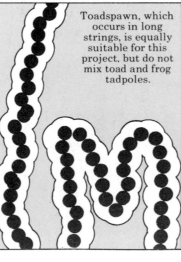

Toadspawn, which occurs in long strings, is equally suitable for this project, but do not mix toad and frog tadpoles.

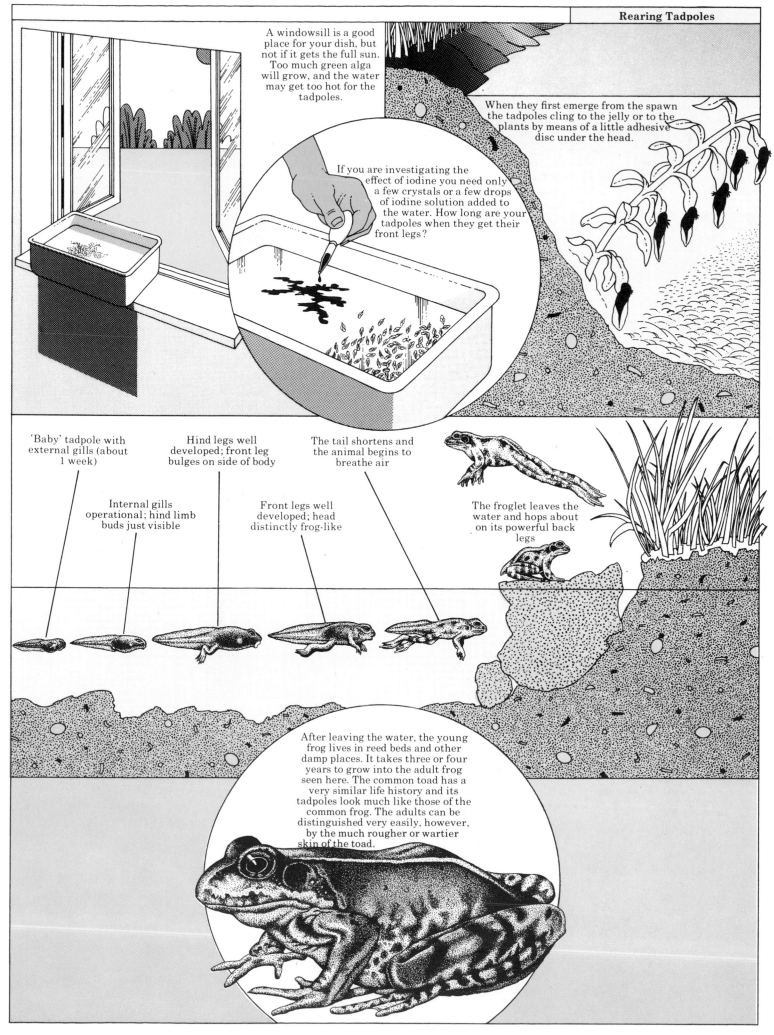

A windowsill is a good place for your dish, but not if it gets the full sun. Too much green alga will grow, and the water may get too hot for the tadpoles.

When they first emerge from the spawn the tadpoles cling to the jelly or to the plants by means of a little adhesive disc under the head.

If you are investigating the effect of iodine you need only a few crystals or a few drops of iodine solution added to the water. How long are your tadpoles when they get their front legs?

'Baby' tadpole with external gills (about 1 week)

Internal gills operational; hind limb buds just visible

Hind legs well developed; front leg bulges on side of body

Front legs well developed; head distinctly frog-like

The tail shortens and the animal begins to breathe air

The froglet leaves the water and hops about on its powerful back legs

After leaving the water, the young frog lives in reed beds and other damp places. It takes three or four years to grow into the adult frog seen here. The common toad has a very similar life history and its tadpoles look much like those of the common frog. The adults can be distinguished very easily, however, by the much rougher or wartier skin of the toad.

STUDYING SEAWEEDS

The nature and types of seaweeds, and the zones they inhabit on a rocky sea shore

Seaweeds are rather simple plants that never have any flowers. Some of them have large sucker-like holdfasts which fix them to the rocks, but their bodies are never divided into true roots, stems and leaves like those of the normal land plants. The seaweed body is generally called a thallus.

Seaweeds belong to the large group of plants called algae. Other members of the group include the blanket weeds that choke ponds in summer and the microscopic plants that turn aquarium water green if left in bright sunlight. Most algae live in water, but there are some terrestrial forms, including those that form green coatings on tree trunks.

You can find seaweeds washed up on almost any sea shore, but to see living seaweeds you must go to a rocky shore at low tide. The first thing you will notice is that the seaweeds grow in distinct zones. Green seaweeds dominate the upper levels of the shore, with abundant brown seaweeds lower down. Red seaweeds begin to appear at about low tide level, and if you dive down into the water you will see that these red seaweeds extend for quite some way out to sea. But the seaweeds do not cover all the sea bed: like land plants, they need sunlight to be able to make their food, and they can grow only in relatively shallow water where sunlight reaches the bottom.

This zonation is clearly determined by the abilities of the seaweeds to withstand exposure to the air and to fresh water when it rains. The uppermost parts of the shore are covered by the sea for only a few minutes each day—the short period around each high tide. The lowest parts of the shore, on the other hand, are covered for all but a few minutes each day.

Green seaweeds are obviously unaffected by long exposure to the air and fresh water, and many grow along the channels in which rain water runs over the rocks. Take care when walking over the green seaweeds because they are remarkably slippery. Apart from the broad-bladed sea lettuce, the green seaweeds include the very common grass kelp and sea moss. Grass kelp covers rocks with long, tubular strands, while sea moss looks like green feathers.

The brown seaweeds which live lower down on the shore contain a brown pigment as well as the green chlorophyll, not instead of it. The brown pigment helps the plants to absorb light more efficiently in the dim conditions. The various species of brown seaweeds are themselves zoned according to the amount of exposure they can stand. Channelled wrack, with its sprays of forking branches, occurs in the topmost zone and often extends well into the green seaweed zone. The plant gets its name from the prominent channel running along each frond. Below it come knotted wrack, bladder wrack, and podweed, all with the familiar bladders which children love to pop but whose real function is to buoy up the plants when they are under the water. Lower down on the shore there are some very large brown seaweeds, including the sugar kelp or sea belt which may be 4 metres (13 ft) long. Oarweed is nearly as long, but its thallus is split into numerous thin strips. The trailing strands of thongweed emerge from funnel-shaped bases among the oarweed. Peacock's tail prefers calmer waters just below low water mark, or rock pools.

Red seaweeds are generally smaller and often much more delicate than the brown species. Few can stand much exposure to the air and they are therefore found low down on the shore or in rock pools. The red pigment is even more efficient at absorbing light than the brown, thus allowing the plants to live at greater depths. Irish moss or carragheen, red laver and *Delesseria sanguinea* are among the most familiar of the red seaweeds. *Delesseria* (it has no common name) often grows on the fronds of oarweed. Some red seaweeds, such as coralweed, are very finely branched and often coated with a layer of limestone. These algae like the calm of rock pools.

While examining seaweeds you will find many animals sheltering among them. Periwinkles are particularly common, and so are the colourful top-shells, but perhaps the most interesting of the animals are the smaller ones that are permanently attached to the seaweeds. Some of these lodgers do not look like animals at all when you find them attached to a piece of limp seaweed in the air, but put the seaweed into a jar of sea water and you can see the animals come to life. What looks at first like a tuft of lifeless hair turns out to be an exquisite animal related to the pond-dwelling hydra (see page 26), and the tiny encrustations of sea mat (see picture at bottom right) put out sheets of minute tentacles to filter food from the water.

A good many families take home a piece of seaweed—usually a piece of oarweed or sea belt—as a weather forecaster. The weed can foretell rain because the mucilage covering it absorbs moisture from damp air and the weed becomes limp, but it reacts rather slowly and all it really does is tell you whether the air is damp or dry at any given time.

You can make a permanent collection of seaweeds by pressing them in the same way as you press other plants (see page 146), but they do not keep their colours at all well. Do not use too much pressure or fibres from the paper will become firmly embedded in the mucilage of the seaweeds and spoil the specimens. Lime-encrusted red seaweeds can be dried in the air as three-dimensional specimens, but they will turn white as they dry. Red laver and several other seaweeds can be eaten if you want to try something different for dinner.

#8 Bladder wrack

A rocky shore of the North Atlantic, showing the three major seaweed zones. The brown zone is largely missing in warmer parts of the world.

1 Herring gulls 2 Sea bindweed 3 Thrift
4 Sea lettuce (with a chameleon prawn in the enlargement) 5 Grass kelp 6 Sea moss 7 Channelled wrack 8 Bladder wrack (with periwinkles in the enlargement) 9 Peacock's tail 10 Sea belt 11 Podweed 12 Serrated wrack 13 Thongweed 14 Oarweed 15 Coralweed 16 *Delesseria* 17 Red laver 18 Irish moss (with sea mat in the enlargement)

THE PLEASURES OF BEACH-COMBING

A guide to the many fascinating natural and man-made objects that can be picked up along the seashore

Twice a day the tide ripples in over the beach and brings with it a rich assortment of driftwood and other material. Much of this is left on the beach, concentrated into a strand-line or tide-line which marks the highest level of each tide. A walk along the strand-lines will reveal an amazing variety of objects.

Try to get to the beach before the gulls and other birds have done too much damage. The birds are mainly after carrion and small animals such as sandhoppers, and they are not really interested in the beachcomber's quarry, but they do have the annoying habit of breaking open the best sea-urchin shells to eat the contents. The strand-line is often particularly rich after a storm on an exposed coast because the stronger waves carry so much more on to the coast, but remember that beachcombing is a very popular pastime—almost a way of life for some people—and the best possible time to walk the strand-line is before anyone else does, i.e. just after high tide. Keep your eyes open and you will be well rewarded.

Driftwood is usually a prominent constituent of the strand-line and it is well worth examining. Even an ordinary-looking board can reveal some fascinating patterns where the water has etched away the softer parts and left the harder parts of the grain standing out. Cleaned and varnished, these pieces of wood make attractive stands for flower arrangements. Natural fragments of wood, such as branches and roots, can be even more interesting: it is astonishing how many 'animal heads' you can see in a piece of driftwood by looking at it from different angles. Many of these pieces need nothing more than a wash to turn them into household ornaments.

Timber is subject to attack by several marine animals, and evidence of such attacks can often be seen in the wood cast up on the shore. If you find a piece of wood peppered with holes about 5 mm ($\frac{1}{5}$ in) across, you can be sure that it has been invaded by hordes of little slater-like animals called gribbles. These eat out narrow tunnels just under the surface and reduce the timber to a sponge-like object. Wider tunnels twisting through a piece of wood, and often bearing a thin, chalky lining, are the work of the shipworm, which is actually a very specialized bivalve mollusc. If you split open a piece of affected timber you will

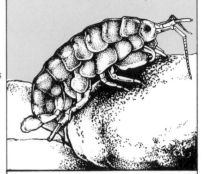

Hordes of sandhoppers live along the strand-line, where they provide a useful scavenging service by rapidly consuming decaying seaweed and other organic matter.

probably find in each tunnel the two tiny shells which the animal uses as drill bits to chew its way through the wood. Pieces of this riddled wood make interesting additions to the collection or the nature table, and if you don't want to keep them you can always put them on the fire. Notice the swarms of little sandhoppers that you disturb every time you move a piece of timber.

The strand-line usually contains many sea shells, although most of them are damaged in some way.

Driftwood sculpture: this gnarled piece of wood needed only a straight cut at one end to turn it into a human torso.

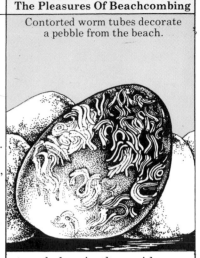

Contorted worm tubes decorate a pebble from the beach.

Crabs' claws are often common and they are particularly fascinating to children if the joints are still flexible enough for the claws to be opened and closed. The crabs' hard body-shields are also common, and can be very attractive. Many of them are covered with twisting white tubes, which were the homes of various marine worms. When a young worm settles on a hard surface, such as a crab shell or a stone, it secretes a limy tube around itself and remains there for the rest of its life. More lime is added to the front of the tube as the animal grows. These worms feed by filtering food particles from the water with feathery tentacles.

Cuttlebones, which are the chalky skeletons of cuttlefish, are common on many beaches and, as long as they are not contaminated with oil, you can take them home for your chickens or cage birds. Wash them well to remove the salt, and your birds will enjoy them. The lime will help their egg shells. Other familiar strand-line objects include the sponge-like balls of whelk egg-cases and the horny mermaids' purses. The latter are the egg-cases of skates and dogfish and other small sharks. Complete starfish and urchin shells can be found if you get to the strand line before the gulls, and they make attractive exhibits if thoroughly dried. Jellyfish are often cast up, but they do not make suitable collectors' items. Some can inflict painful stings, even when they appear to be dead, so be careful how you handle them.

Dead birds and their skulls and skeletons are frequently washed up, and you can deal with these in the way described on page 68. Look for rings on the legs, and send any you find to the address on page 188. Seals and fishes are also marked with metal or plastic tags to find out how far they travel and how long they live. If you find one of these tags you should take it to the local museum, or if there is an address on the tag, send it there.

Many people like to throw bottles into the sea with messages, in the hope that one day a reply will come from a distant land. Scientists do this regularly to discover the speeds and directions of ocean currents. You may find their plastic cards or bottles on the shore, in which case you should send them to the addresses given.

Beaches bordering some of the warmer seas often have strand-lines composed almost entirely of soft brown balls. These consist of the fibrous remains of a marine flowering plant called *Posidonia*. The fibres are rolled into balls by the waves. Great banks of them build up on some beaches.

Strand-lines littered with plastic ropes and bottles are certainly unsightly, but these materials do not do much harm. Some animals even make their homes in them. Nylon fishing lines are a real problem, however, because birds get tangled up in them. Always pick up these lines and take them away. Oil is also a problem on many beaches and the beachcomber must wear old clothes. You can remove grease from your hands with eucalyptus oil. And a final word of warning: never tamper with metal drums or similar containers that might be washed up on to the beach. They might contain dangerous substances and you should report them to the coastguards.

Strand-lines on a remote beach

1 Worm tubes of *Pomatoceros* on a stone
2 Whelk egg-case
3 Glass float covered with barnacles
4 Log with shipworm tunnels
5 Mermaid's purse
6 Sea-urchin shell
7 Bird skull
8 Worm tubes of *Spirorbis* on a stone
9 Ring from bird leg
10 Decaying seaweed
11 Whelk shell
12 Dead crab (upside down)
13 Dead starfish
14 Beach ball (*Posidonia*)
15 Cuttlebone
16 Razor shells

COLLECTING SEA SHELLS

Identifying and displaying the homes of the molluscs – and watching their movements

Sea shells can be collected in abundance on nearly every visit to the sea shore, and their beauty ensures that nearly every family will return from a seaside holiday with at least some shells in their luggage.

With a few rare exceptions, sea shells belong to a group of animals called molluscs. These creatures have no backbones, and their shells serve as both homes and skeletons. Two major types of shells are found on the shore: the bivalve type and the snail type. The bivalve is so called because, in life, the shell is in two parts or valves, joined together at one edge by a hinge and some interlocking teeth. Shells of

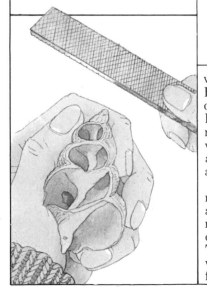

Most sea snails, like land snails, have elaborately coiled shells. You can see how the living-chamber coils round inside the shell by carefully filing away one side of an old shell.

this kind include cockles, mussels, razor shells, clams, oysters, venus shells, scallops and tellins. Mussels and oysters are normally fixed to rocks, but most bivalves live just under the sand or mud. When the tide is in, the elastic hinge causes the shells to gape slightly, and two muscular tubes or siphons emerge from the body. Water is sucked in through one tube and food particles are filtered from it before it passes out through the other tube. You can watch this activity if you dig up a few cockles or other bivalves and put them in a jar of sand and sea water for a short time. When the tide goes out, the bivalves retire down into the sand and powerful muscles hold the valves tightly closed.

Because of their preferred habitats, bivalve shells are most frequently

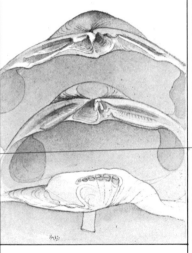

Parts of three bivalve valves, showing the hinge teeth and the scars left by the adductor (closure) muscles. The teeth on one valve fit neatly into slots on the opposing valve and help to hold the two together.

washed up on sandy beaches. Extensive shell banks develop in some places, and luckily you can take as many shells as you like without harm, for the animals that inhabited them are dead.

Sea snails live on both rocky and sandy shores, although they are usually more common on rocky coasts or on coral reefs. They glide about in the same way as land snails and they feed on seaweeds or on other

animals. They are mainly active when the tide is in, and you will find them hiding among the seaweeds when the tide is out, but you might well find them moving about if you go down to the beach with a torch at night. The limpets are among the commonest species on the rocks. They sit exposed when the tide is out, but they protect themselves by pulling the conical shell down very tightly against the rock. In time, the shell wears away a little ring in the rock. The limpet has a remarkable homing ability, as you will see if you mark a few shells with waterproof paint when the tide is out. Put a spot of paint on the rock by each one as well. If you visit them at night, or even dive down to see them when the tide is in, you will probably find them moving about and rasping algae from the rocks, but if you go back the next day when the tide is out you will find each one sitting quietly by its home spot.

Although empty sea shells are very easy to find, they are not always in good condition. The surface gets worn as the shells roll about on the sand, and many shells lose their colours when their surface layers are removed. You might have to search for some time to find a good shell of a particular species, but searching is part of the fun. It should not be necessary to kill the animals to collect the shells, although you will do no harm if you take a few of the common species like winkles and mussels. For a really scientific collection, you might need to collect living animals because this is almost the only way to get the horny 'lids' off the sea snails. These discs are attached to the animals' bodies and they close the shells when the animals retire. The animals can be killed by immersing them momentarily in boiling water, and the flesh can then be removed with a pin or a tooth pick. If the body breaks and leaves the apical part in the shell it is best to let it dry thoroughly rather than to poke about and risk breaking the shell. When properly dry, there should be no smell, but you could

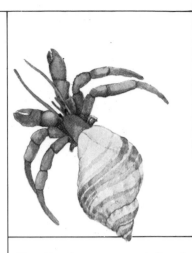

Hermit crabs are commonly found in whelk and winkle shells, which they use to protect their soft bodies. The crab moves to a larger shell as it grows.

employ a few ants to clean out the remains (see page 98).

Empty shells picked up on the beach can be cleaned with water and a soft brush. Never try to varnish them unless you want them purely for decoration, because you need to know what the natural surface texture is like if you are going to identify your shells properly. You can store the shells in match boxes or plastic tubes, in plastic bags, or in a special drawer like that shown on the opposite page. They will keep indefinitely without any further treatment. Unless you have two specimens, bivalve shells should be separated by cutting along the hinge with a razor blade so that you can see both sides of the valves. Soften the hinge by immersing the shell in warm water if necessary.

Sea shells can make up attractive tableaux, their various shapes combined (like pieces of driftwood, see page 36) to suggest other forms. They can also be used to decorate the frame of a seaside souvenir – a painting or a holiday photograph.

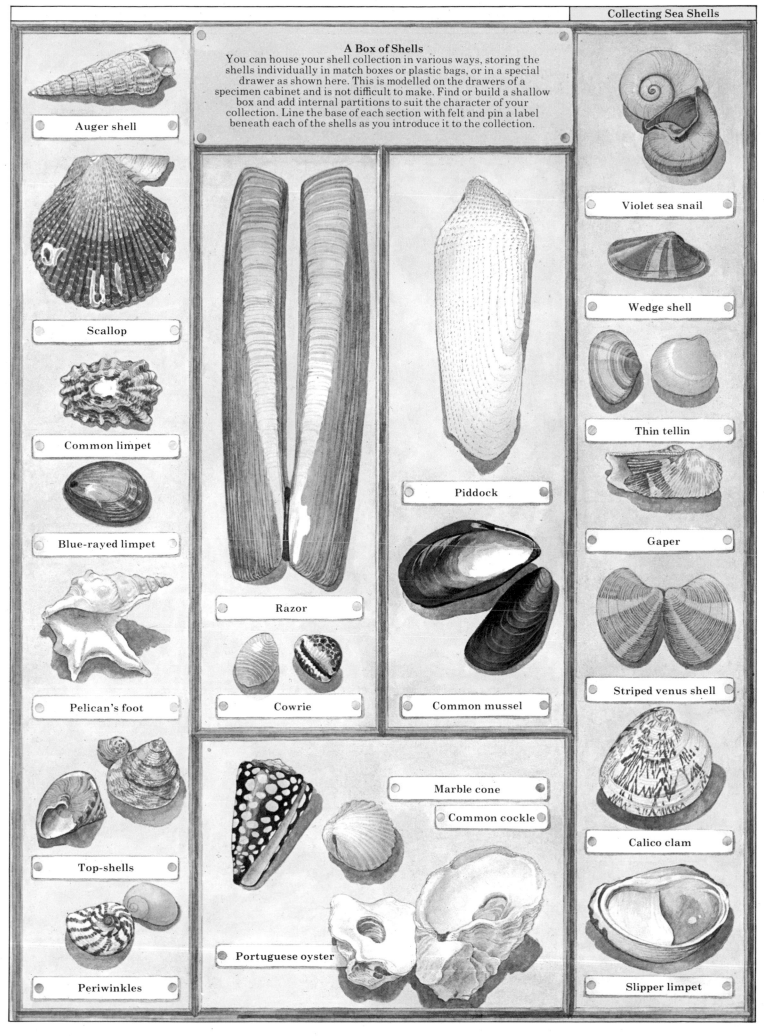

A Box of Shells
You can house your shell collection in various ways, storing the shells individually in match boxes or plastic bags, or in a special drawer as shown here. This is modelled on the drawers of a specimen cabinet and is not difficult to make. Find or build a shallow box and add internal partitions to suit the character of your collection. Line the base of each section with felt and pin a label beneath each of the shells as you introduce it to the collection.

Auger shell

Scallop

Common limpet

Blue-rayed limpet

Pelican's foot

Top-shells

Periwinkles

Razor

Cowrie

Piddock

Common mussel

Marble cone

Common cockle

Portuguese oyster

Violet sea snail

Wedge shell

Thin tellin

Gaper

Striped venus shell

Calico clam

Slipper limpet

Birds are the most widely admired, the most melodious and the most studied of all animals, whether by the professional ornithologist or the amateur naturalist who happens to be interested in their habits and behaviour. Birds far outnumber all the other back-boned animals, or vertebrates, except fishes. They can be found in all types of places from city streets and parks to the highest mountain tops.

All birds have feathers and most of those we see are experts at flying. To enable a bird to fly, the fore-limbs have been modified into wings. All flying birds take off with a great flapping of their wings, but once airborne they can fly in three different ways, and this helps us to identify them at a distance. Some birds such as sparrows, tits, thrushes and warblers 'power fly': they propel themselves through the air by flapping their wings continuously. Others such as gulls, hawks and vultures 'soar', which is the term for wind-riding or gliding. And yet others fly by different combinations of flapping and soaring. Ibises flap their wings several times, then glide for some distance before flapping the wings again. Woodpeckers and nuthatches use a similar method, but they beat their wings faster, and their downward swoop when gliding gives them an undulating flight pattern. With time and patience it becomes easy to identify a bird by the flight-pattern.

Powerful chest muscles flap the wings up and down: one main muscle pulls the wing up and the other main muscle pulls it down. The speed of wing beat is often related to the bird's size. Large herons and eagles flap their wings about once every second, while the tiny hummingbirds vibrate their wings 80 times a second, so fast the wings appear as just a blur.

Wing shapes vary, depending on the way of life of the birds. Gulls and albatrosses spend most of their time in the air and have long narrow wings. The swift, much smaller than a gull, uses its sharply pointed wings for fast flight as it darts after insects.

Slow fliers and birds that hunt in dense woods have short, rounded wings so they can move around obstacles easily. The short broad wings of the goshawk allow it to chase small mammals and birds through bushes. Other birds of prey that hunt in more open spaces have longer wings.

The bird's skeleton is designed to reduce the weight of the bird, making flight easier. A bird's bones are hollow and braced across at intervals with

Seed-eaters, such as the various kinds of finches, have strong, conical bills for crushing seeds. Cross-bills have bills where the tips of each half or mandible cross each other. This odd-shaped beak is used to force open fir cones to extract the seeds. Birds of prey have strong, hooked beaks for tearing flesh. The long beaks of many wading birds such as curlews, herons and stilts are used to catch water animals such as fishes or mud-living creatures. Warblers use their thin, pointed beaks like a pair of tweezers to pick up insects. Birds such as swallows, which catch insects in flight, have short beaks that open very wide.

CHAPTER 3

BIRDS

Equipped with wings for fore-limbs, the ability of birds to fly makes them the most admired and most studied of all animals

bars of thin bone to strengthen them. Break a chicken's bone across, and you will see this structure.

Every bird has some kind of beak or bill which, besides being used to feed, has other important uses. A bird's beak must perform all the actions that the fore-limbs do in other animals (because a bird's fore-limbs are the wings). Thus the beak holds objects, picks them up and puts them down. The intricate nests that many birds make show how well they use their beaks.

The shape of a bird's beak is adapted to its food and its way of feeding.

Like most animals, a bird depends on its senses for survival. The most important senses to a bird are sight and hearing. Smell, unlike mammals, is hardly used at all. If you watch any bird you can soon see that it uses its eyes to obtain most of its information about the world around it.

One thing that attracts us to watch birds is that most are active during the daytime and many are very colourful, which suggests to us, quite rightly, that a bird can distinguish colours.

The various colours of the different kinds of birds

are closely tied to their behaviour and way of life. There are two main groups, birds that have dull colours for concealment (cryptic coloration) and those that advertise their presence with bright colours (phaneric). Those birds that are concealed against their background need to be so coloured to hide from enemies. The female mallard is brown so she can be well hidden from foxes while she is sitting and incubating her eggs on her ground nest. The brilliant hues and colours of birds are also very important during courtship, and for the defence of their territories (see page 42).

Because birds are easier to watch than most animals much of the important research into animal behaviour has been done with them. If you watch birds for a while you will soon see a variety of behaviour patterns emerging, in activities such as feeding, drinking and warning displays; some of these may well have a wider application, being found in many animals other than birds.

When you go out to observe birds, remember to disturb them as little as possible, never take their eggs or nestlings, and do not destroy the vegetation around their nests.

There are laws in most developed countries that protect many animals, including birds and rare plants.

The countries in the European Economic Community follow legislation formulated by the Council for Europe.

Each country also has its own laws to protect valuable wild life. The Protection of Birds Act in Britain, for example, covers game and other wild birds; the original Act was passed in 1954, and has since been considerably strengthened. In the United States the Washington Convention of 1973 protects wild birds, and there is liaison between Canada and the United States over the bird protection laws designed to take care of the migratory species that journey north and south each year.

HOW TO WATCH BIRDS

Hints for bird watchers, including how to make and use a hide

Birds are basically timid creatures, but most of them are active by day and they are easier to watch than most mammals. If you can avoid frightening them you can spend many hours watching them go about their daily lives. Birds have sharp ears and excellent eyesight, so always walk quietly and wear clothes that blend in with the surroundings.

Many bird watchers use hides in which to conceal themselves, especially when they want to photograph birds or watch them for long periods. But a hide is of use only when the birds stay more or less in one place. It is particularly useful for watching birds at their nests, and hides are also widely used for watching birds on a lake.

Professional bird watchers and photographers often build very elaborate hides, even using scaffolding to erect them at tree-top height, but the family naturalist need not go to great lengths to make a hide. Eight strong canes or other twigs cut from a hedge will form a suitable framework, and they can be covered with sacking or old sheets sewn together. Paint the cover green and brown and you have all you really need. If the upright poles have Y-shaped tops the other poles can simply be laid over them as shown in the drawing. Such a hide can be erected with the minimum of noise and disturbance of the birds.

The size of the hide depends very much on the size of the people who are going to use it. Whenever possible it should be tall enough for you to stand up in it. The floor space should be large enough to accommodate yourself and a small stool and, if you are taking photographs, your camera tripod as well. You will need three holes or slits in the front of the cover: one for you to use when sitting on the stool, one to be used while you are standing up, and one for the camera. The two viewing holes allow you to change position every now and then—very important if you are watching for a long time and get uncomfortable.

Birds are very wary of objects that suddenly appear in their surroundings and the ideal thing is to set up the hide several days before you want to use it. This is not usually possible on land with public access, but you might be able to stand up a few branches in the place where the hide will go. Failing that, you could try a portable 'shield' composed of branches attached to a light framework. Hold it in front of you as you approach the birds and move just one or two steps at a time. Stay quite still for a minute or two before you move again, and the birds may not be too bothered about the gradual approach of your shield.

Position your hide or shield so that you get the best views of birds going to and from their nests, but do not attempt to move branches in order to get a better view of the nest itself. This may cause the birds to desert the nest.

As well as using your hide to watch nesting behaviour, you can use it to investigate territorial behaviour among small birds. The 'robin redbreast' is an excellent subject for this. Choose a spot where you know there is a robin and put up a simple model of another robin. It need not be a very good model, as long as it has a red breast. Watch the resident robin attack the model. You can, of course, do this experiment in your garden and watch from the window.

If you place your hide close enough to a nest you may be able to see enough with your naked eye, but for more distant viewing you need binoculars. Some bird watchers use telescopes, but a telescope has very few advantages over a good pair of binoculars and it has many disadvantages. A telescope can give much greater magnifications than binoculars, but it is much more difficult to pick up and follow a moving bird with a telescope. A telescope is therefore useful only when you are watching a distant bird which stays put for long periods (see picture). The

A simple hide set up to watch a family of birds at their nest. The birds will accept the hide as just another bush after a day or two and you can watch them easily. On no account try to bend or remove branches to get a better view. The birds may desert the nest if you do.

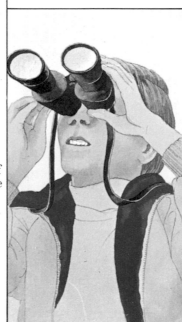

bird watcher on the move needs binoculars which can be focused on a moving bird in the shortest possible time. Pages 166–7 tell you how to choose the right pair of binoculars.

While on the move, always listen for bird songs. Walk quietly and stop to listen after every few steps. The songs will often give away the positions of the birds, and you can then approach them even more stealthily. Birds have a poor sense of smell, so you do not have to worry about approaching from down-wind as long as you keep quiet. Try to learn the songs of the common birds in your area so that you know what bird is singing even if you cannot see it.

While watching birds through your binoculars you might well see some with rings on their legs. These will have been put on by trained bird watchers and they help professional ornithologists to find out how far birds travel and how long they live.

Always keep the strap of your binoculars round your neck to prevent accidents. You can then swing them up to your eyes very quickly.

A telescope in use to watch a heron in the reed beds. This is the ideal situation for a telescope, but you need a tripod for prolonged viewing as a telescope can get very heavy. Because of its high magnification, you need good light to use a telescope.

An infuriated robin attacking a red-breasted model that has been placed in its territory. It is stimulated by the red colour and will attack with equal venom a bunch of red feathers.

Rings are put on birds only by trained bird watchers, either when the young birds are in the nest or when older birds have been caught in special traps.

The bird is held firmly, but gently, in one hand and the ring—the right size for the particular bird—is put on with special ringing pliers.

MIGRATING BIRDS

Tracking the travel patterns of birds as they fly in search of food and warmth

If you watch a place where birds are likely to congregate, perhaps at your bird table feeder (see page 52) or at a particular spot in a wood, you will soon see that the birds regularly come and go at specific times of day. If you watch over a period of months at regular intervals, you will notice that some birds are present all the year round, but many disappear with the onset of the colder weather and return in spring when winter is over and the weather begins to get warm again. Meanwhile, other birds will arrive in autumn and spend the winter months in your area and then disappear again in the spring.

Birds are adapted to travelling distances regularly to obtain food, or to reach sleeping quarters, and they will journey thousands of miles to escape the harsh winters when there is little food available and it gets too cold and wet for their warm bodies.

These comings and goings are termed migrations, and all the movements, whether long or short, whether across half an acre or half a continent, are concerned mainly with survival, reproduction, with the business of staying alive and finding a living.

In recent years, with information gained from special expeditions, from radar scanning and bird-ringing (see page 42) we have learnt a great deal about the routes taken by birds all over the world. We now know that most land birds do not like to cross wide stretches of water, and take the shortest distance between two land masses. The cuckoo and wood warbler journey from Europe in autumn to spend the winter in central Africa, and most cross the Mediterranean Sea near the Straits of Gibraltar, where the sea journey is minimal. Others, however, such as the ruddy shelduck, European crane, and some wagtails do brave a longer sea crossing.

In America the birds do not have to overcome the great obstacles that European birds face with each journey – the Mediterranean Sea, the Alps, the Pyrenees and the Sahara Desert. In North America the main mountain chain, the Rockies, runs in a north-south direction – the same as that followed by the migrating birds – and so it is not an obstacle. The main barrier for those birds that want to reach the tropical areas of South America is the Gulf of Mexico. But the birds can follow the land connection of Central America or use the islands of the West Indies as stepping stones on their way south. The routes the birds take in America are well studied and the American ornithologist Frederick Lincoln mapped four land routes he calls 'flyways', plus a Pacific sea route and an Atlantic sea route.

It is a useful and interesting occupation to note the times of arrival and departure of migrant birds in your study area, and to record the details in your nature notebook (see page 14). Note whether the dates vary from year to year. It is also possible to track the daily migrations that certain birds make from their feeding grounds and their nocturnal roosting places.

Starlings habitually gather in immense numbers in cities in the evening to roost, making a tremendous noise and damaging buildings with their droppings. At dawn they take to the air to fly several miles to feeding grounds in the countryside.

The golden plover covers more than 6,000 miles in its round-trip, returning in spring over land rather than by the oceanic route that it takes on its journey south.

The Arctic tern flies non-stop to the opposite end of the world to enjoy the southern summer. Its annual round-trip is more than 22,000 miles.

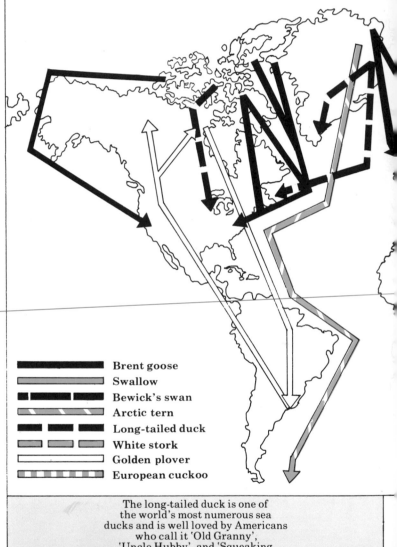

Brent goose
Swallow
Bewick's swan
Arctic tern
Long-tailed duck
White stork
Golden plover
European cuckoo

The long-tailed duck is one of the world's most numerous sea ducks and is well loved by Americans who call it 'Old Granny', 'Uncle Hubby', and 'Squeaking Duck'.

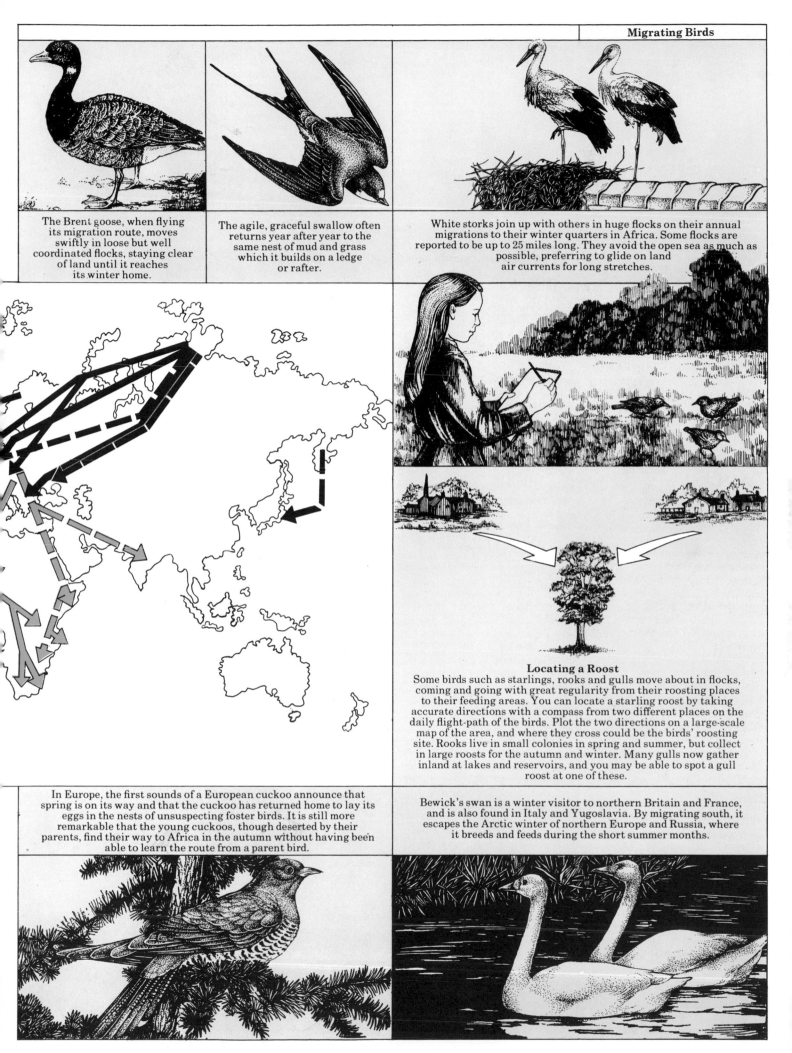

The Brent goose, when flying its migration route, moves swiftly in loose but well coordinated flocks, staying clear of land until it reaches its winter home.

The agile, graceful swallow often returns year after year to the same nest of mud and grass which it builds on a ledge or rafter.

White storks join up with others in huge flocks on their annual migrations to their winter quarters in Africa. Some flocks are reported to be up to 25 miles long. They avoid the open sea as much as possible, preferring to glide on land air currents for long stretches.

Locating a Roost

Some birds such as starlings, rooks and gulls move about in flocks, coming and going with great regularity from their roosting places to their feeding areas. You can locate a starling roost by taking accurate directions with a compass from two different places on the daily flight-path of the birds. Plot the two directions on a large-scale map of the area, and where they cross could be the birds' roosting site. Rooks live in small colonies in spring and summer, but collect in large roosts for the autumn and winter. Many gulls now gather inland at lakes and reservoirs, and you may be able to spot a gull roost at one of these.

In Europe, the first sounds of a European cuckoo announce that spring is on its way and that the cuckoo has returned home to lay its eggs in the nests of unsuspecting foster birds. It is still more remarkable that the young cuckoos, though deserted by their parents, find their way to Africa in the autumn without having been able to learn the route from a parent bird.

Bewick's swan is a winter visitor to northern Britain and France, and is also found in Italy and Yugoslavia. By migrating south, it escapes the Arctic winter of northern Europe and Russia, where it breeds and feeds during the short summer months.

COLLECTING FEATHERS

Feathers are for flight, for keeping a bird warm, and for giving signals. Here are some projects using feathers after the birds have discarded them

A complete wing from a dead bird can be pinned on to a board until thoroughly dry and then stored in a box or a large envelope with some mothballs.

eathers can be picked up on a country walk or in a park at any time of the year. Most of them are probably rather dull in colour, but they can nevertheless be built up into an interesting and informative collection.

Examine a typical feather and you will see that it consists of a horny shaft and a flat vane. The latter is composed of hundreds of slender branches called barbs. You can separate them by pulling the vane gently with your fingers, and you can join them up again by stroking the feather very firmly from the bottom upwards. It is as if the neighbouring barbs are connected by zip fasteners, and this is not far from the truth. If you look at a feather with a good lens you will see that each barb is connected to the next by hundreds of minute branches called barbules. Tiny hooks on the barbules catch hold of the barbules of the barb in front, as shown on the opposite page.

Collect only clean, undamaged feathers and notice that, apart from having different colours, they are of several different types. Some are very stiff and pointed, with the shaft very much off centre. These are the primary flight feathers from the wing-tip. Secondary feathers, from the hind edge of the wing, are less pointed but otherwise quite similar. Contour feathers from the general surface of the body are like small secondary feathers, still with the shaft markedly off centre. Tail feathers may be as long as or longer than the primary feathers, but they can always be recognized because the shaft is in the centre. Some feathers, notably those of swans and various game birds, have a small branch, called the aftershaft, growing out from the base of the vane. You might also pick up some very fluffy feathers without an obvious vane. These are down feathers. They lie under the contour feathers and their job is to keep the bird warm. Some contour feathers have fluffy bases with the barbs not joined together, while the feathers of the ostrich and some other flightless birds are all fluffy. They do not need a smooth, streamlined surface because they do not fly.

Some colourful feathers, such as those from the wings of a goldfinch or a jay, are easy to identify, but most are more difficult. The area in which you find them sometimes gives a clue. Grey feathers picked up in a forest, for example, will tend to belong to one of the pigeons. Some feathers can be identified by reference to books, but the best plan is to take your feathers along to a museum.

When you have identified your feathers you can fix them into a notebook, perhaps devoting half a page to each species. A small slit in the page is all that is necessary to hold the feathers securely.

You will occasionally come across dead birds in the countryside, and you can then improve your feather collection considerably because you can collect all kinds of feathers from a known species. These named feathers will help you to identify some that you find later. You can also see how the various kinds of feathers fit on the bird's body, and you can remove one complete wing for your collection.

Although damaged feathers are not normally suitable for the collection, they do sometimes tell a story. Predatory mammals often bite off birds' feathers in a characteristic way, as shown on the opposite page, and you can then tell how a bird met its death.

Although feathers can be picked up at any time, they are most likely to be found in early spring and mid-summer, when the birds are moulting. The black feathers seen here are from a rook's wing, and that on the right is from a game bird.

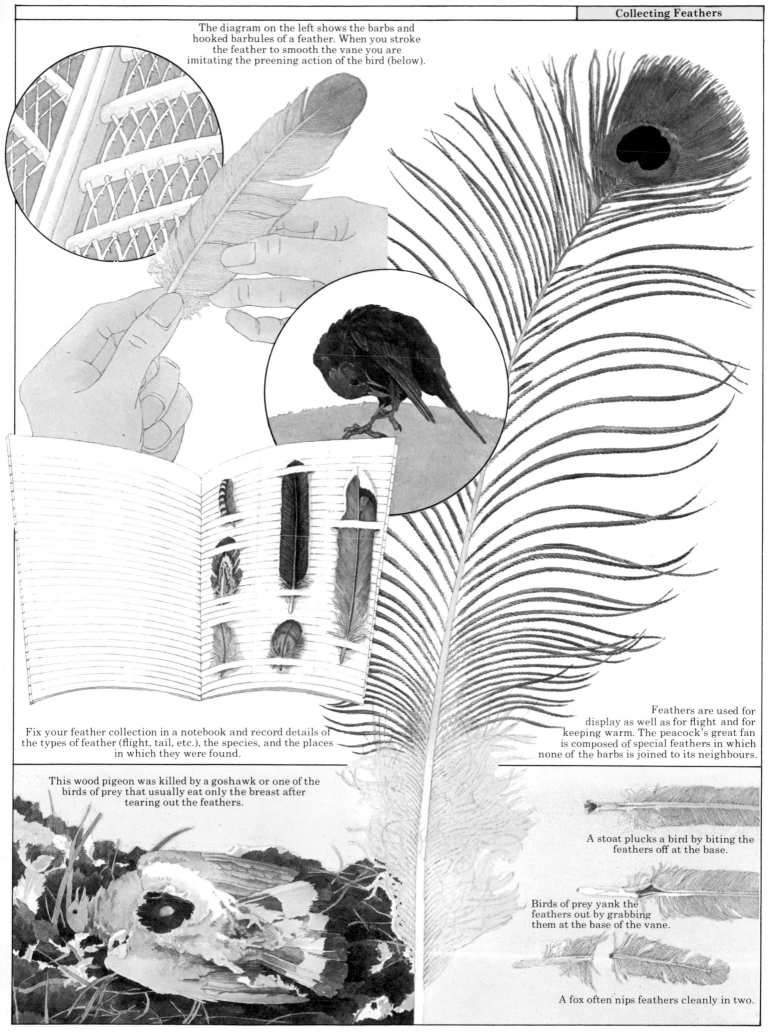

The diagram on the left shows the barbs and hooked barbules of a feather. When you stroke the feather to smooth the vane you are imitating the preening action of the bird (below).

Fix your feather collection in a notebook and record details of the types of feather (flight, tail, etc.), the species, and the places in which they were found.

Feathers are used for display as well as for flight and for keeping warm. The peacock's great fan is composed of special feathers in which none of the barbs is joined to its neighbours.

This wood pigeon was killed by a goshawk or one of the birds of prey that usually eat only the breast after tearing out the feathers.

A stoat plucks a bird by biting the feathers off at the base.

Birds of prey yank the feathers out by grabbing them at the base of the vane.

A fox often nips feathers cleanly in two.

STUDYING BIRD PELLETS

Identifying pellets, and dissecting them to see what the birds have been eating

An owl may eat three or four small rodents or shrews in one night, consuming large amounts of indigestible bones and fur. This material is gradually compacted in the gizzard and then coughed up and ejected during the day in the form of rounded or cylindrical pellets. The bird often produces two pellets in a day, the second being ejected just before it flies off for another evening's hunting. If you know where an owl roosts you will be able to collect plenty of pellets, for a regular roost will have a large pile under it. By dissecting the pellets you can learn a lot about what the owl has been eating.

Don't worry if you don't know where to find an owl: you can often find pellets simply by looking in and around old buildings, especially derelict barns and windmills, and by hunting around the bases of large trees, in woods and even in city parks.

A freshly ejected pellet is coated with mucus, which makes it easy for the bird to bring it up from the gizzard, but this mucus soon dries and the pellet becomes firm and grey. Small bones may be visible on the surface of some pellets, but they are usually firmly bound in with fur.

Barn owl pellets are easily identified when fresh because they are coated with a smooth, blackish crust. They are spherical or cylindrical, with a diameter of 2·5 cm (1 in) or more and a length of up to 5 cm (2 in). Because of the barn owl's association with human habitations, the pellets often contain house sparrow remains as well as the bones of small mammals.

The pellets of the long-eared owl are up to 7·5 cm (3 in) long and about the same diameter as those of the barn owl, but they lack the dark crust. They contain the remains of small mammals and birds and are most often found at the bases of trees in coniferous forests. Pellets of the short-eared owl are similar to those of the long-eared species, but often much longer. They are often pointed at one end and they are found mainly on tussocks of grass and other similar sites in grassland. The short-eared owl feeds very largely on voles. Vole remains thus make up the bulk of the pellets. The tawny owl produces a cylindrical pellet about the

Barns, church towers, and other old buildings are good places in which to look for owl pellets. The birds' white droppings will often tell you where to look, although they are not usually mixed with the pellets.

same size as the barn owl's pellet, but it is often pointed at both ends and it has a much rougher or lumpier surface than the pellets of other owls: bones are often quite obvious on the surface. These pellets, which contain the remains of birds and small mammals, are most often found in coniferous woods.

The little owl, as befits its size and name, produces a much smaller pellet, only about 2·5 cm (1 in) long and little more than half this in diameter. This owl eats large amounts of beetles, and its pellets are often coloured black by the horny wing-cases of these insects. Other owls eat some beetles, but the remains do not contribute significantly to the pellets. Little owls also eat some mice and small birds, and their pellets can be found in old buildings and hollow trees.

Some people might hesitate to pick up and examine what sounds like a rather unpleasant object, but owl pellets are surprisingly clean, and very interesting. Instructions for dissecting them are given on the opposite page.

Owls are not the only birds that eject pellets. Hawks and other birds of prey produce pellets which are superficially very similar to owl pellets, and you often find them in similar places, but you can distinguish them from owl pellets simply by breaking them open. Hawks can digest bones, and their pellets contain little but fur and feathers together with a few claws and the horny coverings of beaks. You cannot easily decide what a hawk has been eating by looking at its pellets.

Crows produce rather loose pellets with a good deal of plant matter in them, and usually some small stones as well. Look under a rookery and you will find lots of yellowish pellets composed largely of straw fragments. Gulls also produce pellets, and these are often very interesting because of the omnivorous and scavenging habits of these birds. Sea shells, insects, plant material, and bones can all be found in gull pellets.

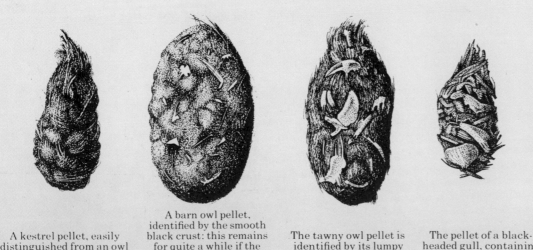

A kestrel pellet, easily distinguished from an owl pellet by the lack of bones inside.

A barn owl pellet, identified by the smooth black crust: this remains for quite a while if the pellet is protected from the weather.

The tawny owl pellet is identified by its lumpy appearance and rough surface.

The pellet of a black-headed gull, containing fish bones and plant fragments.

How to Dissect an Owl Pellet

Dissecting an owl pellet to see what the bird has been eating is a very easy and interesting exercise. There are two main ways of going about it – the wet method and the dry method – but, whichever method you choose, you should first weigh your selected pellet and make a sketch of its size and shape.

The wet method, which is the easier of the two, involves breaking the pellet very carefully into several pieces and putting them into a jar of water. Leave them there for a few hours and then gently shake the jar with a circular motion. Some of the fur or feathers will float to the top and you can pour this debris away. Do not stir the contents of the jar or you will break some of the delicate bones. Re-fill the jar with water after decanting the floating debris, and leave it for a few more hours. Repeat the shaking and decanting several times until you have removed the bulk of the fur or feathers. Pour the remaining material into a shallow dish with some clean water and use a fine pair of tweezers to pick out the tiny bones and teeth. A needle mounted in a wooden handle will help you, and you can use a fine paint brush to remove traces of fur and feathers.

For the dry method, you merely use your needle and tweezers to pull the pellet gently apart, but dried fur and feathers are remarkably tough and it is sometimes difficult to extract the bones without breaking them.

Having extracted the bones, you must bleach them in hydrogen peroxide for a few minutes. Do not leave the skulls in too long or the teeth will fall out. Let the bones dry, and then glue them lightly to a card bearing your drawing of the original pellet and, if possible, the name of the owl that produced it. Try to arrange the bones in groups, so that the skulls are together, the limb bones are together, and so on. The skulls and lower jaws are easy to recognize and identify. The three mammals most likely to contribute to your owl pellet are mice, voles and shrews, and their teeth are very different. Shrews have lots of very small, pointed teeth. Mice and voles both have long, curved yellow teeth at the front and a row of grinding teeth on each side, but the crowns of the grinding teeth differ. Those of voles have a zig-zag pattern, but a mouse's teeth, like our own, have little cusps. There will be lots of delicate skull fragments, and you will also recognize the triangular shoulder blades quite easily. Hip bones have circular sockets to take the ball-joints of the upper leg bones. With practice, you will be able to recognize most of the other bones as well.

You Will Need

Fine tweezers
Needle
Glue
Hydrogen peroxide

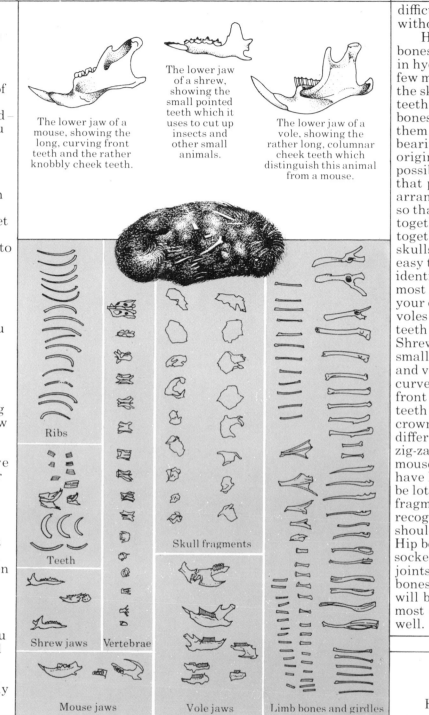

The lower jaw of a mouse, showing the long, curving front teeth and the rather knobbly cheek teeth.

The lower jaw of a shrew, showing the small pointed teeth which it uses to cut up insects and other small animals.

The lower jaw of a vole, showing the rather long, columnar cheek teeth which distinguish this animal from a mouse.

Ribs

Teeth

Shrew jaws

Vertebrae

Mouse jaws

Skull fragments

Vole jaws

Limb bones and girdles

Great care and patience are needed for the dry dissection of an owl pellet. A large pellet will contain hundreds of tiny bones, belonging to several different animals.

OLD BIRDS' NESTS

How and when to collect nests and examine their construction

When the leaves fall from the trees and hedgerows in the autumn a surprising number of vacated birds' nests is revealed—nests which were so well camouflaged that you could never have seen them during the summer breeding season. Bird-protection laws rightly prohibit any interference with nests during the breeding season, but there is no harm in collecting and examining the old nests because, with a few exceptions, birds make fresh nests each year. Species that use the same nests from year to year include herons, rooks and some other crows, and most birds of prey, and these nests should, of course, be left undisturbed. These birds tend to build very large and inaccessible nests high in the trees or on rugged cliffs. An eagle's nest, for example, is usually more than two metres ($6\frac{1}{2}$ ft) in diameter and extremely heavy. The mud nests of house martins, swallows and swifts should also be left alone, and you should not attempt to take nests out of tree holes unless you can do it without enlarging the holes, which spoils them for future nesting.

If you wait until the leaves start to fall from the trees before you start to collect your nests you are very unlikely to disturb any breeding birds, but don't be too surprised if you find a mouse or a dormouse curled up inside a nest: a moss-lined nest makes an excellent bed for one of these small mammals.

Nests are best collected, therefore, in October and November in the temperate regions of Europe and North America, as the weather will not have done too much damage to the nests. You can go on collecting until the end of January, but nests in more exposed positions have usually deteriorated sadly by then.

Most birds make their nests secure by binding them firmly to the twigs of the trees or bushes, but some simply lodge their nests in forks of branches. You will need a pair of secateurs to remove the fixed nests, but do not cut away any more of the twigs than necessary. Cut as close to the nest as you can and lift it out: the twigs around which the nest was constructed will form a skeleton and keep the shape of the nest while you cut it out. Unattached nests are often more fragile and it is worth gently pushing some cotton wool into one of these nests before you try to lift the nest out. Old leather gloves or gardening gloves will save your hands if the bush or hedge is at all prickly, and the gloves may also protect you from flea bites.

Having removed the nest from its site, you can trim away protruding twigs (but not reed stems—see illustrations) and put the nest into a plastic bag with some mothballs or other insecticide. This is to kill the remaining fleas and the carpet beetles, clothes moths and other insects, which would otherwise destroy the fabric of the nest very quickly. Take the nest home and dry it thoroughly and then you can display it in various ways. Nests woven around hollow reed stems can be displayed as shown in the illustrations. Free cup-shaped nests are best displayed on squares of thin board with three small nails sticking up through them to form a triangular support.

You will obviously want to know who lived in your nests when they were in use. Some nests have a very characteristic shape or method of construction and you can usually identify these quite easily with a good illustrated reference book. But remember that nests of a given species can vary quite a lot according to the available building materials: birds in urban areas will often use strips of paper and plastic instead of the more usual straw and leaves. Many small nests do look alike, however, especially when they have been vacated for a few months, and you will have to try to find other ways of identifying them. You might be lucky enough to find identifiable fragments of egg shell around the nest—the parent birds normally throw them out when the youngsters have hatched—or you might even find an addled egg still in the nest. A good knowledge of which birds live in the area will help you to narrow the field, but the only way to be really sure is to see the birds going to and from the nest in the breeding season.

The nest of a reed warbler, carefully woven around the reed stems. Such a nest should be collected complete with the stems that pass through it. Cut the stems a few inches below the nest.

The nest of a thrush, characteristically wedged into the fork of a bush.

Scissors will cut some reed stems, but secateurs are more practical for nest collecting.

Place the nest in a plastic bag with some mothballs. Most of the insects in the nest will crawl out and die.

Remove all but three of the strongest reed stems and lower these three on to three nails placed in the right position on the base board.

Old Birds' Nests

Oval nests can be displayed by fixing them loosely to hardboard or thick cardboard stands.

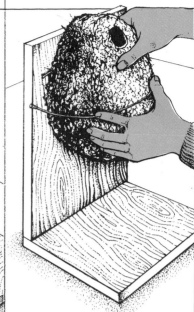

You can then collect the nest in the autumn—not before—and be quite certain who built it.

Instead of displaying or storing the nest, you can photograph it or make an accurate drawing, record the measurements, and then dissect the nest to find out just what it is made from. Remember that the bird started from the outside, so you must start stripping the nest from the inside. Strip it down gently layer by layer, possibly taking photographs or making sketches of each stage. Keep all the components and try not to break any of the small twigs and pieces of grass. Count the number of twigs, straws, roots, hairs, and so on in the nest. Even allowing for the fact that a bird can easily carry several bits back together on one trip, the total number still represents a lot of hard work by one or both parent birds. Glue all the fragments to a card to form a permanent record. You can also attach a small tube containing the various insects from the nest, having first counted and identified them. You should weigh the mud lining of the nest, if one is present, and record the weight on the card. You will find that the mud often accounts for more than half the total weight of the nest—and remember that it was even heavier when it was collected because it was wet. By looking carefully at some of the nest materials, you might get some idea of how far the birds flew to collect them.

You Will Need

Secateurs or scissors
Plastic bags
Mothballs or other
moth-proofer
Tweezers
Old leather gloves

Dissect the nest very carefully with tweezers and try not to break any pieces. Attach them all to a card as shown here, together with a sketch or photograph of the nest and all the relevant details written in. These would include the location and detailed situation of the nest, height above ground, and measurements of the nest itself. Put the name of the bird, if known, at the top of the card.

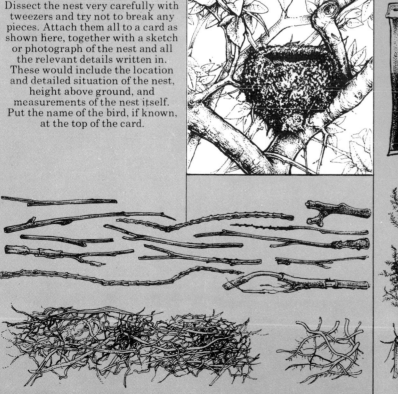

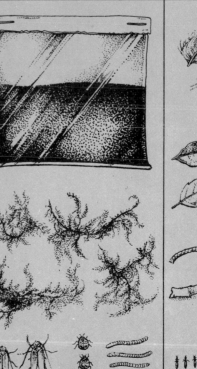

FEEDING WILD BIRDS

Tasty menus to entice wild birds into your garden

Even the smallest and barest garden or window sill will be visited from time to time by sparrows, and probably by starlings and other birds. You can give yourself and the birds a lot of pleasure by putting out additional food. As long as there are no cats about, you can entice the birds right up to your windows where you can watch them at your leisure. By putting out a variety of foods, you can attract many different kinds of birds that you might not otherwise see around your home. This is especially true in winter, when natural foods are often in short supply and the birds cover a large area in their search for food.

Some birds, such as the wren, prefer to feed on the ground, but most species can be tempted on to a bird table feeder. Raised up to window level, the feeding birds are much easier to watch from indoors.

Your table feeder can be fixed to a pole in the ground, hung from the branch of a tree, or fixed to the wall of your house. The birds are happy with any of these situations, but it cannot be stressed too strongly that the feeding platform must be out of the reach of cats. It should be at least 1½ metres (5 ft) from the ground, and if it is hanging from a branch you must ensure that a cat cannot crawl along the branch to reach it. The ideal pole is an unclimbable metal one, but a smooth wooden pole will do the job. If you do have cats prowling through your garden you can try painting the base of the pole with a commercial cat-repellent, and if that does not work you can fit a cat-proof baffle (see illustration opposite).

Some small garden birds, including the tits and robins, are agoraphobic and will not readily come to bird tables out in the open. They like to 'stalk' up to the table, stopping at intervals to survey the scene from the safety of a tree or a bush. Put your table feeder within easy reach of such staging posts, and try to give the table some protection from the wind.

The feeding tray itself should have a perimeter of at least 150 cm (5 ft), so that the birds have plenty of room to perch around the edge without squabbling. A rectangular board 50 cm by 25 cm (20 in by 10 in) will give this perimeter, but your table could equally well be square or even circular. A low rim around the edge stops the food being blown off, but leave a few gaps to let the rainwater run away. A roof is not essential, although it does protect both food and birds from the rain.

Grow cotoneasters and other berry-bearing shrubs to provide food for fruit-eating birds in the autumn.

On the other hand, a roof can get in the way if you are trying to photograph your birds at their dinner.

Any kind of kitchen scraps can be put on the table feeder, but variety is essential if you are going to entice the seed-eaters and insect-eaters to your table. Cheese, bacon rind, dried fruit, porridge oats and other cereals, peanuts and apples are all good bird foods, but it is well worth buying some commercial wild bird food if you want to attract the more discerning feeders. This mixture contains a very wide variety of seeds, specially compounded to appeal to the widest variety of seed-eating species. Insect-eaters can be enticed with fly maggots bought from a fishing tackle shop, while mealworms (see page 106) do the job even better: robins, in particular, will do almost anything to get a feed of mealworms. In the absence of insect food, the tits and other insect-eating species will usually make do with scraps of fat: hang the bone of the weekend joint from the bird table and watch the birds' antics.

In many areas starlings take more than their share from the bird table. They are larger than most visitors and they tend to bully the smaller species. Many bird watchers dislike starlings because of this, although the birds are actually very attractive. You can ensure that the smaller birds get their fill in winter by putting some food out early in the morning and giving a second helping in the afternoon. During the winter the starlings sleep in large roosts, often many miles from their feeding grounds. The smaller birds will have plenty of time for breakfast before the starlings get back to your garden later in the morning. The starlings set off for the roosts again in the middle of the afternoon, and the other birds can have their tea in peace.

You can also outwit the starlings by presenting

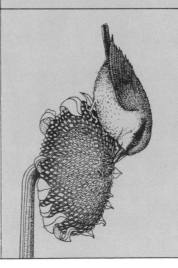

Leave sunflower heads on the plants after flowering. Nuthatches and finches will have a wonderful time pecking out the ripening seeds.

Goldfinches enjoy pulling the developing seeds out of thistle heads. You might not want to grow thistles in your garden, but you could collect some seeds for your 'bird pudding'.

some of your food in special containers as shown on the opposite page. Starlings like to feed with both feet planted firmly on a horizontal surface and they will not usually bother with hanging containers. Tits, finches, woodpeckers, and some other birds seem to enjoy swaying on these devices, however, and it is fascinating to watch them at work. Use fine wire mesh or plastic netting to make a scrap basket. Chopped suet and other fat can go into it, together with various kinds of nuts. Peanuts, either shelled or unshelled, are excellent, but do not use salted nuts. Desiccated coconut is also bad for the birds, but the tits will be delighted with half a fresh coconut hung from the table feeder. When they have finished with it you can fill the shell with 'bird pudding' and hang it out again. The pudding consists of assorted seeds, cake crumbs, cheese, corn flakes or porridge oats, and other scraps which you mix with melted dripping. Pour the mixture into the coconut shell and hang it out when it has set. If you have no coconut shell you can use a yoghurt pot or simply turn the mixture out on to the feeding platform. The solidified mixture can also be pushed into holes drilled in small logs (see opposite).

Whatever method you decide upon for feeding your birds, it is essential that you feed them regularly, especially in the winter. And don't forget drinking water: birds need to drink just as we do. A bowl of fresh water on or near the table will be much appreciated.

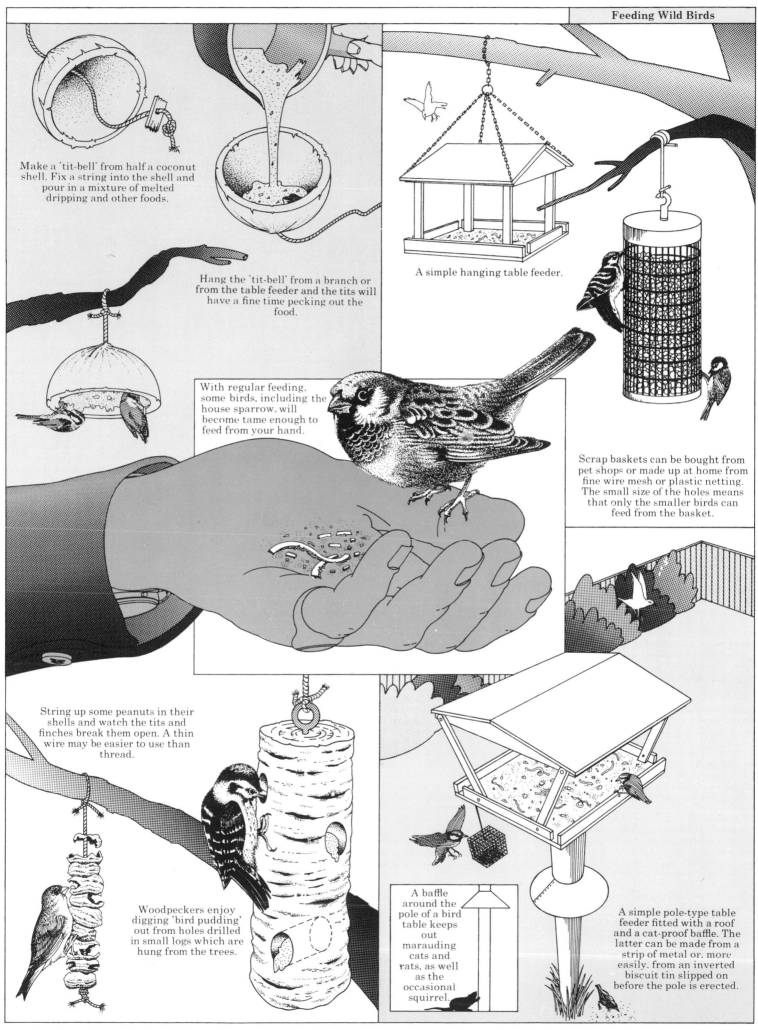

Make a 'tit-bell' from half a coconut shell. Fix a string into the shell and pour in a mixture of melted dripping and other foods.

Hang the 'tit-bell' from a branch or from the table feeder and the tits will have a fine time pecking out the food.

A simple hanging table feeder.

With regular feeding, some birds, including the house sparrow, will become tame enough to feed from your hand.

Scrap baskets can be bought from pet shops or made up at home from fine wire mesh or plastic netting. The small size of the holes means that only the smaller birds can feed from the basket.

String up some peanuts in their shells and watch the tits and finches break them open. A thin wire may be easier to use than thread.

Woodpeckers enjoy digging 'bird pudding' out from holes drilled in small logs which are hung from the trees.

A baffle around the pole of a bird table keeps out marauding cats and rats, as well as the occasional squirrel.

A simple pole-type table feeder fitted with a roof and a cat-proof baffle. The latter can be made from a strip of metal or, more easily, from an inverted biscuit tin slipped on before the pole is erected.

ARTIFICIAL NESTS

How to build nesting places for the birds that visit your garden

An old barrel or other large box fixed high in a tree may encourage an owl to nest.

Having entertained an assortment of birds to dinner at the bird table (see page 52), the enthusiastic bird watcher will no doubt want to encourage them to stay. There is no better way of doing this than to provide them with nesting sites. If the birds can be persuaded to take up residence they will give you immense pleasure as they go about the business of rearing a family, and you will have the added satisfaction of knowing that you are doing something for conservation. The increasing destruction of woodland and hedgerow in many areas is removing millions of potential nesting sites, and a few nest boxes or bird houses in each garden or back yard can do much to remedy this situation.

There are many designs to suit the sizes and nesting habits of different birds, but anyone who can use a saw and a hammer or screwdriver can make a suitable nesting place from a plank of wood. Metal is not a good material because the inside heats up too quickly – remember how hot a car gets on a sunny day – and there are condensation problems in cooler weather.

The most popular artificial nest is a type acceptable to tits, wrens and a whole range of other small, hole-nesting birds such as nuthatches, tree creepers, redstarts, and flycatchers. In its most usual form this is a rectangular box with a hinged lid and a small entrance hole. The stages in making such a box are shown on the opposite page.

Don't worry if you are not a good carpenter: you may well make a better box than a professional because the little gaps where your sides do not quite meet the floor will provide the all-important ventilation and drainage. If you make a box with perfect joints you must make some small drainage holes in the bottom. The wood must be treated with creosote or other preservative, and if you really want your box to look natural you can cover the outside with pieces of dead bark. It is a wise plan to fix a batten to the back of the box and use the batten to attach the box to the tree trunk or wall. This keeps the box away from water running down the surface. On a sloping surface, always fix the box so that the entrance faces downwards.

The size of the entrance hole clearly determines the sizes of the birds that will use your nest boxes. If you want to keep out the ubiquitous house sparrow you must ensure that the hole is no more than 29 mm (1⅛ in) in diameter. This will still let in most of the tits and the tree sparrow, and possibly also the nuthatch and tree creeper if these are about. If you enlarge the hole to a diameter of about 50 mm (2 in) the box will be acceptable to wrens, redstarts, and starlings, but the most likely occupant in a garden setting will be the house sparrow.

A slightly larger box— about 45 cm (18 in) deep and 20 cm (8 in) in diameter —can be built on the same plan to encourage jackdaws and little owls. A rectangular entrance about 12 cm by 10 cm (5 in by 4 in) will let these birds in, but don't be surprised if your boxes are taken by the much commoner sparrows and starlings.

Boxes for hole-nesters can be erected on walls and tree trunks almost anywhere as long as they are out of the reach of cats and not in the full sun. If you have a suitable shed you might like to try an observation box. This has a glass or plastic back and it fits into a hole in the shed wall so that you can see what is going on.

Many birds, such as the robin, the spotted flycatcher, and some of the wagtails, prefer the open-fronted type of nest box shown on the opposite page. This is built to the same plan as the basic nest or bird house mentioned earlier, but the front comes only part-way up the box. Open-fronted boxes should be at least partly concealed in climbing plants on the wall. Larger open-fronted boxes, with a floor area about 50 cm by 30 cm (20 in by 12 in), may attract kestrels, or sparrowhawks, and little owls in suitable areas. These larger boxes can be fixed on walls and high window sills. In open country, as long as there is no public access, they can be sited on poles about 2 metres (80 in) high.

All nest boxes should be put in position long before the nesting season so that the birds can get used to them. If you want summer visitors to occupy them, you may have to block up your boxes until they arrive, otherwise the sparrows will occupy them first. Most birds maintain territories during the breeding season and defend them against other birds of the same species. There is no point, therefore, in putting up large numbers of nest boxes in a small garden.

With sensible precautions for the welfare of the birds, you can make some interesting observations on the development of the family. Grass and other material being carried into the box will indicate that a nest is being built. You can peep in from time to time to see how things are progressing, and you will then learn when the eggs are laid. It is best not to look in after the full clutch has been laid. You will know when the eggs have hatched because there will be some cheeping and the parents will start to bring food to the nest.

Note what sort of food they bring, and how many journeys they make in an hour. Later on you will be able to see the young birds make their first flights, often encouraged by their mother, but do not get too close. Always put the birds' interests first.

At the end of the nesting season, when you are sure that the boxes are no longer in use, take out the old nests (gloves will reduce the number of flea bites you get) and examine them. Give the woodwork a fresh coat of preservative if necessary and leave the boxes for another year.

If you have a large pond on your land you might like to try making a nesting raft from oil drums and other materials. Boxes of soil with reeds and other plants will encourage ducks and other kinds of waterfowl to nest on the raft.

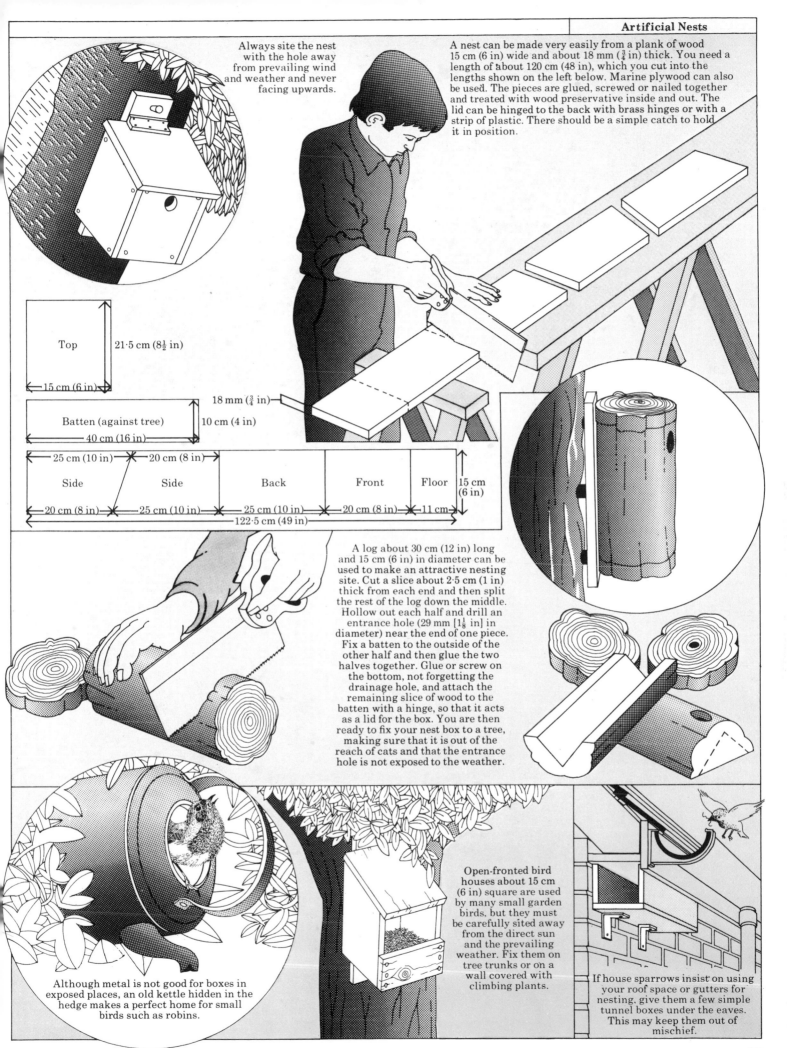

Always site the nest with the hole away from prevailing wind and weather and never facing upwards.

A nest can be made very easily from a plank of wood 15 cm (6 in) wide and about 18 mm (¾ in) thick. You need a length of about 120 cm (48 in), which you cut into the lengths shown on the left below. Marine plywood can also be used. The pieces are glued, screwed or nailed together and treated with wood preservative inside and out. The lid can be hinged to the back with brass hinges or with a strip of plastic. There should be a simple catch to hold it in position.

Top — 21·5 cm (8½ in)
15 cm (6 in)

18 mm (¾ in)

Batten (against tree) — 10 cm (4 in)
40 cm (16 in)

25 cm (10 in) — 20 cm (8 in)
Side | Side | Back | Front | Floor | 15 cm (6 in)
20 cm (8 in) | 25 cm (10 in) | 25 cm (10 in) | 20 cm (8 in) | 11 cm
122·5 cm (49 in)

A log about 30 cm (12 in) long and 15 cm (6 in) in diameter can be used to make an attractive nesting site. Cut a slice about 2·5 cm (1 in) thick from each end and then split the rest of the log down the middle. Hollow out each half and drill an entrance hole (29 mm [1⅛ in] in diameter) near the end of one piece. Fix a batten to the outside of the other half and then glue the two halves together. Glue or screw on the bottom, not forgetting the drainage hole, and attach the remaining slice of wood to the batten with a hinge, so that it acts as a lid for the box. You are then ready to fix your nest box to a tree, making sure that it is out of the reach of cats and that the entrance hole is not exposed to the weather.

Although metal is not good for boxes in exposed places, an old kettle hidden in the hedge makes a perfect home for small birds such as robins.

Open-fronted bird houses about 15 cm (6 in) square are used by many small garden birds, but they must be carefully sited away from the direct sun and the prevailing weather. Fix them on tree trunks or on a wall covered with climbing plants.

If house sparrows insist on using your roof space or gutters for nesting, give them a few simple tunnel boxes under the eaves. This may keep them out of mischief.

BIRD CASUALTIES

Looking after injured and sick birds, with advice on what to do with 'lost' fledglings

Now and again you will come across a sick or injured bird, and it is only natural that you should want to help it if possible. But you must be prepared to devote considerable time and effort to caring for such a casualty: otherwise, it is kinder to have the bird humanely destroyed right away. If you do decide to try to help the bird recover, remember that you must return it to the wild as soon as possible. You must not let the bird become a pet.

One of the most familiar casualties occurs when a bird has flown into a window and been stunned. The crash can make a lot of noise, and there may be quite a lot of feathers scattered around below the window, but the bird is not usually badly hurt. It is more likely to be shocked than injured, and the treatment is to keep it quiet and warm. Pick it up gently and put it into a cardboard box with some soft material. Put the lid on the box and leave it alone until you hear the bird moving about. It is then ready to fly away. In the absence of a cardboard box, you can nurse the bird in your hands, or wrapped gently in your clothes. Give it plenty of support so that it feels secure, and be prepared to sit still and quiet for half an hour or more.

When cats catch birds they usually bite them quite deeply, and the birds often die from shock if not actually from the wound. You might be able to save a bird if you intervene before it is badly bitten. Superficial wounds, such as small cuts and scratches, can then be washed with soap and water and they should heal quickly. Don't be tempted to rescue birds from wild animals. It is perfectly natural for a hawk or a marten to catch birds and you must not interfere.

If a bird is badly injured, with a broken leg or wing, you might find a veterinary surgeon who is prepared to set it, but treatment is expensive and the bird may never recover sufficiently to survive in the wild. A simple break of the lower leg is not too difficult to deal with, and if a bird seems healthy in other respects you could set the leg yourself in the absence of a sympathetic vet. Gently straighten the leg and use a little sticky tape to bind on a matchstick as a splint. Keep the bird in an airy cage and the leg should mend in a few weeks. Broken wings are much more serious and can be dealt with only by a vet, but don't assume that a trailing wing is always broken: it may just be sprained, and if the bird is hopping around without much sign of pain it is worth putting it in a cage for a few days to see if it gets better. If the bird is clearly distressed, however, it is probably better to destroy it at once. Small birds can be killed by squeezing the neck in your fingers, but larger ones should be taken to a vet. If you do keep any of the birds you find you must clearly give them the right kinds of food. Seed mixtures sold for wild birds are ideal for finches and other seed-eaters, while mealworms, maggots (from angling shops), and other small insects will suit the insectivorous species. Birds of prey, which are sometimes picked up under power lines and telephone wires, need raw meat with some fur or feathers on it. Clean water must also be given to adult birds.

If a bird is ill rather than hurt, and you are able to catch it, it will probably not recover, although a vet may be able to suggest treatment. Never put sick birds near healthy ones, and always wash your hands after holding them, because some bird diseases can be transmitted to people.

During the spring and summer, children often bring home 'lost' baby birds. The best thing to do with these is to take them straight back to where they

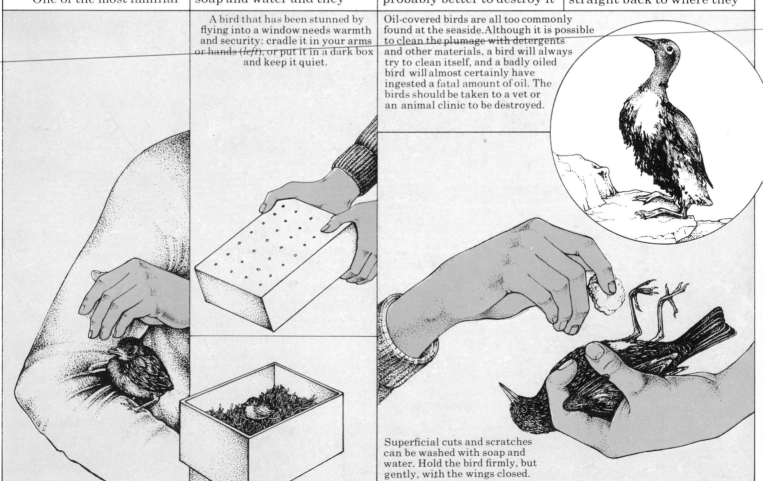

A bird that has been stunned by flying into a window needs warmth and security: cradle it in your arms or hands (*left*), or put it in a dark box and keep it quiet.

Oil-covered birds are all too commonly found at the seaside. Although it is possible to clean the plumage with detergents and other materials, a bird will always try to clean itself, and a badly oiled bird will almost certainly have ingested a fatal amount of oil. The birds should be taken to a vet or an animal clinic to be destroyed.

Superficial cuts and scratches can be washed with soap and water. Hold the bird firmly, but gently, with the wings closed.

were found. A fledgling on its own may look very forlorn, but its parents are nearly always close by, gathering food or anxiously waiting for you to go away. Leave young birds alone!

If you are loath to abandon a young fledgling completely, leave it alone for at least two hours and then go back. If it is still there you can consider hand-rearing it. A young bird needs warmth, so put it in a box lined with hay or newspaper and put it in a linen cupboard or some other warm place. It also needs regular food, and you may have to force-feed it at first (see illustrations). The type of food you offer depends on the species. Finches and other seed-eaters will take a mixture of hard-boiled egg and crushed biscuit moistened with milk. A good pet shop should be able to supply an insectivorous diet suitable for robins, tits, blackbirds, and thrushes. You can also provide small insects such as mealworms, maggots, and ant cocoons. Water is not necessary for baby birds.

If the young bird's droppings are white with

dark streaks you can feel confident that you are feeding it on the right lines. Brown, runny droppings indicate that the diet is unsuitable.

When the orphaned bird is first brought home you should keep it in a fairly confined space, to simulate the nest, but as soon as it begins to move about and feed itself you must give it more room. Put it in a large cage or, if possible, an aviary. After a while the cage can be taken to a safe release point and left for a few hours for the bird to get used to its new surroundings. You can then open the door, but leave the cage in position for a few days so that the bird can return to roost. Continue to put out food for a short while in case the bird has difficulty at first in finding enough. You will probably need help from an expert falconer to teach a bird of prey to hunt for itself.

Lastly, do not be too disappointed if all your efforts are unsuccessful: a sick or injured bird, or an abandoned fledgling would almost certainly have died if left alone.

The most common cause of casualties is the window, but collisions like this do not usually cause permanent injury. You can often get good clean specimens for your feather collection (see page 46) from the scene of a crash.

The fledgling bird on its first excursion often looks rather forlorn, but its parents are usually close at hand to help it. Resist the temptation to bring these birds home.

Most baby birds are fed by the parent thrusting its beak into their throats. To force-feed a young bird, hold its beak between thumb and forefinger and pry it open. Then push the food down with blunt tweezers or a matchstick.

Young pigeons feed by pushing their beaks into the parent's throat. Force-feed baby pigeons by taking a fistful of food and pushing the bird's beak into it.

Man is a mammal and perhaps this is why nearly all mammals are very appealing to us. We can recognize a mammal on sight by the many obvious features that distinguish a mammal from all other animals. A most important feature is that only mammals are covered with hair (or fur, or wool). There are exceptions, however. Of the mammals that have few hairs, the well-known examples are the sparsely haired elephant, and the ocean-dwelling dolphins and whales. There are also naked bats, rhinoceroses, and hippopotamuses. The mammals' furry covering has a most valuable function. It forms a barrier, or insulating layer, which helps to prevent the animal from losing body heat. This is important because, like their relatives, the birds, mammals are warm-blooded.

Mammals get their name from their mammary glands which supply their young babies with milk. No other animal produces milk for its young. The pouched mammals or marsupials of Australia and South America, the opossums, kangaroos, koalas and sugar gliders, are unusual in that they suckle their babies in a pouch. They are very similar to true mammals, however, the other main difference being that the young are born very tiny and underdeveloped. A kangaroo baby looks like an embryo when born after only 33 days' gestation. It is 20 mm ($\frac{3}{4}$ in) long and weighs 0·8 grams (1/35 oz), yet it instinctively finds its way from the birth-canal opening at the base of the mother's tail to her pouch by wriggling and scrambling along a path of fur that has been dampened by the mother's tongue. The duck-billed platypus and the spiny anteaters or echidnas are the only egg-laying mammals, and they live in Australia, and (echidnas only) New Guinea. The eggs are incubated, like a bird's or those of certain reptiles, in a nest. On hatching, these tiny babies lick milk which comes from milk pores on the mother's belly.

Anyone who has watched a bitch with her puppies, a cat and her kittens, or thought about their own family, realizes that most mammals lavish great care, love and attention on their offspring. As every mother knows, a baby takes a tremendous amount of her time in feeding, cleaning, and caring for it. This is the reason why most mammals do not give birth to many babies at one time. Many, such as the elephant, whale, giraffe, zebra, gorilla, seal, antelope and deer usually give birth to one baby: twins and larger numbers of young are rare.

Living on a planet that we dominate, we tend to think ourselves superior to all other creatures and regard mammals as more advanced than the other back-boned animals or vertebrates – the fishes, amphibians, reptiles, and birds. There is some basis for this belief in that the mammals are the most highly organized members of the animal kingdom, just as flowering plants, for the same reason, are dominant in the plant kingdom. It is interesting to note that these major groups of our modern world evolved side by side as successors to the reptiles and the evergreen seed-plants called cycads. These flourished during the Mesozoic era, but by the Tertiary period, about 70 million years ago, many reptiles and cycads had vanished, and the age of flowers and mammals was beginning.

Mammals vary considerably in size, from the tiniest Etruscan shrew, which is some 44 mm ($1\frac{3}{4}$ in) long and weighs under 2·5 gm (1/10 oz), to the blue whale, 33 metres (111 ft) long, and the lofty African elephant, 3·2 metres ($10\frac{1}{2}$ ft) high.

The variations in size and shape of mammals and the different patterns of behaviour are strongly connected with the way they obtain their food. Many search for food mainly at dawn and dusk, so their senses of smell and hearing are better than their sense of sight. A badger, for example, will smell the air on emerging from its set at dusk, listen attentively and then set off along well-worn tracks sniffing out food which ranges from worms and beetles to frogs and mice and some plant material such as windfall apples and acorns.

The mammals that feed on both plant and animal materials are known as omnivores. The hunting flesh-eaters are known as carnivores, and they need good eyesight to be able to catch their prey. Their eyes usually face forwards, giving them overlapping or binocular vision so that they can precisely judge the distance between themselves and the animal they are trying to catch. The members of the hunting group are generally fast-moving and include in their number the wild dogs and foxes; their limbs are more extended to give better leverage and kick while running and leaping, and travelling on the tips of their four toes. The claws of these mammals are used either for digging, as in the fox, or for climbing and catching prey, as in the cats.

The plant-eaters or herbivores such as the deer, antelope, wild sheep and goats are generally long-legged. The nails on their feet have gradually evolved into hooves, and this enables them to speed away on sighting any animal that might be a source of danger. (This tendency in nearly all mammals to flee at any hint of danger makes them difficult to observe.)

Most of the hoofed mammals are hunted for food by the carnivores and their senses are very acute to give them early warning. Their eyes are placed on the side of the head to give as much all-round vision as possible. Their ears, which are movable, are excellent at picking up noises. If you watch a deer or horse you will notice how the ears move independently all the time to pick up the slightest sound. Their sense of smell is also sharp, and if you are observing mammals of any kind in their natural habitat it is most important to stand upwind (see page 60). You may not think you have a very strong smell, but the slightest air current will carry your odour to the mammal you are watching and it will soon be speeding away.

CHAPTER 4

MAMMALS

Introducing the hair-covered, milk-producing creatures that are the most highly organized members of the animal kingdom

WATCHING WILD MAMMALS

How to find these timid animals and observe them in their natural surroundings

family of keen-eyed naturalists out for a walk will usually see plenty of birds around them, but they will not see many mammals—perhaps a few squirrels chasing through the trees, the occasional hare loping across a field, and possibly a fleeting glimpse of a deer, but rarely anything more. This is because most of our mammals are timid and secretive creatures and the majority come out only at night. Special techniques are therefore needed if you want to watch mammals, but if a few simple rules are followed you will find that even a small garden or back yard may contain several interesting species. Hedgerows and woodlands contain many more.

Watching by night is obviously going to be more productive than watching by day, but it is necessary to do a certain amount of 'homework' if you want to have a reasonable chance of success. First of all, you must establish that there are animals of the kind that you want to watch living in your area, and you must find out more or less where they are living. You can do this by looking for burrows, tracks, and various other signs, as indicated on page 70. Then you can make a careful survey of the area to decide the most suitable viewpoint. This survey is especially important if you are going out at night, for it enables you to note the positions of fallen branches, potholes, and other obstacles which might not be so obvious in the dark. You will then be able to pick your way carefully round them without hurting yourself and without disturbing the animals when you go back at night. Ideally, you should select at least two possible viewpoints, because mammals have very good noses and they will smell you very easily if you are upwind of them: with two sites to choose from you do have a chance to get downwind of the animals. You should also be hidden from the animals as much as possible, and you should avoid creating a shadow with your body. The ideal position is sitting with your back against a tree or a rock for support, but this is not always possible and you may well have to put up with some discomfort if you want to watch the animals for long.

It is always worth reading about the animals you want to watch. If you know something of their habits in advance, this can save you a lot of wasted time. Badgers, for example, normally come out soon after dusk and go off for several hours, so it will be no use getting to the set after dark and expecting to see the animals come out. Foxes and rabbits also have a peak of activity soon after dusk, but hedgehogs (among the easiest of mammals to watch) usually come out later.

When the time and place of watching have been settled, you must gather together some essential requirements. Dark clothing is a must (unless you are out in snowy weather) and, if you are planning to remain out most of the night, it must be warm enough. A torch or flashlight is also necessary, and you should cover it with a piece of red glass or red plastic, because the animals are much less sensitive to a red light than they are to the ordinary white light of a torch. Other essentials include a notebook and pencil and an ample supply of patience. Binoculars, a watch and a compass may be useful, and insect repellent is worth applying before you leave home in order to ward off the inevitable mosquitoes. Something to eat and drink will be welcome after an hour or two of patient watching, but make sure you do not carry it in noisy paper bags.

Record all your observations in the notebook—place, state of the moon, wind and weather conditions, details of the animals' activities and the times at which they took place. Photographs add more enjoyment to the project, and simple flash photographs can be taken by anyone with a basic knowledge of wildlife photography (see page 170). But don't be in too much of a hurry to take your pictures, as a single flash may send the animals scurrying for cover, and they may not re-emerge for quite a long time.

Young people should not go out to watch mammals at night unless they are accompanied by an adult, and no inexperienced person should go out mammal watching in areas where bears and other large carnivores exist.

Reconnoitre the site by day, noting fallen branches and other obstacles.

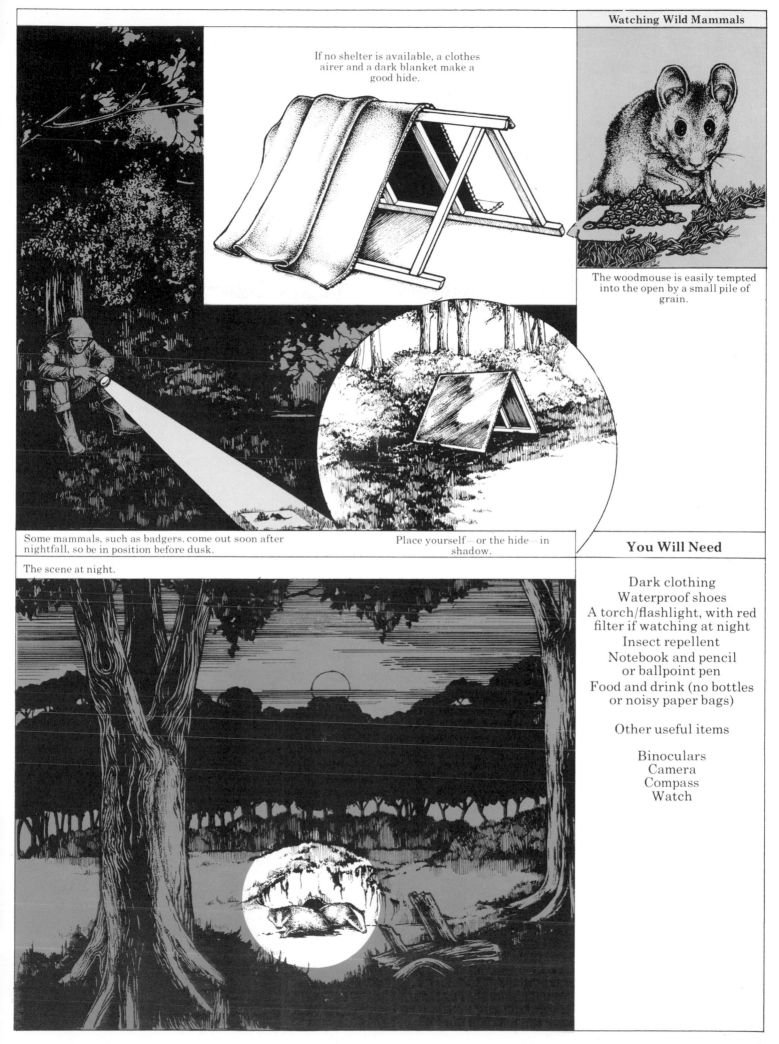

If no shelter is available, a clothes airer and a dark blanket make a good hide.

The woodmouse is easily tempted into the open by a small pile of grain.

Some mammals, such as badgers, come out soon after nightfall, so be in position before dusk.

Place yourself—or the hide—in shadow.

The scene at night.

You Will Need

Dark clothing
Waterproof shoes
A torch/flashlight, with red filter if watching at night
Insect repellent
Notebook and pencil or ballpoint pen
Food and drink (no bottles or noisy paper bags)

Other useful items

Binoculars
Camera
Compass
Watch

SMALL MAMMALS IN THE GARDEN

How to catch and identify the small mammals in your garden, and how to study their movements

The Longworth trap consists of an entrance tunnel and a nesting chamber which clip together to form one unit. The door is held up by a lever, and the animal springs it when it runs over a trip-wire at the far end of the tunnel. The trap should be placed with the tunnel flat on the ground: no water can then run into the nesting chamber.

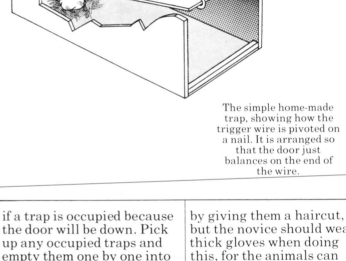

The simple home-made trap, showing how the trigger wire is pivoted on a nail. It is arranged so that the door just balances on the end of the wire.

Although you might never see them, your garden probably supports several small mammals in the shape of mice, voles and shrews. You can find out what species live there, and get some idea of their numbers, by putting out some simple live traps. These traps are designed to lure the animals inside and then trap them alive and without harm. You can let the animals go again afterwards, and they don't seem to mind the experience, for they often enter the traps night after night.

The most commonly used small mammal traps are the Longworth traps, which you can buy from biological supply companies. The traps shown on these two pages are made of metal and consist of two separate parts—an entrance tunnel and a nest chamber.

You can also make yourself a live trap from some strong wood. Form it into a sturdy box about 15 cm (6 in) long and 5 cm (2 in) across as shown in the illustration. Leave one end open and fit it with a hinged lid that can swing up inside the box. There must be some kind of stop to prevent the lid from opening outwards. Fix a nail horizontally through the box near the closed end to act as a pivot for the 'trigger'. The latter is a bent piece of wire which holds the door open and carries the bait on its lower end. When the mammal enters the trap to investigate the bait it disturbs the wire and the door drops down to trap the animal safely inside.

Pitfall traps of the type described on page 100 can also be used for small mammals, but you need deeper jars so that the animals cannot jump out, and you must also leave a bigger gap under the cover.

Grain, cornflakes, or biscuit crumbs can be used as bait for mice and voles, and dried fruit is even better. Just scatter the bait at the inner end of the tunnel in a Longworth trap, or spear a sultana on the trigger wire of a home-made trap. Shrews will sometimes come to this bait, but they are more readily attracted by a little cat or dog food. The traps can get very cold at night, so it is essential to put some bedding in for the animals. Hay is ideal, but crumpled newspaper will do just as well.

Voles can be caught by setting the traps in long grass in orchards and on roadside verges. Mice and shrews are more likely to be caught in hedgerows or along the bottoms of walls. You will often find their runways in such places. If you have a pair of traps you can set them together on the runway, one facing each way so that the animal will go straight in. Never set the traps so that the rain can get inside.

Mice are usually active only at night, but voles and shrews are often active in the daytime. You must therefore examine your traps regularly, for shrews in particular die very quickly from starvation. If you leave traps out at night you must examine them just before you go to bed and again *first thing* in the morning. You can easily see if a trap is occupied because the door will be down. Pick up any occupied traps and empty them one by one into a large plastic bag (see picture on far right). You will be able to tell very easily whether you have caught a mouse, a vole, or a shrew, but there are several species in each group and you should try to recognize each one. Weigh each animal in the plastic bag on a sensitive spring balance —a mouse weighs only about 25 grams (nearly 1 oz). Try to determine its sex (see page 66), and record this, together with the weight and the date and place of capture, in your notebook. Unless you want to keep the animal for observation (see page 64), release it where it was caught, wash the trap thoroughly, and re-set it.

If you put your traps out regularly you might like to mark the animals you catch by giving them a haircut, but the novice should wear thick gloves when doing this, for the animals can deliver some painful bites on the fingers. Never grasp them tightly: firm pressure over the shoulders is enough to keep them still for a few seconds. Clip just a small piece of fur, and this will enable you to recognize the animal again for several weeks. You will know how many different animals you catch if you clip each one on a different part of the back. A trap put in the same place each night will usually catch the same animal, because each one has its own range, so you should try moving the trap around.

You Will Need

One or more live traps (Longworth or home-made)
Large plastic bag
Spring balance
Small scissors (optional)

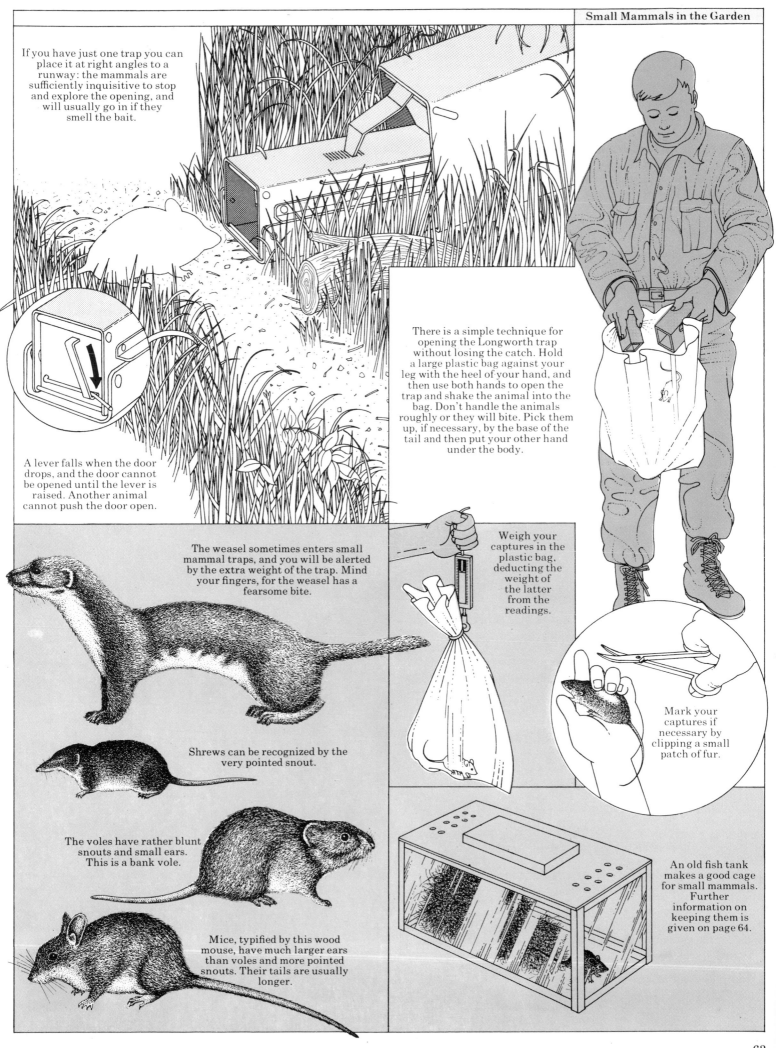

If you have just one trap you can place it at right angles to a runway: the mammals are sufficiently inquisitive to stop and explore the opening, and will usually go in if they smell the bait.

A lever falls when the door drops, and the door cannot be opened until the lever is raised. Another animal cannot push the door open.

There is a simple technique for opening the Longworth trap without losing the catch. Hold a large plastic bag against your leg with the heel of your hand, and then use both hands to open the trap and shake the animal into the bag. Don't handle the animals roughly or they will bite. Pick them up, if necessary, by the base of the tail and then put your other hand under the body.

The weasel sometimes enters small mammal traps, and you will be alerted by the extra weight of the trap. Mind your fingers, for the weasel has a fearsome bite.

Shrews can be recognized by the very pointed snout.

Weigh your captures in the plastic bag, deducting the weight of the latter from the readings.

Mark your captures if necessary by clipping a small patch of fur.

The voles have rather blunt snouts and small ears. This is a bank vole.

Mice, typified by this wood mouse, have much larger ears than voles and more pointed snouts. Their tails are usually longer.

An old fish tank makes a good cage for small mammals. Further information on keeping them is given on page 64.

A SIMPLE VIVARIUM

How to house and feed small mammals and reptiles, and construct an actograph to monitor their cycles of activity and rest

The small mice and voles that you catch in your mammal traps are quite easy to keep in captivity. Their antics as they wash themselves and explore their cages are as amusing as those of the more conventional pets, such as hamsters and gerbils, and the animals are probably more interesting than the domesticated white mice, which have lost a lot of their natural habits. This is particularly true of the wood mouse and other wild mice (not house mice!). They become quite tame after a while and make very good pets, even changing their habits to some extent so that they are active during the day. Voles are not quite so tameable, but still very interesting to keep. Do not try to keep the shrews that you catch, for these animals must eat nearly all of the time and it is beyond most people to keep them supplied with the vast quantities of slugs, worms, and insects that they need.

Mice and voles are rodents and should not be kept in wooden cages, from which they can chew their way out in no time. The standard pet-shop mouse cage is not very suitable, either. The best container is an old fish tank – it does not matter if it is no longer water-tight. You can create a near-natural habitat in it and watch your animals going about their daily lives. Both mice and voles can jump quite well, and unless the tank is at least 50 cm (about 20 in) deep you must put some kind of lid on it.

Wire gauze or perforated zinc will do nicely, but failing that you can use a board with a few ventilation holes. Make sure that there is enough weight to prevent a leaping animal from dislodging the lid.

Put a good thick layer of peat or potting compost in the bottom of the tank and add a log or a stone and a small branch for the animals to run along. Do not let the branch come far off the bottom unless you have a lid on the vivarium, or else your animals will escape. Add some moss and a piece of turf to make the place look as natural and attractive as you can. The turf will soon be grazed and shredded up, but you can always renew it every now and then. Mice and voles – in fact, all rodents – love to shred things up, so give them plenty of straw or hay; much of this will go to make bedding. A jam jar laid on its side usually makes acceptable sleeping-quarters. If you give water in a dish, make sure that it is a wide dish and embed it firmly in the peat or compost so that the animals do not tip it over as they drink. A water bottle would be even better.

Grain and water are all that are really necessary for feeding mice, but they will eat almost anything and they probably appreciate a varied diet as much as we do. Give them occasional handfuls of grass, pieces of apple and other fruit, and a few insects from time to time. They enjoy mealworms (see page 106). Give them some whole hazel nuts from time to time and watch how they gnaw their way through the shells (see page 70). The field voles or short-tailed voles feed mainly on grass, and they will generally thrive with little more than pieces of turf for food, but other voles are more omnivorous. Give them much the same kind of food as you give the mice, with the occasional piece of carrot and a few sultanas as a special treat.

Although some mice are active during the day, especially when in captivity, they are essentially nocturnal animals and they tend to shun the light. In order to watch them in action, you can hang a red lamp over the cage in a dark room at night. You could also try reversing their day and night by darkening the room during the daytime and leaving a light on all night, but this is not usually practical in an ordinary household.

You can use your vivarium for several kinds of animals, not just small mammals. Small terrapins, lizards, slow-worms, snakes (harmless ones!), newts, frogs, and even scorpions can be kept in this kind of cage. Lizards and snakes will be happy with a similar set-up to that used for the small mammals, but if you want to see much activity you will have to keep the vivarium quite warm. The easiest way to do this is to hang a 25-watt lamp just over the top. Your mealworm and blow-fly cultures (see page 106) will

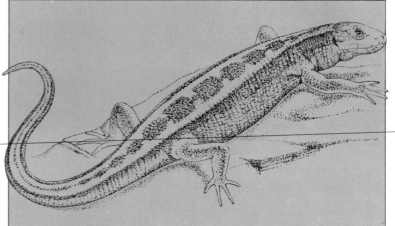

The common lizard will live well in a vivarium with some sandy soil and some turf. Give it a log on which to sunbathe, but release it in the autumn so that it can hibernate naturally.

keep most lizards happy, but snakes are much more difficult to feed because they normally eat larger food such as mice and frogs and they like to catch it alive. Snake-keeping is not a hobby for the ordinary naturalist. Newts, frogs, and terrapins all need moister conditions than those given to the mammals, and plenty of insect food or slugs.

Many small animals have distinct rhythms of activity and rest, perhaps one hour of rushing about looking for food and an hour resting, or perhaps three hours on and three hours off. You would find it tiring to sit and watch the vivarium for hours on end

to find out what sort of rhythms your animals have, but someone with a little mechanical ability could easily construct some apparatus which would also allow the animals to record their activity patterns themselves. Such a piece of apparatus, known as an actograph, is shown on the opposite page.

The animal must be in a fairly small and light cage, such as a plastic box (with ventilation holes) or a small propagator, and you must allow it to get used to the new surroundings before beginning the experiment. The essence of the investigation is that the movements of the animal are transmitted along the pivoted lever and recorded on the revolving drum. The drum may be made from an empty soup can covered with paper which has been blacked by holding it over a sooty candle flame. The

drum is connected to the drive shaft of an old, but working clock, so that it turns once in 12 hours. The really mechanical naturalist could even gear down the drum so that it turns once in 24 hours. A piece of wire, filed to a point, is attached to the end of the lever and bent so that it just makes contact with the revolving drum   enough to scratch the soot off. Periods of activity will be marked by up-and-down traces on the paper, while inactive periods will leave a straight line. When you remove the paper from the drum you can see how much activity there has been in the 12 or 24-hour period.

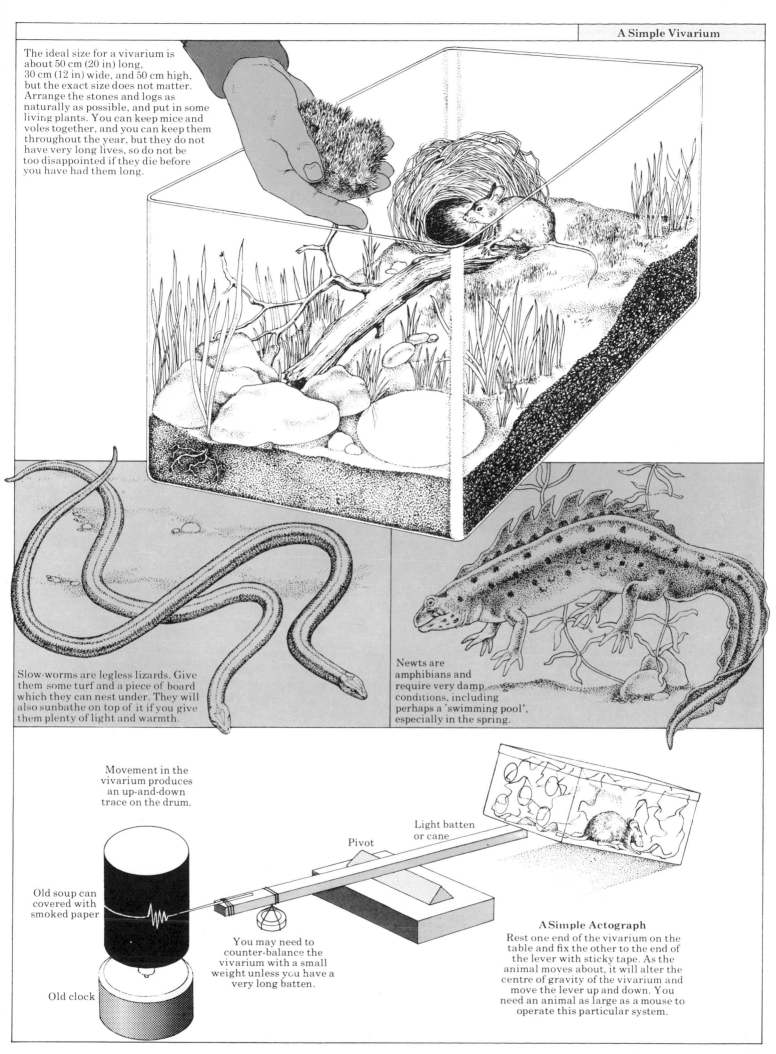

The ideal size for a vivarium is about 50 cm (20 in) long, 30 cm (12 in) wide, and 50 cm high, but the exact size does not matter. Arrange the stones and logs as naturally as possible, and put in some living plants. You can keep mice and voles together, and you can keep them throughout the year, but they do not have very long lives, so do not be too disappointed if they die before you have had them long.

Slow-worms are legless lizards. Give them some turf and a piece of board which they can nest under. They will also sunbathe on top of it if you give them plenty of light and warmth.

Newts are amphibians and require very damp conditions, including perhaps a 'swimming pool', especially in the spring.

Movement in the vivarium produces an up-and-down trace on the drum.

Old soup can covered with smoked paper

Old clock

You may need to counter-balance the vivarium with a small weight unless you have a very long batten.

Pivot

Light batten or cane

A Simple Actograph

Rest one end of the vivarium on the table and fix the other to the end of the lever with sticky tape. As the animal moves about, it will alter the centre of gravity of the vivarium and move the lever up and down. You need an animal as large as a mouse to operate this particular system.

PRESERVING SMALL MAMMAL SKINS

A step-by-step guide to skinning the mammals and preparing the skins for display

I f you have a cat you will probably have dead voles, mice and shrews delivered to your doorstep from time to time. Rather than throw them away, the enterprising naturalist might like to try skinning these small mammals and preserving the skins. You can, of course, do the same with small mammal corpses picked up in the countryside, but such finds are not as common as you might think. Burying beetles and other scavengers quickly bury or otherwise dispose of small carcases in the wild, and only rarely will you come across one still worth preserving.

The skinning procedure itself is very simple as long as your specimen has not been dead too long. Bodies deposited on the doorstep by the cat should be skinned straightaway if possible, but you can leave them until the evening if you store them in a cold place in a closed box or plastic bag. Before starting to skin the animal, you should make a few simple measurements. Weigh the animal and determine its sex if possible. This is not always easy, and it is impossible with young shrews. Mice and voles can be sexed because the area between the anus and the urinary papilla is normally pigmented in males. Measure the total length of the head and body by laying the animal on its back, stretching it fully, and measuring from the tip of the nose to the base of the tail. Measure the length of the tail as well. These details will all go on the label that you attach to the prepared skin.

Begin the skinning process with the animal on its back, either in your hand or on a board. Use a razor blade or fine scissors to make a small cut at the back of each knee. Extend the cuts up the legs until they meet under the base of the tail. Gently loosen the skin with your fingers and cut through the rectum as close as possible to the anus. Push one knee out of the skin and, if you are not planning to keep the skeleton as well (see page 68), cut through the leg bone between the knee and the heel. Repeat the procedure with the other leg. If you do want to preserve the skeleton you must slit the skin down to the ankle and then trim it off.

Loosen the skin at the base of the tail and grip it firmly with your fingers. Grip the flesh of the tail with your other hand or with some tweezers and gently pull the tail out of its skin. A coating of fine sawdust will help you to get a better grip and will also soak up any blood that appears. The skin is completely free from the hind end of the body now and you are ready to peel it forwards. It comes away very easily, but you must be careful when you come to the shoulders. Pull the skin over the shoulders and front legs in the way that you would remove a pullover, and then cut through the leg bones just below the elbow. You must cut the skin and not the bone if you want to preserve the skeleton as well. Continue peeling the skin over the head and use a razor blade to cut the ears very close to the skull. Use the blade to cut round the eyelids as well. The skin will then peel right off the head, and you can cut it free at the lips.

Examine the inner surface of the skin, which is now inside-out, and remove any lumps of fat from it. You might see distinct light and dark bands on the skin, indicating that the animal was about to moult. When you turn the skin the right way out again you might find that the hairs are already falling from the dark areas.

Your skin should dry very easily and should not need any preservation treatment under normal conditions, but if the air is humid you could rub the skin with powdered borax to prevent decomposition while it is drying. You must now decide whether to preserve your specimen as a flat skin or as a round body. For a flat skin, cut a piece of thin card to the shape shown in the picture. Adjust the shape of the 'nose' to fit the snout of the animal, and gently roll the skin on to the card. A little talcum powder may help. Push a cocktail stick or a shaved-down matchstick into the tail, making sure that the skin is not twisted. Staple or wire the tail and back legs to the card, arrange the front legs and the ears nicely, and brush the fur with a small stiff brush. Write the animal's measurements on the card, together with its name and the place and date of discovery. The date is especially important, as the state of the fur varies from season to season. Leave the carded skin to dry for a few days, and then put it into a transparent plastic envelope. As long as the skin is perfectly dry, you can seal up the envelope to keep out insect pests. Alternatively, put a small mothball in with the skin.

A rounded skin is bulkier than a flat one, and it does not really have any advantage because it does not resemble the live animal much more than a flat skin. Only a skilled taxidermist can create a lifelike

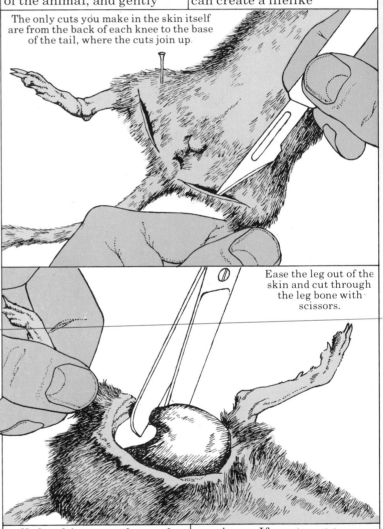

The only cuts you make in the skin itself are from the back of each knee to the base of the tail, where the cuts join up.

Ease the leg out of the skin and cut through the leg bone with scissors.

specimen. If you want to make a rounded skin, however, you merely push cotton wool gently into the skin until it reaches the original length. Extend the legs and support the tail with a stick, and tie a data label to one of the legs. Brush the fur to make it look natural.

You Will Need

Fine scissors
Scalpel or razor blade
Thin cardboard
Talcum powder
Fine fuse-wire or staples

Loosen the skin around the base of the tail. Excess blood can be soaked up with fine sawdust.

The tail can be carefully withdrawn from its skin.

Peel the skin back over the body like a pullover. At this stage you must cut through the front legs below the elbows. You will have to cut the ears close to the skull.

Carefully cut round the insides of the eyelids with a scalpel or razor blade.

Remove the skin from the body by finally cutting through the inside of the lips.

You can rub powdered borax all over the skin to prevent deterioration while drying in humid climates, but this is not normally necessary with small, thin skins.

Gently roll the skin on to a card which has been cut to the right size. Put a cocktail stick into the tail and fix it to the card.

A skin preserved 'in the round', by stuffing it with cotton wool.

A flat skin preserved on a card. Guard against insects attacking your preserved skins.

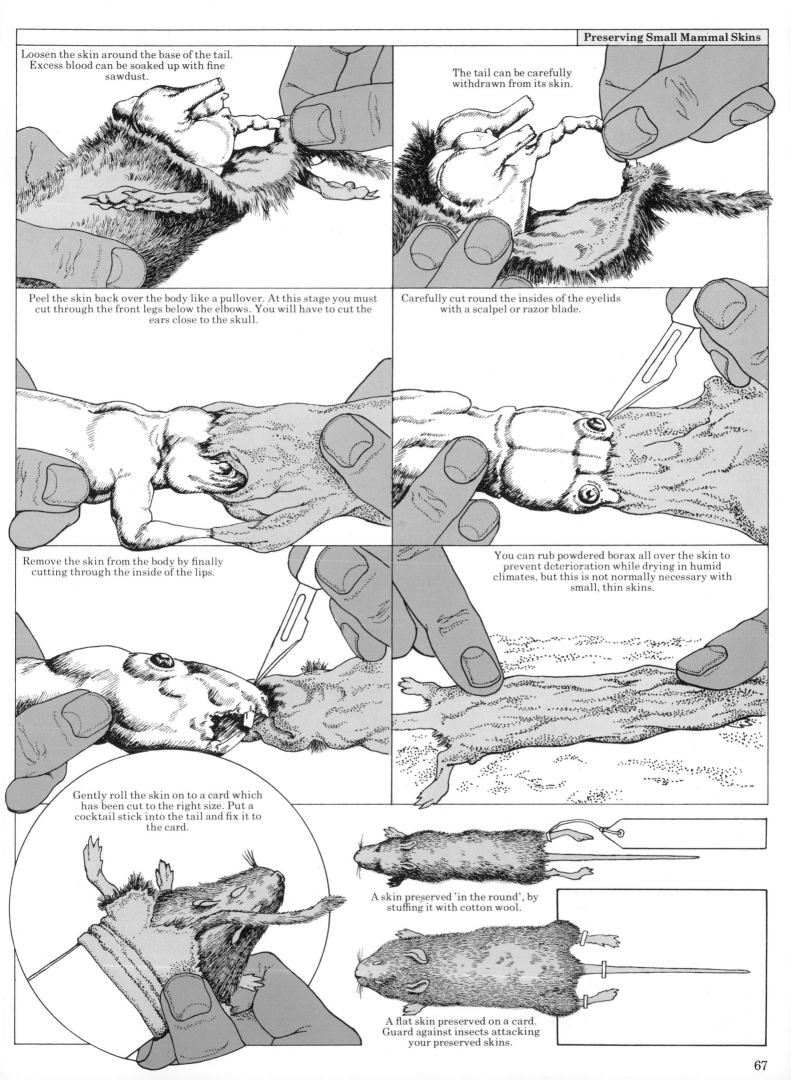

SKULLS AND SKELETONS

How to clean and preserve skulls and other bones, and mount them for display

The small mammals brought in by the cat or picked up in the countryside can yield interesting skulls as well as the skins (described on page 66). Having skinned the animal, you can sever the head quite easily with a pair of scissors and you are then ready to remove the flesh and clean up the bones. The simplest way of doing this is to cook the skull, but this method is really satisfactory only if the flesh is still fresh. Put the skull into an old saucepan with cold water and bring it *gently* to the boil. Rapid boiling will harden the flesh and make it much more difficult to remove. Simmer the material for an hour or two and you should then be able to lift the flesh from the bones with some fine forceps and a small penknife or a dental scraper (your dentist may have an old one he does not want). Take care with the lower jaw, which will usually detach itself

Carpet beetles can be used to eat up a dried carcase and leave you with a clean skeleton, but they take quite a long time.

from the rest of the skull. Use the dental scraper to clean out the inside of the skull, but be extremely careful because the skulls of these little mammals are very thin.

Having scraped away all the flesh, you must bleach the skull, either by leaving it in strong sunlight or by immersing it in hydrogen peroxide for a short time. Do not leave it in the peroxide too long or the teeth will start to drop out. If any teeth do drop out you can fix them back in with glue. Using fine fuse wire, you can re-attach the lower jaw to the skull if you wish, but this is not really necessary. A bent wire will make a suitable cradle for the lower jaw, and you can then rest the skull on it in the correct position. If possible, prop the jaws open to display the teeth.

If you are using skulls which are not completely fresh, it is better to use a different method of cleaning them. Many museums use small beetles called dermestids (see page 106) to clean their skulls and skeletons. The skulls must be dried first, either by placing them on a sunny window sill for a few days or by warming them gently in the oven, but you need not remove the skin. Small skulls dry very quickly, and then you can put them in a jar with the beetles. A hungry colony will strip the flesh from a mouse skull in a few hours, cleaning it perfectly inside and out without any damage. You can also use common carpet beetles (see page 106) in the same way, although they work much more slowly.

You can use tadpoles to clean skulls in the spring, but they are not very efficient and do not get inside the skull. Blowfly maggots can also be used. You can breed your own (see page 106), or you can put a fresh skull out in the garden under a piece of wire netting. Flies will soon lay their eggs on it in the summer and the maggots will do the rest. Ants will do the job equally well if you fix the skull over an ant hill. Cover it to prevent larger animals from taking it away. You must bleach

the skulls in the normal way after any of these biological cleaning treatments, and it is also a good idea to de-grease them. This is done by immersing them in strong household ammonia for a day or two, either before or after bleaching. If you do not de-grease the skulls, they may become discoloured later.

You are most likely to obtain skulls from the cat's victims, but you can use the same methods for other skulls, such as those extracted from owl pellets (see page 48). Keep your eyes open for larger skulls in the countryside. Badgers often die in their sets and their skulls are thrown out by the other badgers during spring-cleaning operations. Foxes sometimes use parts of badger sets and their skulls may be thrown out as well. Rabbit skulls are often found around their own warrens or, usually damaged, around fox holes. If they have been lying around for some time these skulls are generally quite clean and in need only of bleaching and de-greasing.

Bird skulls can be treated in exactly the same way as mammal skulls, although they are more delicate and need greater care. An old toothbrush might be better than a dental scraper on these.

The enthusiast will probably want to try preserving whole skeletons instead of just the skulls. The easiest way of doing this is to boil up the carcase with sulphurated potash, which you can buy from a pharmacy. You must skin the animal first, but if you want to preserve the skin as well you must modify the skinning procedure (see page 66) so as to leave the feet with the skeleton. Remove the entrails and the bulk of the flesh with scissors or a razor blade and scissors, and cut through the tendons running to the feet or else you will not be able to spread the toes. Drop the carcase into a boiling solution of about 15 gm ($\frac{1}{2}$ oz) of sulphurated potash in just over a litre (2 pints) of water. The solution is caustic and will damage a saucepan, so boil it in an old kitchen bowl immersed

in boiling water. Wear rubber gloves. Boil the carcase for about 10 minutes and probe regularly to see when the flesh begins to lift away from the bones. Remove the carcase from the liquid when this happens and scrape away all the softened flesh. The ligaments holding the bones together should not have been affected. Remove the skull and clean out the inside, and then bleach and de-grease the skeleton in the way already described. Use a curved wire to support the arch of the backbone, and pin the legs in the desired positions. A sheet of expanded polystyrene is ideal for this purpose. The ligaments will soon dry and you can remove the pins and mount the skeleton on a permanent board. You can keep the wire under the backbone with larger skeletons, but it is not necessary for the smaller ones. Support the skull on a cradle in the right position and your specimen is complete.

Tadpoles make a good job of cleaning a skeleton, although they cannot get inside the smaller skulls. Change the water regularly to prevent pollution.

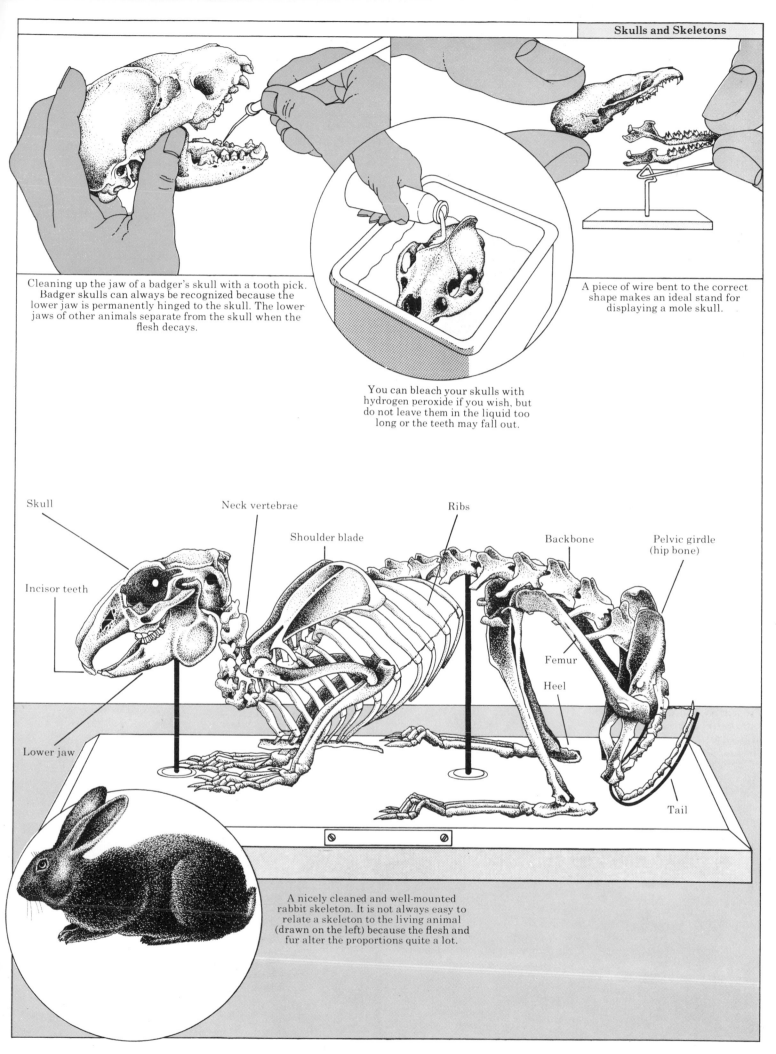

Cleaning up the jaw of a badger's skull with a tooth pick. Badger skulls can always be recognized because the lower jaw is permanently hinged to the skull. The lower jaws of other animals separate from the skull when the flesh decays.

You can bleach your skulls with hydrogen peroxide if you wish, but do not leave them in the liquid too long or the teeth may fall out.

A piece of wire bent to the correct shape makes an ideal stand for displaying a mole skull.

Skull

Incisor teeth

Lower jaw

Neck vertebrae

Shoulder blade

Ribs

Backbone

Pelvic girdle (hip bone)

Femur

Heel

Tail

A nicely cleaned and well-mounted rabbit skeleton. It is not always easy to relate a skeleton to the living animal (drawn on the left) because the flesh and fur alter the proportions quite a lot.

THE WILDLIFE DETECTIVE

Looking for tracks and other signs left by wild animals

An observant and experienced naturalist can walk through a wood and produce a list of animals that live there without actually needing to see any of them. He relies on the evidence that the animals have left behind. This evidence might be a trail of footprints, a half-chewed pine cone, a tuft of hair, or simply a strong smell. If you learn to recognize some of these clues you will be able to play detective as well. Many of the clues, such as food remains and tufts of hair, can be collected and studied to find out more about the habits and anatomy of the animals. Perhaps more important for the amateur naturalist, the clues will tell you where certain animals can be found. By studying the positions of tracks and food remains, you can discover the best places in which to build a hide or erect a camera.

Footprints and tracks are the most common signs, for they are left almost everywhere the animals go as long as the ground is not too hard. A careful study of a woodland trail or the margin of a pond will usually reveal the tracks of several species of mammals and birds. Information on recognizing and preserving some of these tracks is given on page 72.

Feeding signs are also very common and, because each species has its own way of dealing with its food, you can usually tell which animals have been feeding at any given place. The cones of pine trees and other conifers contain nutritious seeds which are eagerly sought by a variety of birds and mammals. Squirrels obtain the seeds by biting off the cone scales one by one, leaving the rather frayed central stalk shown in the illustration. Mice attack cones in the same way, but they usually gnaw through the scales more neatly and closer to the base. Crossbills also attack cones, forcing the scales back to get at the seeds. Pine cones attacked in this way remain distorted, and the scales of spruce cones are actually split right down the middle. Pine cones whose scales are split down the middle have usually been attacked by woodpeckers.

Many birds and mammals eat hazel nuts, and the discarded shells usually show very clearly which animal took the kernel. Adult squirrels, for example, split hazel-nut shells cleanly in two, usually carrying out this operation at a regular feeding station so that large numbers of shells are found at one place. Mice and voles both eat hazel nuts, but they gnaw through the shells in rather different ways (see illustrations), and both tend to feed in protected surroundings. Birds hammer

A pine cone stripped by a squirrel.

their way in to hazel nuts with their beaks and usually leave very jagged edges: the nuts are generally wedged into crevices before they are attacked. Nuthatches use each crevice only once and leave the empty nutshell in the crevice. Woodpeckers use a permanent 'vice', which they often chip out to the right size and shape for the nuts they are eating. As each nut is eaten, the shell is discarded and a fresh one is put in. You thus find quite a pile of broken shells around what is often called the woodpecker's workshop.

Several animals nibble the twigs and bark of trees, often causing serious damage to young saplings by chewing away the leading shoots. You can often identify the culprit by examining the teeth marks on the bark. Deer are common offenders against

A pine cone attacked by a crossbill. These cones tend to open out when kept as specimens, but you can preserve their features by wrapping them in cloth and drying them very slowly.

trees and you can recognize a shoot bitten through by a deer because one side is clean and the other is rather ragged. During spring and early summer deer pull bark from the tree trunks in long strips, often completely denuding slender trunks from ground level to the highest point the animals can reach. Thicker trunks are normally barked only on one side. During the winter the deer remove the bark in small patches and you can see their tooth-marks on the underlying wood.

Voles often gnaw bark from the very bottoms of young trees in the winter and kill many plantation and orchard trees in this way. You can see the finely grooved marks of the lower incisor teeth on the exposed wood. Bank voles often climb well up into the trees and their feeding damage may then resemble that of a squirrel. Rabbits and hares gnaw the lower parts of the trunks, particularly those of young trees, and leave very characteristic marks with their two top teeth. Each tooth has a narrow groove in it, and the mark left by each consists of two deep furrows with a thin strip of bark between them. The two teeth together thus leave four furrows and three streaks of bark.

Carnivorous animals are not very tidy eaters and many of them leave scattered remains, particularly fur and feathers. Foxes are particularly untidy and give away the positions of their earths by leaving piles of fur, feathers, and bones on the ground. Otters leave heaps of fish bones at their favourite feeding places. A pile of feathers with no other sign of a victim may pinpoint the feeding place of a hawk. These birds often pluck their victims in one place and then take the body elsewhere to eat it.

Other well known feeding signs include the 'anvils' on which thrushes break open hundreds of snail shells (see page 90), but perhaps the most unusual signs are left by the shrikes or butcher-birds, which impale insects and other small animals on thorns and barbed wire until they are ready to eat them. Keep your eyes open for owl pellets under trees (see page 48), and don't ignore the droppings of animals. Fresh droppings indicate that an animal is not far away, and you can often identify an animal just from its droppings. Herbivorous mammals generally produce rounded droppings full of plant remains, while carnivores produce elongated droppings, usually full of fur and with a distinct 'tail'.

Finally, do not forget your ears and nose. Many animals produce characteristic sounds and smells and it is not difficult to learn these. They are difficult to describe, however, and the best thing is to go out with an experienced naturalist or to visit a zoo, and to listen and smell for yourself.

A nuthatch with a hazel nut wedged in a crevice.

Young trees stripped by deer. It is the front teeth of the lower jaw that do the damage. The upper jaw has no incisor teeth (see inset).

Above A mouse gnawing a hazel nut. The mouse gnaws at the far side of the shell and the upper incisors leave a row of marks around the outside of the hole. *Below* A bank vole with a nut. The vole gnaws the nearest edge and leaves no marks on the outside.

A twig showing the characteristic toothmarks of a rabbit.

A squirrel holding a hazel nut. It makes a little hole in the top (see drawing above), inserts its lower teeth, and then uses them as a lever to split the nut. Young squirrels have to learn this trick and they gnaw haphazardly at first.

Examine the bottoms of barbed-wire fences for tufts of animal hair, especially in woodland. The hairs could mark a regular runway.

A trampled ring round a bush or tree in woodland indicates the roe deer's courtship area. The male chases the female around this ring many times while they are courting.

MAKING CASTS OF ANIMAL FOOTPRINTS

Plaster casts are easy to make—use them to build up a collection of animal footprints

Many animals leave their footprints in the mud when they come to drink from pools and streams, and you can also find the footprints of animals in the soft ground of shady woodland paths. As well as using these footprints to trace the animals to their homes, you can make a collection of different kinds of footprints in the form of plaster casts.

You will need some plaster of Paris, some strips of thin cardboard about 30 cm (12 in) long and 5 cm (2 in) wide, a few paper clips, a trowel, a small plastic bowl, an old spoon, and some old newspapers. You will also need some water with which to mix the plaster, but you can use clean pond or stream water if it is available and this will save you carrying water from home. You will need a jar or bottle to collect it. Put everything into an old satchel or rucksack.

Look for good, clear footprints that are free from water and dead leaves. Select one with nice sharp edges and then clip a piece of your cardboard into a circle large enough to surround the complete print. Gently push the ring of cardboard into the mud around the print, and you are then ready to mix the plaster in your bowl. Use enough to fill the depression made by the animal's foot and to form a layer about 2·5 cm (1 in) deep above it. Stir the mixture with your spoon until it is about as runny as treacle, and then pour it *gently* into the print. Wash the bowl and spoon

straightaway.

The plaster which you have poured into the footprint will get warm while it is setting and it will harden in about 15 minutes. The whole thing can then be dug up with the trowel and wrapped in newspaper to be taken home. It is not wise to remove the cardboard or the mud at this stage because the plaster does not get really hard for several hours and there is a danger of breaking pieces from the cast.

When you have got your casts home you can begin to clean them. Remove the cardboard strips and use a gentle stream of water from the tap to wash away the mud. Use an old toothbrush or soft scrubbing brush to loosen the mud from awkward crevices, and then leave the casts to dry. Always try to identify the animals whose footprints you cast. You can then write the name and any other details on the plaster.

Your casts are, of course, not true copies of the original footprints, for your casts stand up above the plaster instead of being sunk into it. You can paint the raised part of the cast and use it to make a flat print on paper, or press the cast into soft modelling clay and make a true replica of the original footprint. If you make all your casts the same size you can store them in a long cardboard tube, with foam rubber between them and with labels on the side to show where each cast is. Failing that, you can can keep them in drawers, or even in shoe boxes as long as you wrap them in paper.

Don't devote all your time and effort to individual footprints. Look and see if there are any continuous tracks. If so, you might be able to work out which prints were made by each foot. Take casts of each foot, but before you do this make some sketches showing the distances between each print and the angles of each print to the line of the track. In this way you can tell whether the animal was walking or running, and you can also use the sketches to reconstruct the whole track on a sheet of modelling clay.

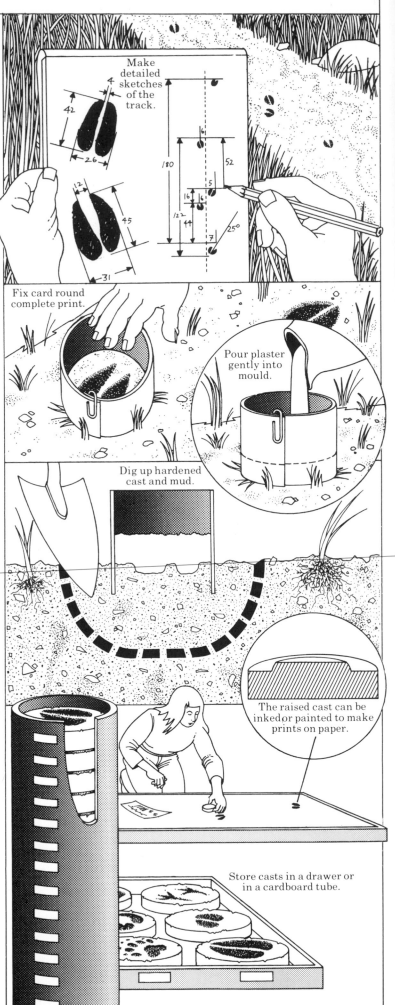

Make detailed sketches of the track.

Fix card round complete print.

Pour plaster gently into mould.

Dig up hardened cast and mud.

The raised cast can be inked or painted to make prints on paper.

Store casts in a drawer or in a cardboard tube.

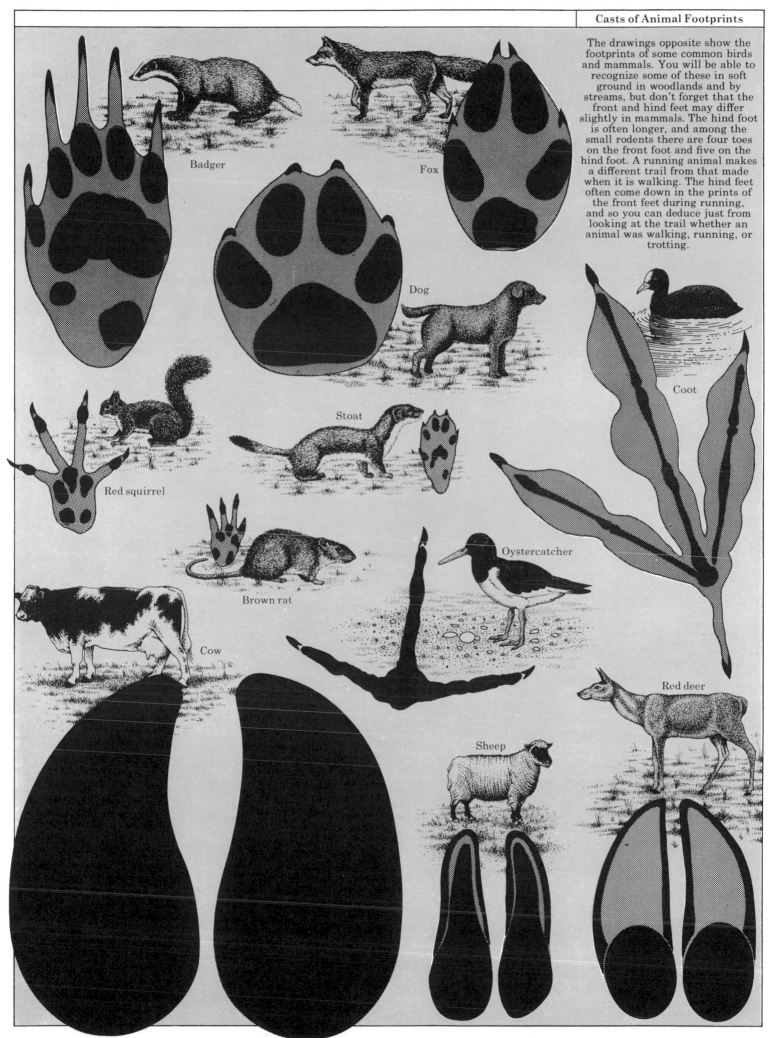

The drawings opposite show the footprints of some common birds and mammals. You will be able to recognize some of these in soft ground in woodlands and by streams, but don't forget that the front and hind feet may differ slightly in mammals. The hind foot is often longer, and among the small rodents there are four toes on the front foot and five on the hind foot. A running animal makes a different trail from that made when it is walking. The hind feet often come down in the prints of the front feet during running, and so you can deduce just from looking at the trail whether an animal was walking, running, or trotting.

Badger

Fox

Dog

Coot

Stoat

Red squirrel

Oystercatcher

Brown rat

Cow

Red deer

Sheep

73

74

he animals with which we shall be dealing on the next few pages are all members of the vast assemblage called the invertebrates. This means that they have no backbones. There are far more species of these small spineless creatures than there are of the backboned creatures such as the mammals and birds: in fact, there are something in the region of a million known kinds of insects alone. Although the majority of these invertebrate animals are small, they are not all small. Several insects are larger than the small shrews and various birds, while some marine invertebrates are veritable giants – squids with bodies five metres long and arms three times that length, and huge clams weighing much more than a man.

Hardly any insects live in the sea, but they live just about everywhere else, and there are very few plant or animal materials that they do not eat. Run through the natural materials in your mind: timber, blood, dung, wool, and so on – there are insects that feed on them all. They obviously require different equipment to deal with these various materials, but this has been no problem for the insects. Watch a caterpillar munching away at a leaf, and then watch the adult butterfly of the same species delicately sucking nectar or fruit juice with its tubular 'tongue' (see page 82), and you will see just how wonderfully the insects have coped with the various foods at their disposal. Try to watch a house-fly or bluebottle as well, and see how it uses its sponge-like mouth to mop up fluids. Many flies, such as the mosquitoes, have mouths like hypodermic needles and they use them to suck blood from other animals. The aphids and their relatives, which all belong to a group known as bugs, have similar mouths, which they use for feeding on plant sap or on other animals. Many of the bugs are likely to be

mistaken for beetles, because of their hard wing cases – actually the front pair of wings – but the needle-like piercing beak just under the head will always identify a bug. You are most likely to meet bugs when sweeping the vegetation or beating trees (see page 92).

As well as eating just about every possible material, the insects are themselves eaten by a wide variety of other animals, and many of them have evolved the most amazing forms of camouflage and other habits as protection against these enemies (see page 94). Stick insects and many caterpillars look just like twigs and the birds take

Quite a number of insects employ sounds in their courtship behaviour. The loudest 'singers' are the cicadas, which are found mainly in the warmer parts of the world. The males 'sing' by vibrating little drum-skins on the sides of their bodies at very high speeds. This produces a shrill, warbling noise which can be quite deafening in some areas. The other famous insect songsters are the grasshoppers and crickets, but these use a very different method to make their sounds. The male grasshopper has a line of minute teeth on the inside of each back leg – you need a microscope to see them – and as he moves

extremely long antennae, sing by rubbing the bases of their wings together. Their songs are usually pitched rather higher than those of the grasshoppers and they are more difficult to imitate.

Some bees and wasps and all the ants and termites are social insects, living in large or small colonies and working for the good of the whole community instead of just for themselves as most insects do. The honey bees (see page 86) have some really marvellous ways of communicating with the other members of the colony. Ants also communicate with each other a great deal and they lay scent trails for their fellow workers to follow. The ants on page 74 are busily demolishing a plum and carrying its sweet juices back to their nest in their stomachs: a long column of two-way traffic stretches between the plum and the nest.

We have already met several invertebrate animals in the chapter on aquatic life, and the present chapter will concentrate on land-living invertebrates. Vast numbers of these can be found in and around the house, or in the park, so you will not have to go far to look for many of them. But a great many hide away during the daytime because they do not have waterproof coats and so risk desiccation. They are quite safe at night, however, because the air is then always cooler and damper, and little water is lost from their bodies. You can go out to look for these animals at night, or else you can set traps for them or try to find their daytime shelters. All of these methods can be instructive.

You will meet a considerable number of different animal groups if you decide to do any of the projects in this section, and it is therefore worth looking at the classification of the invertebrates in some detail so that you will recognize what you find. Many people tend to lump all the invertebrates together as 'insects', but you will see that there are some very big differences between the insects and some of the

CHAPTER 5

INSECTS AND OTHER SMALL ANIMALS

The crowded world of the animals without backbones – the worms, slugs and snails, woodlice or sow-bugs, millipedes and centipedes, insects and spiders

no notice of them; leaf insects, many bush crickets, and numerous moths, including the lappet moth, look remarkably like living or dead leaves; and many insects look just like the bark of the trees on which they rest. Some insects, such as the wasp shown on page 74, possess weapons and unpleasant tastes that protect them from their enemies, or at least from some of them, and these armed insects often bear bright colours and bold patterns. Birds soon learn to recognize these colours and patterns and, having once tried one of the insects, they leave them alone.

his legs quickly up and down the teeth strike a hard vein on each wing and set up the familiar vibrations or chirps. Each species has its own song, and the female responds only to that song. It is possible to imitate the songs and attract the females to yourself, but you have to get the pitch and duration of each song just right. You will probably have more success if you make a tape-recording of the singing male (see page 164) and play that back out in the field.

Crickets and bush-crickets, which can easily be distinguished from grasshoppers by their various other groups.

Worms

Apart from the tiny protozoans that you might see if you put some soil under your microscope (see page 168), the simplest animals that you might come across in any natural setting, are various worms. The best known, of course, are the ordinary earthworms (see page 84), which belong to a large group of animals called annelids – a name which refers to the numerous rings or segments of which they are composed. Not many people give earthworms a second thought, but they really are incredibly valuable animals to have around. They exist in immense numbers and their ploughing activities are vital for the maintenance of the fertility of the soil. Apart from the 'ordinary' earthworms, there are some smaller species which prefer to live in the richer and moister surroundings of the compost heap and other rotting material. The brightly banded red and orange brandling worm lives in such places, from where it is regularly dug out by anglers because of its attraction for fishes. Many small white worms also live in decaying vegetation. These are known as pot-worms and they are often found in dense clusters. Thousands of even smaller worms called roundworms or nematodes live in the soil, but these do not have ringed bodies and they are not annelids. You are unlikely to see any unless you really look for them. One way to collect them in their hundreds is to put a small piece of meat, raw or cooked, in the soil, placing it in a little bag of wire gauze to stop larger animals from taking it. Hundreds of tiny nematodes will swarm to the meat, and if you look at it under your microscope (see page 168) you will see their tiny bodies writhing all over it.

Slugs and Snails

The molluscs are another very important group of invertebrate animals, second in terms of numbers to the insects, although still a very long way behind them. On land, they are represented by the slugs and the snails, while aquatic examples include cockles, limpets, and octopuses. All have extremely soft bodies, but the majority have some kind of shell to protect them. Slugs are really no more and no less than snails which have almost or completely lost their shells. Both groups glide along on a flat, fleshy organ known as the foot, or sometimes the head-foot because there is no clear division between the head and the rest of the organ. The animals' passage over the ground is lubricated by copious

secretions of slime or mucus from glands under the head, and the animals almost swim in this fluid. If you allow a slug or snail to crawl on a piece of glass, or on the inside of a jam jar, you can look at the underside of the foot – the sole – and you will see lots of light and dark bands moving forward. These are the muscular ripples produced as the animal picks up each part of the sole in turn and lifts it forward.

Some snails have separate male and female individuals, but most garden-dwelling species, like the worms, are hermaphrodite, meaning that they have male and female organs in one individual. The slugs are also hermaphrodite. Mating still has to take place, however, and in this respect the animals perform some amazing rituals. Garden snails crawl all over each other and each one of a pair actually fires a chalky 'love dart' into its partner as a prelude to the actual mating.

The mating of the great grey slug is even more astounding, although few people have been lucky enough to witness the fascinating chain of events leading up to it. Having met on the ground, the two animals climb up a tree or a wall and then lower themselves gradually down again on a thick rope of slime which may be well over 50 cm (20 in) long. They gyrate around each other in this position for up to an hour before actually exchanging sperm and then either falling to the ground or climbing back up the rope, eating it as they go.

Woodlice

Woodlice or sow-bugs, also called slaters and many other names, are very common in almost any damp situation. They are among the very few truly land-living members of the great crustacean group, which includes the crabs, lobsters, shrimps, and barnacles. But, although they live on the land, they are still very much dependent on moisture and they are never found in really dry situations. They normally venture out into the open only at night (see page 80). Except on the odd occasions when they turn their attention to young seedlings, the woodlice are quite harmless in the house and garden. They may even be beneficial, because they feed mainly on rotting material and they help to return valuable nutrients to the soil.

The woodlice and all the other crustaceans form just one division of the vast group of invertebrates known as arthropods. These animals all have jointed bodies and jointed limbs encased in tough outer skins. These skins do not grow in the way that ours do, and the animals have to change them periodically. This skin-changing process is called moulting and it can take place anything up to 25 times in an animal's life. At each moult, the old skin splits and the animal crawls out of it, already equipped with a new, looser coat ready to accommodate the next stage of growth.

Millipedes

Millipedes can be found in much the same sorts of places as woodlice, and they feed on the same kinds of materials, although some millipedes are much more attracted to living plants. The most familiar millipedes are the shiny black ones which live under logs and stones and under loose bark. They have slender, cylindrical bodies and they coil up like watch-springs when they are disturbed. Some millipedes, however, are much shorter and fatter and they are often confused with woodlice. The millipedes can always be distinguished because they have many more legs. Woodlice have just seven pairs of legs, but millipedes have two pairs of legs on nearly every segment of the body. This feature will also distinguish the brownish flat-backed millipedes from the centipedes. The latter, which belong to yet another group of arthropods, have only one pair of legs on each body segment.

Centipedes

Whereas the millipedes are generally rather slow-moving plant-eaters, the centipedes are carnivorous animals. They move much more quickly than the millipedes and they have a pair of large, poison claws at the sides of the head. Some of the large tropical species are dangerous to man. Centipedes that live right in the soil are generally very long and slender, with many pairs of legs – but never exactly the hundred legs suggested by their name. Their bodies are amazingly flexible, enabling them to double-up and turn round in confined spaces. The shiny brown centipedes that you find under stones generally have shorter and wider bodies, with just 15 pairs of legs. The last pair trail out behind the body and act like an extra pair of feelers or antennae.

Insects

The enormous assemblage of insects is divided up into about 30 different sections or orders, largely according to differences in their life histories and their wing structures, although it must be realized that a great many insects do not actually have any wings. The typical insect body has three main parts: the head, the thorax, and the abdomen. The head carries a pair of feelers or antennae, some kind of feeding apparatus, and usually a pair of eyes, although these are nothing like our own eyes. The thorax, which is the middle part of the body, bears three pairs of legs and, in winged species, one or two pairs of wings. Only adult insects have functional wings. The abdomen may have some 'tails' at the hind end, but it does not have any legs in adult insects.

The most primitive kinds of insects, such as the familiar little silverfish, belong to a group called bristletails. They do not really change much at all during their lives except that they get larger. The tiny springtails that abound in soil and leaf litter (see

page 80) also change little during their lives. Neither group has any wings. Most other insects, however, undergo a greater or lesser amount of change (metamorphosis) during their lives. The greatest changes are undergone by the butterflies and moths, the flies, the beetles, the bees and wasps, the caddis flies, and a few other groups. The young stages of these insects look nothing like the adults and they are called larvae. They have to pass through a pupa or chrysalis stage during which they are converted into adults (see page 96). Dragonflies, earwigs, grasshoppers, stick insects, and aphids (greenfly and

their relatives), and some others do not pass through a chrysalis stage: the young insect, called a nymph, changes gradually into an adult, getting more and more grown-up each time it changes its skin.

Arachnids

The last major group of arthropods which the ordinary naturalist is likely to meet are the arachnids. These include the scorpions, spiders, harvestmen, ticks, mites, and a few other small creatures. The arachnids are the animals most likely to be confused with the insects, but the distinction between the two groups is

really quite clear. Insects all have three pairs of true legs – some larvae have additional stumpy legs at the back – but the arachnids have four pairs of walking legs. In addition, the arachnids never have antennae, and their bodies do not show the three divisions – head, thorax, and abdomen – which are so clearly seen in almost all insects. No arachnid ever has wings, nor has any other non-insect invertebrate.

Scorpions

Scorpions are found mainly in tropical and sub-tropical regions. They are easily recognized by the long 'tail', which is tipped by a curved sting, and by the large claws or pedipalps. The stings of some species are extremely dangerous, although some of the smaller species are relatively harmless, with stings no worse than those of bees or wasps. Some of these smaller species can be kept in a vivarium and fed on mealworms (see page 106).

Spiders

Spiders, in which the body is generally quite clearly divided into two sections, are probably among the most disliked animals in the world, but they are at the same time among the most fascinating. They are, for

example, among the very few animals that make traps to catch their food, and their silken webs are some of the most intricate of all animal constructions (see page 104). Not all webs are alike, however, for each species builds to its own pattern, and each web is designed to catch a particular kind of prey: some catch flying insects, while others trap crawling species. Some spiders make no webs at all, and simply chase after their prey or lie in ambush for it. One group, known as jumping spiders, creep up on their prey like cats and then pounce when they are within range. This kind of behaviour requires very good eyesight and if you look at the face of a jumping spider with your lens you will see that it has huge eyes staring out from its face like the headlamps of a motor car.

Harvestmen

The naturalist will also come across plenty of harvestmen in the garden and the field, especially in the autumn. These animals look very much like spiders, but their bodies are not divided into two clear sections and their second pair of legs are always the longest. Harvestmen make no silk and have no poison fangs.

Mites

Mites are the smallest of the arachnids. The ones that you are most likely to see are red velvet mites crawling on paths and plants, but the most abundant mites are the tiny ones that live in soil and leaf litter (see page 80). You need a strong lens, or preferably a microscope, to see these properly. Many mites are responsible for the growth of plant galls (see page 126), particularly the little red pustules that occur on maple leaves. Other tiny mites infest the skin of various animals, and many a naturalist has had cause to curse the little harvest mite that causes such intense itching when it digs itself into groin or armpit. Mites, like insects, get almost everywhere.

SLUGS AND SNAILS

Observing the movements, resting places and eating habits of slugs, snails and woodlice

In common with most other ground-living invertebrates, the slugs and snails, also the woodlice or sow-bugs, generally come out to feed only at night, when the air is damp and there is little risk of their drying up.

Slugs and snails will also come out after a daytime shower, but not while it is actually raining.

If you look at a recently mown verge after rain you will see hordes of slugs and snails feasting on the rotting grass cuttings, which they much prefer to our vegetables.

Woodlice do not like the light under any circumstances, and you will have to search for them under stones and logs during the day. Large numbers also hide in bark crevices and the gaps in old walls, and if you go out with a torch at night you will be surprised at how many you find in such places.

By paying attention to the relative humidity of the air and the low levels of light intensity at dusk, you will find that the darker and more humid the environment becomes, the more woodlice come out. If you get up very early in the morning you will be able to watch the reverse movements, with the animals scurrying for shelter as the light intensity increases and the humidity drops.

The experiment described on the opposite page will show you how some of these reactions are produced.

Toothy Slugs

When you bite into an apple or a piece of cheese you leave tooth marks, but did you know that slugs and snails also leave tooth marks? They are, of course, much smaller than your own, but you can see them if you look carefully. The slugs and snails carry their teeth on a horny strap called a radula. As they crawl over their food, they push out the radula and the rows of sharp teeth leave little scratch marks. One of the best ways to see these is to melt a little fat and, just before it sets again, pour it into the lid of a plastic container. Collect a few slugs from your garden or from the roadside verge and put them into the container – do not use the very large, black or brown slugs. Put the lid on and leave the slugs alone for a few hours. They will wander about on the hardened dripping and leave trails of tooth prints in it. You can see the little furrows quite easily, but if you then bring your lens into play and focus on these furrows you will see the individual tooth marks. Each species has its own pattern, for the individual teeth are arranged in different ways in different species.

How Far Do Slugs Wander?

Slugs hide under logs, stones, and other suitable objects during the day and venture forth at night. To see how far they travel, and whether they go back to the same hiding places every morning, carry out the following experiment, for which you need a number of bricks or, better still, some squares of sacking, and a large patch of ground. The experiment is best carried out in spring or autumn, but you can do it any time if the weather is not too dry or too cold. Collect about 100 slugs of either the netted or the garden variety (see illustrations) and feed them for a day or two on bran to which you have added some neutral red dye. The dye will stain the slugs without harming them.

Lay out the bricks or sacking (about brick size) in concentric circles, with each object about 60 cm (24 in) from the next, and then release the slugs at night in the centre. Each day for the next week or so, examine each brick or piece of sacking to see how many of the dyed slugs are hiding under it. You will probably find that the slugs move out from the centre quite rapidly during the first few nights but then, as they become less crowded, there is less pressure on them to move. They then stay in approximately the same place in the daytime, and come back to it each morning after following a more or less circular course during the night.

The netted slug is easily recognized by its mottled fawn colour and milky slime. After eating the dyed bran it turns a delicate pink.

The garden slug is black with a bright orange sole, which becomes pinkish after eating the dyed bran. (These two species are by far the worst of the garden slugs in terms of the damage they do.)

Do Garden Snails Have a Home?

While tidying up the garden you will undoubtedly come across clusters of sleeping garden snails under logs and stones and in unused flower pots. During the winter or the driest part of the summer these snails will actually be hibernating or aestivating, but at other times they will merely be resting until it is time to get up and go out in the evening. Do they come back to the same shelters each night? There is a simple way to answer this question, and that is to mark each snail in one shelter with a small spot of paint – not a bright colour that will make it more obvious to its enemies. Look under the shelter each morning and see if all the marked snails are at home. If not, have a look around at some other likely shelters, and if you find any marked snails you will get some idea of how far the animals travel. If all your marked snails do return home each morning, it may be because there are no other suitable shelters, or because they know their home base by its smell. Put out some other similar shelters and see how quickly they are adopted by the snails.

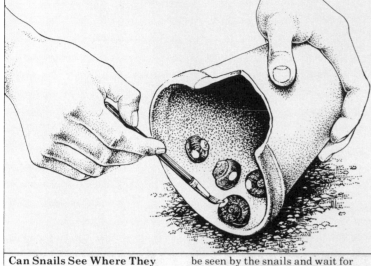

Water just one half of the tray of soil.

Add equal numbers of woodlice to each side and watch their different reactions.

Cover the tray for a few minutes and all the animals will move to the damp side. To investigate the effect of light, moisten both halves of the tray but leave one side uncovered; the woodlice will stream across to the dark side and settle down.

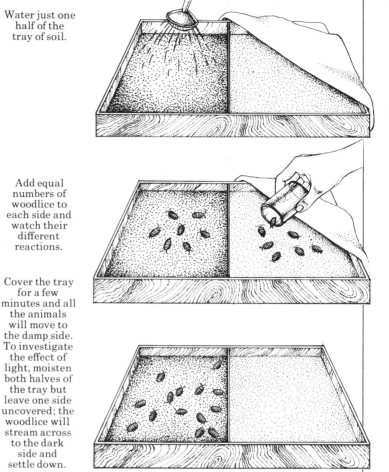

Can Snails See Where They Are Going?

Put a sheet of thick plastic at least one metre square on the ground near a wall or a hedge. Place some bricks in a circle on the edges of the sheet away from the wall or hedge, leaving fairly small gaps – about 10 cm (4 in) – between them. Mark their positions with waterproof ink. As night falls, release about 20 snails – garden snails or banded snails (see page 90) will do very well – in the centre of the sheet. Move away so that your outline cannot be seen by the snails and wait for developments. The snails will gradually disperse, but do they clearly see their way through the gaps between the bricks, or do they first bump into the bricks and then find their way through? If you dust the sheet with talcum powder in the morning, you will get the answer. The talc sticks to the snails' slime trails and shows that they nearly all go straight through the gaps. In other words, the snails do sense the light and they make straight for it.

How Do Woodlice Find Shelter?

During the daytime, woodlice or sow-bugs are always found in moist, dark places, usually with both back and belly in contact with something. How do they find such places after their nocturnal wanderings? You can answer this with a fair degree of certainty by giving the animals a simple choice-chamber. You need a seed box or similar tray which you fill with dried earth, and then you water just one half. Put about a dozen woodlice in each half and watch their reactions. Those in the dry half immediately start running about in an agitated fashion, while those in the wet half move lethargically if at all. Cover the tray with a cloth or newspaper to cut out the effect of light, and within a few minutes all the woodlice will probably be in the wet half, and fairly still. This response is quite automatic; the animals do not search for the damp places. Finding themselves in dry conditions, they walk rapidly about in various directions until they eventually leave them. Then they automatically respond to damper places by slowing down and perhaps stopping altogether. This behaviour tends to keep them in the damp places. Their tendency to run away from light also helps them to find the damp, dark nooks. But what makes them come out in the evening? Hunger perhaps, or the fact that they absorb too much water if they stay under cover too long.

ANIMALS IN LEAF LITTER

How to extract and examine the small and fascinating forms of life that live among the fallen leaves

Next time you scuffle through the dead leaf litter on the woodland floor pick up a handful of damp leaves and examine it with your lens. You will be surprised at the number of tiny animals that you see. It is very easy to extract these animals and examine them in more detail at home.

Collect some litter in a plastic bag or a small sack, and make sure that you get a high proportion of the damper leaves from below the surface. The dry leaves right on the top contain very few animals. The simplest way to examine the litter when you get home is to put it into a sieve and shake it vigorously over a large sheet of white paper on the table. Sieve just a little at a time, and knock the sieve sharply to dislodge animals clinging to the leaves. Shine a reading lamp over the sheet and use a small twig or a paint brush

to turn over the particles. The animals are light-shy and you will see them scuttling for cover again when you disturb them.

Some of the more common types of animal found in the leaf litter are shown at the bottom of this page. Some feed directly on the decaying leaves, while others are carnivorous animals and feed on the plant-eaters. A rough and ready way to distinguish them is that the carnivores tend to rush around, while the plant-eaters crawl more slowly, but there are exceptions to this rule. The false scorpions, for example, are entirely predatory, but they creep about very slowly unless they are disturbed. If you touch one with the tip of your paint brush it will draw in its large pink claws and rush backwards at high speed. The mites are usually the commonest animals in the leaf litter, but you will need a very sharp pair of eyes to spot them all. A large reading glass (see page 18) is a great help in finding them. Looked at under a more powerful lens or a microscope, the mites reveal themselves as bizarre, bristly, but strangely beautiful creatures with a wide variety of shapes. Most of them are vegetarians and they play an important role in breaking down the dead leaves; but there are also a number of predatory species. Springtails are also very common in the litter. They are small, wingless insects

which normally crawl slowly among the leaves, but if you disturb them they leap into the air. They shoot forward by means of a tiny forked spring at the hind end. This is not easy to see in the living animal, but it is released when the animal dies and you can see it protruding very clearly from the back of the body.

You might be surprised to find so many delicate flies in the litter, but these do not live there permanently. The ones you find have probably just emerged from their pupae and they are waiting to fly away at night.

It is very difficult to keep these animals alive away from their natural environment because they dry up so easily, but it is easy to make a collection of dead specimens. You can pick the animals up on the tip of a moist paint brush and put them straight into a bottle of alcohol. For permanent storage you can put each kind of animal into a separate tube of alcohol.

For large-scale extraction of litter animals, it is best to use a piece of apparatus known as a Tulgren funnel, which you can make very easily as shown in the illustrations. The central feature is a container such as you get with canned fruit or instant coffee. Remove the top and bottom and replace the latter with some wire gauze or perforated zinc with holes up to 5 mm ($\frac{1}{5}$ in) across. Half-fill the container with leaf litter

and stand it in a funnel as shown. Support the funnel in some way—a cardboard box with a hole in it is quite suitable—so that its lower end dips into a jar containing some alcohol. A low-powered light bulb—25 watts is ideal—is then fitted into a properly wired-up lamp holder and lowered into the container above the litter. Switch on the lamp and leave the apparatus for several hours. The heat from the lamp will drive the animals down through the litter and into the alcohol. Put them into stoppered tubes and examine them at your leisure. You can put them on to microscope slides (see page 168) to identify them and to examine their detailed structure.

Collect litter from different woods and compare the animals. You will find some surprising differences between the litter in a deciduous oak wood and that in a pine wood.

You Will Need

A large plastic bag
Sieve
Large sheet of white paper
Strong light
Funnel
Jam jar
Some glass tubes or small bottles
An empty can
Some wire gauze
A properly wired-up lamp holder and 25-watt lamp
Some alcohol
Paint brush
Pooter, made from a small jar and some tubing

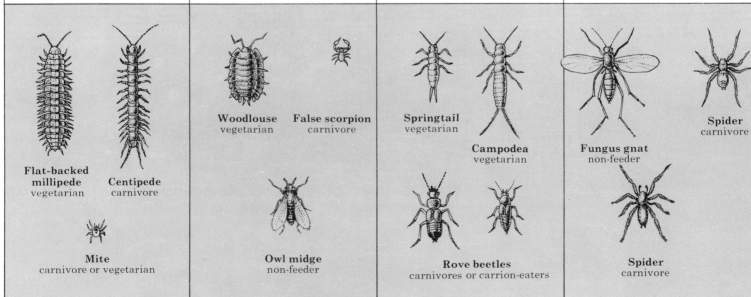

Flat-backed millipede vegetarian   **Centipede** carnivore

Mite carnivore or vegetarian

Woodlouse vegetarian   **False scorpion** carnivore

Owl midge non-feeder

Springtail vegetarian

Campodea vegetarian

Rove beetles carnivores or carrion-eaters

Fungus gnat non-feeder

Spider carnivore

Spider carnivore

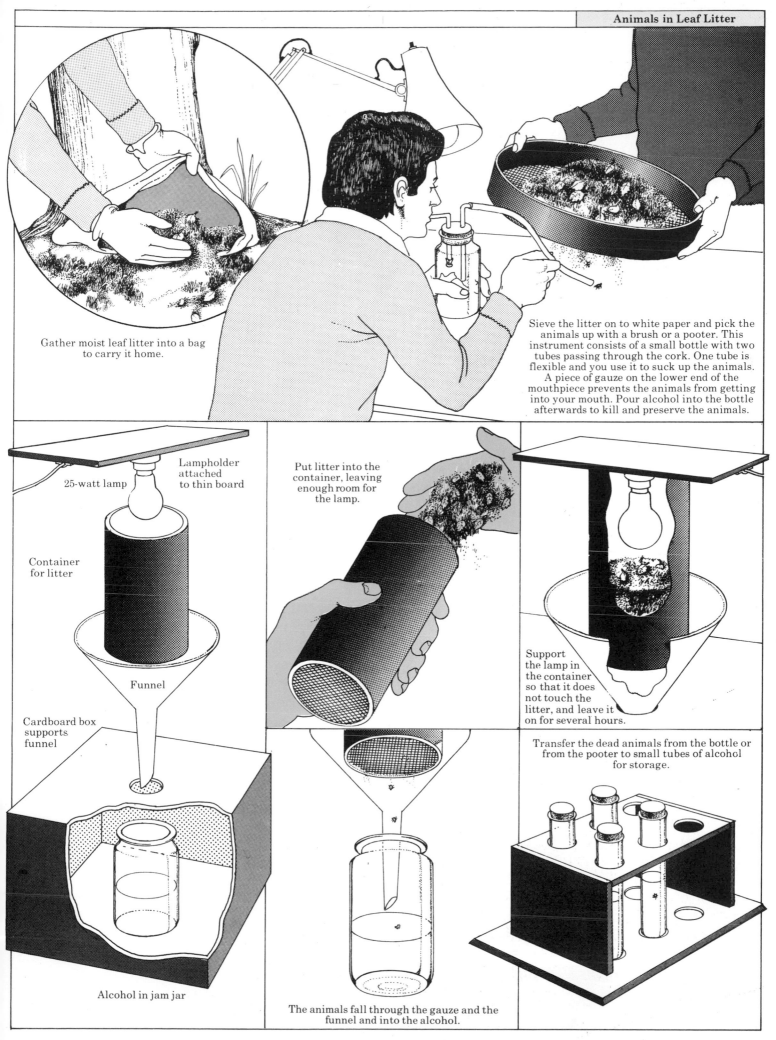

Gather moist leaf litter into a bag to carry it home.

Sieve the litter on to white paper and pick the animals up with a brush or a pooter. This instrument consists of a small bottle with two tubes passing through the cork. One tube is flexible and you use it to suck up the animals. A piece of gauze on the lower end of the mouthpiece prevents the animals from getting into your mouth. Pour alcohol into the bottle afterwards to kill and preserve the animals.

25-watt lamp

Lampholder attached to thin board

Container for litter

Funnel

Cardboard box supports funnel

Put litter into the container, leaving enough room for the lamp.

Support the lamp in the container so that it does not touch the litter, and leave it on for several hours.

Alcohol in jam jar

The animals fall through the gauze and the funnel and into the alcohol.

Transfer the dead animals from the bottle or from the pooter to small tubes of alcohol for storage.

BUTTERFLY GARDENING

**Attracting butterflies
by growing
the right kinds of
flowers**

Many people brighten their gardens by growing the so-called improved strains of flowers, with bigger and better blooms. These might be very colourful, but they are static. You can have a moving display of colour if you plan your garden with butterflies in mind. Grow the right kinds of plants, and the butterflies will come of their own accord to dance around your garden

throughout the summer. You can even entice these insects into town gardens in this way, as there is usually a nearby river bank or railway embankment from which they can spread. These ribbons of semi-natural habitats are extremely important for the maintenance and spread of butterfly populations.

Butterflies feed on nectar, which they obtain by plunging their long tongues into the centres of flowers. They are attracted only by those flowers which produce worthwhile supplies of nectar, and these are the flowers you should try to grow. The new giant strains of flowers which you see in your seed catalogues rarely interest the butterflies because their extra size and additional petals have been developed at the expense of scent and nectar.

You must select a range of plants that will bloom from early spring until the last days of autumn, and then you will have butterflies nearly all the year round.

A small selection of good

butterfly flowers is shown on these pages, together with some of the butterflies that visit them, but there are many more that you can grow. Good spring flowers include the perennial yellow alyssum or gold-dust, which many people grow on rockeries and walls, and the attractive polyanthus. Wallflowers, especially the plain yellow varieties, also attract butterflies well. Red valerian, another plant that likes sunny walls, comes into flower in late spring and remains a focal point for butterflies for much of the summer.

Some of the common summer bedding plants are very useful lures for butterflies. They include ageratum and the sweet alyssum. The latter comes in both white and purple varieties, but the purple one is best for butterflies. The dwarf phlox of the rock garden is another favourite. Hyssop, sometimes known as the butterfly bush, and thyme are well worth planting along with lavender to attract summer

butterflies, and hebe is a good shrub to go with the buddleia. Some of the late-flowering dahlias are useful in the autumn, but you must plant the single varieties which still produce nectar, not the huge 'double' flowers.

Butterflies do not live by nectar alone, however, for their young stages—the caterpillars—feed on the leaves of various plants. These are not normally the ones from which the adults get their nectar, and so if you want your butterflies to settle with you permanently you must cater for the caterpillars as well. Many of the brightly coloured species, such as the red admiral and peacock, feed on stinging nettles in the caterpillar stage. The browns feed on grasses, while the small copper caterpillar feeds on docks. You will probably hesitate to grow these weeds in your garden, but it is well worth trying to accommodate some in an odd corner, or under the hedge if you have one.

Aubretia flowers early in the spring and attracts the small tortoiseshell, the brimstone, and other butterflies which hibernate through the winter and wake up with the first spring sunshine.

Honesty comes into flower in April or May and it is visited by small tortoiseshells and the orange-tip. The latter species may lay its eggs on the flower buds.

Sweet rocket flowers with the honesty and is also attractive to the orange-tip, both as a source of nectar and as a food plant for the caterpillars.

Petunias flower for much of the summer and their deep-throated blooms are particularly attractive to long-tongued moths such as this day-flying hummingbird hawkmoth.

Several garden butterflies hibernate as adults, and may enter the house to go to sleep. If any wake up before the flowers are open, you can feed them artificially with a little sugar solution on your finger.

Stinging nettles *(above)* are the food plant of the red admiral, peacock, and small tortoiseshell caterpillars. Painted lady and comma caterpillars will also eat nettle leaves, although they prefer thistle and hop leaves respectively. Stinging nettles are thus very important to the butterfly gardener,

and a place should always be found for them in or very near the garden. The pictures above show the early stages in the life of a red admiral butterfly. The eggs are on the left, the caterpillar is in the middle, while the picture on the right shows the adult butterfly breaking out of its chrysalis case.

Buddleia attracts so many butterflies in mid-summer that, together with the hyssop, it is often called the butterfly bush. It is quick-growing and well worth planting. Here, some clouded yellow or sulphur butterflies are feeding on it.

The broad pink heads of the ice plant *(Sedum spectabile)* attract huge numbers of tortoiseshells, red admirals *(below)* and other butterflies in late summer. The butterflies often get 'drunk' on the nectar.

Lavender's rich scent and nectar attract a wide range of summer butterflies, including the comma, identified by its 'ragged' wings, and the painted lady *(right)*.

Michaelmas daisies give the peacock butterflies a last chance to stock up with nectar before going into hibernation for the winter.

A SIMPLE WORMERY

How to keep and observe earthworms at home

A mature earthworm, showing the 'saddle'. Earthworms are hermaphrodites, which means that each animal has both male and female organs. All mature worms have a 'saddle'. When the worm is about to lay eggs, the 'saddle' produces a detachable collar, which slides over the front end of the worm and collects some eggs as it goes. It then forms the cocoon seen on the right.

If you have a garden you will undoubtedly know the earthworm, although you might not realize that there are several different kinds of earthworm in your soil. The worms live there in vast numbers and they play a vital role in aerating the soil and keeping it in good condition.

You can get some idea of the earthworm population by doing a simple experiment on your lawn. Mark out an area about one metre (3 ft) square and then dissolve about 14 gm ($\frac{1}{2}$ oz) of potassium permanganate crystals in $4\frac{1}{2}$ litres (1 gallon) of water. Pour the solution evenly over the marked area of lawn and watch the worms wriggle out of the ground. You will be surprised how many there are, and even then not all of them will emerge. For best results, do the experiment during a damp spell in early summer.

Earthworms are particularly common under lawns because they are undisturbed there and the grass roots provide them with plenty of decaying food. If you dig down into an old lawn you will notice that there are very few stones in the upper layers. This is due to the ploughing action of the worms. They swallow soil as they plough through the ground, and they void the material again as worm casts on or just under the surface. Only the finest material can pass through the worms, and so the stones gradually sink as material is taken from under them and re-deposited above them.

You can watch this ploughing activity for yourself by making a simple worm cage called a wormery. All you need is a length of batten, a few screws, and two sheets of rigid transparent plastic. The exact size does not matter, as long as the plastic sheets are the same size. Make up the wooden framework as shown in the illustration and then screw on the plastic to make a thin box. You can glue on the plastic if you wish, but you will not then be able to get it off to clean the inside later. Glass sides can be used if you cut grooves for them in the framework.

Having put the wormery together, fill it with layers of soil of different colours or textures. Finely sieved garden soil, peat, fine sand, and chalky soil will be ideal. Each layer should be about 2·5 cm (1 in) thick, and you can have more than one layer of each kind. Water

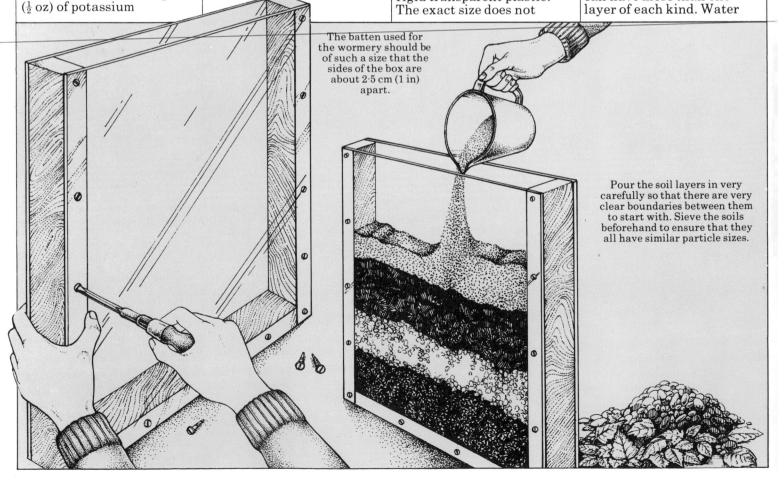

The batten used for the wormery should be of such a size that the sides of the box are about 2·5 cm (1 in) apart.

Pour the soil layers in very carefully so that there are very clear boundaries between them to start with. Sieve the soils beforehand to ensure that they all have similar particle sizes.

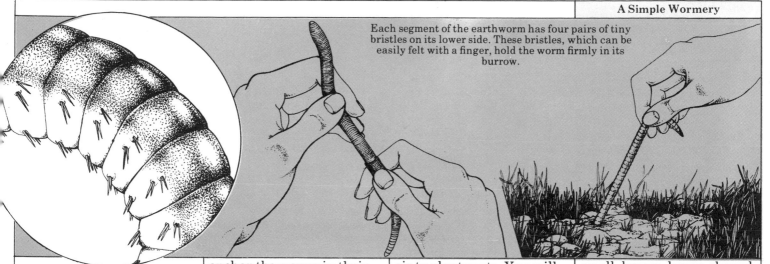

Each segment of the earthworm has four pairs of tiny bristles on its lower side. These bristles, which can be easily felt with a finger, hold the worm firmly in its burrow.

the wormery thoroughly (but not enough to waterlog the soil if you have glued the sides on), and you are then ready to introduce the worms. A dozen fully grown worms should be sufficient for a wormery about 30 cm (1 ft) across and you should have no difficulty in digging these up in your garden. You will know if they are mature by the prominent 'saddle' about a quarter of the way along from the front (pointed) end. While handling the worms, rub your finger along the underside of the body from back to front and feel the little bristles on each segment. These are what anchor the worms in their tunnels and make it so hard to pull them out. Put the worms into the wormery and scatter a thin layer of gravel on the top. Cover this with some dead leaves or grass cuttings to feed the worms, and put a light-proof cloth over the whole wormery. Earthworms do not like light and they are actually killed by bright sunshine.

Leave the wormery alone for a few days and then lift the cover to have a look. You will see numerous tunnels through the layers, and the layers themselves will be beginning to merge as the worms plough them up. In nature, the tunnels play a major role in bringing air to plant roots. You will also notice that the worms have been pulling the dead leaves down into the soil, and there will also be worm casts on or near the surface. Worms increase soil fertility by burying dead leaves and eating only small parts of them, and they also bring mineral-rich soil up from the lower layers. Cover the wormery again and examine it every few days. See how the originally distinct soil layers are becoming mixed.

When you have seen enough of the worms' activity empty the wormery on to a tray and examine the soil carefully. You will probably find a number of small, brown, lemon-shaped objects about as big as a grain of rice. These are the worms' egg cocoons. Put the soil and the worms back in the garden and dismantle and wash the wormery. You can use it again for ants if you make a cover for it (see page 98).

You Will Need

Two sheets of glass or rigid transparent plastic about 30 cm (1 ft) square (the size is not critical)
A length of batten about 2·5 cm (1 in) wide, long enough to go round three sides of your glass or plastic
Some screws
A sheet of black plastic or other light-proof material

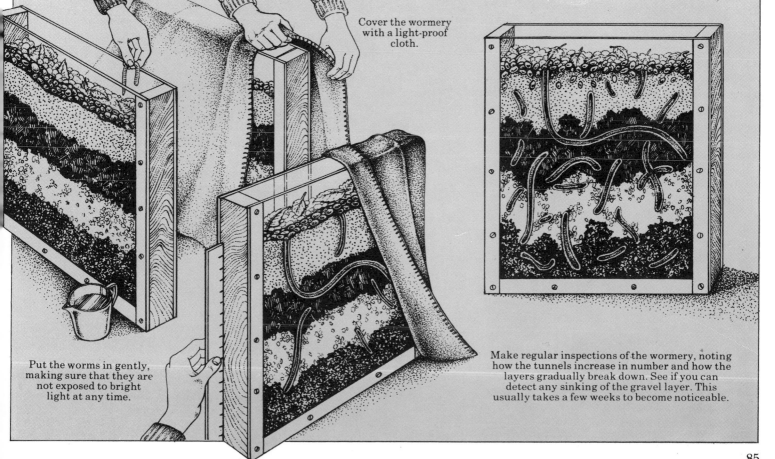

Put the worms in gently, making sure that they are not exposed to bright light at any time.

Cover the wormery with a light-proof cloth.

Make regular inspections of the wormery, noting how the tunnels increase in number and how the layers gradually break down. See if you can detect any sinking of the gravel layer. This usually takes a few weeks to become noticeable.

CAN BEES SEE COLOURS?

Simple experiments with honey bees to test their perception of colours

Since Karl von Frisch, the famous Austrian biologist, started to study honey bees more than 50 years ago, many scientists have investigated the behaviour of these wonderful little insects. Many of the experiments are very complicated, but some are remarkably simple and can be performed in any garden. Few gardens are without honey bees, even in the middle of cities, for the insects frequently fly two or even three miles from their hives to look for the nectar which they convert into honey.

The following experiment, based on the work of von Frisch, can be carried out to find out whether or not the bees can see colours. You need a white-topped table or some similar flat surface in the garden, some pieces of plain glass about 7.5 cm by 5 cm (3 in by 2 in), and some pieces of coloured paper about the same size. These should be red, blue, green, yellow, black, and various shades of grey. Alternatively, the pieces of glass can be painted in these colours on one side only. You also need a small amount of honey, a small paint brush, and a pot of quick-drying plastic paint. The experiment can be carried out at any time during the warmer months of the year when bees are on the wing.

Set out the coloured papers (not the grey ones) on the table and cover each with a piece of glass; or if you are using painted glasses, put them on the table with the painted side downwards. Put a small amount of diluted honey on the blue glass and then go in search of a bee. If there are bees visiting the garden flowers, they can often be enticed away with a *small* drop of honey on the end of a slender twig or grass stem. Gently push the twig under the bee's head and encourage her to transfer her attention to the honey. This is not too difficult because the honey has more sugar than the nectar, and the bee will then cling to the twig and feed. Don't worry about getting stung – this is most unlikely, as the bees are far too busy collecting food to bother about stinging the inquiring naturalist. Having persuaded your bee to cling to the twig, walk carefully back to the table with her. You may find that the bee flies away before you get there, but this will be because she has a full stomach and not because she dislikes your treatment of her. When you reach the table with a bee, transfer her carefully to the honey on the blue glass. Don't dump her in the honey, but encourage her to feed from it. While she is feeding, you can put a *tiny* spot of the quick-drying paint on her thorax (this does no harm to the bee). Use a bright colour that will show up from a few yards away. You can then sit back and watch.

The bee's stomach will soon be full and she will fly up from the table, circle around a few times to get her bearings, and then fly off to the hive. You will need patience at this point, for if the hive is a long way off the bee may not return for some time. You can use the interval to entice more bees to the honey, and thus increase your chances of success in the experiment.

In all probability, the original bee, identified by her spot of paint, will return to feed, and she may well be followed after a while by some of her sisters. She will have told them about the honey, and she will also have given them instructions for finding it by dancing excitedly on the honeycombs in the hive. Mark all the bees while they are arranged round the honey and then, when they fly away, replace the blue glass with a clean one without honey. When the bees come back again, the marked ones will fly straight to the blue plate, showing that they can remember colours and pick out the blue from the others. This does not prove that the bees see colours in the way that we do, however: they could achieve these results merely by seeing the coloured glasses as different shades of grey.

In order to prove that the bees really do see the different colours, give them some more honey on the blue plate and then, while they are away again, clear the table and re-lay it with a clean blue plate amid a range of greys. The bees will come back unerringly to the blue one, proving that they see it as a colour and not as a shade of grey. Carry out these experiments with the other colours, and you will find that the bees can distinguish all of them except red. They cannot distinguish red from similarly dark shades of grey.

You can also carry out this experiment with the common wasps or yellow-jackets in the early part of the summer, but it is not easy to get hold of the wasps in the first place. The best way is to put out some honey on a blue glass and hope for the best. While the wasps are busy rearing their brood a worker wasp will take honey back to the nest for the other workers (not for the young grubs), but the wasps do not communicate with each other like honey bees and the original worker will not bring others along.

Anatomy of a Bee	A Common Wasp	A Solitary Mining Bee
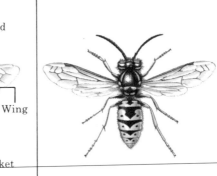		
The orange bands on the body show that this worker belongs to the Italian strain of honey bees. Several other strains exist without the orange bands.	The bright yellow and black colours distinguish the wasps from most of the bees, and their bodies are less hairy.	Many solitary bees (see page 88) occur on the flowers in the spring and summer. Some are very like honey bees, but their bodies are much flatter.

Antenna
Eye
Head
Thorax
Wing
Abdomen
Pollen Basket

You Will Need

Squares of coloured glass, or plain glass and squares of coloured paper
White-topped table
Honey
Paint brush
Quick-drying plastic paint

Place a small blob of honey on the blue glass.

Set up the table in the garden, not too near a flower bed.

Take a twig and persuade a bee to feed from honey on the end of it. Then carefully carry the bee over to the table and put her down on the blue glass.

Put a tiny spot of paint on the bee's back while she is feeding.

Replace the blue glass with a clean one. The bees will come back to the blue glass even when it has no honey on it.

The bee flies off and returns with other workers.

Leaving the blue glass on the table, replace the other colours with different shades of grey. The bees will still go to the blue glass.

NESTBOXES FOR BEES AND WASPS

Attract these interesting and useful insects to your garden and watch them breed

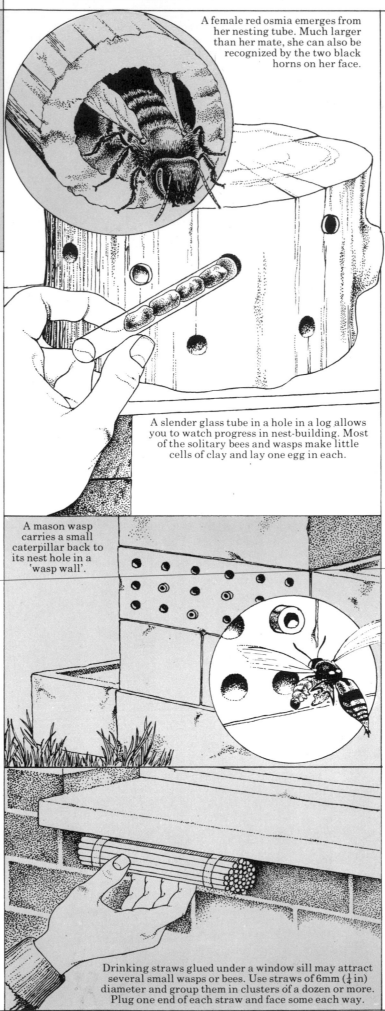

A female red osmia emerges from her nesting tube. Much larger than her mate, she can also be recognized by the two black horns on her face.

A slender glass tube in a hole in a log allows you to watch progress in nest-building. Most of the solitary bees and wasps make little cells of clay and lay one egg in each.

A mason wasp carries a small caterpillar back to its nest hole in a 'wasp wall'.

Drinking straws glued under a window sill may attract several small wasps or bees. Use straws of 6mm ($\frac{1}{4}$ in) diameter and group them in clusters of a dozen or more. Plug one end of each straw and face some each way.

The idea of attracting bees and wasps might not appeal to many gardeners at first, but you really can derive a great deal of interest from doing this. Your garden will also benefit, because the bees pollinate the flowers and enable them to set fruits and seeds, while the wasps destroy large numbers of aphids and other insect pests. To allay the gardener's fears, it is not suggested that you attract the highly social wasps or yellowjackets that annoy us in the late summer, and we are not concerned with keeping bees for honey. It is the solitary bees and wasps and the furry bumble bees that you should encourage to take up residence in your garden.

Most of the solitary bees and wasps are somewhat smaller than their social counterparts, and their life histories are very different. After mating, the female of a solitary species goes off and makes some kind of nest. She stocks the nest with food and then lays some eggs in it. A few species come back periodically to replenish the food supplies as the young grubs feed, but most abandon their nests completely when they have laid their eggs and sealed up the entrances. The new generation of bees or wasps emerges some months later, and the cycle begins again. It is not always easy to distinguish solitary bees from solitary wasps, but the bees are usually much hairier than the wasps and you will often see them covered with pollen or else with bulging pollen baskets on their legs. The hind legs of the bees are relatively broad. There is also an important difference in the behaviour of the two groups: bees collect pollen for their grubs, while wasps all collect some kind of animal food. There are actually two rather distinct groups of solitary wasps that you are likely to find in your garden —the digger wasps and the mason wasps. Nearly all digger wasps are either black and yellow or plain black. Many have distinctly square heads, and they all lay their wings flat over the body when at rest. The mason wasps are usually black and yellow and they fold their wings along the sides of the body when at rest.

The eggs of the solitary bees and wasps are laid in a variety of situations, but the most common form of nest site is some kind of tube or tunnel, either pre-existing or excavated by the parent insect. By providing some ready-made tunnels, you will greatly increase the chances of these insects settling in your garden. The insects' bodies vary a good deal in size and, as they like tunnels that are fairly tight, you should provide holes of various sizes from about 4 mm ($\frac{1}{6}$ in) in diameter to about 1 cm ($\frac{2}{5}$ in).

The simplest way of providing these nesting holes or tunnels is to drill holes in some logs. Stand the logs up on end along the garden path or on the patio. They can make quite an attractive feature if you stand some potted plants on top of them. Make sure that the logs are in the sun, as the insects like heated quarters and you will find that they always choose the sunny sides of the logs.

Another way of attracting the insects is to build a small wall with a few house ventilation bricks. The holes in these bricks are rather too large for most bees and wasps, but you can cut pieces of bamboo and other hollow stems and lay them in the ventilation bricks. Make sure that the inner ends of the tubes are plugged with modelling clay or some other material. Alternatively, you can

An up-turned flower-pot, partly filled with an old mouse nest and buried in the ground, might attract a queen bumble bee (*left*) and persuade her to make her nest in it. Cover the hole to protect it from the weather.

make a basket with wire netting and fill it with hay. Fix it to a shed wall or a tree trunk and simply push in the lengths of tube. You can also affix lengths of hollow stems under window sills. Many of the smaller species will even nest happily in paper drinking straws fixed in similar places. Fix the straws in bunches, as for some reason this makes them more attractive to the insects.

One of the commonest visitors to your logs or wall will probably be a rather rounded, rusty-coloured bee called the red osmia (see illustration). Both males and females may take up residence in the holes and tubes, although only the females will make nests. You will see them arriving with loads of mud to make the cells of their nests, and going head first into the holes. After a while the insects back out, and they may then turn round and back in again to sit looking out of the entrance. The most interesting activities, of course, go on inside the nest hole, and you can try to see this by putting glass or plastic tubes in some of the larger holes. Make sure the inner ends are plugged. If you are lucky a bee will take up residence, and you can then see how building is progressing by gently pulling the tube out from time to time. Make sure the bee is out foraging when you do this. When she no longer visits the nest, you can remove the tube for good and keep it in a container to await the emergence of the

As an alternative to glass observation tubes, you can use wooden tubes which have been split down the middle so that you can open them. This tube contains the nest of a leafcutter bee.

The ruby-tailed wasp is a brilliant red and green insect which parasitizes several of the bees and wasps.

This very slender black wasp called *Trypoxylon* stocks its narrow nest tunnel with small spiders.

Ectemnius is a black and yellow digger wasp that will nest in hollow canes, although it prefers to dig its own tunnels, throwing out coarse sawdust in the process.

A leafcutter bee approaching its nest with a piece of leaf rolled under its body. The leaf sections are neatly cut to exactly the right size.

new bees. You may have to wait until the following spring.

Among the most interesting bees you may attract are the leafcutters. You will recognize them by the pieces of leaf which they carry to the nest holes. If you can persuade a female to nest in an observation tube you will be able to see the neat sausage-shaped cells which she makes with the leaf fragments. Try to follow her when she leaves the nest, and you might be lucky enough to see her actually cutting pieces out of leaves—usually rose leaves—and curling them up under her body to carry them home.

The larger digger wasps usually dig their own tunnels in decaying wood, but the smaller ones are happy to nest in the tubes that you provide. You can watch them bringing small flies, aphids and other insects to their nests when they have finished making the clay cells inside. Mason wasps often nest in narrow canes and drinking straws, but some merely make their clay cells in crevices and daub more clay or mud over them. You might find these on the walls of your house.

Bumble bees nest on or under the ground, and you might be able to encourage one or two queens to take up residence in your garden in the spring by providing them with some furnished accommodation. The furnishing must be in the form of old bedding from a mouse nest, for the bumble bees normally take over old mouse nests for their homes and they seem to require the scent of mice to persuade them to settle down. You can get some old mouse bedding from a pet shop if you explain what you want it for. A simple flower-pot nest is shown in the illustration, but you can make other subterranean dwellings for them. A metal or wooden box is very satisfactory if you fit it with a short pipe leading diagonally up to the surface of the ground. Protect the opening from the worst of the weather by putting a brick close to it. This will also help to guide the bees back to the nest.

SNAIL SHELL PATTERNS

A demonstration of their value as camouflage

If you look around you in the countryside you will often find large stones surrounded by masses of broken snail shells. These stones are the feeding places or 'anvils' of the thrushes. The birds collect snails and bring them to the anvils to break them open. Various species of snails meet their end in this way, but a high proportion of the broken shells will belong to two species called banded snails. These have basically yellow shells with a greater or lesser amount of brown banding. The two species are very much alike, except that one has a white lip around the mouth of the shell and the other has a brown lip. For the purposes of this project, you can treat the two species as a single population. Both species are widely distributed in Europe, but only the white-lipped snail is common in North America: the brown-lipped snail has been introduced, but it occurs in only a few places.

Both species of banded snails are extremely variable. Though the basic shell colour is usually yellow, it can also be brown or pink. On the typical shell there are five narrow brown bands running round each whorl, but any or all of these bands may be missing, and any two or more may be fused together to give wider bands. Shells with the two upper bands missing are said to be effectively unbanded, because the banding is not visible from the top. Fusion of all the bands, or just the upper ones, makes the shell appear very dark from above.

The different varieties of shells are not evenly distributed, and you can prove this for yourself by collecting shells from different habitats. Start by collecting broken shells from the thrushes' anvils in open grassland. If you do this in the summer, when the grass is nice and green, you will find that most of the broken shells are clearly banded. Then turn your attention to the surrounding grassland and search carefully for whole shells, with or without snails in them. Collect as many as you can and you will see that almost all of them have a yellow ground colour. Divide the snails into two groups: unbanded or effectively unbanded, and clearly banded. Then make two simple histograms in your notebook to show the percentage of yellow shells and the percentage of unbanded and effectively unbanded shells in the grassland. You will find that the majority are unbanded or effectively unbanded, thus appearing plain yellow from the top. This coloration clearly has a protective value, for the birds cannot see the plain-coloured shells so well in the grass and they take mainly the banded ones. Later in the year, when the grasses are browning, the banded shells are better camouflaged and the birds take a higher proportion of unbanded ones.

Investigate hedgerows as well as open grassland. Choose a shady hedgerow if possible and you will find that, although most of the shells still have a yellow ground colour, a high proportion have fused bands and appear very dark. Make two more histograms, as shown on the opposite page, to indicate the percentage of yellow shells and the percentage of unbanded shells in the habitat. When you look at the anvils in hedgerows you will see that the unbanded shells are taken in greatest numbers: these are the ones that show up most. Keep the empty shells that you find.

In woodlands, you will find that the yellow ground colour of the shells gives way very largely to pink or brown, in association with the darker surroundings. Most of the shells are unbanded or effectively unbanded, for plain shells merge more completely with the dead leaves. Make a third pair of histograms to show the percentages of yellow and unbanded shells as before. Banded shells show up easily and these are the ones which are most numerous at the anvils.

Clearly, the shell colours and patterns provide efficient camouflage, and you can use the empty shells to prove this even more clearly. Take 20 plain yellow, 20 banded, and 20 brown shells and fill each with a mixture of bread and meat paste. Mix the shells thoroughly and place them in two lines in any of the three habitats studied. Leave them for a couple of days and then go back to see which ones the thrushes have removed.

An immature banded snail showing the thin, horny region which has just been added to the edge of the shell. When mature, the lip will produce the toughened brown or white rim seen in the two shells on the left.

Some of the many forms assumed by the brown-lipped and white-lipped snails

Typical form, with five separate bands

All five bands fused together to give an effectively brown snail

Unbanded yellow snail

One-banded yellow snail (effectively unbanded when seen from the top)

Unbanded pink snail

Grassland

Hedgerow

The thrush breaks open the snail shell by gripping the lip in its beak and bringing the shell down sharply on to the stone. It sometimes takes several knocks to break the shell enough to get out the snail.

Woodland

Young glow-worms feed on snails, and you might well find some of them while collecting banded snails. They usually have their heads well inside the shells. Put them in the dark and they will probably light up next time you disturb them.

Wood   Grass   Hedge

Make histograms in your notebook to show the percentage of yellow shells in the three habitats. There are far more in hedgerows and grasslands than in woodlands. A second set of histograms shows the percentages of unbanded shells (including effectively unbanded ones) in the three habitats: woodland and open grassland have most unbanded shells.

91

AN INSECT COLLECTION

How to catch and preserve insects, and build up a reference collection

The keen-eyed entomologists of the 19th century took great pride in filling their cabinet drawers with long rows of butterflies, and the more they had of each kind the better they liked it. There is nothing to be gained from this kind of collecting today, and, with many species on the decline, there is everything to lose. A great deal of fascinating information about insect behaviour and habits can be discovered without making a permanent collection at all (see page 96), but a reference collection with examples of the major groups of insects is a must for the serious student of entomology and also for the enthusiastic amateur. It is a first-class way of learning how different insects are constructed and how they are classified.

For the purposes of catching them, insects can be divided into flying forms and crawling forms. Flying insects, such as butterflies and moths, dragonflies, bees, wasps, and true flies, are best caught with the conventional butterfly net. This should be at least 30 cm (12 in) across and the bag should be at least 50 cm (20 in) deep. It should be made of fine, soft netting, preferably black or dark green so that the insects will not see it coming so easily. You can put a long handle on it, but you might find this difficult to control. A 10-cm (4-in) handle is usually adequate.

Crawling insects in grass and other low-growing vegetation can be collected by careful searching. You will learn a lot about their habits and their fine camouflage, but you might not get many insects in a short time. A better method is to use a sweep net, one design of which is shown at the bottom of this page. The insects that you are likely to catch include earwigs, grasshoppers, bush-crickets, bugs, beetles, and small flies. You will also catch large numbers of spiders. Insects on trees can be caught with the aid of a beating tray (see illustration opposite). Don't forget to search the tree trunks for resting moths and other insects. Put out pitfall traps (see page 100) for ground-living insects.

Night-flying insects can be collected by hanging a light bulb, properly wired, over a white sheet. Moths will fly to the light and you can catch them with a net. If you cannot spare the time to stay and watch, you can make up a simple trap with the light over a funnel in a cardboard box (see opposite page).

Having caught your insects, you must kill them swiftly and efficiently. The best way is to use a wide-mouthed killing bottle, fitted with a tight cork stopper. Pour some plaster of Paris into the bottom of the bottle and let it set. When it is thoroughly dry you can start using the bottle. Ethyl acetate is one of the best killing agents. Simply pour a few drops on to the plaster in your bottle and put the cork in. Insects placed in the bottle will die quickly.

Most insects are preserved simply by pinning and drying them. Butterflies and others with flimsy wings are 'set' on setting boards first (see opposite page). Always use stainless entomological pins, obtainable from dealers. Ordinary pins are too easily corroded. Tweezers are useful for handling the pins and pinned insects. Beetles and bugs, if wanted purely for display, can be carded: they are put down on to a lightly glued piece of white card and their legs and antennae are brushed gently into position. Like setting, this operation can be carried out only when the insects are in a fresh and relaxed condition. Bugs and beetles required for serious study should be pinned if they are large enough. Otherwise they can be lightly glued to the tip of a

The butterfly net in use: when the insect is in the net, turn the handle to trap it.

small triangle of card, which is itself pinned into the collection.

Your collection can be housed in special entomological store-boxes, but these are very expensive. Cardboard boxes lined with expanded polystyrene or foam rubber will be suitable, although they do not show off your insects as well as a proper store-box. Don't forget to label your specimens with their names and the date and place of capture, and don't forget to add some moth-proofer to kill the inevitable pests.

A sturdy sweep net in use. Whatever design you use, the frame and bag must be able to stand up to hard wear. Light canvas with a reinforced hem around the rim should be used for the bag. Sweep the net to and fro in front of you as you walk through the grass, and examine it after every two or three sweeps.

You Will Need

Killing bottle and fluid

Entomological pins

Setting boards

Storage boxes

Net

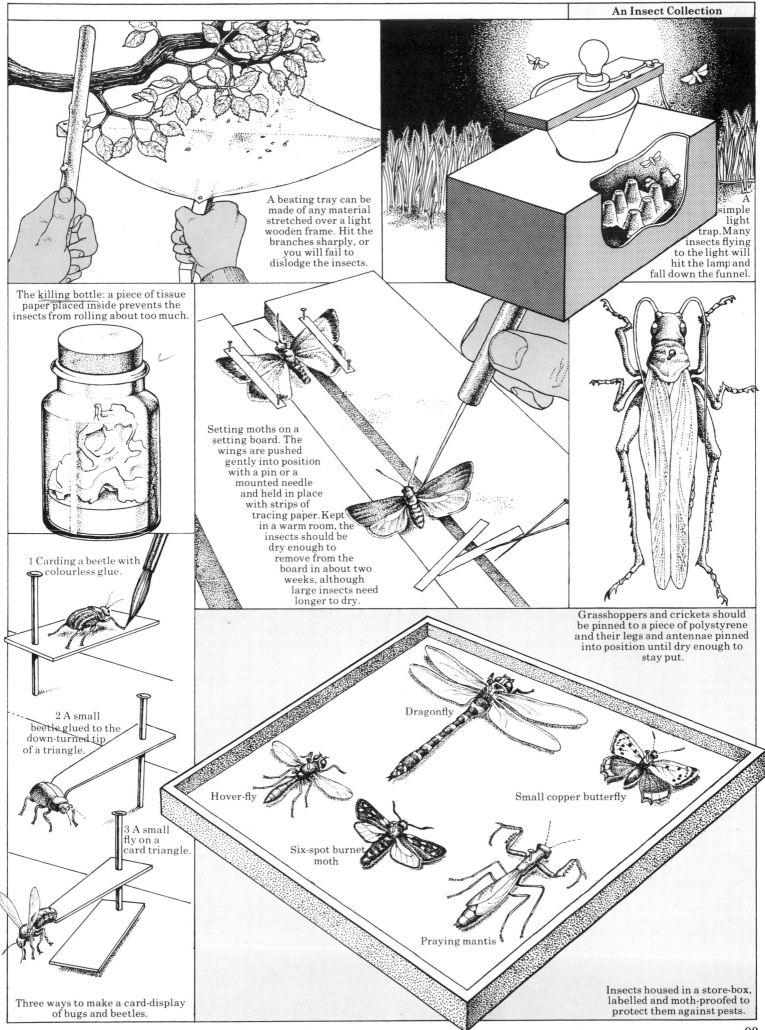

A beating tray can be made of any material stretched over a light wooden frame. Hit the branches sharply, or you will fail to dislodge the insects.

A simple light trap. Many insects flying to the light will hit the lamp and fall down the funnel.

The killing bottle: a piece of tissue paper placed inside prevents the insects from rolling about too much.

Setting moths on a setting board. The wings are pushed gently into position with a pin or a mounted needle and held in place with strips of tracing paper. Kept in a warm room, the insects should be dry enough to remove from the board in about two weeks, although large insects need longer to dry.

1 Carding a beetle with colourless glue.

2 A small beetle glued to the down-turned tip of a triangle.

3 A small fly on a card triangle.

Three ways to make a card-display of bugs and beetles.

Grasshoppers and crickets should be pinned to a piece of polystyrene and their legs and antennae pinned into position until dry enough to stay put.

Dragonfly

Hover-fly

Small copper butterfly

Six-spot burnet moth

Praying mantis

Insects housed in a store-box, labelled and moth-proofed to protect them against pests.

93

INSECT CAMOUFLAGE

The amazing ability of insects to merge with their surroundings, even changing colour to match different backgrounds

The merveille-du-jour moth spends the daytime resting on tree trunks. It is usually found resting on lichen-covered bark, which it matches with astonishing precision. The pattern on many moths' wings is similar to bark patterns, and the moths always sit in such a position that the wing patterns run parallel with and tend to merge with those of the bark.

The insects might not be as clever as the chameleon or the cuttlefish when it comes to changing their colours, but they nevertheless employ some wonderful forms of camouflage to protect themselves from their enemies. Both colour and behaviour are involved, and these features have become part and parcel of the insects' whole make-up. Although there are some very remarkable exceptions, as we shall see below, the majority of insects have evolved colour schemes which closely match those seen in their natural habitats.

Take a sweep net into a grassy field and sweep it to and fro through the grass. If you do this in the summer you will catch numerous bugs, grasshoppers, and other insects. Look at each one carefully and decide which is its dominant colour. If an insect has two colours, such as brown and green, more or less equally distributed, allow both colours. When you have recorded the colours of all the insects you have caught, count them up and see which colour is the most common. You will not be surprised to find that the majority of the insects are green or perhaps light brown – two colours which blend in extremely well with the grass.

Carry out the same investigation on heathland or on the woodland floor, where the dominant colour of the surroundings is brown. You will find that most of the insects in such places are brown or black. Repeat the investigation without a sweep net: just use your eyes to search for the insects. You will not find nearly so many, and those that you do find will usually be the more obvious ones, proving even more conclusively that insects are very well camouflaged in their natural habitats.

Search tree trunks for resting moths early on a summer morning. Leafy lanes and woodland paths are the best places to do this. Note whether the moths you find match the colours of the tree trunks. They usually do, but is this because they deliberately select trunks of the right colour, or because the birds have already eaten those that landed on the wrong kinds of trees? This is a difficult question to answer, but you might like to investigate the problem if you have a greenhouse or a conservatory. Collect old pieces of bark of various colours and scatter them at random in the greenhouse: stand some up in their natural attitude, and lay others down. Collect as many moths as you can from tree trunks in the daytime or from street lamps or moth traps (see page 92) at night and release them in the greenhouse. Next morning look to see whether the moths are randomly distributed on the pieces of bark, or whether they favour those that match their own colourings best. Some species have colours and patterns that are amazingly similar to bark.

See how many other examples of camouflage you can find. Tropical insects generally provide the best examples – the fascinating stick and leaf insects and small bugs that look just like flower buds or thorns on twigs – but good examples of camouflage are to be found everywhere. Many caterpillars look just like slender twigs, even to the extent of standing out rigidly from the larger branches. They are ignored by the birds, and a number of moths also escape detection because they look like living or dead leaves. This form of camouflage, in which the insects actually resemble some other object, is called protective resemblance.

Although the colour of an insect is usually more or less constant and has evolved to match the environment, some insects can change their colours to match different backgrounds. You can investigate simple colour change with the common laboratory stick insect (*Carausius morosus*), which you can obtain from dealers and pet shops and often get free of charge from friends who have too many – the insects breed very readily in captivity.

Select a dozen or more adults with fairly light brown colouring and divide them into three equal groups. Put one group on some light coloured leaves, another on dark leaves, such as ivy, and the third group on dark coloured leaves in complete darkness. Leave them all alone for a day or two, and then examine them. Those on the light coloured leaves will still be light in colour, while those on the dark leaves will be darker. Those insects kept in the dark will not have changed, indicating that the insects kept under normal conditions can detect the colour of their surroundings and change colour accordingly. Put the dark insects back on to light leaves and they will gradually become pale again. Some changes are irreversible, however, as shown in the experiment on the far right.

Some insects are very brightly coloured, and yet they do not seem to be attacked by birds, Tiger moths, wasps, the black and red burnet moths, and the boldly banded black and yellow cinnabar moth caterpillars are good examples. They are not eaten because they taste very nasty, and the bold colours act as a warning to the birds. A young bird will try a few of these insects, but it will soon learn to leave them alone. Some edible insects also have these colours, however, and they are also avoided by the birds. This phenomenon is called mimicry, and it is very well shown by many hover-flies which mimic wasps.

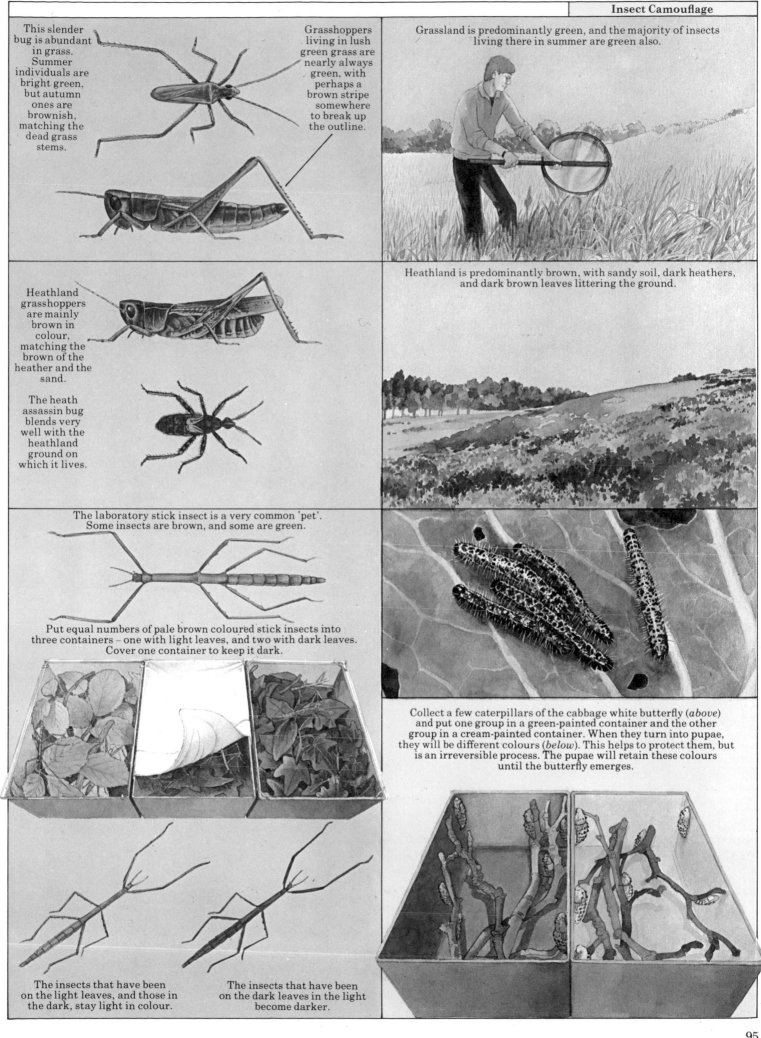

This slender bug is abundant in grass. Summer individuals are bright green, but autumn ones are brownish, matching the dead grass stems.

Grasshoppers living in lush green grass are nearly always green, with perhaps a brown stripe somewhere to break up the outline.

Grassland is predominantly green, and the majority of insects living there in summer are green also.

Heathland grasshoppers are mainly brown in colour, matching the brown of the heather and the sand.

The heath assassin bug blends very well with the heathland ground on which it lives.

Heathland is predominantly brown, with sandy soil, dark heathers, and dark brown leaves littering the ground.

The laboratory stick insect is a very common 'pet'. Some insects are brown, and some are green.

Put equal numbers of pale brown coloured stick insects into three containers – one with light leaves, and two with dark leaves. Cover one container to keep it dark.

Collect a few caterpillars of the cabbage white butterfly (*above*) and put one group in a green-painted container and the other group in a cream-painted container. When they turn into pupae, they will be different colours (*below*). This helps to protect them, but is an irreversible process. The pupae will retain these colours until the butterfly emerges.

The insects that have been on the light leaves, and those in the dark, stay light in colour.

The insects that have been on the dark leaves in the light become darker.

Do This

BREEDING INSECTS

Simple ways to rear butterflies, moths and stick insects

There can be few households that have not had caterpillars in a jam jar at some time or other. Wriggling caterpillars fascinate children and they are regularly brought home as 'pets'. You can't exactly cuddle a caterpillar, but if you feed it properly you can witness some of the most amazing transformations that occur in the animal kingdom.

You can collect caterpillars of many kinds from hedgerows and trees in spring and summer, but don't collect too many at first because they need quite a lot of looking after. Get some experience with a few common kinds first. You can bring the caterpillars home in almost any small container, but remember to put some food plant in with them. Don't forget which plant you found them on, because they will probably refuse anything else and you will have to make regular trips to collect fresh supplies of of the original kind.

When you have brought them home, you must give your caterpillars some roomy accommodation. A purpose-built larval cage like that shown on this page can be bought from dealers, or else you can make your own with a round container and some stiff, transparent plastic glued into a cylindrical shape. Fit the cylinder into the container and make a few small holes in the lid. Stand the food plant in the cage in a small jar of water to keep it fresh, and stuff tissue paper in the mouth of the jar to prevent the caterpillars from drowning themselves. Change the food plant as soon as it shows signs of turning yellow.

After a few days you might notice that some caterpillars have stopped feeding and moving, and you might also notice a swelling behind their heads. Don't worry: the caterpillars are only going to change their skins, but do not touch them at this time, for they are very easily injured. You may be lucky enough to see one of them split its old skin and wriggle out of it. Its new, looser skin soon hardens and it can begin to feed again. Most caterpillars change their skins four or five times during their lives, and then they are ready to turn into chrysalises or pupae. You will usually know when they are about to do this, because many of them walk round and round in search of a suitable site, and quite a number change colour from green to pink or brown.

Some butterfly caterpillars pupate among the bases of the plants on which they feed, but most hang themselves up in some way on twigs and other surfaces. Most moth caterpillars pupate either under the ground or in silken cocoons among the vegetation. Use gardeners' potting compost or peat for those species that burrow into the ground. Ordinary garden soil is not good because it contains sharp little particles which get into the delicate joints of the insects. Moss and straw are useful for those species which pupate among vegetation, while a few twigs or pieces of bark stood up in the cage will provide sites for the butterfly larvae to pupate.

Some species remain in the pupal stage for a very long time, but as a general rule those insects that pupate by the late spring will emerge later in the same year; those that do not pupate until early summer or later will usually not emerge until the following spring. Keep the pupa cage in a fairly cool place during the winter (not indoors) and give it an occasional sprinkling with water.

Examine it frequently in case any insects have emerged. With luck, you will see the incredible spectacle of a butterfly or moth dragging itself from its pupa, crawling up a stem, and gradually spreading and drying its crumpled wings.

If you have only one specimen of a kind, it should be released in its natural habitat, but if you have both sexes you can try to breed from them. Many moths breed very readily in captivity, mating in a confined space and laying their eggs on virtually anything. Butterflies are more particular and generally demand plenty of space in which to fly about before they will breed. A greenhouse is a good place in which to breed them.

The stick insects are another group of insects that are very easy to breed. Many of the species are parthenogenetic, which means that the females can lay eggs without mating. Indeed, in some species, males are hardly ever found. Stick insects must be kept in fairly tall cages so that they have plenty of room to change their skins. You must search for their eggs at the bottom of the cage, for the insects scatter them at random. Stick insects have no chrysalis stage: they simply get larger and larger until they are fully grown.

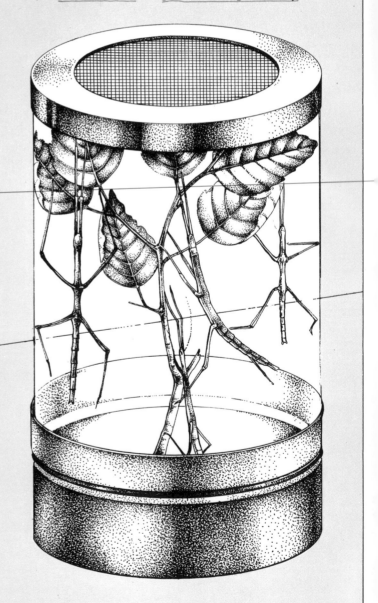

purpose built larval cage

A typical breeding cage containing some stick insects. All stick insects are vegetarians and most are quite easy to breed as long as you keep them warm and give them enough humidity.

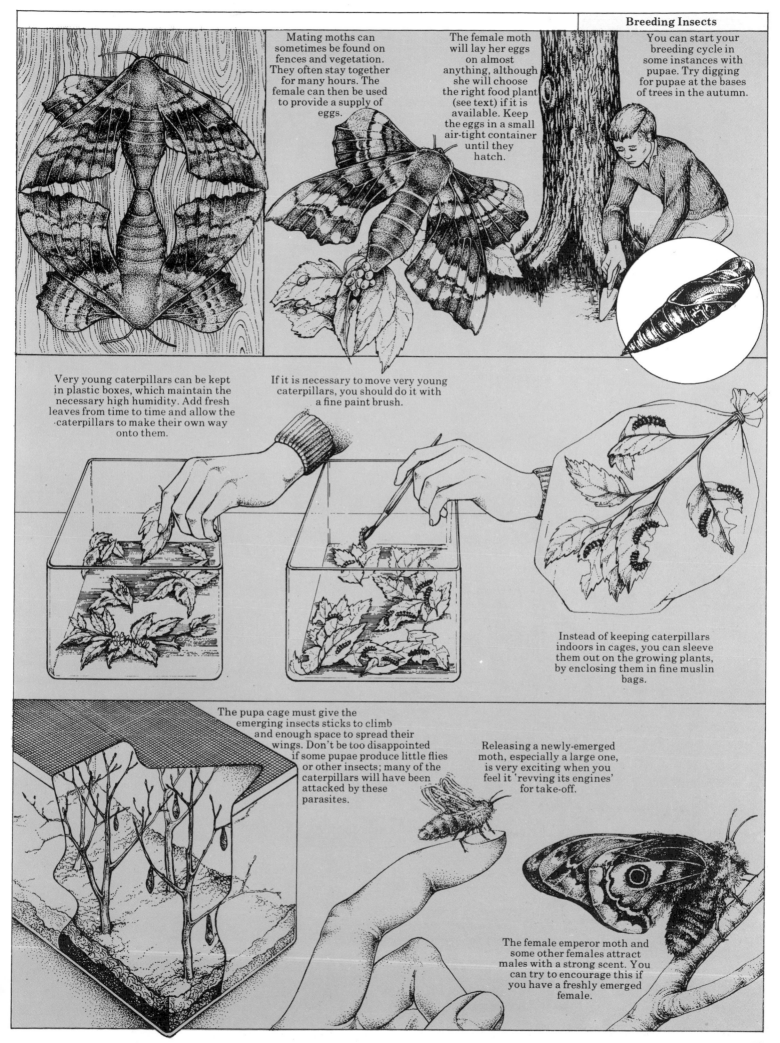

Mating moths can sometimes be found on fences and vegetation. They often stay together for many hours. The female can then be used to provide a supply of eggs.

The female moth will lay her eggs on almost anything, although she will choose the right food plant (see text) if it is available. Keep the eggs in a small air-tight container until they hatch.

You can start your breeding cycle in some instances with pupae. Try digging for pupae at the bases of trees in the autumn.

Very young caterpillars can be kept in plastic boxes, which maintain the necessary high humidity. Add fresh leaves from time to time and allow the caterpillars to make their own way onto them.

If it is necessary to move very young caterpillars, you should do it with a fine paint brush.

Instead of keeping caterpillars indoors in cages, you can sleeve them out on the growing plants, by enclosing them in fine muslin bags.

The pupa cage must give the emerging insects sticks to climb and enough space to spread their wings. Don't be too disappointed if some pupae produce little flies or other insects; many of the caterpillars will have been attacked by these parasites.

Releasing a newly-emerged moth, especially a large one, is very exciting when you feel it 'revving its engines' for take-off.

The female emperor moth and some other females attract males with a strong scent. You can try to encourage this if you have a freshly emerged female.

KEEPING ANTS

How to make an ant farm or formicarium, and maintain a thriving colony of ants

Ants are often described as the most industrious insects on earth. They are certainly very busy creatures, and you can follow their activities closely by making a simple ant farm or formicarium. You can use your wormery cage (see page 84) as long as you make it escape-proof by adding a lid and standing it in a tray of water with a film of paraffin over it. Fill the cage with fine soil and add the ants. The insects will then excavate numerous tunnels.

With that method, however, many of the ants' activities will be hidden from view. A better idea is to make a proper formicarium along the lines shown in the illustrations on these pages. The basic materials are a sheet of glass, some pieces of wood, some putty or modelling clay, and some plaster of Paris. In effect, you make the ants' tunnels and chambers for them, in positions where you can watch what goes on.

All ants are social insects, living in colonies of various sizes. Each colony is ruled by one or more queens. If you gather up a few ants and put them into your formicarium you may be able to keep them alive for a few weeks, but you will not have a thriving colony unless you collect a queen, for only the queen can lay eggs and keep the colony at its full working strength. The best ants to collect are the small black garden ants (*Lasius niger*) that nest under stones and garden paths, but you can also

collect the yellow ants that make the conspicuous mounds in grassy places. Neither of these species can sting. Dig into the nest with a trowel and collect as many ants as you can without getting too much soil. Search carefully for the queen, who is quite easy to recognize because of her much larger size. Put the queen and the other ants into your formicarium and give them some food to make them feel at home. The common ants are omnivorous and will eat almost anything you give them, but ripe fruit, seeds, and small pieces of meat will

be particularly appreciated, and the occasional spoonful of honey or jam will be a real treat for them. Provide water in a 'sponge' of blotting paper or foam rubber. The food and drink should normally be given in the 'feeding trough', but larger pieces, such as bananas or oranges, can be put into a jar attached to the flexible tube.

You must keep the nesting part of the formicarium covered for most of the time, because the ants are used to living in the dark, but you can leave the feeding area or trough uncovered. Lift the

cover from the nesting area every now and then to see how the various chambers are being used for different purposes: one might be a nursery, another a larder, and another might even be a cemetery. Don't stand your formicarium in the sun, and don't let the insects get too dry. If you keep the conditions just right the colony should thrive indefinitely. You might even get a swarm of winged ants waiting to emerge one day in the summer. These are the males and new queens, which fly away and mate before the queens begin new colonies.

You need a piece of glass at least 30 cm (12 in) square, and a wooden board a little larger. Lay the glass on the board and surround it with a framework of battens about 2·5 cm (1 in) thick. The battens should touch the glass on one side, but there should be a gap of about 10 mm ($\frac{2}{5}$ in) on the other sides.

Arrange some strips and blobs of putty or modelling clay on the glass to form a network, and put a small block of wood on the glass near the end opposite that which touches the framework. The tube, if used, should abut on to this block.

Use modelling clay to hold the tube firmly in place in the gap in the frame.

With the glass in position, pour freshly mixed plaster of Paris into the frame until level with the top. Leave it to set hard.

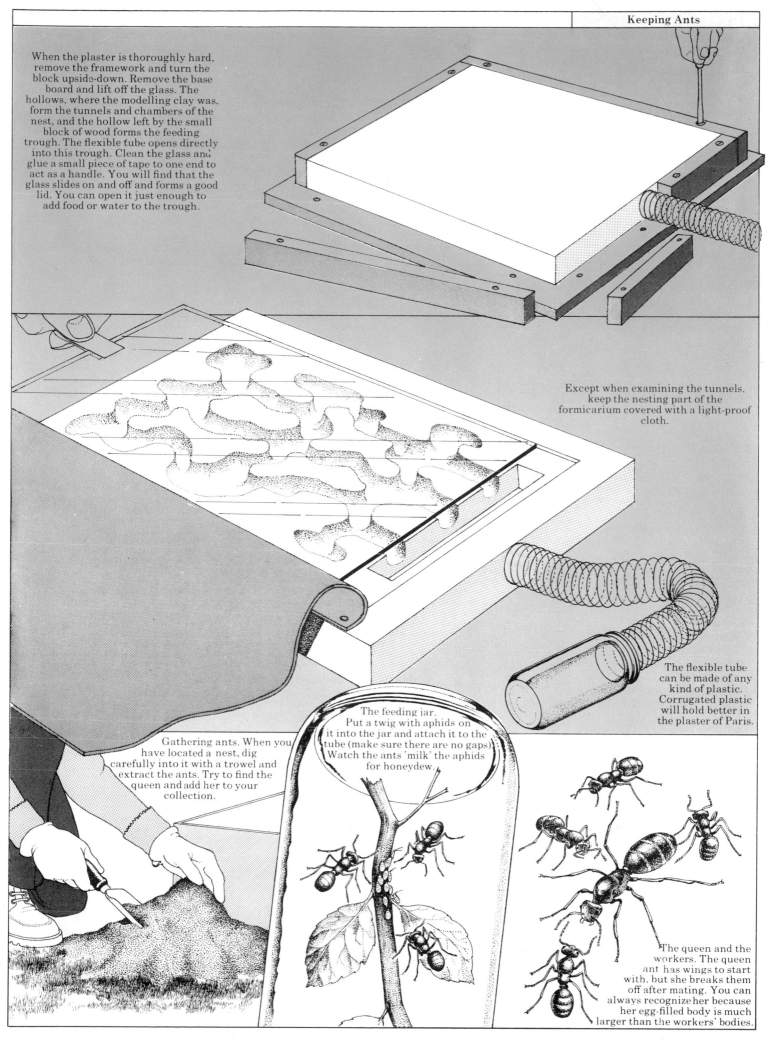

When the plaster is thoroughly hard, remove the framework and turn the block upside-down. Remove the base board and lift off the glass. The hollows, where the modelling clay was, form the tunnels and chambers of the nest, and the hollow left by the small block of wood forms the feeding trough. The flexible tube opens directly into this trough. Clean the glass and glue a small piece of tape to one end to act as a handle. You will find that the glass slides on and off and forms a good lid. You can open it just enough to add food or water to the trough.

Except when examining the tunnels, keep the nesting part of the formicarium covered with a light-proof cloth.

The flexible tube can be made of any kind of plastic. Corrugated plastic will hold better in the plaster of Paris.

Gathering ants. When you have located a nest, dig carefully into it with a trowel and extract the ants. Try to find the queen and add her to your collection.

The feeding jar. Put a twig with aphids on it into the jar and attach it to the tube (make sure there are no gaps). Watch the ants 'milk' the aphids for honeydew.

The queen and the workers. The queen ant has wings to start with, but she breaks them off after mating. You can always recognize her because her egg-filled body is much larger than the workers' bodies.

PITFALL TRAPS FOR SMALL ANIMALS

Sink jars in the ground to discover some of the tiny animals that swarm about during the night.

I f you shine a torch round a garden or any other habitat at night, you will see all kinds of small creatures wandering about on the ground, especially when the ground or the atmosphere is damp. Most of these animals have to lead nocturnal lives because they have no waterproof coats and they would rapidly dry up in the daytime. You can get some idea of the distribution and variety of this nocturnal animal life by setting out some simple pitfall traps in the garden or along a stretch of road-side verge or hedgebank. These traps consist merely of glass jars which are sunk into the ground at various points. Small animals scampering over the surface fall into the jars and they are then unable to escape because they cannot climb the smooth sides of the jars.

When sinking the traps, it is essential to put the rims flush with the surface, and it is also necessary to cover each trap with a piece of slate or wood which is raised up on small stones to allow enough headroom for beetles to enter. The cover is to prevent rain from entering the trap and drowning the captives, and also to prevent mice from getting in and making a meal of the trapped animals. Glass can be used for the cover, but there is always the danger in summer that the sun will be up before the naturalist and will shine into the

traps before they are emptied. Sunlight is lethal to some of these small animals.

The siting of the traps is very important if you want to make a proper assessment of the animal life in the study area, for there may be quite different animals living in different parts of a garden. You would not expect to find the same kinds of creatures on a dry lawn as in a damp compost heap, for example. Six traps is a reasonable number for an average garden, and they should be scattered over the whole area so that each distinct habitat is covered. In a typical garden, traps can be sunk in the lawn, in or around the compost heap, in the herbaceous and vegetable gardens, under the shrubs or hedges, and in the inevitable neglected corner where there might be a few bricks or old logs lying about. If one part of the garden is distinctly damper than another, traps should be sunk in both parts.

The animals that you can expect to find in your pitfall traps when you

examine them in the morning include springtails, ants, ground beetles, rove beetles, burying beetles, earwigs, woodlice, centipedes, millipedes, and harvestmen. Spiders also occur in some traps, but their ability to spin silken ladders and life-lines enables them to escape fairly easily from the jars. The numbers of animals trapped will depend very much on the siting of the traps and also on the weather. Very few will be caught on cold winter nights or during very dry spells in the summer, but mild, overcast nights may yield scòres of insects and other creatures. It can be very interesting to relate the catch on particular nights to temperature and humidity records for the locality.

It is not necessary to bait your pitfall traps in order to catch the animals, but bait can certainly be used if you wish, and baited traps do often bring in extra species and numbers. Small pieces of meat, fish, or cheese are the most suitable baits, and over-ripe fruit can

also be used. Earwigs, ground beetles, rove beetles, burying beetles, and ants are more commonly caught in baited traps than unbaited ones, while baited traps also attract a fair number of blow-flies during the daytime. Most other creatures seem to fall into baited and unbaited traps with equal readiness. If you use baited and unbaited traps in your investigations, it is essential that you separate baited traps from unbaited ones by at least 2 metres (6½ ft). Unless you do this, you may get animals attracted to baited traps blundering into unbaited ones, and so upsetting your results.

The simple pitfall trap

Slate

Small stones

Glass jar

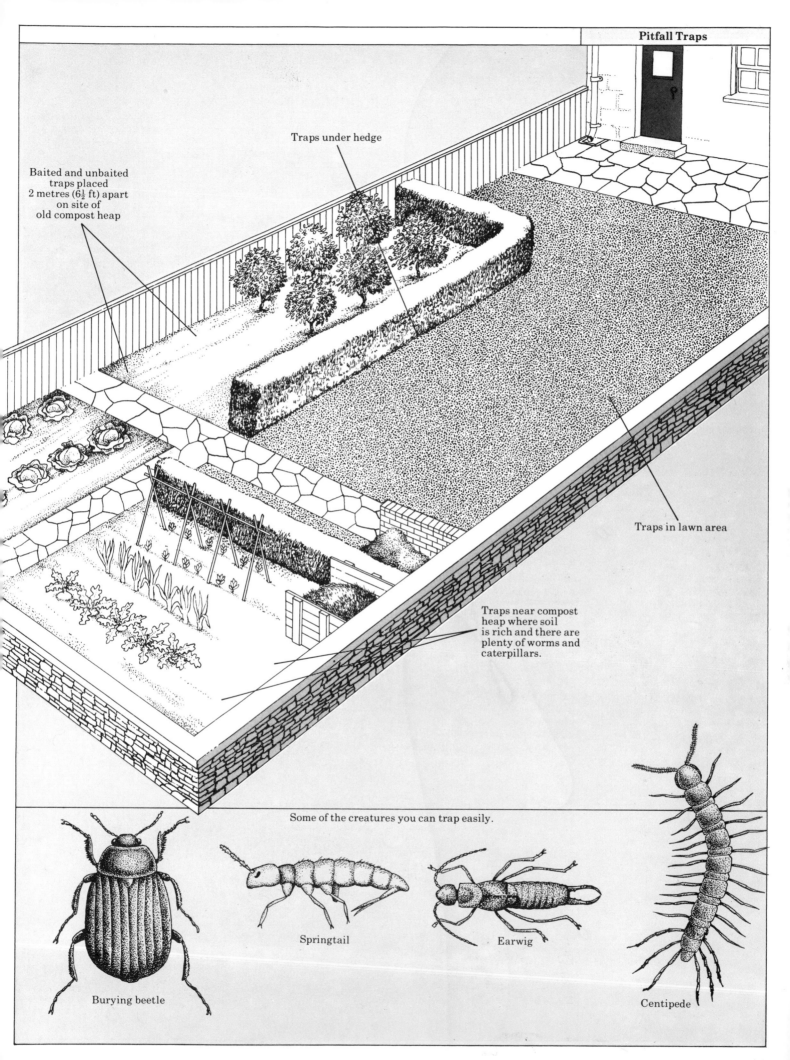

Traps under hedge

Baited and unbaited
traps placed
2 metres (6½ ft) apart
on site of
old compost heap

Traps in lawn area

Traps near compost
heap where soil
is rich and there are
plenty of worms and
caterpillars.

Some of the creatures you can trap easily.

Burying beetle

Springtail

Earwig

Centipede

ANIMAL COMMUN-ITIES

Methods for defining just how many animals live in a particular habitat

When observing animals it is sometimes possible to count exactly how many animals of one kind live in a particular area. You can count the number of deer in a herd, or the number of birds in a nesting colony, or waterfowl on a lake. You can even count the number of dragonflies breeding over a small pond if you use binoculars and have a great deal of patience. However, when it comes to quite large numbers of animals moving about freely in a certain habitat, it is very difficult to estimate by simple counting methods just how many live there.

About twenty years ago two ecologists were studying two different kinds of animals. Roger Tory Peterson was studying plaice, and Frederick Lincoln water-fowl, and they both worked out a marking method from which the total population may be estimated. The basis of this principle is that if a proportion of the population you are studying is marked in some way and then released among the original population, these animals will quickly reintegrate. If a second sample of the animals is then captured, the number of marked individuals in the second sample will have the same ratio to the total number in the second sample as the total of marked individuals originally released has to the total population. This may sound rather complicated to read, but it is a matter of simple algebra and the details are given in the box at the bottom of the opposite page.

Finding out how many animals there are in a given community is an interesting and simple project, but is most important to choose the correct marking method. You must be sure that the marking technique chosen for the animals whose population you are going to calculate will affect neither their behaviour nor their life-span in any way. A conspicuous blob of paint, for example, may well destroy an animal's natural camouflage. A green grasshopper sitting on a green blade of grass is well hidden from any bird that is looking for an insect to eat. However, if you put a bright red dab of paint on the top of its thorax, it will be very noticeable to the hunter and may well be quickly taken. Choose a part of the body that is normally hidden from view. In an insect such as a grasshopper this is usually under its thorax. Another thing to allow for is that if you make a conspicuous mark you are more likely, when capturing animals for your second sample, to capture the conspicuously marked animals, and this will affect the accuracy of your calculations.

A third problem is the choice of paint. Some paints, especially cellulose lacquers, may flake off leaving your animal virtually unmarked. Many oil paints and powder paints wash off in a heavy dew or a shower of rain. A good artist's oil paint (not student's oil paint) is probably the best marking material to use. It can, of course, be obtained in a variety of colours and has been used successfully for marking many different kinds of small animals including butterflies, moths, locusts, grasshoppers, flies, beetles, and even bed bugs.

To apply the paint to your captured animals it is probably best to use a fine camel-hair brush, but you can be more imaginative depending on the animal you wish to mark. You can use an entomological pin, a sharpened match-stick, a single hair, or a fine dry

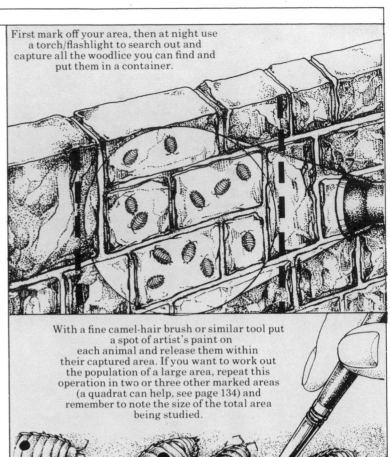

First mark off your area, then at night use a torch/flashlight to search out and capture all the woodlice you can find and put them in a container.

With a fine camel-hair brush or similar tool put a spot of artist's paint on each animal and release them within their captured area. If you want to work out the population of a large area, repeat this operation in two or three other marked areas (a quadrat can help, see page 134) and remember to note the size of the total area being studied.

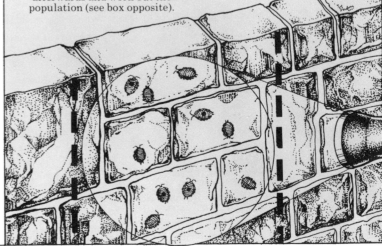

The following night capture all the woodlice in the areas they were caught the previous night and note the total number of animals caught and the numbers of marked and unmarked animals. Release them again afterwards and work out the population (see box opposite).

grass stem.

The capture-recapture method described here is used by thousands of ecologists all over the world. Although many use these same simple marking techniques, some experts favour alternative methods. Fluorescent paints are sometimes used since these stand out in ultra-violet light at night, and so are useful when studying nocturnal animals. Bands and rings, which are mainly used on birds and mammals, can be used on certain butterflies and locusts, though the small size of most insects usually makes this impractical.

A comparatively new but exciting method of marking is by radio-active isotopes. Ecologists using these isotopes either mark the animal with a radioactive label or feed it with material containing radioactive isotopes. The advantage of the latter method is that the mark is invisible to any predators, and is not shed when the insects moult and lose their external covering. Such procedures are rather too complex for most amateur naturalists, and fortunately the simpler methods are more than adequate for finding out a great deal about animal populations.

On these pages, methods are shown for woodlice, or sow-bugs, and butterflies, but you can choose any insect that is common in the area you are studying. If you have looked at the project on woodlice described on page 79, you will find that these animals prefer damp places to dry ones and in many damp areas they are very numerous. If you have actually done the project, you will probably have noticed that they hide by day in damp, dark places, and come out at night to scavenge for food. It is therefore important to capture your animals when they are on their nightly feeding trips.

Choose your area and measure it fairly accurately. Although it should be quite large, you cannot hope to capture all the woodlice living there, so mark the area off into smaller squares.

If you have a quadrat (see page 134), this can be used to do the job for you.

Capture all the woodlice in one particular square and put them in a box. Dab a spot of artist's oil paint on the tip of their bodies or, if you become expert enough, on the underside. When they are all marked, release them inside the area in which they were caught.

The next night capture the woodlice in the same area and note the total number caught as well as the number that are marked with oil paint. Release the animals, and then work out your calculations according to the method shown in the box on this page. If you have studied two or three zones within a larger area, work out the population for each one, take an average of these and multiply the number by the number of times one studied area goes into the whole area. This will give you the total population of the whole area.

Butterflies or grasshoppers are also good subjects. The best time to catch butterflies is in the morning before it gets too warm. If you are going to work out the population of a field, a piece of woodland or waste ground, remember to measure it first and note down the dimensions. If the butterflies appear to be very numerous in the area, you should try to catch at least 100. If there are not so many butterflies, then of course you will have to modify your plans.

Catch the butterflies in a net and keep them in a dark place in a box or black, fine-mesh bag. Remember to handle the butterflies gently. Put a spot of artist's oil paint on the underside of a front wing and do the same to each butterfly.

Release your marked insects at three or four different spots within your area so they can mix freely. Return the next day and capture about as many as you caught before. Note the number of marked and unmarked butterflies, and then, after releasing them, calculate the population according to the method shown in the box.

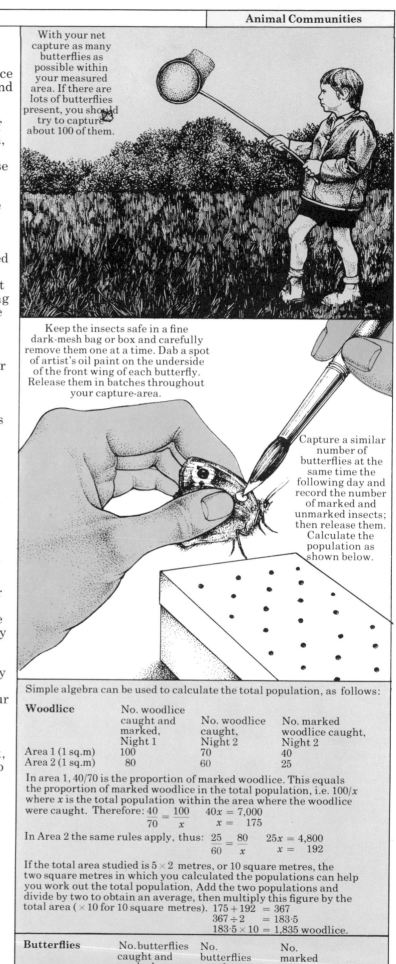

With your net capture as many butterflies as possible within your measured area. If there are lots of butterflies present, you should try to capture about 100 of them.

Keep the insects safe in a fine dark-mesh bag or box and carefully remove them one at a time. Dab a spot of artist's oil paint on the underside of the front wing of each butterfly. Release them in batches throughout your capture-area.

Capture a similar number of butterflies at the same time the following day and record the number of marked and unmarked insects; then release them. Calculate the population as shown below.

Simple algebra can be used to calculate the total population, as follows:

Woodlice	No. woodlice caught and marked, Night 1	No. woodlice caught, Night 2	No. marked woodlice caught, Night 2
Area 1 (1 sq.m)	100	70	40
Area 2 (1 sq.m)	80	60	25

In area 1, 40/70 is the proportion of marked woodlice. This equals the proportion of marked woodlice in the total population, i.e. $100/x$ where x is the total population within the area where the woodlice were caught. Therefore: $\dfrac{40}{70} = \dfrac{100}{x}$ $\quad 40x = 7,000$ $\quad x = 175$

In Area 2 the same rules apply, thus: $\dfrac{25}{60} = \dfrac{80}{x}$ $\quad 25x = 4,800$ $\quad x = 192$

If the total area studied is 5×2 metres, or 10 square metres, the two square metres in which you calculated the populations can help you work out the total population. Add the two populations and divide by two to obtain an average, then multiply this figure by the total area ($\times 10$ for 10 square metres). $175 + 192 = 367$
$367 \div 2 = 183 \cdot 5$
$183 \cdot 5 \times 10 = 1,835$ woodlice.

Butterflies	No. butterflies caught and marked Day 1	No. butterflies caught, Day 2	No. marked butterflies caught, Day 2
	100	70	20

Therefore: $\dfrac{20}{70} = \dfrac{100}{x}$ $\quad 20x = 7,000$ $\quad x = 350$ The population of the butterflies over the area studied is 350.

STUDYING SPIDERS' WEBS

**How webs are built and
how they work,
with suggestions on
how to collect and
preserve them**

he spiders are among the very few animals that set traps to catch their food. The delicate webs might not look very efficient in this respect, but if you examine a web in the summer you will see that it really is a deadly snare for the small insects that the spider eats. But do not think that all spiders make webs: many of them go hunting and pounce on their prey like most other predatory animals, while others lie in wait and grab passing insects.

Although they do not all make webs, all spiders produce silk in glands in the hind part of the body. Several different kinds of silk are produced and used for life-lines and for wrapping up the eggs as well as for making the webs. The silk is a sticky fluid when it is made, but as soon as it is drawn out from the spider's spinnerets it solidifies into a slender, but very strong and elastic thread. A thread in a typical orb-web, such as you might find hanging from a window frame or the garden fence, may be only 0·003 mm in diameter, but if you pull it with your finger it will stretch considerably before it breaks. This is clearly very important in a web which must withstand high winds and also hold struggling insects like blow-flies and wasps. In fact, the spider's silk is stronger in terms of breaking strain than a steel wire of the same thickness.

Look around you almost anywhere and you will see lots of different kinds of webs made by many different kinds of spiders. Old walls, for example, often bear numerous white webs which look like small and rather ragged pieces of lacework. These belong to spiders of the genus *Amaurobius*. The spiders themselves sit in crevices and wait for crawling insects to get their feet trapped in the fine, lace-like mesh of the web. The most abundant webs, however, are the domed sheets of the little money spiders and their relatives in the family Linyphiidae. Looking like up-turned hammocks, these webs cover shrubs and hedgerows and all low-growing vegetation. They are present throughout the year, but they are most numerous and most noticeable in the autumn, when there may be as many as three million of them to the hectare (over a million to the acre). Imagine how many insects are trapped by these webs. The webs are not sticky, but if you look at them carefully you will see numerous threads like scaffolding above the sheet, and the spider hanging below it. Small flying and hopping insects blunder into the scaffolding and fall on to the sheet, where they are snapped up by the spider before they can recover. The large, sheet-like cobwebs in the corner of the shed work in much the same way, although they have more of a system of trip-wires on the surface than an array of scaffolding above.

The most familiar webs, however, are the more or less circular orb-webs belonging to the garden spider and other members of the family Argiopidae. You can find them in spring and summer, but they are most noticeable in the autumn, when they are full-size and often spangled with dew. The spider may be sitting in the middle web, but more often it will be hiding nearby and maintaining contact with the web by means of a silk thread. You can sometimes lure it out by tickling the web with a piece of grass, but it is incredibly difficult to imitate the actions of a fly and you will not fool the spider very often.

The orb-web is not perfectly circular, for its shape depends to some extent on the frame supports that are available. There are often noticeably more arcs below the hub than above it. Nevertheless, its construction is a wonderful feat of engineering.

If you go out early in the morning or after a spell of windy weather, you may see the spider repairing or rebuilding its web. It may start again from scratch, or it may rebuild within the original framework. The first stage in building a completely new web is to make the bridge thread from which the rest of the web is hung. The spider may let the wind carry the bridge thread at random until it catches on a suitable support, or else the animal may actually drop down from one support and then, still dragging a thread behind it, climb up to another support and pull the thread tight. Some of the stages in the building of the web of a garden spider (*Araneus diadematus*) are shown on the opposite page, but the exact procedure varies with the positions of the available supports. How long does your spider take to build or rebuild its web? You could try taking the animal indoors and giving it some twigs. It might build a web for you.

The webs get bigger as the spiders grow, and you can investigate this by watching a spider for several weeks in the summer and keeping a record of the web. Measure its diameter every few days and count the number of radii or spokes. You will find that the number gradually changes.

The web of *Segestria senoculata* on an old wall. When a crawling insect blunders into one of the radiating trip wires the spider rushes out to catch it.

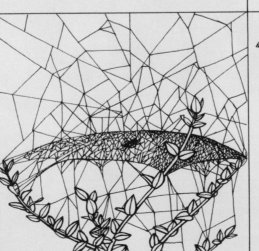

The hammock web of a linyphiid spider, showing the scaffolding threads which bring down small insects. The spider waits underneath the sheet.

The orb-web of *Zygiella*, a very common spider on window frames. The web can always be recognized by the two empty sectors at the top.

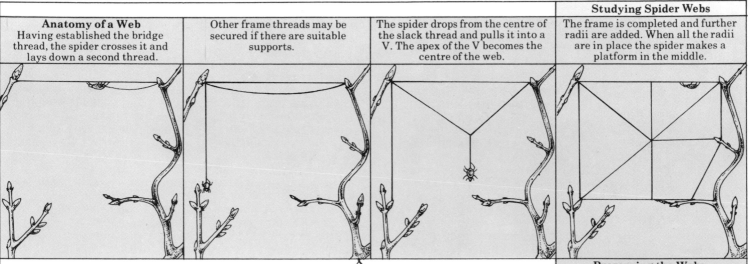

| **Anatomy of a Web** Having established the bridge thread, the spider crosses it and lays down a second thread. | Other frame threads may be secured if there are suitable supports. | The spider drops from the centre of the slack thread and pulls it into a V. The apex of the V becomes the centre of the web. | **Studying Spider Webs** The frame is completed and further radii are added. When all the radii are in place the spider makes a platform in the middle. |

The completed web of the garden spider (*right*) shows the strengthening platform in the middle and the sticky spiral which actually traps the insects. Before the sticky spiral is laid down, however, the spider spins a more open spiral on the completed radii. This open spiral is not sticky and the spider uses it as scaffolding when spinning the final threads. Starting from the outside of the dry spiral, the spider walks round and deftly uses its hind legs to pull silk from the spinnerets. The legs are also used to attach the new thread to the radii, and the spider is incredibly accurate with its measurements. It is a joy to watch one stretching the back leg out and putting the thread down in just the right place. See how even are the spaces between one turn of the spiral and the next. There may actually be several distinct threads in the sticky spiral, with the outer region consisting of several concentric arcs, but they are still perfectly placed. The spider eats the silk of the dry spiral as it goes round and finishes the sticky spiral a little way from the central platform. The threads of the sticky spiral are coated with gum (from another gland in the spider's body) as they are spun, and the gum breaks up into tiny droplets as the silk is stretched into place. The spider does not get trapped in its own web because its feet are covered with an oily secretion. When a victim arrives, the spider detects the vibrations and runs straight out to the prey, bites it, and wraps it in a silken shroud.

Preserving the Webs

The collection and preservation of delicate objects like spiders' webs (*below*) is a real challenge, but one which can be met with patience and ingenuity. The fine threads are hard to see in their natural state, but you can dye them with various biological stains. Eosin is a useful red stain which can be bought from biological supply companies. The stain must be sprayed very lightly to avoid damaging the web, and one of the best ways to do this is to use an old nasal spray container. Partly filled with the dye, this will produce a very fine spray. Having stained the web, you must put a light coating of glue on to a suitably sized piece of card and then bring the card up very gently behind the web (*bottom centre*). The idea is to get the web to stick to the card without becoming distorted, so you must try to get all parts of the web on to the card at once. Stop pushing as soon as you have made contact, and then cut through the supporting threads. Spray the carded web with several coats of varnish or artist's fixative to make a permanent specimen. If you find it difficult to card the web without damage you can spray the whole web with a fine coat of varnish after staining. This will give it more strength. If you prefer to mount your web on black card you can first spray the web with talcum powder or zinc oxide powder to make it white (*bottom right*). This technique is also suitable for preparing webs for photography.

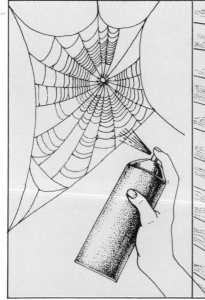

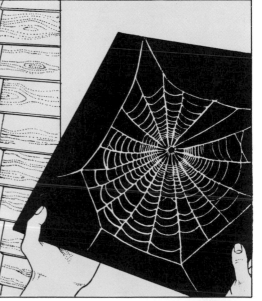

MEALWORMS AND MAGGOTS

How to breed your own supplies of insects to feed pets, attract birds, and clean skeletons

Mealworms

Mealworms are the yellowish grubs of a shiny black beetle called *Tenebrio molitor*. They were once serious pests in flour mills and granaries, but insecticidal treatment of such places has now reduced the populations so much that it is sometimes difficult to find the insects at all. It is best to buy some from a pet-shop to start with, and use them to start your own culture. For satisfactory results, you must keep the culture between 25°C (77°F) and 30°C (86°F). At lower temperatures they will breed so slowly that you will not get enough mealworms for your needs, but you must not keep them at temperatures above 32°C (89°F).

The best container for your mealworms is a large earthenware jar, but you can use a glass jar if you cover it with brown paper or keep it in a dark place. A large biscuit container will also be satisfactory. Half-fill the container with a mixture of bran, flour, and thoroughly dry bread. Add your mealworm culture, which should preferably consist of adults and young, and cover the container with a cloth. Add more dried bread or biscuit from time to time, and give the insects an occasional treat in the form of a small, dried ham bone. Water the cloth *very lightly* every week or so. Use the grubs to feed birds, lizards, and many other animals, but do not give small birds more than four mealworms each day.

Many naturalists keep insectivorous pets, such as lizards and preying mantises, and derive a great deal of enjoyment from them. Feeding the animals is often something of a problem, however, because many of these creatures will take only living food. You can sometimes buy live food from pet-shops and angling shops, but you can save a good deal of money and have some extra 'pets' into the bargain if you breed your own insects to use as food. Freshwater turtles or terrapins and many aquarium fishes will appreciate some of this food, and you can also use your insects to attract wild birds into your garden (see page 52). Many birds are extraordinarily fond of mealworms and will forget all about being shy if they are offered some. Hedgehogs are also fond of these crunchy little grubs, and if you are a fisherman you will always be able to use any surplus maggots.

These two pages provide some simple hints on rearing three useful insect species, two of which are used for feeding other animals. The third species – the dermestid beetle – is a most valuable aid in cleaning up the skulls and skeletons of dead animals (see page 68). Breeding blow-flies and their maggots is a slightly smelly occupation, best carried out away from the living quarters of the house, but the other two species can be reared with very little fuss as long as you can keep them fairly warm.

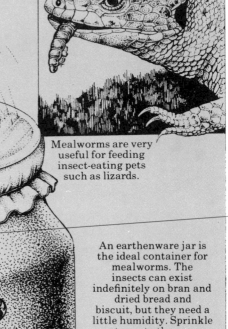

Mealworms are very useful for feeding insect-eating pets such as lizards.

An earthenware jar is the ideal container for mealworms. The insects can exist indefinitely on bran and dried bread and biscuit, but they need a little humidity. Sprinkle water onto the cover but never enough to make the bran wet.

Extract the mealworms from the jar with the aid of a fine sieve. Put the fine material back into the jar – it may well contain lots of eggs. Always leave enough mealworms to grow up into the next generation.

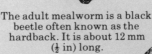

The adult mealworm is a black beetle often known as the hardback. It is about 12 mm (½ in) long.

The mealworm itself is yellowish and rather like a wireworm. It is up to 30 mm (1¼ in) long.

Mealworm Life Cycle

An adult female will lay perhaps 600 eggs during her ten-week life, and at 25–30 C (77–86 F) the eggs will hatch in a little over a week. The larvae take about six months to mature, and then they spend two or three weeks as pupae before producing adult beetles. If you have the facilities you can keep cultures at different temperatures and see just how much more quickly the warmer insects complete their life cycle.

Blow-flies

Blow-flies or bluebottles are very easy to rear, although somewhat smelly. The best place to keep them is in a cellar or an out-house, where you can maintain a temperature of about 20°C (68°F).

You can acquire your stock by buying maggots from an angling shop, or you can merely leave a piece of fish or meat under a piece of wire netting and wait for the flies to lay their eggs in it. You can buy a cage or make one easily enough with a few battens and some perforated zinc or muslin. The bottom should be solid, and covered with sawdust.

Put the maggots in a shallow dish buried up to its rim in the sawdust, and keep them supplied with rotting meat or fish. When fully grown, they will wriggle out into the sawdust and turn into pupae. Within a few days your cage will be full of flies. Add food to the cage at night, when the insects are drowsy and less likely to escape.

Dermestid Beetles

Dermestid beetles, usually members of a species called *Dermestes maculatus*, are widely used in natural history museums for cleaning the skulls and skeletons of various animals (see page 68). It is easy to keep a culture going in a warm kitchen or linen cupboard once you have your original stock. Biological supply companies may keep them, or you may be able to beg a few from a museum. A dozen are enough to start a culture.

Use a large glass jar for your dermestid culture, and ensure that it has a well-fitting lid. Put a layer of meat meal in the bottom and add a teaspoonful of dried yeast before introducing your beetles. Add some cotton wool or similar material to provide shelter. The insects eat a surprising amount of meat, so keep them well provided. Transfer the beetles to clean jars every two or three months, and they will clean any small skulls you like to give them.

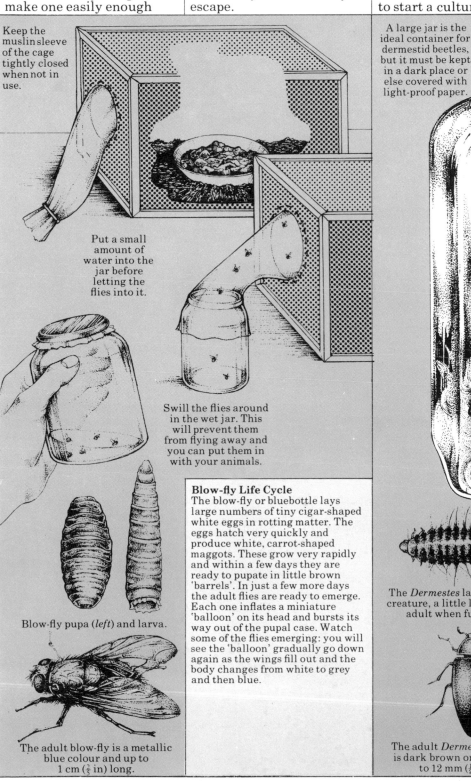

Keep the muslin sleeve of the cage tightly closed when not in use.

Put a small amount of water into the jar before letting the flies into it.

Swill the flies around in the wet jar. This will prevent them from flying away and you can put them in with your animals.

Blow-fly pupa (*left*) and larva.

The adult blow-fly is a metallic blue colour and up to 1 cm ($\frac{2}{5}$ in) long.

Blow-fly Life Cycle

The blow-fly or bluebottle lays large numbers of tiny cigar-shaped white eggs in rotting matter. The eggs hatch very quickly and produce white, carrot-shaped maggots. These grow very rapidly and within a few days they are ready to pupate in little brown 'barrels'. In just a few more days the adult flies are ready to emerge. Each one inflates a miniature 'balloon' on its head and bursts its way out of the pupal case. Watch some of the flies emerging: you will see the 'balloon' gradually go down again as the wings fill out and the body changes from white to grey and then blue.

A large jar is the ideal container for dermestid beetles, but it must be kept in a dark place or else covered with light-proof paper.

The *Dermestes* larva is a bristly creature, a little longer than the adult when fully grown.

The adult *Dermestes maculatus* is dark brown or black and up to 12 mm ($\frac{1}{2}$ in) long.

Dermestid Life Cycle

Dermestes maculatus, often known as the hide beetle or leather beetle, has a life history similar to that of the mealworm, although it grows up much more quickly. The carpet beetle illustrated on page 68 is a close relative and you can rear it in much the same way; you need to leave the fur or feathers on the small animals that you give them to clean. They are very useful for cleaning bird skulls, which are often too delicate to be plucked.

sked to name the largest living thing in the world, most people would probably choose the blue whale, but they would be wrong. The giant redwoods and sequoias or 'big trees' of western California are far larger than any whale.

The largest of these giant trees is one called General Sherman. It grows in the Sequoia National Park in California and it stands about 83 metres (272 ft) high. Measured at about 1.5 metres (5 ft) above the ground, it has a girth of just over 24 metres (about 79 ft), and it has been estimated to weigh about 2,030 tonnes (2,145 tons) or 20 times the weight of an average-sized blue whale. It has also been estimated that this green giant contains enough timber to build about 40 five-roomed bungalows. But the General Sherman is by no means the tallest tree. That distinction goes to a redwood called Howard Libby, whose height was recently recorded as just over 110 metres (362 ft). The trunks of the redwoods are much more slender than those of the sequoias, however, and so the trees are far less massive.

When you realize that these giants grow from seeds not much bigger than pin-heads, it is not surprising that the American Indians worshipped them as gods. The immense size of the trees is the result of the climate in which they grow: it is warm for most of the year, and rainfall is extremely heavy on the coast-facing slopes. Warmth and water, as any greenhouse-owner knows, are the two main requirements for growth, and so the trees go on growing and growing. The common oak shown on the left is a midget by comparison, although we tend to think of it as a mighty tree. The tallest British oak is a mere 39 metres (128 ft) high, while the fattest is about 13 metres (43 ft) in girth. But even General Sherman

is far from being the fattest tree. A sweet chestnut tree growing at the foot of Mount Etna was once reported to have a girth of 64 metres (210 ft), and several of the strange baobabs or bottle trees of Africa have girths of more than 30 metres (97 ft).

Although many people talk of trees on the one hand and plants on the other, it is important to realize that trees *are* plants. They make their food and they reproduce themselves just like most other green plants, and many are actually very closely related to the small plants that we grow in our gardens. The Amazonian forests, for example, contain numerous achocon trees,

the conifers and the flowering trees. The conifers all bear their seeds in cones (see page 116), but the flowering trees have proper flowers and fruits. The redwoods and sequoias, the pines, firs, and larches are all conifers. The majority of them have tough, needle-like leaves. Familiar flowering trees include the apples and other fruit trees of our gardens and orchards, the horse chestnuts or buckeyes, and the magnolias. Oaks, poplars, birches, and elms are also flowering trees, but you will have to look at them quite closely to see the flowers. They are all pollinated by the wind and they do not need colourful

northern Europe and Asia, and then right across Canada. Relatively few conifers live in the Southern Hemisphere, although there are several, such as the rimu and the kauri pine, in New Zealand. There are also forests of monkey puzzle or Chile pine trees on the slopes of the Andes in South America. The leaf structure of the conifers enables them to survive the great cold of high latitudes and high mountains, but the tough leaves also help some conifers to live in hot, dry climates.

The flowering or broad-leaved trees include large numbers of deciduous species – trees that drop their leaves during the unfavourable season. Most of these live in the north temperate zone, just to the south of the coniferous taiga, and they drop their leaves in the autumn. This prevents loss of water (see page 138) at a time when the roots cannot absorb much from the cold soil. A number of tropical trees also drop their leaves at the beginning of the dry season, but the flowering trees that make up the dense equatorial forests are all evergreens: there they receive abundant warmth and water all the year round.

As well as being very large, many trees are very long-lived. Some giant redwoods that have been felled have revealed annual rings (see page 110) showing that they were at least 3,000 years old, and many trees are undoubtedly older. The bulk of a tree, however, consists of non-living material. Almost all of the trunk is made of dead tubes which merely carry water up to the leaves. The living part of the trunk is a relatively thin cylinder just under the bark. Ring-barking a tree, which is the removal of a complete ring of bark, will immediately kill the tree because no food material will be able to travel down from the leaves to keep the roots alive. The very centre of an old tree does not even carry water and often rots away to form a hollow tree, which can grow quite happily as long as the outer section is healthy.

CHAPTER 6

TREES

The most majestic of plants, trees include in their number the largest of all living things

which reach heights of more than 20 metres (65 ft), yet they belong to the same family as the little violets and pansies that we grow.

We can define a tree as a plant which, under normal circumstances, has a single, thick, woody stem or trunk. Some small trees are frequently called shrubs, but this term should be restricted to woody plants that always have several main stems coming from more or less ground level. A tree stump that is throwing up lots of shoots may look like a shrub, but it is still really a tree.

There are two very distinct groups of trees –

flowers (see page 132). Flowering trees tend to have broad leaves and they are often simply called broad-leaved trees in order to distinguish them from the conifers.

Nearly all of the conifers are evergreens, meaning that they keep their leaves throughout the year. The larches are the only major exceptions to this rule. Most conifers grow in the climatically more hostile parts of the world, and they are particularly associated with the northern regions. A huge belt of coniferous forest known as the taiga encircles the globe across

MEASURING TREES

Some methods of measuring the heights of trees, and estimating their ages

here are few people who do not stop, however briefly, to admire the beauty of a well-grown tree, and fewer still, perhaps, who do not get some deep enjoyment from walking among the trees in an ancient forest. When looking at a sturdy oak or a lofty pine, it is sometimes difficult to realize that it has grown from a small seed, and it is not surprising that trees played such an important part in the cultural lives of people in earlier times. Although we no longer worship trees and woodlands in the way that our ancestors did, trees still play a big part in our lives. We get timber and many other products from them, but to the naturalist a tree, whether standing resplendent in a park or mingling with others in the forest, is something to be admired for itself and also for the wealth of animal life that it supports. Literally hundreds of kinds of insects and other animals may live on and beneath a single tree (see page 120).

All naturalists, both young and old, are intrigued by size, and one of the most frequent questions must be 'How tall is it?' The illustrations on these two pages show how you can set about answering this question. Apart from idle curiosity about how tall a certain tree is, the naturalist may also want to know how much a tree grows in a year. The height of the trees is also an important factor in studying the whole woodland community.

The Proportional Method

This is a very easy way of measuring the heights of fairly small trees. All you need are a straight stick about 2 metres (6½ ft) long, a tape measure, and a friend to help you. Starting from the base of the trunk, you must pace out 27 strides in a straight line. The size of your strides does not matter as long as you keep them regular. Get your friend to hold the stick vertically on the ground exactly 27 strides from the tree, and then you must take three more strides in the same direction. Mark the spot and then get your eye right down on to the ground at that point. Look up at the top of the tree and ask your friend to move a finger up or down the stick until the finger coincides with the top of the tree, and then mark the position of the finger with chalk. Because the tree is ten times as far from you as the stick (30 strides as opposed to 3), the height of the tree will be ten times the height of the mark on the stick. If you are measuring trees more than 20 metres (65 ft) high you will need a longer stick, or else you will have to use one of the other methods shown on these pages.

The Pencil Method

This is another very easy method of measuring the height of a tree, requiring only a pencil or a short stick and the assistance of a friend. Hold the pencil or stick vertically in front of you at arm's length, and position yourself so that the bottom of the pencil coincides with the bottom of the tree trunk and the top of the pencil with the uppermost part of the crown. Don't move from your position, but turn the pencil into the horizontal position. Keep one end in line with the base of the tree, and ask your friend to walk away from the trunk at right angles to your own position. Tell your friend to stop as soon as he or she appears to be at the end of your pencil. The distance between your friend and the base of the trunk, which you can easily measure with a tape or by pacing it out, should equal the height of the tree. Remember that you must always hold the pencil at the same distance from your eye, and the easiest way to do this is to keep it at arm's length.

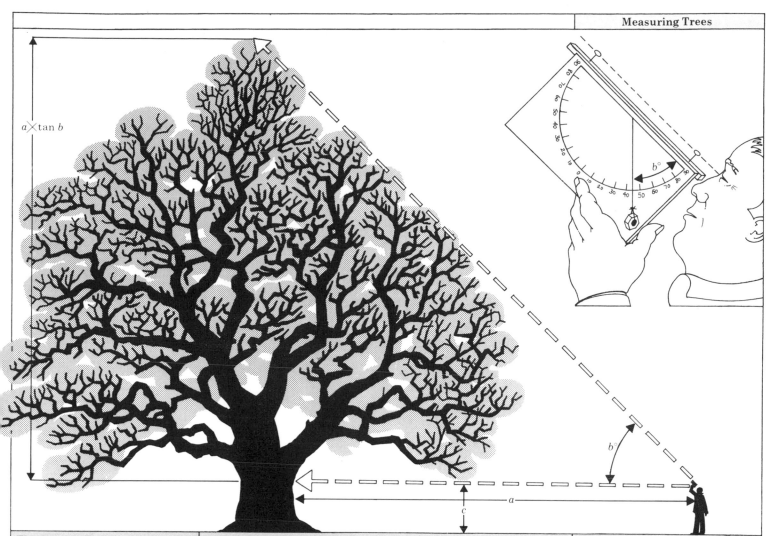

$a \times \tan b$

The Age of a Tree
It is well known that a tree produces annual rings in its trunk. The rings are formed by the new water-carrying tubes laid down just under the bark each year. They are most obvious in trees growing in the cooler regions, where growth ceases in the winter, because there is a distinct junction between the narrow autumn-produced tubes and the wider ones of the following spring. By counting the rings, you can get a pretty accurate idea of the age of the tree, but you cannot count the rings without cutting down the tree, of course. You can, however, estimate the ages of many trees from other evidence. Alan Mitchell, a world-famous expert on trees, has discovered that trees of very many different kinds all grow at more or less the same rate. Most trees with a full crown have an average of 2.5 cm (1 in) of girth for each year of their lives. A tree 2.5 metres (about 8 ft) in circumference would thus be about 100 years old if growing by itself. In a wood, where it has to compete with other trees, such a tree might be 200 years old. Always take your measurements at about $1\frac{1}{2}$ metres (5 ft) above the ground, and don't use this method for very young trees. A few trees do not conform to this rule at any time. They include many poplars and most of the giant conifers of America's west coast, all of which grow two or three times faster than the above rate. Scot's pine, horse-chestnuts or buckeyes, and many of the smaller species grow more slowly.

Canopy Maps
Trees growing under different conditions often develop very different shapes and crowns of very different sizes. It is easy to make maps showing the shapes of the various crowns or canopies. Measure the girth of the trunk at ground level, and then pace out the farthest extent of the branches in at least eight directions. Make scale drawings of your results. The left-hand 'map' is of a tree growing in open woodland, while the right-hand one represents a tree of the same species growing on a wind-swept hillside.

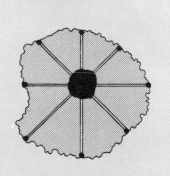

wind direction

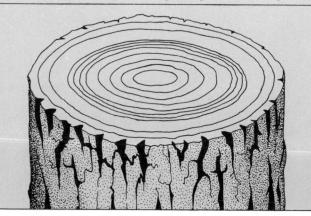

Measurement by Angles
This method of measuring heights is more complicated than the other two, but it is also more accurate, as long as the tree is growing on level ground. You need a tape measure, and a clinometer for measuring the angles, A simple clinometer is shown in the drawing above. It consists merely of a protractor and a plumb line attached to a piece of wood. Two screw eyes at the top give you a sight-line, and you could also shape the board to make a comfortable hand-grip. The simplest way to use the instrument is to walk away from the tree until, when you take a sighting of the top of the tree, the plumb-line hangs at an angle of 45°. At this point, the distance from you to the tree plus your own height from the ground to your eye is equal to the height of the tree. Armed with a set of mathematical tables, the mathematically-minded naturalist will be able to calculate the tree's height from any position. If a is the distance from the observer to the tree, b is the angle shown on the clinometer, and c is the height of the observer's eye, then the height of the tree is equal to $c + (a \times \tan b)$. You find the value of $\tan b$ by looking up natural tangents in the mathematical tables. The tangent of 45 is 1, and this is why it makes life easier if you can move around until you get a reading of 45°. This is not always possible, however; spreading branches may hide the top of the tree from some positions, and you will then have to move back and rely on the mathematical tables.

BARK RUBBING

Make a collection of bark impressions from the trees in your area.

ach kind of tree has its characteristic bark pattern, and it is usually possible to identify trees in the temperate regions just from their bark. Beeches, for example, normally have very smooth bark, while plane trees and many maples have bark which regularly peels off in thin flakes or strips. Most other mature trees have a more rugged bark, with prominent ridges and crevices breaking it up into its characteristic pattern. Some of these barks are most attractive in terms of colour as well as pattern, but it is not practical to collect bark because its removal will damage or even kill a tree. It can be stripped from dead stumps and logs, but it is usually past its best then, and in any case bark is a rather bulky thing to store. It is much better to make a collection of the bark patterns by the process known as bark rubbing. This is very similar to the brass rubbing which many people do in churches and it requires the very minimum of equipment.

First and foremost, you need a tree with a clear bark pattern that is not obscured by mosses or lichens. Then you need a sheet of strong, but not very thick paper. Its size is not very important, but it should not be less than about 30 cm (12 in) square if you want to obtain a faithful representation of the bark pattern. The paper can be fixed to the trunk with string tied tightly round it at top and bottom, or it can be fixed with pins or blobs of modern adhesives. It can also be held against the trunk by hand, but great care must then be taken not to move the paper once rubbing has started.

Traditionally, the paper is rubbed with a cobbler's heel-ball – a ball of black, waxy material which cobblers use for blacking the edges of shoes – but perfectly acceptable results can be obtained with large wax crayons, and crayons have the advantage that you can produce rubbings in different colours. Colourful effects can also be achieved, however, by using a black heel-ball on different coloured papers. The wax must be rubbed firmly and smoothly all over the paper covering the chosen section of bark, and the pattern of blocks or ridges will then be transferred to the paper – the raised parts of the bark coming out dark and the crevices pale or uncoloured.

Having made your rubbings, it is important to label them. Put the name of the tree on the front, and you can add further information on the back of the paper. This should include an estimate of the height of the tree and its girth, and also an estimate of its age (see page 110). It is also important to write down the height above the ground at which the rubbing was made, for bark patterns often change as the tree gets taller and older.

While making bark rubbings, the naturalist will come across plenty of loose and fallen bark which has come adrift through the action of bark beetles. Ash and pine trees are both susceptible to these insects, but the best known victim is the elm, whose bark beetles have been responsible for the spread of Dutch elm disease and the consequent death of millions of elm trees in Europe and North America The beetles and their grubs tunnel in the food-rich layers of the inner bark, leaving a fascinating pattern of grooves on the inside of the bark and also on the underlying wood.

When the beetles are especially numerous, the bark becomes completely separated from the wood and the patterns become visible. Pieces of the detached bark can be collected, but again they are bulky and it is more fun to make rubbings of the galleries. This can be done on the bark itself, or else on the wood. The latter gives a firmer surface on which to work, but the grooves are usually rather more shallow there. You will probably have to clean out the grooves with a brush before you make your rubbing.

Your bark rubbing collection can be stored in a drawer or a flat container, but particularly exciting patterns can be framed and put on a wall, where they make surprisingly effective room decorations. But don't put them opposite a sunny window or on a chimney breast, or you may find that the wax melts and spoils the picture.

You Will Need

Sheets of strong paper

String or pins or blob-type adhesive

Cobbler's heel-ball or wax crayons

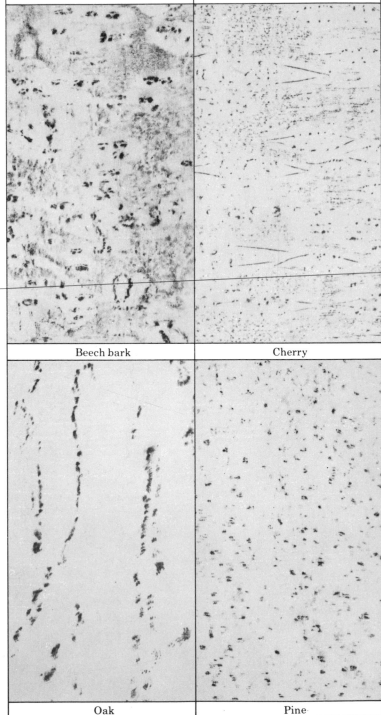

Beech bark

Cherry

Oak

Pine

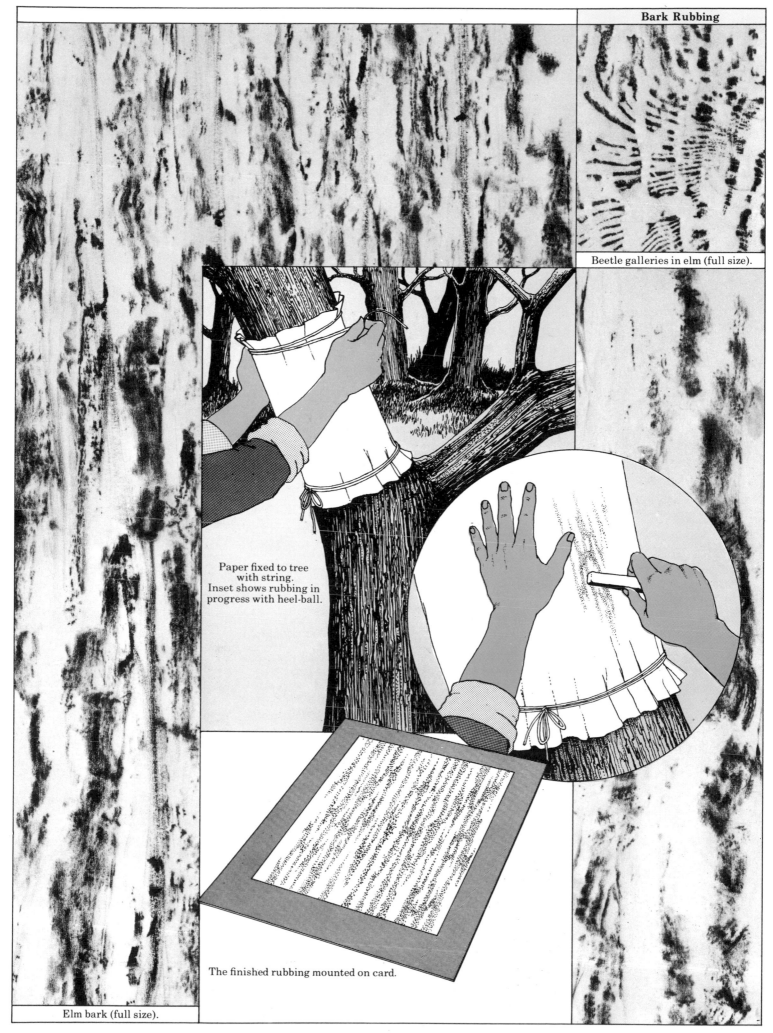

Beetle galleries in elm (full size).

Paper fixed to tree
with string.
Inset shows rubbing in
progress with heel-ball.

The finished rubbing mounted on card.

Elm bark (full size).

113

TWIGS AND BUDS

The wonders of watching buds burst into bloom in your own home, and producing more plants from cuttings, and by grafting and budding

On a walk in the countryside in winter you can take a few twigs from various kinds of trees and bring them home to watch them develop. Use a good illustrated reference book to identify any twigs you are not familiar with. In the warmth of your home put the twigs in clean fresh water and place the jar in a warm, draught-proof, light position.

A bud is a 'condensed' shoot. Inside its thick protective scales is a very short stem, and leaves so small and close together that they overlap, each one wrapping round the next one above it. The leaves are crinkled and folded because they have to cram the large surface area of the growing leaf into such a small space. The outside of a bud is made up of scales, usually black or brown, which protect the more delicate, inner leaves from drying up, stop birds or insects from nibbling at them. At the end of the bud's short stem is either a developing flower or a growing point: as the bud opens, so new buds down the stems are formed.

The buds formed at the ends of main shoots or branches during the season's growth are called terminal buds. If you look at any twig you will find there are also buds in the axils of the leaves. These are called axillary or lateral buds. Sometimes they stay as tight buds all year, and do not grow until the following year, in which case they are called dormant buds.

Terminal buds that grow are responsible for making a tree taller, whereas axillary buds make new branches and twigs. Both types may produce a flower instead, or a leafy shoot and a flower. If a terminal bud produces a flower, growth stops when the flower dies and drops away. The next season, the lateral buds below this point grow and so the developing tree continues to grow taller, but there will be a fork in the trunk. Look around you on your next walk and you will see numerous examples where this has happened.

The buds on the twigs in your home will soon start to open and grow because the warmth of your home indicates to the twig that spring has arrived and growth spurts ahead (see illustration below).

If you look closely at winter twigs you will find scars on them. This is where a leaf fell from the twig the previous year with the onset of winter. Each different kind of tree has a certain kind of leaf scar and they help to identify the species. On the scar is a pattern of dots. These show where the canals (vascular bundles) carrying food and water from the twig to the leaf were situated. They seal off when the leaf drops so that the rest of the twig does not lose vital food and water. Twigs also bear narrow scars, occurring close together and extending from a quarter to half-way

Growing Buds
Given warm surroundings your buds will soon begin to grow. The horse-chestnut or buckeye bud *(far left)* has sticky dark brown scales that keep out insects and diseases. As it grows, the bud scales are gradually pushed apart: at the same time the stem grows and spaces out the leaves, which unfold and spread out their surfaces. The bud scales curl back and in a few weeks drop off when their work is done, leaving a ring of scars. When the leaves open and unfurl to the light they are very pale, but they soon deepen in colour as the green chlorophyll inside the cells fully develops, and photosynthesis begins soon after. The latter is the process by which green plants build up carbohydrates from carbon dioxide in the air and water absorbed through their roots.

round the twig; these are scars left by bud scales from a previous year. They are called girdle scars and mark the position of each year's terminal bud; the length between each set of girdle scars is thus the amount the twig has grown in one year.

Propagation, the process of growing plants and multiplying their numbers, is one of the most fascinating of the gardener's arts, and you can gain tremendous pleasure and sense of achievement from watching your young plants grow.

The methods of propagation are many, but in this book we have concentrated on the following: growing from seeds (see page 138), taking cuttings, budding, and grafting. It is fairly easy to get cuttings to grow, and with a little experience

budding and grafting can soon be mastered – as long as you are not discouraged if you have one or two early setbacks and failures.

With most woody plants, the easiest, cheapest and quickest way to obtain new ones is to take cuttings. The term 'cutting' refers to any portion removed from the stem, leaves or roots of the parent plant; if properly prepared and cared for, a cutting will grow into new plants that look exactly like the parent plant. You can take cuttings from your own plants, but for greater variety try asking friends or neighbours if you can take a few cuttings from their plants; you can always repay them with a young

plant grown from one of your own stock.

Budding is used most often to propagate roses and is a form of grafting, usually carried out in mid-summer. On a country walk you may find wild briar roses, and if you take stem cuttings from these and grow them for a year, they will then make suitable stocks for bush roses. The stages in budding a rose are explained in the second column below.

Grafting is the practice of joining two or more living parts of plants so they form a permanent, growing union. One part of this union is a growing, rooted plant with a main stem, and the other (though there may be more than one) is called the scion, and is a piece of the previous year's wood from another plant. This method is usually applied to fruit trees and some shrubs, and the best time to do it is at the end of the dormant season. Various types of grafting are explained below.

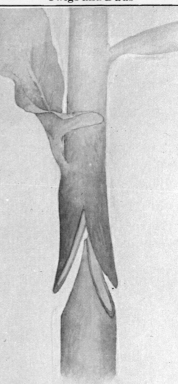

Saddle grafting is often used to join a named rhododendron variety to a common rhododendron stock. Stock and scion are of equal size.

The scion should contain one terminal bud and the V-shape or saddle in the scion fits exactly over the shaped stock and is bound with raffia.

Place the plant in a warm, closed propagating frame. This type of grafting requires no grafting wax. After one or two months the union should be complete.

Cuttings

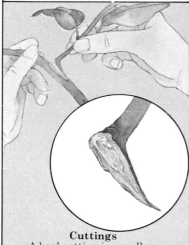

A heel cutting is usually a half-ripe or hardwood cutting of a side-shoot. Pull the side-shoot firmly away from the main shoot.

Insert the cutting up to a quarter of its length in seed compost, and place it in a shaded, closed frame; alternatively you can put a plastic bag on a wire or wood frame over the pot and place it on a window sill.

Budding

In budding the bud is carefully cut from the parent bush.

The bud cutting consists of a leaf stalk and a shield of bark.

A T-cut is made in the stock plant and the bud inserted.

Soak some raffia in water and then tie in the bud above and below the T-cut.

Split the raffia at the back about one month later.
The following spring cut back to about 2½ cm (1 in) above the bud and in summer you will see your reward.

Grafting

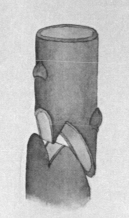

Whip and tongue grafting is where a scion (see text) is given a slanting cut and tongue and placed on a stock.

Crown or rind grafting is where a scion with a slanting cut is inserted between the bark and wood and then tied with raffia and the top and side covered with wax. This method is suitable for rejuvenating fruit trees.

CONES, FRUITS AND SEEDS

How the cone of a fir tree is produced, and how some of the seeds and fruits of trees and shrubs are dispersed

e can recognize conifers because most of them have small, narrow leaves called needles and they are evergreen trees. The group includes such well-known types as Christmas trees (spruces and firs), monkey-puzzles, pines, yews, larches, cedars, and cypresses. These trees do not produce flowers, but the familiar cones that we see growing on a conifer house the pollen and seeds of the tree. These cone-bearing trees make up a large part of the vegetation in cooler parts of the world. They stretch in an unbroken belt from Norway to eastern Siberia and right across Canada. Coniferous trees grow more quickly than the broad-leaved trees and this is why conifers are so widely grown for timber. Their wood is usually softer and is in fact called softwood; it does not last as long as hardwoods, being more prone to rot.

The large, beautiful cones that we see growing on a conifer or scattered beneath it are the female cones; the male ones are usually found on the same tree but they are quite small and yellowish; although rather inconspicuous individually, they are easily seen in the tree itself where they are grouped into large clusters at the bases of new shoots. Both types start to grow in the spring: the female cones develop near the tips of new shoots and are red when they first begin to grow.

If you find a fallen cone, look at it carefully and you will see that it consists of a series of over-lapping scales which are really very special kinds of leaves. The scales of the male cone carry the pollen sacs that are full of yellowish pollen. In spring the wind carries the male pollen to the female cones and the small female cones begin to swell and become woody as fertilized seeds develop between the scales. The seed itself has a thin 'wing' growing from it, and when the cones open the seeds fall out and are carried away on the wind. If a seed falls on suitable soil it will grow into a new conifer.

You can find out what makes a cone open and close by a simple experiment. Collect a few cones on a walk, and when you get them home separate the ones that are open from those that are closed, putting them in two separate groups. (You may find that they are all either closed or open, but this need not affect the experiment.) Put some of the cones in a dry, warm place such as a linen cupboard, and others – from the same group – in a damp, moist place. This could be inside a plastic bag to which you have added a little water, or perhaps on a shelf in the bathroom. Look at your cones in a day or two and see what progress they have made.

The cones open and close due to the moisture in the air. The process is controlled by moisture-sensitive cells at the base of each scale. In dry conditions the cones open and in wet conditions they close. This is a necessary adaptation because if the cones opened in wet, rainy weather the seeds would fall straight to the ground and not be carried to a new growing site. So the cones open when the air is dry and the seeds have a better chance of scattering.

Some people put cones outside their homes because they believe that they can forecast the weather (see page 16). This is not strictly true since the cones open and close as the weather changes from dry to wet, and vice versa, and not in advance of these changes.

Fruits and berries are produced by every flowering plant (see page 136) and they contain the seed which will grow into a new flowering plant if the conditions are favourable. Some of these fruits are swollen and attractive to birds and mammals that carry them away and eat the juicy, fleshy portion and leave or excrete the pip or stone; this then germinates some distance away from the parent plant.

The juicy fruits you buy to eat from shops are of two main kinds – the true fruits and the false ones. True fruits grow from the ovary of the flower, and there are two types among wild plants: the drupes, which are stone fruits and include plums, damsons, cherries and sloes, and the berries, which include cranberries, bilberries, elderberries and gooseberries. The false fruits are those which develop from other parts of the flower as well as the ovary. Hips, haws, apples and pears have this structure.

Cones

Seed production in conifers is centred on the cones. The male and female cones begin to grow in spring. The male cones are small, yellowish and grouped in large clusters at the base of a new shoot. The female cones grow at the tip of the new shoot. In the female cone each scale carries a pair of ovules and wind carries the pollen from the male cones which fertilize the ovule and a seed develops. This occurs in dry weather, which causes the female cones to open a little to allow the pollen to enter. The female cone now begins to grow and the seed develops. In the pine tree illustrated here the process takes two years, although in most conifers it takes only a year. When the seed is fully formed with a wing, the cone opens in dry conditions and the seeds are scattered by the wind.

New female cone

Last year's female cone

Mature female cone

Male cone

Needles

Seeds

Elm fruit

Maple fruit

Winged fruits, sometimes called helicopters by children who love to throw them into the air and watch them twirl and ride the breeze, are produced by many different trees including the elm and maple illustrated here. The fruit or ovary has extensions from its wall which make the wing-like structures. When the winds blow the fruits from their branches, the fruit spins to prolong its fall and increase its chances of being carried away from the parent tree in air currents. In some fruits such as the lime, the wing is a leaf-like bract on the stalk which bears the fruit.

The waxwing is an important dispersal animal in many parts of Europe and North America, stripping trees in autumn of their berries. One bird was recorded that ate its own weight in 2½ hours.

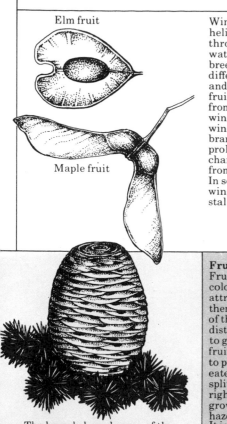

The barrel-shaped cones of the cedar grow to 8 cm (3 in) with a flattened, often hollow top. The cone grows upwards, the tree looking as if it is covered with squat pink-brown candles.

Fruits and Berries
Fruits and berries are sometimes colourful, soft and juicy in order to attract animals to come and eat them, so ensuring that numbers of their seeds are carried some distance away and are more likely to grow into new plants. Other fruits are provided with hard coats to protect the seeds from being eaten by animals; the hard covering splits when the conditions are right for germination and the seed grows out. A good example is the hazel-nut.
It is important that the fruits or seeds of a tree or plant are adapted in such a way that they are distributed over considerable distances away from the parent plant or tree. This helps to prevent over-crowding among, and competition between, members of the same species, and also results in the colonization of new areas. Many favour dispersal by the wind, among them the conifers, some broad-leaved trees (see opposite) and many flowering plants (see page 136). Some plants such as gorse and broom 'explode' the seed case to expel the seeds as far as possible. On a walk or in your garden on a hot summer's day you may hear popping noises as these plants explode.
Fleshy, succulent fruits like the blackberry, plum and elderberry are eaten by birds and mammals. The hard pips containing the seeds inside are undigested and pass out with the animal's droppings far away from the parent plant. Even if the seeds are not swallowed, the fruit is often carried away before the seeds are dropped, as happens with the rosehips. Other examples are sticky fruits such as the yew and mistletoe, which are rubbed off from the carrier bird's beak far away from the parent plant.

The seed of the horse-chestnut or buckeye is protected inside a green spiky case until it is ready to fall in the autumn. The case then splits and lets 1 round, or 2–3 flat-sided, shiny, mahogany 'conkers' fall to the ground.

The yew berry attracts many birds to feast on it. The sticky flesh adheres to the bird's beak and the seed is carried some distance before it is rubbed off.

The cones of the Norway spruce are 12–15 cm (5–6 in) long and hang downwards; they are green at first but turn brown by autumn.

The wild strawberry grows in woods and shady hedgerows, and its summer fruits are eaten by many kinds of birds and some mammals such as badgers and hedgehogs. It is a false fruit (see text)

The female cones of the European larch often grow in clusters of up to six. The cones are 2–3 cm (about 1 in) high; dead cones that have scattered their seeds remain on the tree for up to 10 years.

The many different kinds of blackberry all have fruits ready for eating in late summer by animals which carry them long distances before the seeds pass out unharmed in droppings.

Although protected during summer as they develop inside the green, soft-spined husks, the triangular brown nuts of the beech tree are released in autumn, and this 'beech mast' is eaten by squirrels, jays, rooks, pigeons, and even badgers.

REPLICAS IN PLASTER

How to make and display plaster casts of tree bark, fruits and plants

If you look closely at the trunks of the trees in your garden or local park, or while on a country walk, you will find that each one you look at is different. Even if the trees are of the same kind, the patterns of the bark will be slightly different. Some of them you will find very beautiful and attractive, so much so that you may be tempted to strip off a piece of bark and take it home with you. This would damage the tree and it may not survive. Many mammals such as rabbits and deer damage trees by eating the bark (see page 70), especially when food is short in winter, and sometimes the tree is killed as its protective covering is destroyed and it can no longer draw water and food up to all its twigs, leaves and branches. So, instead of taking a piece of bark, make a cast of it and take that home.

For this project you will need to buy a large lump of modelling clay from a handicraft or modelling shop. You should make sure it is reasonably soft, and you may need to wedge it to get rid of air holes. This means you should knead the clay as a potter does or in the same sort of way as you might knead a piece of dough.

When you have chosen your piece of bark, press the modelling clay firmly onto it, using an even pressure. Then gently and carefully peel back the clay and you will see the imprint of the bark in it. Have a protective box ready for transporting your clay home, so that the print does not get damaged.

On your work table, gently bend the clay into a curve with the bark's impression on the inside. Then with some more modelling clay make two walls to fit at each end and so form a sealed mould. You can prevent the mould from wobbling about by putting wedges of clay underneath it, or by placing it in a tray of sand.

You now prepare your plaster as for making casts of animal footprints (see page 72). Make enough to fill the mould almost up to the brim and leave until it is completely dry. To remove the plaster from the clay, first peel the end walls away and then carefully remove the middle clay. You now have a perfect replica of the tree's bark in white plaster. All you have to do is to paint it in its true colours.

You can also make plaster casts of different parts of a tree or bush. Winter twigs, which you can collect on a walk, make attractive casts. Remember to take only one or two twigs from each kind of tree. This time make your clay into square or rectangular tablets (like tiles). Lay the twig on the clay and press it firmly into the clay. After pressing it in, lift the twig up from the clay, holding it by the lower end of the stalk. A clear impression of the twig is left in the clay and is the exact size and shape of the twig. If you do not want to go to the trouble of making a plaster cast of your impression you can make up several clay tablets, some of which might have several twig impressions on the one tablet. However, making plaster casts does give you a more lasting record, as clay tablets are very fragile.

To make a plaster cast of a twig, cut a strip of card and fix it securely around the tablet, making sure it is about twice the depth of the clay. Then mix your plaster of Paris with water until it is like thick cream (see page 72), and spread it over the clay, after first moistening the clay surface with vaseline or liquid soap. When the plaster is dry, break down the sides and peel the clay gently away from the plaster. You will now have a cast of the twig resting in relief on the plaster tablet. Paint it in its natural colours and remember to label the back with details of the twig, where you found it and the date.

You can also make plaster replicas of fruits and seeds collected in autumn, and of leaf prints (single ones or a spray). The important thing is to make sure that a good impression is made in the clay. Try mixing leaves and fruits to make a decorative plaque which you can mount on a wall.

Another way to display the features of a tree is to make a wall display of all the parts of its life cycle. This would include a finished cast of its bark; a leaf – pressed, rubbed or cast; fruits – real or replicas in plaster; flowers – dried or made in plaster, and buds in winter, or the leaves just opening – either real or replicas in plaster. Mount the various things you have made on light board, or a cork tile, or on strong card. Your display could take the form of a decorative collage or an information board, with notes alongside the various items.

As you become more expert at making plaster casts of plants and trees you will no doubt become more adventurous and extend the range of your casts. You may also like to experiment with colour, using purely decorative ones such as gold and silver instead of the natural colours of the subjects.

Finally, remember always to give your finished work a coat of clear varnish. This can be shiny or matt, depending on the subject and your preference.

You Will Need

Modelling clay
Plaster of Paris
Penknife
Water
Paint brush
Clear or matt varnish
Paints
Strips of card
Mounting board, card
or cork
Sand (optional)

Compiling a Wall Display
An interesting and attractive way of displaying a tree's life is to make a permanent wall display (see below) of various parts of the tree collected at different times of the year and preserved by different methods. A wall display of a horse chestnut or buckeye is seen here, but you can make a similar one with most kinds of trees. The leaf is pressed, the fruit and flower are dried, and the bark is a plaster replica. But there are many other ways to show the tree's parts (see page 130). All of these can also be reproduced effectively as plaster casts. The size of the clay tablets must be chosen in advance so that when all the parts are completed at the end of the season, the plaster casts will fit together well in your display.

The illustration on the right shows the various items of equipment you will need for making plaster replicas and a few examples of finished casts. The clay tablets do not need to be square or rectangular, you can have circular ones for seeds or leaves or you can try more difficult shapes as you become more expert, e.g. stars, diamonds, and wavy shapes.
Paint brushes of different thicknesses are important. The thick ones are for the broader areas and the fine-pointed ones are for the veins of leaves and for putting the finishing touches to your painting. In some of your casts you can produce a beautiful effect by using gold and silver paint. For example, give autumn leaves highlights in gold, or a leafy spray a background of silver paint. They can make attractive gifts for friends. Finish all your painted replicas with a clear coat of varnish.

Put the shaped piece of modelling clay onto your piece of bark and press it on gently; then carefully peel back the clay and take it home in a protective container.

Make the clay with the bark's imprint into a sealed mould by curving it slightly upwards, and with some more clay add two ends to the mould, making sure there are no holes in it. Keep the mould in position with sand or clay.

Mix the plaster of Paris with water to form a thick cream and pour it into the mould until it almost reaches the brim, then leave it to dry.

When the plaster is completely dry, gently and carefully remove the clay mould – first the ends and then the curved part. Clean any bits of clay still sticking to the plaster cast, then paint and varnish your bark replica.

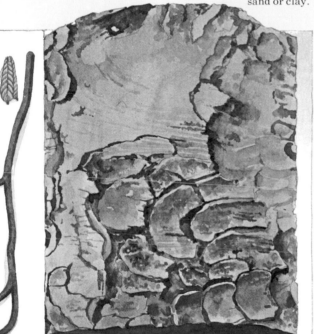

THE TREE COMMUNITY

Learning to distinguish the many kinds of plants and animals that are associated with an individual tree

A single tree is the framework of a very complex community of plant and animal life, and the naturalist looking for a long-term project could derive an immense amount of pleasure and knowledge by 'adopting' an individual tree and studying it throughout the year. The idea is to see exactly what lives on the tree, or in close association with it, and to find out how the various forms of life interact with the tree and with each other. You can choose a tree in your garden or in the local park, or in a hedgerow, or a forest. Make sure that you choose a species that is native to your own area: introduced trees generally have few animals associated with them. Make some estimates of the height and canopy spread of your tree and try to work out its approximate age (see page 110). Dig down close to the trunk to find out what sort of soil the tree is growing in. Dig small holes farther away from the trunk and see if you can find out how far the roots spread: they often spread about as far as the canopy.

Observation is at the heart of this project, and binoculars are useful for examining the upper branches. Examine the bark carefully for lichens and mosses (see page 142) as well as for small animals such as woodlice and earwigs. Do not remove strips of bark from living trees to see what is underneath: pull loose bark gently away, then go back at night with a flashlight and see what has emerged from the bark. Examine leaves and twigs for insects, spiders, and galls. You can often spot things by looking up through the leaves. Use a beating tray (see page 93) to collect insects.

Look at the plants on the ground around the tree as well: the amount of shade cast by your tree will affect the ground flora. Many fungi are physically connected with tree roots and always associated with certain species. Examine the leaf litter in the way described on page 78 to see what animals live among the dead leaves from your tree.

List everything that you find associated with your tree, and try to find out what effect each organism has on the tree. On what part do they live? Are the animals vegetarians or carnivores, and what exactly do they eat? Always distinguish in your records those animals which actually feed on the tree, whether as vegetarians or carnivores, from those which simply use the tree as a home or a temporary resting place. Many moths, for example, will rest on the bark by day without having any other connection with the tree, but it is still instructive to record them.

Always record the dates on which you discover the various animals on your tree, and then you will have a diary of your tree as well. You will not be able to put a name to everything you find on your tree, but you will be able to recognize the commoner species and groups of animals with the aid of reference books (see page 188).

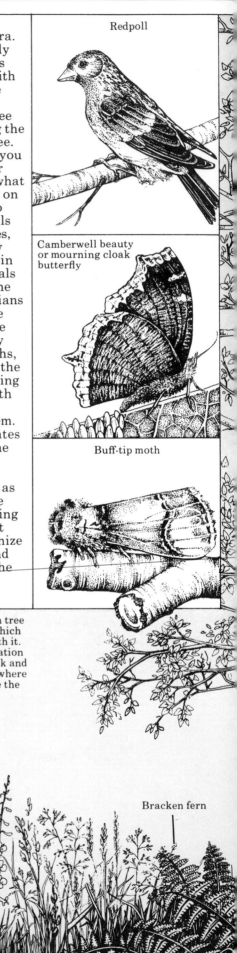

Redpoll

Camberwell beauty or mourning cloak butterfly

Buff-tip moth

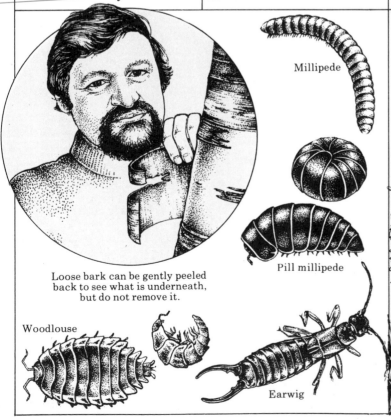

Loose bark can be gently peeled back to see what is underneath, but do not remove it.

Woodlouse

Millipede

Pill millipede

Earwig

The illustrations show a birch tree and some of the organisms which you might find associated with it. Notice how the ground vegetation is very sparse close to the trunk and more luxuriant farther away, where there is less shade and where the tree roots are less dense.

Bracken fern

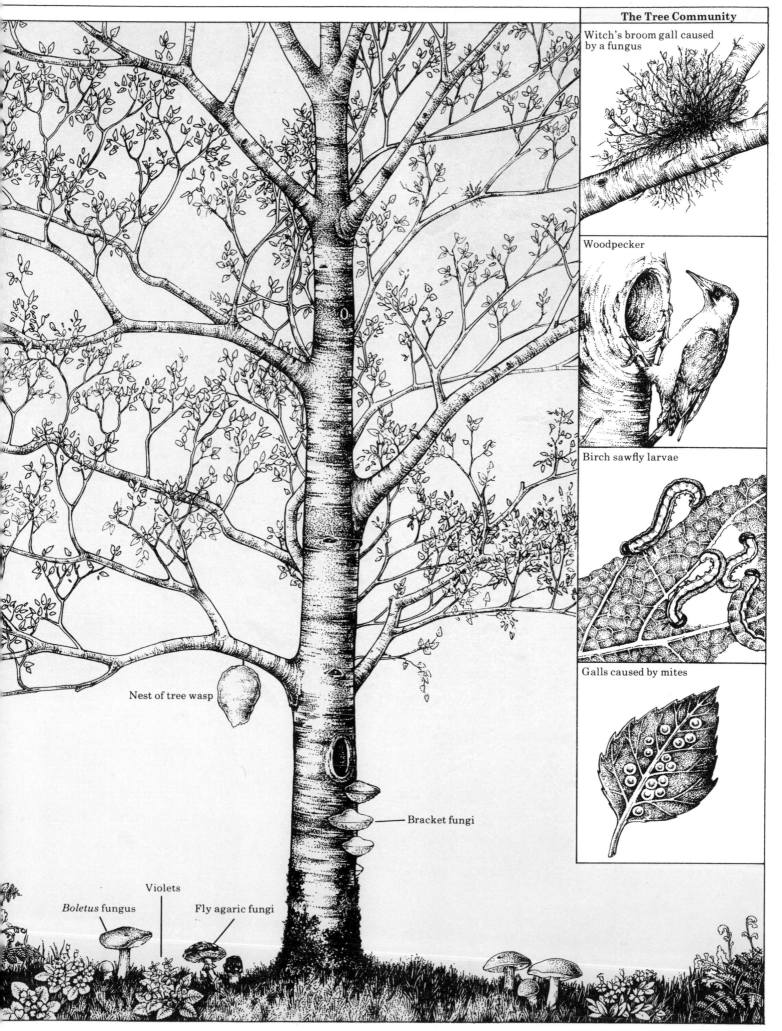

The Tree Community

Witch's broom gall caused by a fungus

Woodpecker

Birch sawfly larvae

Galls caused by mites

Nest of tree wasp

Bracket fungi

Violets

Boletus fungus

Fly agaric fungi

121

LOOKING AT HEDGEROWS

The natural history of hedges, fences, and other man-made boundaries, and how to determine their age

Hedges are prominent features in the landscape of many parts of the British Isles and western Europe, and are also found in some eastern areas of the United States. They are not natural features, but boundaries or barriers organized by man. Large numbers of British hedges were planted in the 18th century, when a great deal of the land was being enclosed, but there are also many older hedges. The Domesday Book (1086–87) mentions village hedges, and it is clear that many early hedges marked the parish boundaries.

Hedgerows, together with fences and old stone walls, are always fascinating to explore. When they reach maturity, or become overgrown, either through design or neglect, they are havens for wildlife. Some farmers deliberately leave an uncultivated strip along a fence to encourage the growth of trees and bushes. These provide sites for nesting birds, while foxes like to make their dens among the rocks of an old stone wall.

Whereas in the United States fences and hedgerows are largely a feature of the East, in the West and Midwest cultivated areas tend to be huge and unfenced. In the East, fields are smaller, fences are more numerous, and the regular rainfall means that a variety of trees and shrubs is always ready to spring up on any piece of uncultivated land. Many hedges are found on plantations in the South.

In the early days of the United States, there was a plentiful supply of material for fencing and hedge-laying, just as in Europe, hundreds of years earlier, there had been forests in abundance. Since the settler's first job is always to clear the land for planting, there were plenty of logs, tree-limbs, shrubs and piles of stones with which to build boundaries for the new farms. Split logs made fences, while in New England, for example, the rocky land made stone walls a necessity. These stone walls are still part of the landscape; some have been kept in good repair but the majority have begun to collapse. When they fall down, the surrounding area soon becomes overgrown. Spaces among the fallen rocks make excellent seed beds for many plants. Among the trees, grey birch, chokecherry, shadbush and red cedar are usually the first to grow, and later the maple, oak and hickory take over. If a whole field is uncultivated for long, it all goes back to forest, which is why the remains of old stone walls can often be found in woods, the stones covered with moss and surrounded by ferns.

Where hedges predominate, it is a fascinating exercise to try and work out their ages and origins. The newer hedges are generally quite easy to recognize because they tend to be straight and many contain only two or three kinds of shrubs and trees. Hawthorn is by far the most common shrub in planted hedges in Britain; others, less commonly found, are elder, ash, blackthorn, privet, wild rose and elm.

The older hedges tend to follow more irregular courses and they usually have quite a number of woody species in them. With numerous broad stumps throwing up coppice shoots, these old hedges have a very different character from the planted hedges of more recent times. Often called mixed hedges, they contain such shrubs as hazel, maple, dogwood, and guelder rose.

The older hedges may have been planted – probably with a mixture of species taken from the nearby woodland – but some undoubtedly sprang up spontaneously on the uncultivated no-man's-land between villages. You can usually recognize the hedges that originated from woodland because they tend to contain a good number of woodland herbs, such as dog's mercury, primroses, and bluebells.

By counting the number of woody species in various

Hedge-laying involves cutting the stems down to a few feet in height and then cutting almost right through the stumps and bending them obliquely. The laid stems are held in place by strong stakes, and further sticks are woven along the top to prevent the cut stems from springing up again. The cutting stimulates the growth of strong new shoots from the base and a dense hedge results. The laid stems form a strong barrier against cattle and sheep until the new shoots are well grown. Laying is a very good way of managing hawthorn hedges, and laid hedges are still quite common in certain cattle-rearing areas of the English Midlands.

lengths of hedgerow you can get a good idea of the ages of some hedges. The method was worked out by Dr Max Hooper of the British Nature Conservancy Council, and, although it cannot be absolutely accurate, it has proved to be a remarkably good guide.

All you have to do to estimate the age of a hedge is to select a 27-metre (30-yard) stretch at random and count the numbers of tree and shrub species in that stretch. Include roses, because these can form free-standing bushes on their own, but ignore brambles and other climbers. If you find five species of trees or shrubs, the hedge is likely to be about 500 years old, and if you find nine species the hedge may well be about 900 years old. For a more accurate result you should make counts on several 27-metre stretches and average the results. Do not include gateways or the ends of hedges in your surveys, for these parts are often not typical of the hedge as a whole. You must also take the general appearance of the hedge into account. Some 18th-century hedges, for example, were planted with two or three species to start with, and this would radically affect your calculations.

Old hedges, on the other hand, can appear much younger than they really are in some places because there is a lack of suitable trees to provide the seeds of the invasion force. You would be wise to date at least one old hedge and one newer one in your locality from maps or other documents. This will tell you if the shrub-counting method is reasonably accurate in your area.

The verge of a typical roadside hedge *(right)* contains lots of grasses which can withstand trampling. Daisies, plantains, and dandelions also grow near to the road, but most other flowering plants grow further back where there is less trampling. Hogweed and other large, white-flowered umbellifers decorate the verges in the summer.

1 Hogweed
2 Stitchwort
3 Dog violet
4 Couch grass
5 Greater plantain
6 Red clover
7 Lesser celandine
8 Field maple
9 Dog rose
10 Hawthorn or may

11 Chaffinch
12 Linnet
13 Yellowhammer
14 Hazel
15 Honeysuckle
16 Orange-tip butterfly
17 Traveller's joy
18 Bramble
19 Lords-and-ladies

20 Bluebells
21 Cockchafer
22 Dunnock
23 Hedgehog
24 Cocksfoot grass
25 Drinker moth caterpillar
26 Frog

Roadside hedges often have drainage ditches along one side, and the hedges themselves grow on banks. Many of the older boundary hedges also grew on wide banks, which were probably the original boundaries. Roadside hedges also tend to have grass verges with attractive flowers. The low-growing flowers in the hedge bottom and on the verge usually bloom early in the year, before too many of the hedgerow leaves come out to shade them. Notice also that the shrubs flower much earlier on the sunny side of the hedge than on the shady side. The mixed nature of this hedge shows it to be one of the older hedges, and the presence of bluebells suggests that it originated from a piece of old woodland.

WORKING WITH WOOD

Revive an old country craft and make useful and amusing objects

Wood can offer you hours of pleasure if you have the time and patience to make things from it. Pieces of driftwood found along the strand-lines can be made into polished sculptures or used to enhance your flower arrangements (see page 36). On a country walk you will sometimes come across a fallen dead tree with interesting-looking branches, or a fallen branch, which also can be carved and sanded down, oiled, or polished and varnished to give a pleasing shape.

In the not-too-distant past craftsmen worked wood of every kind to produce ornaments and all kinds of objects for houses, farms, churches, and various outdoor activities. Today this skilled craft has almost vanished, although cottage industries that have sprung up in recent years are once more helping to popularize the art of working with

wood. As a substance, wood renews itself fairly quickly, and provided you are careful where you take it from, and remove only very small quantities, your efforts are unlikely to harm the local environment. But remember always to ask the landowner's permission.

Before you embark on a project, it is worthwhile reading about the woods that the traditional craftsmen used for specific jobs; this will also tell you a great deal about the properties of the particular woods. Ash, for example, is both tough and supple and resists shock without splintering. It is therefore widely chosen to make handles for tools and garden instruments, as well as oars, frames, wheel rims and skis. Elm is chosen for outdoor furniture because it is strong, tough and durable if exposed to the weather. This wood is the one to choose if you want to attempt fine carvings. The creamy-white wood of the lime is also chosen for carving since it is easily worked and very stable. The pale cream-coloured wood of the sycamore is another that is used for carving.

If you haven't worked with wood before, you will no doubt want to start by making something fairly simple. Most of us need a broom for the garden, for example, and a traditional besom is easily made from binding twigs of the birch together on the end of a long pole or branch.

Walking sticks can be made from many different

kinds of trees. Find a pollard when you are out on a walk. This is a young broad-leaved tree which has been cut across some 2 metres (6½ ft) from the ground, and has young fresh shoots growing out to form a bushy crown. Oak, beech, hornbeam and willow were often pollarded in the past to provide lengths of wood for fencing, basketry, or firewood. It is still possible to find them in woods, along stream banks, and in lanes. A very simple walking stick can be made from a blackthorn stem which you trim and then polish to a smooth finish.

Give your stick a ready-made curved handle by leaving it attached to its tree of origin and pinning it to the ground with a U-shaped stake. Over a period of months your stick/branch will grow towards the light and in so doing will develop a natural curve (see illustrations below).

Although the flowers of the honeysuckle are fragrant and beautiful to look at, this plant can distort and ruin young trees by climbing about on them. On touching a young growing tree, the wiry main stem of the honeysuckle twines itself spirally round the tree's trunk constricting its growth so that it becomes deformed. You can turn this trick of nature to your advantage by cutting the trunk to make an attractive stick (see illustrations); the curves will look as if they have been hand-carved.

The tough twining stem of a honeysuckle will soon deform a young tree's trunk.

The deformed young tree-trunk can be made into an attractive walking stick by removing the honeysuckle stems, stripping off the bark and polishing the wood to a high finish.

Find a young sturdy branch growing not too far from the ground and gently pull down the tip to reach the soil. Pinion the branch firmly to the ground with a U-shaped stake so that the tip is free.

Leave the branch for several months, and you should find that, in the process of growing towards the light, it will have developed a natural bend.

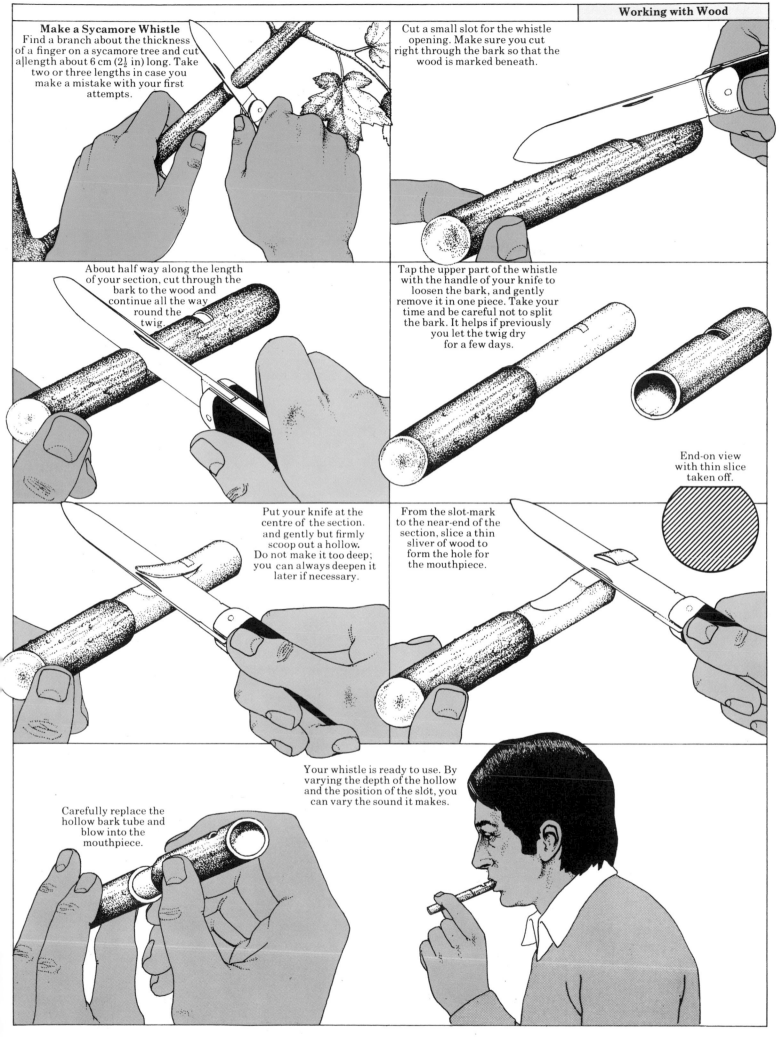

Make a Sycamore Whistle
Find a branch about the thickness of a finger on a sycamore tree and cut a length about 6 cm (2½ in) long. Take two or three lengths in case you make a mistake with your first attempts.

Cut a small slot for the whistle opening. Make sure you cut right through the bark so that the wood is marked beneath.

About half way along the length of your section, cut through the bark to the wood and continue all the way round the twig.

Tap the upper part of the whistle with the handle of your knife to loosen the bark, and gently remove it in one piece. Take your time and be careful not to split the bark. It helps if previously you let the twig dry for a few days.

End-on view with thin slice taken off.

Put your knife at the centre of the section. and gently but firmly scoop out a hollow. Do not make it too deep; you can always deepen it later if necessary.

From the slot-mark to the near-end of the section, slice a thin sliver of wood to form the hole for the mouthpiece.

Carefully replace the hollow bark tube and blow into the mouthpiece.

Your whistle is ready to use. By varying the depth of the hollow and the position of the slot, you can vary the sound it makes.

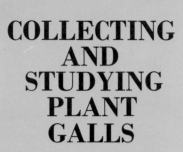

COLLECTING AND STUDYING PLANT GALLS

The strange growths that appear on the leaves and stems of trees and other plants

If you take a walk along the edge of an oak wood in late summer and examine the oak leaves you will almost certainly find a number of small, button-like objects attached to their lower surfaces. These objects are spangle galls, and they are caused by the presence of tiny insects called gall wasps. Detach a few galls and split them open with a fingernail and you will see that each one contains a little white grub. Oak trees are especially prone to attack by these interesting little insects, whose adults look like little black or brown ants, with or without wings. Hundreds of different kinds of galls can be found on the various species of oak. The female gall wasps lay their eggs on the trees, and when the eggs hatch the presence of the grubs stimulates the trees to form the galls. Nutritious tissues swell up around the grubs and give them a constant food supply. Each species of gall wasp induces the formation of a particular kind of gall. Some of the insects look so similar that even experts have difficulty in telling them apart, but they must have chemical differences because they may induce very different galls on the same leaf.

As well as the several different kinds of spangle galls, there are many other types of galls on the leaves and the twigs. They include the familiar oak apples and the hard, round marble galls. Some galls develop on the trunks and roots of the trees. Young trees and those with low-growing branches are especially vulnerable to attack by gall wasps, and this is why it is usually more profitable to search the edges of a wood than the centre. You can sometimes find huge numbers of spangle galls on a single tree—often a hundred or more on a single leaf—but they do not appear to do the trees any harm.

It is very easy to collect galls and breed out the insects at home. Spangle galls should be collected in the autumn when the leaves are beginning to fall. The galls fall from the leaves at about this time but you should keep them with some of the leaves in a small plastic box. Keep the leaves fairly damp and you will see that the galls continue to grow. Insects will start to

'Pineapple' galls induced by aphids on spruce twigs. The scales separate to let the young aphids out, and the galls then turn brown.

emerge early in the spring if the galls are kept in a cool place. Spangle galls usually produce just one insect from each gall, but the emerging insect might not be the rightful occupant of the gall. The gall wasps are attacked by many parasites, which either eat the gall wasp grub or cause it to starve by eating its food. The parasite then emerges instead of the original cause of the gall.

Galls on twigs will sometimes go on developing if you cut the twig and keep it in water, but it is best to delay cutting the twig until the gall is fully formed. Alternatively, you can tie a sleeve of muslin or similar material around the branch and wait for the insects to emerge. A large gall, such as an oak apple, will yield numerous gall wasps and parasites.

The oak-dwelling gall wasps have some very strange life histories, which you can investigate quite easily with spangle galls. When your insects hatch out from the galls in the spring put them on to a twig of a living oak tree and enclose them with a muslin sleeve for a few days. They will lay their eggs on the oak buds, and you can then remove the sleeve. Keep a close watch on the twig and you will possibly see some new galls developing on the young leaves in late spring, but these will not be like the galls you collected in the autumn. If you started with the common spangle gall (see illustration opposite) your new galls will be like blackcurrants on the

'Bean' galls induced on willow leaves by the grub of a small sawfly. The grub pupates in the soil when fully grown, so many mature galls are empty.

leaves or on the male catkins. The insects inside them will also be different. Those that emerge from the spangle galls are all females which can lay eggs without mating, but the currant galls yield both male and female insects, which have to mate before the next generation of eggs is laid on the leaves. The two generations are normally found on the same tree, but some gall wasps use two oak species.

Gall wasps are not found only on oaks. Several species induce galls on wild roses, the best known gall being the robin's pincushion or bedeguar gall. This looks like a fluffy red ball in the summer, but the hairs hide a very hard, woody core with lots of separate chambers in it. You can

breed out the insects very easily by collecting the galls in the winter, by which time they have stopped growing and turned brown. Males are extremely rare in this species and the females emerging from the galls in the spring lay eggs on the roses without mating.

Many herbaceous plants also play host to gall wasps. The stems of various hawkweeds swell up around gall wasp grubs, and the stems of the European ground ivy produce some beautiful red swellings.

Galls are also caused by other animals invading the plant tissues, and also by some fungi. Aphids induce pouch-like galls of various shapes, which are always open to the air. Other insects which induce galls include many midges and other flies,

The robin's pincushion gall on a wild rose. Each gall contains several woody chambers. Despite the barrier of fluffy hairs, many parasites get into the gall.

and some sawflies. Mites are responsible for the little red pustules on the leaves of maples and other plants, but the animals are too small to see without a strong lens.

Many galls can be put into a permanent collection. Woody galls, such as the marble gall, dry very easily, and the spangle galls also keep well after the insects have left. Thin galls can be pressed with the leaves in the normal way. You can also try making plaster casts of your galls (see page 118), and you can try sand-drying (see page 148) for the softer types. Always cut open a gall to see the internal structure. Mount the insects that emerge beside their empty galls. The easiest way to mount them is on little cardboard points (see page 92).

The gall wasp responsible for the marble gall is called *Andricus kollari*. The grub lives in a central chamber and the adult chews its way out in the autumn, leaving a neat round exit-hole.

Marble galls on the common oak start off green *(above)* and become golden brown *(right)*.

'Purse' galls induced by aphids on the leaf stalks of poplar. The insects escape through a small hole at the end of the purse.

These striking galls, up to 30 cm (12 in) long, are induced by aphids on the shoots of pistachio bushes.

There is room in a marble gall for several guests as well as the rightful occupant. This gall has 31 exit holes, each marked with a pin, showing that 31 insects grew up in it.

The common European spangle galls develop on oak leaves in mid-summer *(left)*. Collect galled leaves when the leaves are turning brown *(top left)* and put them in a plastic box. Some damp peat in the bottom will help to keep them moist. Remove any mould that appears, and when the insects emerge *(above)* sleeve them out in some muslin on an oak twig. If currant galls *(right)* develop on the leaves you can collect the insects and start the cycle again.

LEAF PRINTS AND SKELETONS

Experiments with leaves – making prints of their shapes, patterns, skeletons and colours

Leaves picked in high summer in their bright green tones, or in autumn when they have turned deep brown, red or yellow, can be preserved in several ways. You can press them (see page 146) or take prints of them. There are various methods of making leaf prints, all of which will give you interesting results.

A simple way is just to record the shapes of the leaves. Take a leaf and lay it down on a piece of paper and hold it firmly in position with your finger. Take a fairly thick paint brush and paint over the outline of the leaf and onto your paper so that the complete edge of the leaf is recorded. Using this method you can build up a record of the leaves from all the trees in your area.

Another easy method is to take a leaf rubbing in the same way that you make bark rubbings (see page 112). Place your leaf on a firm piece of card and put a sheet of strong white paper over it. Take a heel-ball or a wax crayon and rub over the leaf area with even, parallel strokes. The veins and ribs of the leaf will stand out with surprising sharpness. Choose autumn leaves that are dry and hard for good results. Remember, too, that fresh summer leaves are doing a very important job making food for the tree, so do not take too many of these. Wax crayons can be bought in a range of colours, and you can either try to reproduce the true shades of a leaf or experiment with different colours.

Oil paints or shoe polish, even soot from a candle flame, can also be used to make leaf prints. Use your fingertips, a small stencil brush or a polish brush to spread the colour on the back of your leaf. If you want to use soot, collect it by holding an enamel plate or saucer over the flame of a lighted candle. Mix the collected soot with a little linseed oil and use this black oil paint in the same way as the other materials. After painting, place your leaf on a piece of paper, and proceed as described in the illustrations.

An unusual way of preserving leaves is to make leaf skeletons which can be mounted on card to make attractive pictures; you can also use the skeleton to make a photograph which will show the image of the leaf skeleton in reverse. Quite large leaves with strong ribs and veins make the best skeleton prints. The first step is to remove all the soft vegetable matter from the leaf so that only the skeleton is left. Put your leaves in a saucepan with a litre (about 2 pints) of water, bring to the boil and simmer for half an hour. Strain off the liquid into a bucket or pail and allow to cool. Make sure the leaves are still in good condition, and then let them lie for several days in the water in which they were boiled. It is wise to place the bucket of water away from living quarters during this period because after a few days the liquid begins to smell. Have a look at your leaves after a week or so and gently turn them in the liquid. When the vegetable material has softened considerably, remove the leaves from the bucket and rinse them very gently in clean water. Take a soft-bristled paint brush to dislodge any remaining leaf material, so that only the leaf skeleton is left.

An alternative way of removing the leaf material from its skeleton is to use washing soda. Make up a weak solution of soda and heat it to just below boiling point. Remove the saucepan from the heat and put in your leaves. It is advisable not to let children follow this method by themselves as great care must be taken not to get the soda solution on the skin, and especially not in the eyes. It is best to wear rubber gloves. Take out each leaf carefully and you will find that the solution will have rotted away the leaf so that only its skeleton remains.

Whichever method you have been using, the next stage is to place the leaf skeletons on a piece of clean newspaper and leave them in some warm place to dry. When the leaves are dry, take them out and look at them. You will find that the skeletons are now a dirty brown colour, and you may wish to bleach them, especially if you intend to

Most trees and plants can be identified just by the shape of the leaf. Hold a leaf on a piece of paper and paint in short, steady strokes from the edge of the leaf onto the paper. An exact outline will be left when you lift up the leaf.

put them in a display. To do this, just lay the leaf skeleton in a weak solution of bleach and water. After a few hours remove the leaves and allow them to dry. The skeleton can then be mounted or made into a decorative card.

An interesting extension of the leaf skeleton project, especially to anyone interested in photography, is to make a photographic leaf skeleton. The skeleton does not need to be bleached as it is only used as an image. The shape, design and pattern of the skeleton are all that matter.

If you are a keen amateur photographer you will probably have printing equipment and perhaps an enlarger that you can use to enlarge very small leaf skeletons. The method shown here is a simple one, however, and uses basic equipment that most of us will have at home. You need only to buy developer, fixative, photographic paper, and a red light bulb (a red plastic filter on an ordinary bulb will do). Choose a leaf that is quite flat and take it into a room that you have completely darkened; the red light can be switched on and will not damage your photographic paper. Set up a spotlight or anglepoise lamp above a flat board and position it at such a height above the board that when it is switched on, only the board is lit up. When all is ready, switch off all lights except the red one and follow the instructions shown in the illustrations opposite.

You Will Need

Wax crayons or heel-balls
Paper
Blotting paper
Boot polish, or oil paints or a candle and linseed oil
Bleach or washing soda
Bucket or pail
Saucepan
Spotlight or anglepoise lamp
Photographic paper
Developer
Fixative
Red bulb
3 flat plastic dishes

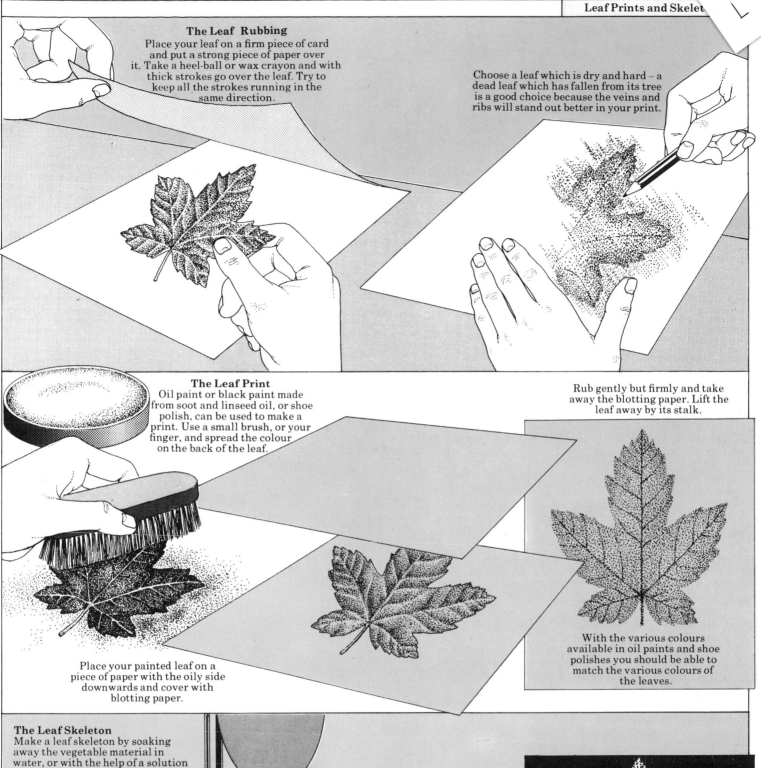

The Leaf Rubbing
Place your leaf on a firm piece of card and put a strong piece of paper over it. Take a heel-ball or wax crayon and with thick strokes go over the leaf. Try to keep all the strokes running in the same direction.

Choose a leaf which is dry and hard – a dead leaf which has fallen from its tree is a good choice because the veins and ribs will stand out better in your print.

The Leaf Print
Oil paint or black paint made from soot and linseed oil, or shoe polish, can be used to make a print. Use a small brush, or your finger, and spread the colour on the back of the leaf.

Rub gently but firmly and take away the blotting paper. Lift the leaf away by its stalk.

Place your painted leaf on a piece of paper with the oily side downwards and cover with blotting paper.

With the various colours available in oil paints and shoe polishes you should be able to match the various colours of the leaves.

The Leaf Skeleton
Make a leaf skeleton by soaking away the vegetable material in water, or with the help of a solution of washing soda (see text). To make a photographic leaf skeleton, you will need a dark room lit by a red light. Put a piece of photographic paper below a spotlight or anglepoise lamp. Place your leaf on this paper and switch the light on for 8 seconds. Remove the leaf and immerse the photographic paper in developer for 3 minutes. You will see the skeleton emerge on a dark background. Put the print into a tray of water (stop bath) for 30 seconds. Next put the print into a tray with fixative for 3 minutes. Then immerse the print in a water-filled tray for an hour to wash. Take out and dry. Note: depending on your light source the time of exposure may have to be altered. Trial and error will soon indicate the best exposure time.

MAKING TREE CHARTS

How to build up your own 'picture' of a tree using your bark rubbings, plaster casts, and pressed leaves

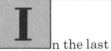n the last few pages you have seen how to make plaster casts of various objects, how to make bark rubbings, how to press leaves, and so on. Instead of keeping all these objects separately, you might like to make up a chart for each kind of tree that you have studied. A large sheet of coarse paper is a good base on which to build your chart, but you do need a *large* sheet if you are to get on all the aspects of each tree at each season of the year (see illustration).

The central feature of the chart should be a bark rubbing from the trunk, and you can cut the rubbing into the shape of the trunk, including a few stubby branches if you wish. Glue this rubbing evenly onto the chart. Using strong glue or sticky tape, you can then fix on twigs from the tree to look like branches. Use both summer and winter twigs, so that you can see what the leaf arrangement is like on the twigs and also what the winter buds look like. In order to keep the summer leaves in something like their natural condition, you could try standing the twigs in a 50/50 mixture of water and glycerine for a few days – until the glycerine starts to ooze out of the leaves. Wipe off the excess glycerine before attaching the twigs to the chart, and the leaves should stay fresh-looking for quite a while. You can always replace items on the chart with fresh ones from time to time.

You can use pressed leaves as well as prints and rubbings on the chart, but make sure that you include some with the autumn coloration when dealing with deciduous trees. Some species, such as the maples, go through a wide range of colours as they prepare for the autumn leaf-fall. If your chart has room, you could also show how the leaf size gradually increases in the spring. Pick a leaf from the same branch each day as soon as the buds start to open, and go on until you find no further increase in size. Press all the leaves and fix them onto your chart in chronological order.

Include pressed or dried flowers on your chart, and if the tree has separate male and female flowers, as most wind-pollinated and many insect-pollinated trees do, make sure that you have a specimen of both. Dried fruits or plaster casts of the fruits may be incorporated into the chart, and you should also have a seed or two from inside the fruit when this is significant. It is worth including the fruit and the seed (conker) of the horse chestnut or buckeye, but do not bother to take the casing off an acorn to expose the seed. Include any galls that you find on the trees and possibly also the insects that emerge from them; put the insects in small tubes which you can attach with sticky tape.

Make sure that you label your chart fully with the name of the tree and the dates on which you collected each piece. It would be ideal to make up your chart from a single tree, but this is not essential.

Your charts, which are in fact scientific collages, make very attractive and informative wall decorations. Having made them up for all the common trees, you should never again have to wonder about identifying trees.

The tree being mounted in this picture is an oak

A bark rubbing cut into the shape of a trunk. Indicate the height at which the rubbing was taken on the original tree.

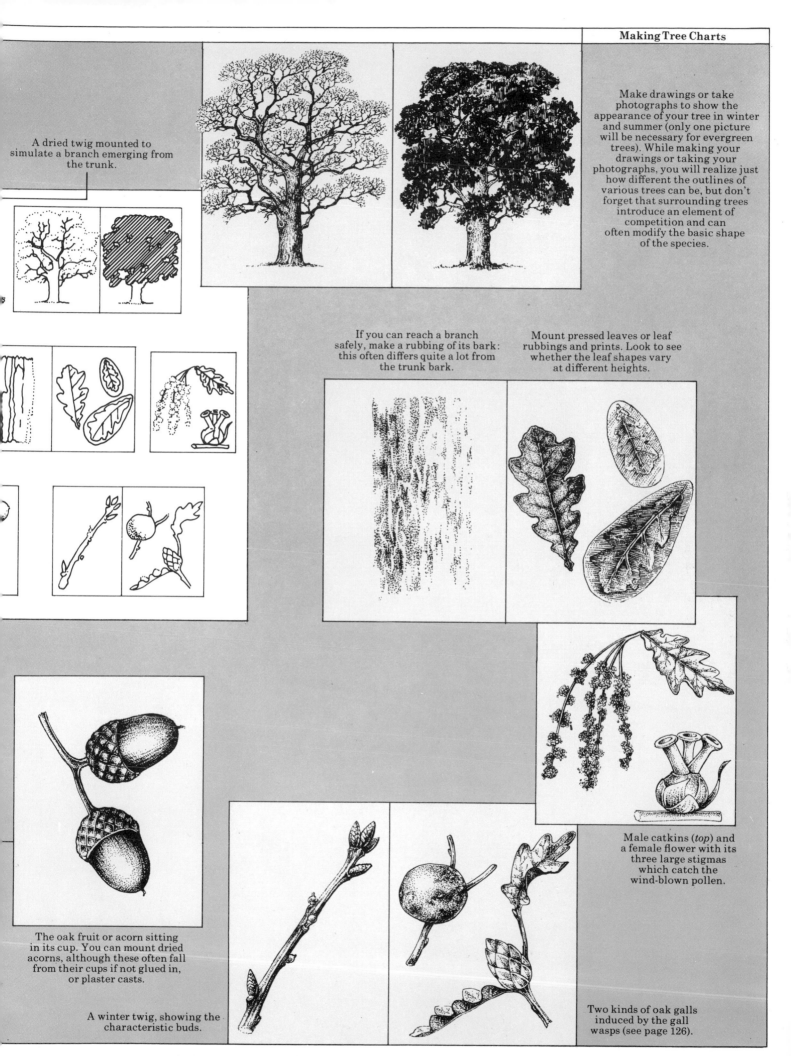

A dried twig mounted to simulate a branch emerging from the trunk.

Make drawings or take photographs to show the appearance of your tree in winter and summer (only one picture will be necessary for evergreen trees). While making your drawings or taking your photographs, you will realize just how different the outlines of various trees can be, but don't forget that surrounding trees introduce an element of competition and can often modify the basic shape of the species.

If you can reach a branch safely, make a rubbing of its bark: this often differs quite a lot from the trunk bark.

Mount pressed leaves or leaf rubbings and prints. Look to see whether the leaf shapes vary at different heights.

Male catkins (*top*) and a female flower with its three large stigmas which catch the wind-blown pollen.

The oak fruit or acorn sitting in its cup. You can mount dried acorns, although these often fall from their cups if not glued in, or plaster casts.

A winter twig, showing the characteristic buds.

Two kinds of oak galls induced by the gall wasps (see page 126).

erbaceous plants are those which have little or no woody tissues in their bodies, as opposed to the trees and shrubs which are composed almost entirely of woody material. Some herbaceous plants develop somewhat woody stems late in the year, but these stems do not remain alive and continue from year to year. A good example is the familiar michaelmas daisy, which dies back to ground level each autumn and sends new shoots up in the spring.

The thousands of species of herbaceous plants belong to several major groups, of which the simplest are the algae. These nearly all live in water, and the best known of them are the seaweeds (see page 34). Many live in fresh water, however, and they are responsible for turning pond water green in the summer. Some are minute single-celled organisms that swim or float freely in the water, while others form the tangled masses known as blanket-weed. Some algae live in moist situations on land. The green coatings on tree trunks and damp walls are formed from tiny algae. Although some of the seaweeds are brown or red, all algae contain the green pigment called chlorophyll, and, like all green plants, they use it to make food by the remarkable process called photosynthesis. This is, in fact, a very complex process, but it boils down to the essential fact that the plants trap the sun's light with the aid of chlorophyll, and then use this energy to combine water and carbon dioxide. This makes sugar which is the plants' basic food, and oxygen is given off in the process. The chemical side of the process is exactly the reverse of that involved in animals' breathing: animals take in oxygen and give out carbon dioxide. There is thus a continuous re-cycling of these materials in the atmosphere – the so-called carbon cycle.

The fungi form another group of rather simple plants, but they differ from all other groups in not having any chlorophyll. Some biologists do not even consider them to be plants. The fungi, which include all the moulds and toadstools, can grow in the dark, but they cannot make their own food. They absorb food from other plants and animals, either living or dead. Those that take food from living organisms are called parasites: those that feed on dead material are saprophytes. One reason why fungi are so common in woodlands is that there are such enormous quantities of dead leaves for them to feed on. The fungi have no flowers and they reproduce by scattering clouds of minute spores (see page 148).

The strange group of plants called lichens (see page 142) is now generally regarded as a group of specialized fungi which use algae to help them get their food, for each lichen is actually a combination of a fungus and an alga. Lichens are the hardiest of all plants, except that they cannot tolerate air pollution.

Mosses and liverworts are fairly simple green plants that belong to a group known as the bryophytes. They are usually confined to damp places. Like the fungi, they reproduce by means of spores, but they have a more complex life history than the fungi.

Ferns and their allies (see page 144) belong to a group called the pteridophytes. Unlike the mosses, they have water-carrying tubes in their bodies and they can therefore grow much larger. Some, known as tree ferns, are more than 20 metres (65 ft) high, although their trunks are not quite like those of real trees. Ferns have no flowers, but they have complex life cycles involving spores and two quite separate types of plant.

The flowering plants all belong to the highest division of plants – the spermatophytes. This group also includes the cone-bearing trees. There are two major sections of flowering plants – the monocotyledons, which include the grasses and other narrow-leaved plants, and the dicotyledons. The latter have relatively broad leaves as a rule, but the real difference between the two groups lies in the seed. Monocotyledons have just one seed leaf or cotyledon in each seed, while the dicotyledons have two.

Flowering herbaceous plants range from minute floating duckweeds to great banana plants. The latter look like small trees, but they do not have real trunks – just thick clusters of leaf stalks. There are normally four parts to the plant: the root, the stem, the leaf, and the flower. The latter is the seat of reproduction and it also has four main regions, although one or more of these may be missing in certain flowers.

The sepals form the outermost part of the flower, which is known as the calyx. They are generally green and leaf-like and they protect the flower when it is in bud.

The petals, which form the corolla, are generally brightly coloured and their main job is to attract insects to the flowers for the purposes of pollination.

Before a flower can set seeds, it must be pollinated, meaning that pollen of the right kind must reach the carpels. Most flowers are so designed that their own pollen cannot reach their carpels – perhaps because the stamens scatter their pollen before the carpels are ready to receive it – and if the pollen does reach the carpels it often cannot grow on them. The flowers thus rely on cross-pollination, with pollen from another flower of the same kind, and they nearly all rely on the wind or insects to carry the pollen.

Wind-pollinated flowers are usually very dull in colour, with small petals or none at all. Grasses, plantains, and stinging nettles are among the best known of the wind-pollinated herbs, although many trees are pollinated by the wind as well (see page 109). The wind-pollinated flowers hang loosely, or else the stamens hang well out of them, and the wind scatters the pollen.

Insect-pollinated flowers generally have brightly coloured petals, and they also have attractive scent and sweet nectar. All kinds of insects come to sip the nectar, and while doing so they accidentally pick up pollen on their bodies. Some of this pollen is then brushed on to the stigmas of the next flower to be visited. The pollen grows down into the carpel and fertilizes a cell there to form a seed. The carpel itself forms the fruit, and when this is ripe the seeds inside it are scattered.

CHAPTER 7

HERBACEOUS PLANTS

These are the 'non-woody' plants, and range from tiny, floating algae to huge banana plants

MAKING A PLANT SURVEY

How to record plants in their own habitats and build up a picture of the different plant communities in your area

Recording where plants live reveals a great deal about their life histories. A simple way to begin is to make a record of all the plants you can find in one fairly small area, say about a 20–30 metre (or yard) square. You can record the plants in the form of a map, choosing symbols for each different kind of plant. Do not worry about drawing your map exactly to scale when you first start your field work. Mark off your chosen site with string and measure the length and breadth of it. Draw a similar shape on your map paper and write in the measurements and other details. Shrubs and trees will serve as landmarks, so mark these first.

Then note the positions of other groups of plants, such as a clump of nettles or a patch of ground ivy. There will usually be so many individual plants that you will not be able to mark each one separately, hence the need to work in groups. Don't forget to make a key of all the symbols used in your map. You can make an interesting long-term study of the locality by mapping it at regular intervals, so building up a year-round record of the plants and the changes that take place.

Once you have got used to making field surveys, you may like to try working on a smaller scale and with much more precision, studying different plant habitats in detail. For this you will need an ecological tool called a quadrat. This is simply a square frame, which can be made by bending a stiff piece of wire into a square, or by nailing together four pieces of wood of the same length. If you are making your own quadrat, allow 100 cm (3 ft) for each side, then the area you survey will be 1 square metre (1 sq yd). To help record the ground plants' positions accurately, divide the quadrat with string into smaller squares of equal size. At the same time prepare a map on a similar grid, keeping the proportions of the quadrat.

Go to the piece of ground you plan to investigate, and throw your quadrat over your shoulder so that it falls at random. Then study the plants within the square, identifying and noting all their names, and enter this information on your map. Remember not to pull up flowers, and try to disturb the ground as little as possible.

A variation on this project is to compare an untrampled area with a trampled area of ground. This will reveal which plants do not like being trodden on and which can tolerate the pressure of our heavy feet — and, more to the point, that of the local wildlife. The illustrations opposite show how to go about these experiments. Remember not to choose your area exactly but to throw the quadrat over your shoulder. This is so that random samples are obtained, thereby giving a more balanced picture than if you selected the precise area yourself.

For some surveys you can mark out a permanent quadrat by driving corner stakes into the ground, and visiting the site at regular intervals. This is useful for following changes that take place in the area, either through the seasons or because of some interruption such as a fire, the felling of nearby trees, ploughing, and so on.

Another interesting exercise is to make a plant profile known as a line transect. This marks the position of plant species along a particular line (see illustration at the foot of the page). Choose a section that will bring out any contrasts in ground level and changes in vegetation, such as would be caused by a pond or stream, a path, or a ditch. If the transect can cross different types of soil, so much the better.

To make the transect, drive two poles into the ground, one at each end of the ground you are going to study, and stretch a strong piece of string between them. If you have a spirit level, use it to make sure the string is horizontal. It is a good idea to mark off your string at regular intervals with pieces of thin wire or thread. You may need to put in extra support poles to keep the string horizontal, depending on the length of the transect. Take the measurements and other details of all the plants growing along the line. When you return home you can make a detailed plant profile on graph paper, using symbols for the plants you have identified.

You Will Need

For a quadrat
Four equal lengths of wood
Nails or stiff wire
String
Notebook and pencil

For a transect
Two or more poles
String marked into measured lengths
Long tape measure
Notebook and pencil

When you have made your quadrat and chosen the area you wish to study, turn your back to it and throw the quadrat over your shoulder. Leave it exactly where it falls and then begin to identify all the plants within the square, noting down the names and giving them symbols. Then draw the square on graph paper, putting in each individual plant in its exact position. You can repeat this many times in the same type of habitat and build up a precise record of the plants that live there.

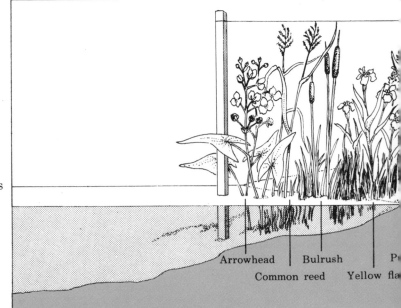

Arrowhead   Bulrush   P
Common reed   Yellow fla

Untrampled grassy areas allow different kinds of plants to survive, such as buttercups, dandelions and sowthistles.

This is a survey of a trampled area of lawn. Only those plants survive that can tolerate being trodden on; they generally include various grasses, daisies and plantain.

Below

When you have placed your poles in position for a line transect, measure the height of each pole and note it down. Then begin at one end and work your way along the string, which you have marked at regular intervals, perhaps in 10-cm (4-in) sections. As you go, note down the name of each plant, the distance from the string to the plant tip, and the distance from the string to the ground. When you get home you can build up a picture on graph paper of the plant species that occur along the length of the transect, the undulations of the ground, and the heights of the various plants.

If some grasses are difficult to identify, take a specimen of each home and identify them at leisure. Take a note of the types of soil and also any changes that may occur as you move along. In the transect illustrated, the soil changes from mud in water to dry soil, interrupted by a patch of compacted soil where the line crosses a footpath.

The point frame, made from some nails and a piece of wood, can be used to study plant communities. Stick it into the ground in various places, and count the number of plants that actually touch the nails. Note which kind of plant is most common in each habitat.

Meadowsweet

strife   Greater willowherb   Meadow buttercup   Rye grass   Daisy   Plantain   Daisy   Meadow buttercup   Yarrow

135

FRUITS AND SEEDS

A look at the fruits and seeds of herbaceous plants, and how they are scattered to perpetuate the species

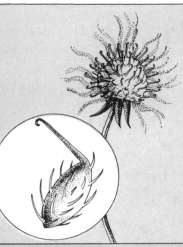

The avens fruit; its hook is formed from the style of the flower. This is a long projection from the carpel or seed-box.

The egg-shaped burrs of the cocklebur are clothed with hooks formed from leaf-like bracts. Each burr contains two fruits.

Burdock hooks are also formed from bracts surrounding the flower heads.

Next time you come home from a country walk and find your clothes covered in sticky burrs, don't merely pull them off and throw them away: take a close look at them – with your lens if necessary – and examine the wonderful construction of the tiny hooks that get caught in your clothing. They are extremely efficient grapnels, designed specifically to hook into fur and wool. The burrs are the fruits of various plants, and the hooks provide an excellent means of scattering them. Consider, too, how far you carried the burrs, and how far other animals such as hares or deer might carry them.

All the flowering plants reproduce by scattering seeds, although some have other methods of reproduction as well. The seeds all grow inside the fruits and they are scattered when they are ripe. Some herbaceous plants bear juicy fruits whose seeds are scattered by birds in the same way as those borne on trees (see page 116), but most herbaceous fruits are dry when they are ripe. In many species the fruits themselves are scattered, while in others the fruits stay on the plants and split open to release the seeds. It is quite easy to decide if an object is a fruit or a seed after it has left the parent plant because a fruit always has two scars on it – one showing where it was attached to the plant, and one showing where the stigma of the flower was attached to it (see page 146).

A seed has only one scar, called the hilum, showing where it was attached to the inside of the fruit.

Some herbaceous plants, such as buttercups, simply drop their fruits or seeds on to the ground beneath them, but the majority have some definite method of dispersing their seeds. This is of great importance for the survival of the species, as explained on page 116. The use of hooks to ensure dispersal by animals has already been mentioned, but if you study the hooked fruits carefully you will see that the hooks have several different origins. The burrs of the burdock are actually complete fruiting heads and they contain numerous small, one-seeded fruits.

When a burr becomes attached to an animal it can be carried for many miles, and the small fruits gradually get shaken out. Other burrs can also be carried long distances before the animal manages to scratch or rub them off.

The wind plays an important role in the dispersal of many fruits and seeds, as will be obvious to anyone who has blown a dandelion 'clock' or seen the clouds of thistledown drifting away from a field of ripe thistle heads. Many of the weeds that spring up in your garden originally arrived on the breeze. The parachutes of the dandelions and thistles and other composites are outgrowths from the little single-seeded

fruits and they can carry these fruits for many miles.

The seeds of poppies, foxgloves, and many other plants are also scattered by the wind. The seed capsules are carried on slender, but rather stiff stems which sway in the breeze and flick out the seeds as they return rather sharply to their upright positions. Collect a few ripe heads of poppies or columbines by cutting their stems as low down as possible, and then fix them firmly into a clothes peg or some other holder and place them on top of an old sheet. Bend the stems gently back and let them go. Watch the seeds shoot out and measure how far they travel over the sheet. You will be surprised

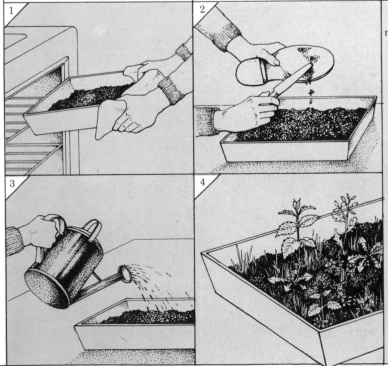

Many seeds that don't appear to have any special dispersal mechanism become sticky when wet and they then attach themselves to the feet of birds and other animals. You will often bring seeds home in the mud on your shoes. Carry out the following simple experiment to see just how many seeds you do bring home. Sterilize some soil in a metal tray by heating it in an oven (1). Scrape the mud from your shoes on to the sterilized soil (2) and water it well (3). Cover the tray with glass and leave it in a warm place for a week or two. You will be surprised how many plants, mostly common weeds, come up (4). Try the same experiment with the dust collected from your pockets after a country walk.

The hooks of the agrimony form a ring around the top of a two-seeded fruit.

The fruit wall of the goosegrass or cleavers is covered with tiny hooks.

Willowherb fruits are long and slender and they split open to release clouds of fluffy seeds.

Goldfinches and other birds eat lots of plantain seeds, but they scatter many more which can grow into new plants.

how far they go, and remember that this distance will be greatly increased in windy conditions because the seeds themselves are light and easily blown about.

Not all plants rely on outside agencies to scatter their seeds: many employ explosive methods to throw their seeds out of their fruits. The best known perhaps is the balsam, whose scientific name of *Impatiens* is very apt: you have only to squeeze the ripening fruits gently for them to fire their seeds out in all directions. Liquid pressure building up in the pods is responsible for the rupture of the balsam fruits, but most other explosive fruits split open as they dry out. Collect some ripe fruits of vetch, or garden peas or beans, and dry them out thoroughly in front of a fire. Notice how the pods split along two sides and throw the seeds out with some force. There is often a loud bang as they split. See how far the seeds travel. The fruits of the violet squeeze their seeds out as the fruits' valves contract on drying, and so do the fruits of the caper spurge. The seeds of the latter are thrown out so vigorously that they can crack a window.

Make a collection of different kinds of fruits and seeds, labelling each with its method of dispersal. Many of the fruit capsules make attractive decorations when dried; they can also be sprayed with paints.

The dandelion 'parachute' is beautifully designed to carry the fruit away on the lightest breeze. See how far you can blow the fruits with a single puff.

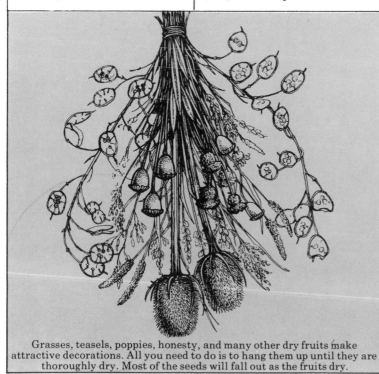

Grasses, teasels, poppies, honesty, and many other dry fruits make attractive decorations. All you need to do is to hang them up until they are thoroughly dry. Most of the seeds will fall out as the fruits dry.

The bean seed clearly shows the scar (hilum) where it was fixed inside the pod.

Stresses build up in the bean pod as it dries, and it eventually splits along both edges to throw out the seeds.

137

THE GROWING PLANT

Simple projects to see how plants live, and respond to their surroundings

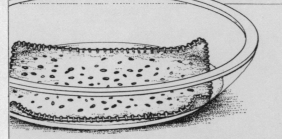

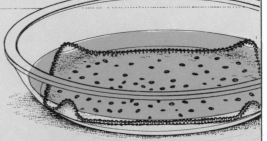

Conditions for Growth
Seeds will not grow just anywhere or any time: they require certain conditions before they will burst into growth. This simple experiment can be used to demonstrate these conditions to young children.

1. Seeds of mustard or cress will not grow on dry flannel.

2. Seeds will not grow if they are immersed in boiled water (from which the dissolved oxygen has been driven out) and which is then covered with a thin film of cooking oil to keep out the oxygen.

A green plant's life revolves mainly around light, water, and carbon dioxide from the air. These are the three things it needs to make its basic food materials of sugar and starch, although other minerals are needed for efficient growth (see page 140).

Light is, of course, normally obtained from the sun, and it is trapped by the green chlorophyll in the leaves where its energy powers the food-making process called photosynthesis. If you examine the arrangement of the leaves on a plant, especially by looking up through the branches of a tree, you will see that they are spread out to catch as much light as possible. You will not find one leaf immediately under another.

When a plant is illuminated on just one side, it automatically bends over towards that side. You can see this very clearly when you keep pot-plants on the window sill. The bending movements, called tropisms, are brought about by the faster growth of the shaded side of the stem, an effect which itself is brought about by the greater concentration of growth-hormones on that side. The movements are actually controlled by the tip of the shoot, however, and you can prove this very easily with a simple experiment. Sow some onion or grass seeds, or better still a few oat or other cereal seeds gleaned from the fields, and put them on the window sill. As they grow, you will see the

seedlings bend over towards the light. Turn the dish round and the seedlings will bend back and straighten up. Then cap some of them with tiny hoods made of aluminium foil. The hooded seedlings will continue to grow straight, but the others will bend towards the light again.

If you keep plants continuously in the dark they will be unable to make the green chlorophyll and they will become very pale. In an attempt to reach some light, they will go on growing upwards and become very spindly, and they will eventually die if kept in the dark.

Plants make other kinds of bending movements in response to gravity. If you turn a small potted plant on its side the shoot will very soon bend upwards again, and the root will turn downwards. You can also see this effect by growing seeds in a jam jar as shown on the opposite page. The roots will always grow downwards, no matter what position the seed is in.

You can observe other kinds of movement in flowers such as crocuses and lawn daisies, which open and shut according to the weather. Such movements are not tropisms because they are not directional. They are called nastic movements. Crocus opening is controlled by the temperature, but daisies open and shut according to the light intensity. Some of the carnivorous plants, such as the sundews and the venus fly-trap, move their leaves when stimulated by insects that land on them, and the movements are

designed so that the insects become trapped. The best-known movements, however, are those of the sensitive plant (*Mimosa*), which literally folds up its leaves when touched. If you have one of these plants, touch it to make it collapse and then see how long it takes to recover. Special thin-walled cells at the bases of the leaves release water when the plant is touched, and this causes the collapse.

Plants absorb water from the soil and distribute

it through their bodies in a system of fine tubes or veins. These are easily seen in leaves, and you can see them when you cut thin sections of the stem to examine under the microscope (see page 168). You can also see the arrangement of the veins in the stems by dipping the stems into water containing ink or dye, and leaving them for a few hours. Cut through the stems and you will see circles of coloured dots – these are the bundles of veins. Red ink or dye is

The stems and leaves of green plants always turn towards the light, as you will know if you have ever kept a potted plant on the window sill. This is a natural reaction which ensures that the plants get the maximum amount of light with which to make food.

You can prove that it is the tips of the stems that are sensitive to the light by covering the tips with aluminium foil. The covered tips do not bend over.

3. Seeds will not grow if placed in a refrigerator, even if they are kept moist.

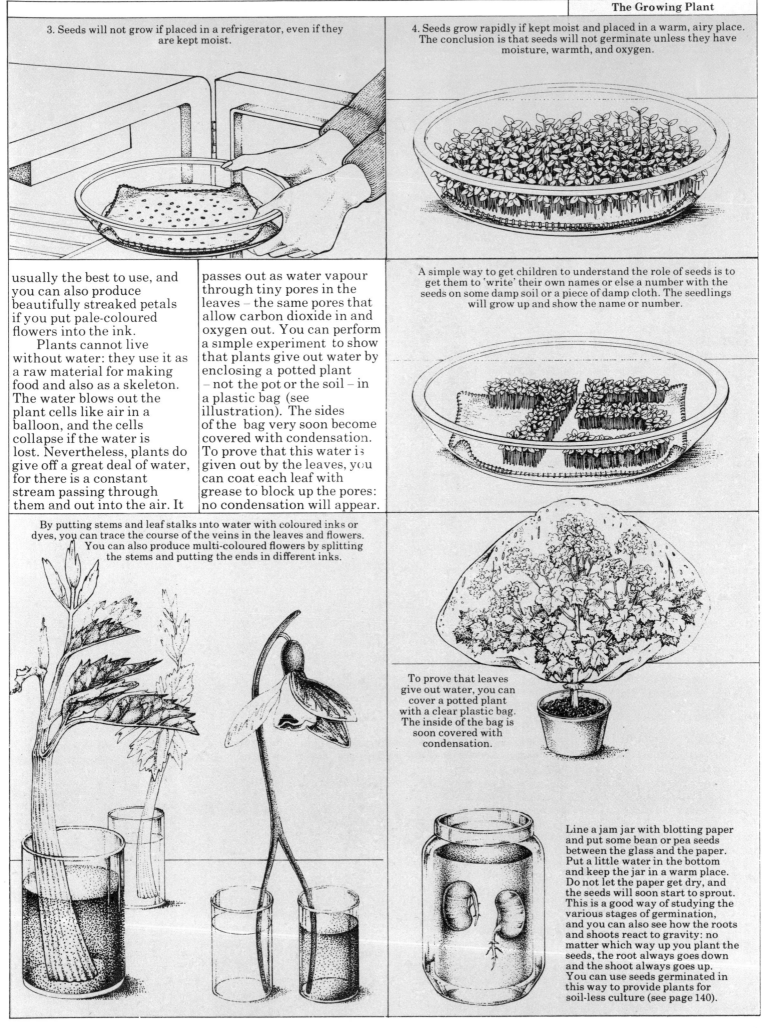

4. Seeds grow rapidly if kept moist and placed in a warm, airy place. The conclusion is that seeds will not germinate unless they have moisture, warmth, and oxygen.

usually the best to use, and you can also produce beautifully streaked petals if you put pale-coloured flowers into the ink.

Plants cannot live without water: they use it as a raw material for making food and also as a skeleton. The water blows out the plant cells like air in a balloon, and the cells collapse if the water is lost. Nevertheless, plants do give off a great deal of water, for there is a constant stream passing through them and out into the air. It passes out as water vapour through tiny pores in the leaves – the same pores that allow carbon dioxide in and oxygen out. You can perform a simple experiment to show that plants give out water by enclosing a potted plant – not the pot or the soil – in a plastic bag (see illustration). The sides of the bag very soon become covered with condensation. To prove that this water is given out by the leaves, you can coat each leaf with grease to block up the pores: no condensation will appear.

A simple way to get children to understand the role of seeds is to get them to 'write' their own names or else a number with the seeds on some damp soil or a piece of damp cloth. The seedlings will grow up and show the name or number.

By putting stems and leaf stalks into water with coloured inks or dyes, you can trace the course of the veins in the leaves and flowers. You can also produce multi-coloured flowers by splitting the stems and putting the ends in different inks.

To prove that leaves give out water, you can cover a potted plant with a clear plastic bag. The inside of the bag is soon covered with condensation.

Line a jam jar with blotting paper and put some bean or pea seeds between the glass and the paper. Put a little water in the bottom and keep the jar in a warm place. Do not let the paper get dry, and the seeds will soon start to sprout. This is a good way of studying the various stages of germination, and you can also see how the roots and shoots react to gravity: no matter which way up you plant the seeds, the root always goes down and the shoot always goes up. You can use seeds germinated in this way to provide plants for soil-less culture (see page 140).

PLANTS WITHOUT SOIL

An introduction to hydroponics – an absorbing hobby and a potentially important way of growing food

Green plants make their basic food materials, which are sugars, from water and from carbon dioxide gas in the air. The plants also need a number of other vital substances, such as nitrogen, phosphorus, potassium, and so on. The roots absorb these materials with the water from the soil, but the soil itself is not an essential requirement for plant growth. Many water plants float freely in the water, and it is possible to grow most other plants without soil as long as they are provided with a solution of the right mineral salts. It may be that in future times much of our food will be grown in soilless cultures.

You can do some simple investigations yourself to see what minerals are necessary for the proper growth of plants. Each mineral has a particular function, and by omitting the various minerals from your culture solutions (see below) you can get some idea of what this role is (see illustrations).

Start off some broad bean or cereal seeds in jam jars with blotting paper, as shown on page 138. The seedlings will grow quite well to start with because there is a good food reserve in the seed. When the seedlings are large enough, transfer them to the experimental jars, each of which has a different solution in it. Some kind of lid is necessary, and the simplest is a piece of cardboard taped to the jar. Cut a hole large enough to take the plant, which can be supported if necessary by a plug of cotton wool. Another hole is necessary for aeration, because roots need oxygen and you must pump some air down into the water each day with some kind of bellows. Do not simply blow into the water, as this will introduce carbon dioxide instead of oxygen. The jars must be surrounded by black plastic or paper to keep out the light: unless this is done, algae will grow in the water and quickly clog the roots.

The major elements needed by plants are nitrogen (which is almost always used in the form of nitrates), phosphorus, potassium, magnesium, calcium, iron, and sulphur. These are all used to build new plant material and growth is stunted to a greater or lesser degree if the plant cannot get enough of them. There are also a number of other elements, such as molybdenum, manganese, and boron, which are needed in minute amounts to keep the plant working properly. They are called trace elements and they are perhaps the plant equivalent of vitamins.

One of your culture jars must contain all the major elements listed above, and this is called the control jar. The plant in it should grow well, at least for the duration of the experiment. (You need not bother to include the trace elements because they are needed in such minute amounts that enough are probably present as impurities in the other minerals that you use. Some will also be provided in the original seeds.) The formula for making up the complete solution is given in the column on the right. Each of the other culture jars has one of the important elements missing, but you need not test every element if you are just doing the investigation for fun.

Always dissolve the minerals in distilled water to prevent contamination. Tapwater always has quite a lot of minerals dissolved in it, and you can try growing a plant in it just to see what it does and does not contain. You can buy distilled water from a chemist or a garage (it is

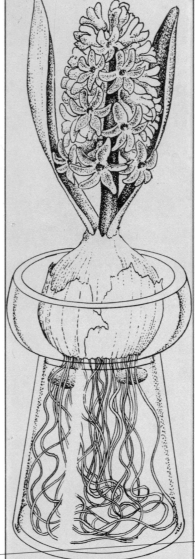

Many people grow hyacinths and other bulbs on the hydroponic principle. You can get the bulbs to flower by sitting them in plain water, but here, of course, the leaves are drawing on food stored in the bulb. After flowering, the bulb must be put into the garden, or into a complete culture solution to allow it to build up more reserves.

used for car batteries) or else you can obtain some by melting down the ice that builds up around the freezer in your refrigerator. Try growing a plant in distilled water – there should be no growth at all.

An alternative method of growing plants without soil is to grow them in pots of pure, washed sand. These stand in or are watered by the complete culture solution. The sand has no nutrient value and cannot be called soil. The advantage of this method is that you do not have to bother about aeration: the sand is very porous and plenty of air finds its way into the spaces around the plant roots.

Formulae for the Culture Solutions

The Complete Solution for the Control Jar
1 gm calcium sulphate
1 gm calcium phosphate
1 gm magnesium sulphate
3 gm potassium nitrate
0·02 gm (a *minute pinch*) ferric chloride
0·2 gm common salt (sodium chloride).

Dissolve these substances in 4 litres (0·88 gallon) of distilled water.

The amounts involved here are very small (remember that there are 28 grams in one ounce) and you will need a scientific balance to weigh them accurately. Absolute accuracy is not essential, but you must not overdo things too much because an excess of one nutrient can prevent the roots from absorbing enough of another. Excess nutrients can poison the roots.

The Solution without Magnesium
Use ½ gram of potassium sulphate instead of the magnesium sulphate.

The Solution without Calcium
Use 1 gram of potassium sulphate instead of calcium sulphate, and 3 grams of sodium phosphate instead of calcium phosphate.

The Solution without Iron
Simply omit the tiny pinch of ferric chloride.

The Solution without Potassium
Use 2 grams of sodium nitrate instead of the potassium nitrate.

The Solution without Phosphorus
Use ½ gram of calcium nitrate instead of the calcium phosphate.

The Solution without Nitrogen
Use 2 grams of potassium chloride instead of the potassium nitrate.

The Solution without Sulphur
Use ½ gram of calcium chloride instead of calcium sulphate, and 1 gram of magnesium chloride instead of the magnesium sulphate.

Without Magnesium
The plant is very yellow, because magnesium is necessary for the formation of green chlorophyll.

Without Calcium
Growth of root and shoot are both stunted, because calcium is an important building material.

Without Iron
The plant is stunted and yellow because it cannot make chlorophyll.

The Control Plant
Growth is vigorous in all parts (the light-excluding cover has been cut away so that you can see the roots), and the leaves are a healthy green.

Use a simple form of bellows or a cycle pump to blow air down through the solution, employing a piece of plastic or glass tubing to ensure that the air really does get right down to the bottom. The air will escape again around the base of the plant.

If you use sand-culture methods to grow your plants you do not need to worry about aerating the roots. Stand the pots in clean sand and water this regularly.

Without Phosphorus
The leaves die at an early stage, and the growth of the whole plant is very stunted because food is made very slowly.

Without Potassium
Early growth is not much affected, but leaves become yellowish later and do not produce good flowers or fruit.

Without Nitrogen
Most plants show very little growth, because nitrogen is an essential constituent of all living matter.

Without Sulphur
The plant is stunted and pale in colour, for sulphur is an important constituent of many living tissues.

Plant Growing in Tapwater
The results vary according to the nature of the tapwater, but the plants are usually stunted through lack of nitrogen.

FERNS AND SPORES

The fascinating life histories of the ferns and related flowerless plants

The ferns and their allies – the horsetails and clubmosses – are all flowerless plants belonging to a large group known as pteridophytes. Like the mosses described on the previous page, they all reproduce by spores, but their life histories are somewhat more complicated.

The leaves of most ferns are finely divided and, apart from the tree ferns of tropical regions, they all spring from underground stems. The way in which the leaves uncurl is very characteristic and this makes it easy to identify most ferns. Most common ferns carry their spores on the undersides of the ordinary leaves or fronds, and you can clearly see the spore-bearing regions on a mature leaf. They look like little rusty patches, although in some ferns the delicate spore-capsules are covered with a protective shield. Try shaking the fronds on a dry day, and you will see clouds of minute spores drifting away on the breeze. Like the mosses, the ferns release their spores only when the weather is dry, and you can see how they arrange this by carrying out the simple experiment shown on the far right.

The spore of a typical fern, falling on suitably moist ground, will soon germinate and grow into a little heart-shaped green disc called a prothallus. This looks nothing like the parent fern, but it is a key stage in the life history of the species. It is a very clear example of

Life Cycle of a Fern

The spores of a fern are extremely small and they are produced in little stalked capsules which are normally borne on the undersides of the ordinary leaves. Each spore is a single cell with a tough wall around it, but this tiny cell carries enough 'information' in it for it to be able to grow into the heart-shaped prothallus. When it first germinates, the spore puts out a minute green thread, which immediately starts making food and then gradually produces the new cells which make up the prothallus. A number of root-like hairs hold the prothallus on the ground. After fertilization of the female cell or the prothallus (see text), a tiny new fern plant begins to grow. It takes food from the prothallus at first, but gradually starts to make its own food as its own leaves start to grow. The first few leaves are often very simple and quite unlike later ones. Watch the stages of growth by scattering some spores on to some potting compost in a plastic box and keeping it moist. Plant the new ferns back in the wild, or in your garden.

what biologists call the alternation of generations. The prothallus is, in fact, the equivalent of the whole moss plant, because it is here, on the prothallus, that the male and female reproductive organs are produced. As in the mosses, the male cells are attracted to the female cells by a chemical stimulus, and they swim to them in the film of water covering the prothallus. This reliance on a film of water for the reproductive process means that, although some individual fern plants can survive a good deal of drought, fern communities are usually found only in rather moist situations – shady forests, the banks of streams, and so on. Some species even live in water, although they do not look much like ordinary ferns

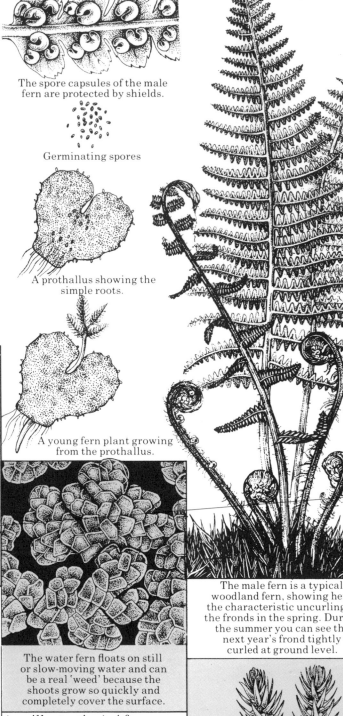

The spore capsules of the male fern are protected by shields.

Germinating spores

A prothallus showing the simple roots.

A young fern plant growing from the prothallus.

The male fern is a typical woodland fern, showing here the characteristic uncurling of the fronds in the spring. During the summer you can see the next year's frond tightly curled at ground level.

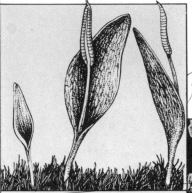

The adder's tongue fern looks quite unlike a normal fern. Its spore capsules are clustered around the central spike.

The water fern floats on still or slow-moving water and can be a real 'weed' because the shoots grow so quickly and completely cover the surface.

(see illustration). After fertilization, the female cell gradually develops into a new fern plant.

All the pteridophytes are much less significant in the world's vegetation today than they were 300 million years ago. Then, they included huge tree-like forms which spread over vast areas and formed the coal forests.

The clubmosses and horsetails were especially large in those ancient times, but today they are all small plants, rarely more than a

Clubmosses are so named because they carry their spores on special leaves which are grouped into club-shaped cones. Apart from this, they look much more like mosses than ferns.

metre (39 in) high. Both groups have a prothallus stage in their life history.

The ripe horsetail cone opens up and each scale looks like a little up-turned box, from which the spores can fall.

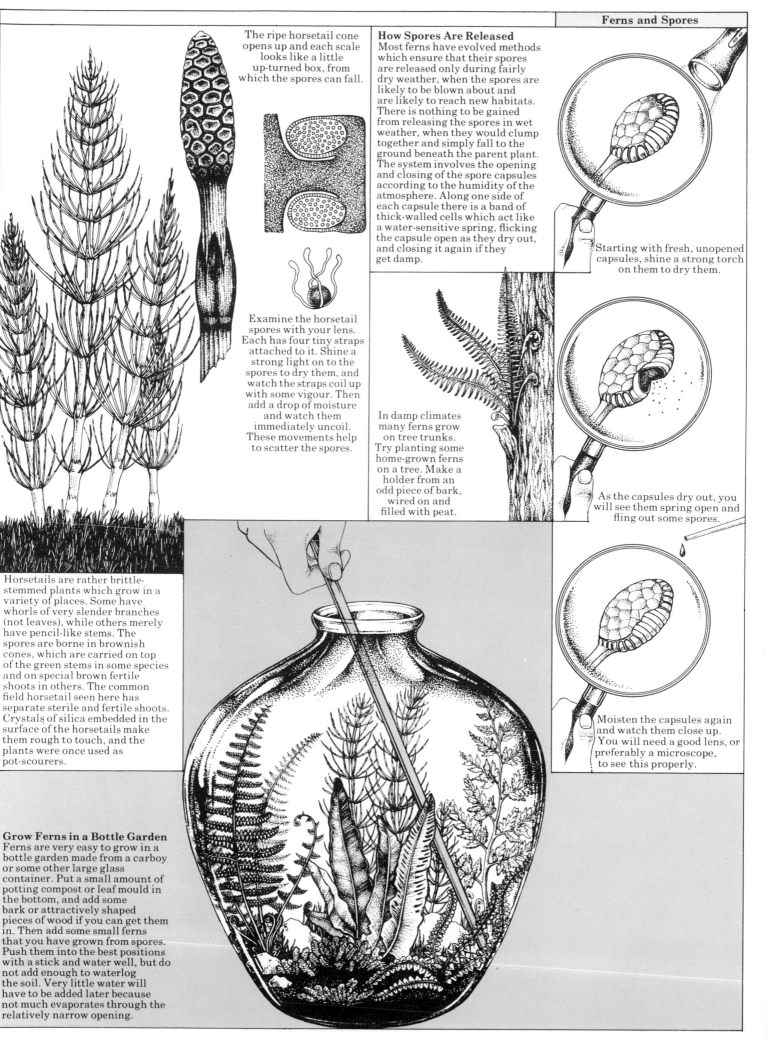

How Spores Are Released
Most ferns have evolved methods which ensure that their spores are released only during fairly dry weather, when the spores are likely to be blown about and are likely to reach new habitats. There is nothing to be gained from releasing the spores in wet weather, when they would clump together and simply fall to the ground beneath the parent plant. The system involves the opening and closing of the spore capsules according to the humidity of the atmosphere. Along one side of each capsule there is a band of thick-walled cells which act like a water-sensitive spring, flicking the capsule open as they dry out, and closing it again if they get damp.

Examine the horsetail spores with your lens. Each has four tiny straps attached to it. Shine a strong light on to the spores to dry them, and watch the straps coil up with some vigour. Then add a drop of moisture and watch them immediately uncoil. These movements help to scatter the spores.

In damp climates many ferns grow on tree trunks. Try planting some home-grown ferns on a tree. Make a holder from an odd piece of bark, wired on and filled with peat.

Starting with fresh, unopened capsules, shine a strong torch on them to dry them.

As the capsules dry out, you will see them spring open and fling out some spores.

Moisten the capsules again and watch them close up. You will need a good lens, or preferably a microscope, to see this properly.

Horsetails are rather brittle-stemmed plants which grow in a variety of places. Some have whorls of very slender branches (not leaves), while others merely have pencil-like stems. The spores are borne in brownish cones, which are carried on top of the green stems in some species and on special brown fertile shoots in others. The common field horsetail seen here has separate sterile and fertile shoots. Crystals of silica embedded in the surface of the horsetails make them rough to touch, and the plants were once used as pot-scourers.

Grow Ferns in a Bottle Garden
Ferns are very easy to grow in a bottle garden made from a carboy or some other large glass container. Put a small amount of potting compost or leaf mould in the bottom, and add some bark or attractively shaped pieces of wood if you can get them in. Then add some small ferns that you have grown from spores. Push them into the best positions with a stick and water well, but do not add enough to waterlog the soil. Very little water will have to be added later because not much evaporates through the relatively narrow opening.

143

MOSSES AND LICHENS

Exploring the anatomy and habitats of these low-growing plants

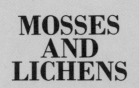

Mosses and lichens are two groups of relatively lowly plants that frequently grow together and are often confused with each other. In fact, they are quite unrelated. The mosses are leafy plants, while the lichens are rather special kinds of fungi. Neither group has any flowers.

The mosses usually grow in neat cushions or mats, but if you examine them closely you will see that each clump is composed of numerous separate stems, up to several centimetres long. Each stem has a number of very delicate leaves, but no real root. At certain times of the year you might see tightly packed

generally found only in damp habitats, although some can survive a fair amount of drying. After fertilization the female cell grows into a spore capsule, which rises up on a stalk from the top of the moss stem. The young capsule may be upright or hanging, but it always has some kind of hood on it. This eventually drops off and reveals another cap. As the spores ripen inside, this cap becomes detached in one way or another and in many species it reveals a set of radiating teeth (see illustration opposite). The teeth are sensitive to humidity and remain closed in damp weather, but if you collect some capsules and dry them out you will see the teeth curl back to allow

related to mosses, although their spore capsules are much simpler. Some liverworts look very much like mosses, but others (see illustration opposite) look more like flat green seaweeds. They generally grow in even damper places than mosses – wet woodland paths, stream banks, and the sides of waterfalls being favourite places. Many possess little cups containing detachable buds called gemmae. The buds are washed out by raindrops and they may be carried away by surface water. They eventually grow into new liverworts.

Lichens are extremely hardy plants that consist of a combination of a fungus and an alga (see page 134). They are often found high

'fingers' closely pressed to the surface. These flattened forms grow extremely slowly, but at a fairly constant rate in a given area. They can be used for getting a rough idea of the age of old buildings. Look at some lichen patches on gravestones in your local cemetery, and measure their diameters. Dates on the gravestones will give you the maximum ages of the lichen patches.

Although lichens are very hardy in most respects, they are very intolerant of atmospheric pollution and you will not find many in large towns. You can actually do a simple experiment to see how their numbers are affected by pollution. Starting from the town centre, or from some

Mosses are always green and the wall-dwelling species are always on the shady side.

Wall-dwelling lichens are generally grey or orange. They are found mainly on the drier side of the wall, where they are not overshadowed by the larger mosses.

Mosses are best preserved by drying them thoroughly and putting them into clear plastic bags, which you can attach to the pages of a loose-leaf book.

clusters of leaves, almost like flowers, at the tops of some stems. Male and female cells are formed here, and the male cells swim to the female ones to fertilize them. Fertilization cannot take place in dry conditions, and so the mosses are

the spores to escape. Shake some spores on to some damp blotting paper and keep it moist. You will see the spores put out minute threads, from which new moss plants will grow.

Liverworts are small plants which are closely

on mountain crags where the temperature rarely rises above freezing point, and they can also grow on rocks which get so much sun that they are too hot for us to touch. Many grow on sea cliffs, walls, tree trunks, and poor heathland soils. The fungus partner absorbs minerals from the surroundings, while the alga makes food by photosynthesis. The fungus passes minerals to the alga and receives sugars in return, so both partners benefit. Grey and green are the dominant colours of lichens, but there are also red and orange species.

There are three main shapes among the lichens. Some, including the pixie-cups, grow more or less upright and look like tiny trees or bushes. Some form crusts on rocks, while others consist of spreading

other source of pollution such as a large factory site, move away towards open country. At suitable intervals, count the number of lichen patches on a 10-metre (33-ft) stretch of wall (make sure all the walls you examine are of similar construction) or on a tree trunk (again, make sure the trees are of the same kind). You will find that the farther you go, the more numerous the lichen patches. If you want to collect lichens, you will need a strong knife to slice pieces from tree trunks, and a hammer and chisel to chip out pieces of lichen-encrusted rock. Once you have taken your specimens you need do nothing to them apart from keeping them dry and free from dust. They have virtually no water in them and they are best placed in clear plastic bags.

A mature moss plant with capsules in various stages of development.

A highly magnified view of the mouth of a dry moss capsule, showing how the teeth are curled back to allow the spores to escape. Not all mosses have teeth like this.

Pixie-cup lichens, which are usually about 2 cm (¾ in) high, grow on tree stumps and on the ground in many different habitats.

Marchantia, a liverwort, has a number of crown-like cups (gemmae) which contain buds. Try dropping water into them to see how far the gemmae are scattered.

Reindeer moss is one of the shrub-like lichens. It grows on mountains and moorlands, but is especially abundant in the Arctic region, where it is a major food of the reindeer.

Collect lichens from bark with a sharp knife, but take only a thin sliver of bark with each one.

The dog lichen is especially common on sand dunes and in other grassy places, where its steely grey lobes spread over the ground.

Mosses are very easy to grow at home as long as you give them plenty of humidity. An old fish tank covered with a sheet of glass makes a good container, or you can use a gardener's propagator as shown here. Arrange logs and stones on potting compost and lay the mosses on them.

145

PRESSING AND DRYING WILD FLOWERS

How to make a collection of wild flowers, with due regard to the conservation of rare species

One of the pleasantest things about a country walk is to see the wild flowers in the fields and on the roadsides. The temptation to pick the flowers and take them home is understandable, but it is much better to leave them for others to see and for them to reproduce themselves. Remember that it is the flowers that produce the seeds, and without seeds there can be no future generations of flowers for you and your descendants to enjoy. Wholesale picking of flowers seriously threatens seed production and can do nothing but harm to the future of the countryside. In some countries legislation makes it an offence to pick some of the rarer flowers, but the responsible naturalist will not do any harm by picking an occasional specimen of the commoner species. This is sometimes necessary for the accurate identification of certain species which are classified on the basis of minute differences in structure.

Now that one can record flower colours faithfully by means of colour photography, the traditional hobby of pressing flowers has lost much of its charm, but photography cannot record the minute details which the botanist often needs to see, and a reference collection of pressed plants still has its uses. The following information will help the amateur naturalist to build up a good reference collection of common plant.

The first essential piece of equipment is a container in which to put your flowers when you have picked them. You can buy special containers called vascula (see illustration opposite), but a biscuit tin or a plastic freezer container will do just as well, and a simple clear plastic bag is quite adequate as long as you are careful not to squash it. The essential point is to prevent your specimens from wilting before you get them home. Do not lay your container in the sun, for this is a sure way to cook the plants. You can pick most herbaceous stems without aid, but the tougher ones should be cut with scissors or secateurs to prevent damage to the rest of the plant. Cut the stems as low down as possible, so that you get examples of the lower leaves as well as the upper ones, but do not dig up the roots. If you take more than one piece from each plant – you will need to do this with plants like dandelions which bear their leaves and flower stalks quite separately – be sure to tie the pieces together before putting them into your container. Label the material at this stage, for you can easily forget just where you collected it.

The usual way of preserving the flowers and other parts of the plants which you collect is by pressing them, and for this you need some sheets of clean, absorbent paper. Blotting paper is good, but not essential. You need some kind of press as well, because the method really involves squeezing all the moisture out of the plants. You can buy specially made plant presses from biological supply companies. They are usually made of strong steel mesh (see opposite), but you can make a perfectly good press with two sheets of hardboard or plywood about 45 × 30 cm (18 × 12 in). Drill a few holes in the boards to allow evaporation, and tie an old belt or luggage strap around them to apply the pressure.

Put some sheets of newspaper on the lower half of the press and cover these with one or two sheets of blotting or other clean, absorbent paper. Your specimens can then be arranged on this paper. The stems of tall specimens can be bent into zig-zags, or even cut, but in general try to get the plant looking as natural as possible. Turn the leaves so that you can see the upper surface of one and the lower surface of another, for the textures of the leaf surfaces are often important in identifying specimens. Tubular flowers and the bulky flower-heads of plants like thistles can be cut down through the middle so that you can see their internal

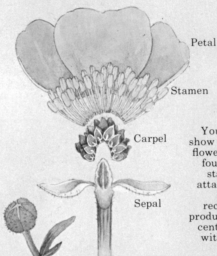

Your pressed specimens should show the detailed structure of the flower as far as possible. There are four main parts: sepals, petals, stamens, and carpels. All are attached to the swollen tip of the stalk, which is called the receptacle. The carpels, which produce the seeds, are always in the centre, but they may be enclosed within the receptacle some way below the petals.

structure. Having arranged your plants to your satisfaction, cover them with one or two more sheets of absorbent paper and then some more newspaper before putting on the top of the press and tightening it. You can, of course, press several layers of plants at one time as long as you separate each layer by two sheets of absorbent paper. Leave the press for a few days, preferably in a warm room, and then open it up and renew the paper if necessary. Small and delicate plants should not need this treatment, but the bulkier specimens might need several changes of paper before all the moisture has been absorbed.

The time needed to dry your specimens thoroughly obviously depends on the amount of moisture in them to start with and on the temperature of the room, but you can usually remove them from the press after about three weeks and put them into your collection. A loose-leaf folder with large sheets makes a good container for your specimens. Attach the plants to the sheets with small pieces of gummed paper as shown in the illustration. If you collect seeds from the plant at a later date you can attach them to the sheet in a small transparent envelope. Label each sheet as fully as possible with the name of the plant, the date and locality in which you collected it, and the type of soil in which it was growing. These details all make your collection more valuable, because you can compare the sizes and other features of specimens growing under different conditions. Your flowers will always lose a lot of their original colours, and you will find it useful to make a small sketch at the time of collection to show what the colours were like. Attach the sketch to your herbarium sheet. Store the folder in a dry place to prevent mould growth on your specimens, and spray the sheets periodically with moth-proofer to prevent insect damage.

If you have to pick a specimen, take the smallest adequate piece of the plant, so that you leave the bulk of it for others to enjoy. Competitions for wild flower collections and arrangements should be discouraged, as these lead to heavy collection in one area.

You Will Need

A metal or plastic container
Some large sheets of blotting paper and newspaper
A press, made from steel mesh or hardboard
A large scrapbook or folder

Here are some common plants which you can press without fear of harming the populations. Below are some rarities which should not be picked under any circumstances.

Buttercup

Thistle

Daisy

Clover

Convolvulus

Mayweed

Scarlet pimpernel

Speedwell

Fritillary

Wild gladiolus

Snowdon lily

Spring gentian

The traditional botanist's vasculum, used for bringing home the plants.

Arranging the plants carefully on the absorbent paper of the plant press. The wire press shown here allows the moisture to evaporate away quickly, and so speeds drying, but you can make your own press from pieces of board. Failing that, you can press small plants under a heavy pile of books, as long as you use plenty of absorbent paper around the plants themselves.

Pressing flowers always distorts them, and if you want to preserve them in their true form you can try drying them in a sand bath. They will lose most of their colour, but they retain much of their minute detail. Full details of the method are given on page 148.

A loose-leaf folder is ideal for storing your collection of pressed plants, because new specimens can be added next to their relatives. Notice the packet of seeds, collected from the plant at a later date.

"Seen in The fall"

TOADSTOOLS AND OTHER FUNGI

Learning about toadstools, making spore prints from them, and growing spores in jelly

Every autumn a fine crop of toadstools pushes up through the fallen leaves on the woodland floor. Many are attractively coloured, and some advertise their presence with a nauseous smell: some are good to eat while others are deadly (see Chapter 10). These toadstools belong to a very large group of plants called fungi and none of them has any chlorophyll – the green colouring matter with which ordinary plants make their food. The fungi all absorb ready-made food from their surroundings – usually from the dead leaves and twigs. The toadstools which you see in the autumn are only a part of the fungus plants, for the majority of the fungus is in the form of fine threads absorbing food from deep down in the leaf layer. The toadstools are the reproductive parts of the plants and their job is to scatter the minute spores which eventually grow into new fungi. The spores of a typical toadstool are produced under the cap, either on the surfaces of radiating gills or on the linings of numerous tubular pores, and they drop down to be scattered by the wind. Other fungi use different methods. The stinkhorn, for example, carries its spores in a smelly fluid around the top. Flies are attracted to the fluid and they carry the spores away. Puffballs contain millions of spores and fire them out in clouds when touched by an animal or a rain-drop, or even when blown by the wind. The soft and transient

nature of most toadstools makes them better subjects for the artist or the photographer than for the collector, but you can make permanent specimens of some of them without much trouble. Whole toadstools can be 'pickled' in alcohol, and this is the way scientists often preserve them.

You can also preserve toadstools in their original shape by drying them carefully in a sand-bath. You need a metal dish and enough fine sand to bury your specimens. Lay the toadstools carefully on some sand in the bottom of the dish and then very gently pour sand over them until they are completely covered

to a depth of at least 2·5 cm (1 in). The sand must be completely dry to start with. Put the dish into a hot oven and leave it until the fungi are dry. You will need to experiment a few times to get the time and the temperature just right: the fungi must be properly dried, but you must avoid over-cooking, which will turn them into charcoal. A safer method for prize specimens is to lay them on sand in the dish and then pour on sand which has been heated in the oven. You can then leave the dish to cool slowly.

The dried toadstools are extremely fragile. Remove the sand from over them with a fine brush, and lift

the specimens out by the stalk. They lose a lot of colour, but they look very lifelike. Keep them upright in a closed glass container. The method works best with the smaller and more delicate species, which have less water in them.

Another very simple way of making a record of a toadstool is to make a spore print. You need a young toadstool with a freshly opened cap. It must be of the plain umbrella type, with a smooth lower margin for good results. Pick the toadstool and take it home carefully. Cut the stalk away flush with the cap and lay the cap, gills down, on a piece of paper. If the gills

are white, use black or coloured paper: if they are coloured, use white paper. Cover the cap with a jar or a basin to keep out draughts. A second cap of the same age is handy because you can use it to judge the time needed to make your print. Pick it up from time to time to see how the spores are building up on the paper. You may need an hour, or you may need several hours, depending on the ripeness of the cap. When you consider it is ready, remove the basin from your main specimen, without causing any draught, and very carefully lift up the cap. You will see the radiating pattern of the gills clearly reflected by the

Toadstools carry their spores either on the surfaces of radiating gills (*left*) or on the linings of tiny tubes or pores under the cap (*below*).

neat rows of spores that have been released. If you have left it too long, the spores will have formed little walls between the gills, and these walls will soon collapse.

Your new spore print is easily damaged because the spores are loose, but you can preserve it by spraying it *very lightly* with a fixative spray or varnish such as artists use on crayon or charcoal drawings. Test the very edge of the print with a fine brush, and if any spores come away you must give the print a further coat. Carry on with fine coats until there is no more smudging, and then give a final coat for permanent protection.

You can make prints from toadstools with pores as well as from those with gills, but it is difficult to find them with even edges to support them: if the pores sit right on the paper they will smudge the print when you lift the cap. Bracket fungi are not suitable for spore prints, nor are puffballs and stinkhorns, but you can examine the 'cloud patterns' of puffballs by tapping them gently.

If you have a good lens, or better still a microscope, you might like to grow some of the spores. Make up some gelatin and pour it into a shallow dish containing a few dead leaves. Let the jelly set and cool, and then scatter your spores on it. Keep it well covered and examine it every day for spore growth. Tiny threads will soon start to creep through the jelly if you keep it fairly warm. Better results can be obtained on special nutrient jelly which can be bought from biological supply companies.

You Will Need

For Making Spore Prints
A sharp knife or razor blade
Coloured and white paper
or thin card
Fixative spray
Basin

For Sand Preservation
Fine, dry sand
Metal dish

For Growing Spores
Gelatin

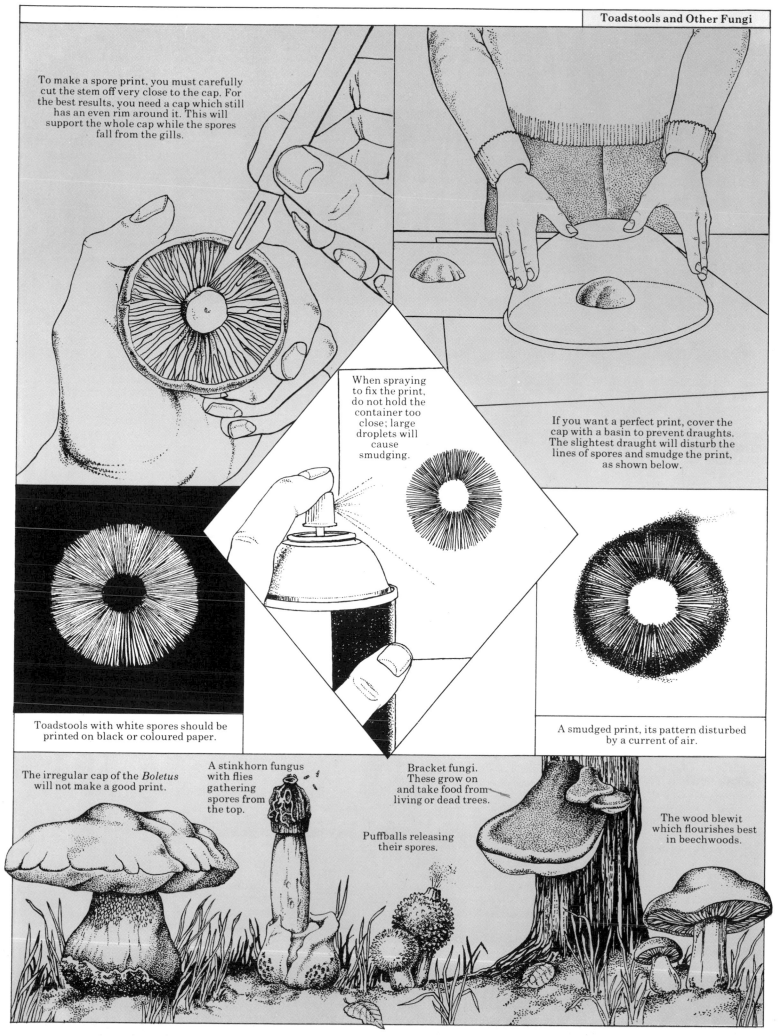

To make a spore print, you must carefully cut the stem off very close to the cap. For the best results, you need a cap which still has an even rim around it. This will support the whole cap while the spores fall from the gills.

When spraying to fix the print, do not hold the container too close; large droplets will cause smudging.

If you want a perfect print, cover the cap with a basin to prevent draughts. The slightest draught will disturb the lines of spores and smudge the print, as shown below.

Toadstools with white spores should be printed on black or coloured paper.

A smudged print, its pattern disturbed by a current of air.

The irregular cap of the *Boletus* will not make a good print.

A stinkhorn fungus with flies gathering spores from the top.

Bracket fungi. These grow on and take food from living or dead trees.

Puffballs releasing their spores.

The wood blewit which flourishes best in beechwoods.

VEGETABLE DYES

Boil up your own dyes from wild plants, and experiment with the shades and colour variations yielded by different dyestuffs

Boil up the vegetable material with the required amount of water and stir constantly. Some dyes must be boiled for longer than others.

Make sure there is plenty of room in your bowl for the alum and the wool, and do not stir too much.

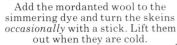

Add the mordanted wool to the simmering dye and turn the skeins *occasionally* with a stick. Lift them out when they are cold.

In the days before artificial chemical dyes were available, nearly all colouring materials were produced from wild plants. A few of these plants, such as woad and indigo, were actually cultivated, but most dyestuffs were required in smaller quantities and the wild-growing plants were able to provide enough material. The dye-yielding plants are still plentiful in the countryside and, although dyeing with them is certainly more trouble than using a packet of commercial dye, there is something exciting about making up your own dyes, especially if you also collect and weave your own wool. You cannot achieve the range of colours obtainable with artificial dyes, but the natural dyes do produce some very attractive shades.

Silk, linen, and cotton can all be dyed with natural vegetable dyes, but they are more difficult to handle. The beginner is advised to stick to wool, and the information given on this page is concerned only with the dyeing of wool.

Lichens of various kinds (see page 142) can be used for dyeing, and they have the advantage that the wool does not need any prior treatment. *Xanthoria parietina*, the bright golden lichen that grows so commonly on old walls and roofs, gives a rich yellowish brown colour to wool. The method is to collect about 500 gm (about 1 lb) of lichen for every 500 gm of wool and boil the lichen in a large bowl of water for two or

three hours. Let it get cold, and then add the wool, which should be thoroughly wetted first. Boil it all up again until the wool has the required depth of colour. Let it get cold before removing the wool, which you must then wash thoroughly in cold water. The best time to collect lichens for dyeing is in the winter, or after heavy rain. They can be scraped from the substrate more easily at such times.

When using most other vegetable dyes you must first treat the wool with a mordant, otherwise the dye will not hold fast. Several chemicals can be used as mordants, but the most frequently used is a mixture of alum and cream of tartar. For 500 gm of wool you need about 100 gm of alum and 25 gm of cream of tartar dissolved in a large bowl or saucepan of cold water. Start to boil up the water, and add the wool as the water gets warm. Bring to the boil and then simmer for about an hour – slightly less for fine wool, which also requires slightly less alum. Lift the wool out while still warm, gently squeeze the water out, and put the wool into a container until you are ready to dye it. You can dye it straight away, but it is better to leave it for a day or two to soak thoroughly.

The method for other dyes is much the same as that used for lichens. Put the plant material into cold water and bring it to the boil slowly, simmer for a while, and then add the wool. You should stir regularly while boiling the dyestuff, but do not stir after you have added the wool, for this will cause the wool to

mat together. Use a smooth stick to turn the wool a few times and to lift it out after dyeing. Plastic sticks, such as large knitting needles, are very useful for this. The wool should be simmered gently until it has acquired the right depth of colour – remember that when wet it always looks darker than it really is – and you should then leave it in the liquid until cold. Lift it out, squeeze out the excess dye and wash the wool thoroughly.

The following recipes will help you to produce the colours shown on the opposite page. The quantities given are all for dyeing about 500 gm (about 1 lb) of wool, and the wool should have been mordanted with alum in the way described above.

1. One kilogram (about 2.2 lb) of fresh birch leaves produces a pleasant yellow colour.

2. 500 gm of birch bark boiled for about two hours before the wool is added will dye the wool any shade from dull yellow to deep gold, according to how long it is left. 50 gm of cream of tartar should be used in the mordant.

3. Add about 25 gm of salt and an extra 25 gm of cream of tartar to the mordant solution, and 500 gm of blackberries will yield a bluish-grey colour.

4. 500 gm of young bracken shoots, simmered for two hours before adding the wool, produces a yellowish green.

5. 500 gm of elderberries give a violet colour to alum-mordanted wool, and a more lilac colour if salt is added to the mordant. Elder leaves

produce a green colour.

6. One kilogram of chopped dog's mercury produces a yellow colour, becoming blue with long boiling.

7. About 750 gm of well-bruised privet berries produce a bluish-green dye.

8. About one kilogram of young ling (heather) flower shoots produces an olive-yellow. Simmer the shoots for several hours and cool and strain the liquor before adding the wool and boiling again, otherwise you will never get the flower buds out of the wool. You need about 50 gm of cream of tartar in the mordant.

9. Walnut husks and shells give a dark brown colour to unmordanted wool, and a paler colour to mordanted wool.

10. 500 gm of ragwort flowers produce a lovely yellow colour.

11. 500 gm of oak bark gives a deep brown colour to wool.

12. 750 gm pine cones, broken up and boiled for several hours, produce a reddish-yellow colour.

13. The dried roots of the madder (*Rubia peregrina*) produce a rose-pink dye.

You Will Need

Several large galvanized iron bowls, buckets, or enamel saucepans for boiling the mordants and dyes

Scales

Some stout sticks

Alum (potassium aluminium sulphate)

Cream of tartar

Rubber gloves are useful, and you will, of course, need the dyestuffs and some material, e.g. wool, to dye.

1 Birch leaves

2 Birch bark

3 Blackberries

4 Bracken buds

5 Elderberries

6 Dog's mercury

7 Privet berries

8 Ling (heather)

9 Walnuts

10 Ragwort

11 Oak bark

12 Pine cones

13 Madder

eology is the study of the earth. As such it embraces all the other sciences and deals with the earth's history, its structure, the forces that affect it and the life-forms that existed on it in times past. It is such a broad subject that it is subdivided into a number of more specialized sciences dealing with different aspects. Many of these have long and rather daunting names, but they are only labels to distinguish one branch of geology from the others. Mineralogy, for example, deals with minerals, petrology deals with rocks, stratigraphy with the changing environmental conditions, palaeontology with fossilized animal and plant life, geomorphology with landscapes, and geophysics and geochemistry with the physical and chemical processes that have taken place in the earth and are taking place today.

Most of these sciences are very complex and are worthy of years of study but there is a great deal that the amateur can observe and learn. The pioneer geologists were nearly all amateurs who made observations, compiled notes and then started interpreting what they saw and drawing conclusions.

Take a walk in the country or in a park, and look at the lie of the land. Is it hilly or flat? Are there any rivers or streams crossing it, and, if so, are they slow or fast, do they run in deep ravines or flow gently over flat land in sweeping meanders? At the seaside, is the land eaten away in towering cliffs or are there broad belts of sand dunes? When you look at these things you are studying geomorphology.

If there is a quarry, a road cutting, a river gorge or some other fresh outcrop of rock near your home, have a look at the lumps of rock broken off. See whether the rock shows distinct layers, or strata, like the different layers in a cake, indicating that it is a sedimentary rock formed

from successive beds of mud, sand or clay laid down in some long-gone sea. It may, on the other hand, be hard with no visible internal structure, suggesting that it is an igneous rock solidified from a melt. If it shows structures that give the rock the appearance of having been crushed and twisted in the depths of the earth, it is probably what is called a metamorphic rock. Such considerations are part of the science of petrology.

If the rock is coarse enough to contains crystals that are visible with the naked eye or a hand lens, look at the crystals closely. See whether they have good crystalline shapes or are

intergrown with one another. Are they hard or soft – can they be scratched by a penknife, a fingernail, a piece of glass? Are they glassy in appearance, or metallic or pearly? With the results of these observations and a good reference book you can identify the minerals. This is the science of mineralogy.

If the rocks in your exposure are obviously sedimentary, look at their thickness and see what sort of sequence they form. If they are very thick and fine-grained, this would suggest that they have been deposited very slowly over a long period of time; if they

are thin, they will probably have been deposited over a relatively short period. Perhaps the grains are of different sizes and are jumbled up together as if they had been dumped quickly, with no time for water currents to sort them out. Perhaps there is a sequence of different beds, beginning with a limestone bed with fossil seashells, through one of shale formed by mud, to one of sandstone with river-current structures in it. This is a fairly typical sequence and suggests that, in times gone by, a sea area on this spot was encroached upon by a river delta. If the rock is a sandstone, see whether its structures

resemble those you can find today in sand and mud, e.g. ripple marks and mud cracks. These will give you some idea of the environment in which the rock was formed. The science to which these studies belong is called stratigraphy (see page 162).

If there are fossils in the sedimentary rock, see whether they are of shells and other things you recognize. If you cannot identify them immediately take them home and see if they compare with illustrations in books of fossils or the hard parts of animals. Are they recognizable as species

that exist today in seawater, fresh water, the tropics or temperate waters? This is the science of palaeontology.

Look at the sedimentary rocks in your area. They will either be lying flat, in other words in the same position as when they were deposited, or tilted. If the latter, check to see whether they are tilted to the same degree in other quarries or cuttings in the area. Perhaps they are deformed and thrown into folds; perhaps they have been split and displaced by cracks or faults.

These considerations belong to a branch of geophysics called tectonics – the study of the final shape and aspect of the rocks of an area.

Once you have decided on a likely area for your studies, collect the proper equipment for an expedition. Sturdy shoes or boots are necessary if your locality is far from the road. Waterproof clothing should be taken – as light as possible since a specimen bag full of rocks will be heavy to carry home. A geological hammer should be obtained but, failing that, a coal hammer and a masonry chisel will do. You will find a hand lens (see page 18) useful for studying small crystals and small-scale structures in rocks.

Once in the field it is worth remembering that indiscriminate hammering is the mark of a novice. It is often stated that one of the most potent agents of erosion is a geological field party, and because of this many unique sites in national parks are closed to geologists. Remember, therefore, to hammer only what you need. Before hammering, select your spot carefully.

Geology is a hobby that can become quite compelling. As you learn to look at your local countryside with a 'geological' eye, you will want to know more about the rock that forms it and the earth processes that have shaped it. Your petrological and palaeontological collections will begin to grow and later will give you lasting pleasure.

CHAPTER 8

ROCKS AND SCENERY

An introduction to earth sciences, the study of our planet as it used to be

EXPLORING THE LANDSCAPE

Decode the landscape in your area by looking at the rocks that have gradually shaped it

The shape of a particular landscape is determined by a number of factors, the most important being the nature of the rock. Where a very hard rock such as granite is found in a mountain range, it will preserve that area as an upland for a very long time – long after the surrounding softer rocks have been eroded away. A porous rock, through which water percolates, will also remain as an upland for a very long time since the usual surface run-off of rainwater, which is an important agent of erosion in most areas, does not occur. Instead the water seeps through the rock and collects where it meets an impervious layer.

Low-lying areas may be areas of fairly hard rock that have been exposed to the forces of erosion for many millions of years, or they may be areas where deposition is actively taking place today. This can happen in regions where sand dunes and sand spits are being built out into the sea, or in salt marshes where river sediments are being deposited in estuaries.

The most dramatic rock outcrops are found in regions of sedimentary rocks where there is an alternation of hard, resistant rock such as sandstone or limestone, and soft, easily eroded rock such as shale. A rock sequence like this, where exposed, will give a stepped outcrop with the hard beds protruding beyond the soft. Several of the more common types of landscape are described here and overleaf.

Granite Landscapes

Granite is a coarse igneous rock that is found underlying broad areas of land. It occurs as batholiths – vast underground reservoirs of molten material that have solidified and whose tops have been eroded away. The rock is basically made up of three minerals – milky-white or pink feldspars that may form large, rectangular crystals; glassy quartz, and sparkling plates of mica. Iron ore is usually present as well, but in such small quantities that it cannot be seen with the naked eye.

Granite landscapes are characterized by damp moors often covered with peat. The granite is usually cut through by cracks called joints, and where the rock is exposed, as in sea cliffs and the protruding knolls called tors, it weathers along these joints giving a characteristic appearance reminiscent of brickwork. China clay forms as the feldspar decomposes, and the white spoil heaps from china-clay workings can often be seen in granite areas.

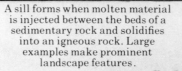

A sill forms when molten material is injected between the beds of a sedimentary rock and solidifies into an igneous rock. Large examples make prominent landscape features.

When molten rock pushes upwards to the surface of the earth it bursts out violently, building up a cone of igneous rock called a volcano. After millions of years the volcano becomes extinct and is eroded away completely, leaving only the column of igneous rocks to represent the tube up which the molten matter travelled. This is called a plug.

Metamorphic Rocks

Metamorphic rocks come in two types contact metamorphic, which are limited in extent and form and occur where an igneous body has cooked the rocks for a few feet on each side, and regional metamorphic where whole areas have been altered by mountain-building activity. Regional metamorphic rocks are found in mountainous areas and can be recognized by their hardness and their contorted nature. Slate is a typical metamorphic rock found in such areas and is the only metamorphic rock that is economically important – although veins of copper and lead are often associated with this kind of terrain. Slate quarries can be seen as vast pits in the sides of mountains.

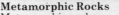

Chalk Landscapes

Chalk is a particularly pure form of limestone. It was deposited in clear shallow seas mostly in the Upper Cretaceous period between about 100 and 65 million years ago. The particles of calcium carbonate forming the chalk are the hard skeletons of minute water plants that existed in the warm Cretaceous seas. The beds tend to be massive with few bedding planes. The startling white coloration of chalk shows up well in chalk pits and sea cliffs and in some places the topsoil is removed to produce huge decorative shapes, such as human figures and horses, that are visible for miles. The chalk is very porous and so rainwater tends to sink in without forming streams. Chalk landscapes usually occur in downland and feature rounded hills and dry valleys covered with short grasses.

Limestone Landscapes

Limestone, like chalk, is porous and so limestone landscapes are generally very dry also. They tend to lack soil and vegetable cover, and produce a barren type of landscape that is known as a karst. In such areas the rainwater collects in underground streams, enlarging and eroding caves along the joints between the rocks until great hollows are formed. As rainwater percolates through the rocks into these hollows, particles of calcium carbonate are left attached to the cavern roofs. This accumulation of carbonate produces stalactites (see inset) whereas stalagmites are formed on the cavern floors where carbonate is deposited by the impact of drips of water.

The Geology of Coalfields

Coal measures usually show the kind of varied geology formed by unstable delta conditions. When a shallow sea was encroached by the sands of a delta, the sandbanks formed were quickly colonized by thick plant growth. If the area then became submerged, the plants were buried and converted into coal by the pressure of the later beds lying on top of them. A coalfield usually consists of a number of fairly thin seams of coal separated by beds of barren limestone, shale or sandstone. Most large coal deposits were laid down during the Upper Carboniferous period about 300 million years ago, and they are usually marked by the black pit heaps and hoists of coal mines. An area that has supported a coal-mining industry for many years may show subsidence in roads and farmlands where the mining has caused collapse in the upper layers of rock.

Irregular Sequences

In areas of shallow water, where deltas were constantly being formed and submerged, irregular sequences of rocks were deposited. Clear sea water gave limestone, muddy water gave shale, and the river mouths themselves gave sandstone.

Folds in the Rock

After rocks have been deposited and solidified, they may be subjected to all sorts of deformation before we see them exposed in the field. The most common type of deformation is the fold. Different types of fold can often be clearly seen in thinly stratified sedimentary rock. A fold in which the beds sag downwards, like a slack piece of string held at each end, is called a syncline. A fold in which the beds are curved upwards is called an anticline. Often, as in the example shown, the two are found together. Folds do not usually have any effect on the topography of an area; being small-scale structures, the erosion surface usually cuts right across them rather than following the ups and downs of the underlying strata.

Faults in the Rock

Faults occur where one block of the rock cracks away from another and moves in relation to it. This can take place on a scale of a few inches – no more than a slight step in the strata – or it can involve a displacement of many hundreds of miles, like the San Andreas Fault in California, which has moved over 800 miles and is still on the move, causing frequent earthquakes in the area.
A fault can be a normal fault, in which one block has slipped down in relation to the other; a thrust fault, in which one block has ridden up over the other, or a lateral fault, in which the blocks have moved sideways, either to the left or the right, in relation to one another. Whole areas may be thrown up or down between parallel faults, giving rise respectively to horsts and rift valleys.

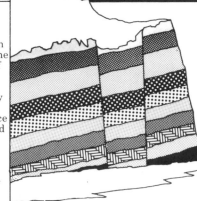

Glacier Landscapes

Landscapes that have been recently subjected to cover by glaciers – and this includes great tracts of the Northern Hemisphere – are usually associated with distinct scenic features. In mountainous areas, where most of the glaciers originated, these consist of valleys deepened by the weight of ice.

Pyramidal peak
A mountain top accentuated by the formation of corries around it.

Corrie
A hollow in a hillside where a glacier originated.

U-shaped valley
A valley broadened and deepened by the weight of a glacier.

Hanging valley
A smaller valley that meets a deepened U-shaped valley.

Arête
A ridge left between two corries or U-shaped valleys.

Esker
A long, winding deposit of sand and gravel following the path of a river beneath a glacier.

Drumlins
Regular heaps of sand and gravel left by retreating glaciers.

Erratic block
A boulder that has been carried a great distance by a glacier.

Salt Marshes

These usually form where the fine material brought down by a river is not washed out to sea but is built up near the river mouth. They are characterized by networks of tidal creeks and mud banks. The mud banks build up above sea level and are stabilized by grasses and salt-resistant plants. When the sea level changes they are eroded away to leave miniature cliffs and sea stacks.

Sand Landscapes

A sand landscape, like a salt marsh, is a landscape of accretion rather than of erosion. It is usually found where winds blow up off the sea, bringing with them rock particles eroded from elsewhere. There may be broad beaches backed by sand dunes and, inland from these, older sand dunes covered with coarse grasses. Where sand is found inland the land is very dry and heaths develop, covered with bracken or gorse. Coniferous forest is often planted on such land. Along the coast where the accretion is still taking place the actions of waves and sea currents combine to give longshore drift, which transports sand particles along the beach. Sand spits are formed by this process, a river mouth being gradually blocked off by a growing finger of sand which eventually causes the river to change its course. Longshore drift is also seen where fences called groynes are built out into the sea to prevent coastal erosion. Sand builds up behind the groynes to give a zig-zag coastline.

Clay Landscapes

Clay landscapes are formed either from glacier deposits or where there have been extensive river deposits in the last 50 million years. The landscape is very wet with ponds in the hollows, and the original forests have usually been cleared for farmland.

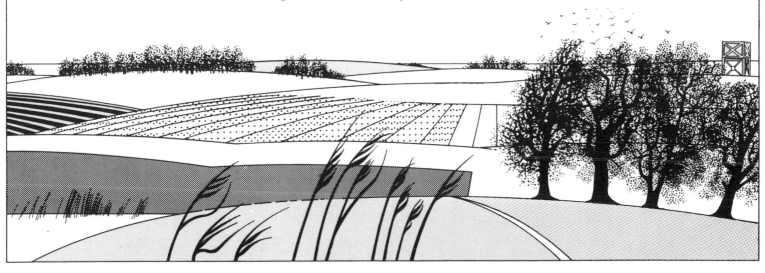

COLLECTING ROCKS AND MINERALS

Some of the interesting rocks and stones that you can pick up in the park or countryside

ocks are everywhere around you. They may be covered with soil in many areas, but there are still many places in which you can see the rocks in their naked glory – mountains, river beds and banks, road cuttings, and sea cliffs. Beaches are also excellent places for looking at rocks, although here they are in the form of water-worn pebbles.

Because of the wonderful colours, patterns, and textures found in the rocks, the collection of rocks and pebbles can be an absorbing hobby. There is also the chance that you may find gem-stones, and a study of the rocks will help you to understand the landscapes in your area among which you live.

The rocks that compose the earth are of two main kinds – igneous and sedimentary. The igneous rocks are those 'borne of fire' – in other words they have solidified from molten material originating deep down in the earth. Volcanic lava and other igneous rocks that poured out on to the surface of the earth tend to have a very fine crystalline structure, whereas the granites that solidified slowly deep down in the ground have much larger crystals. These igneous rocks may have joints showing where they cracked as they cooled, but they do not have the distinct layered structure of the sedimentary rocks. The latter were laid down as sediments – usually in the sea – and later compressed to form solid rocks. Examples of the sedimentary rocks include clays, sandstones, limestones, and shales. The coal seams are also sedimentary rocks, but they are rather special in that they are composed almost entirely of the remains of ancient plants. The particles that make up the other sedimentary rocks were derived from the wearing away or erosion of previously existing rocks. Wind, frost, rain, and other agencies gradually cause the rocks to crumble, and the particles are eventually washed into the sea. This cycle of erosion and deposition is going on all the time, so new rocks are being formed under the sea today from the sand and silt brought down by the rivers.

In addition to the igneous and sedimentary rocks, there is another group of rocks called metamorphic rocks. These are rocks which started out either as igneous or sedimentary types but which have since been changed by intense heat or pressure associated with mountain-building and volcanic activity. They are often very hard and many are characteristically banded as a result of flowing under pressure.

All rocks are composed of materials called minerals. The most abundant of the rock-forming minerals are compounds of silicon – especially quartz or silica. The latter is a major constituent of granite, and it also forms the bulk of the rocks called sandstones and the bulk of the sand on our beaches. Compounds of aluminium are also extremely common in the earth's crust. The majority of rocks consist of several minerals in combination. Granite, for example, consists of silica, feldspars, and mica (see opposite). Chalk, on the other hand, is almost pure calcium carbonate, while sandstones consist almost entirely of silica.

Occasionally, one kind of mineral becomes concentrated in a small area – often in narrow 'veins' running through other rocks, or else filling up small hollows in the rocks. Specimens from such deposits are called mineral specimens rather than rock specimens and they are much prized by collectors. Many of them are metallic ores, such as galena and iron pyrites (see opposite).

The two essential tools for collecting rock and mineral specimens are a sturdy hammer and a chisel. Special geological hammers are best because they are made to withstand constant pounding on the rocks. Sooner or later a geological map will be useful so that you can pick out areas of different rocks to visit. Look for suitably exposed pieces of rock – the corners of blocks are particularly good – that you can chip off with a few swift hammer blows. The chisel is not necessary if you can find a suitable corner to attack, but it is very useful on a more uniform rock face. Look for a small crack on which to begin your attack. Goggles are sometimes useful when working with particularly hard rocks like granites. Always try to get a specimen showing one weathered surface and one freshly cut surface. It is not necessary to collect very large pieces: not only is this wasteful, they are also very heavy to carry home. All you need is a piece large enough to show the range of component minerals and the texture.

Stick a piece of adhesive tape on to each specimen and write on it the date and locality in which you found it. Wrap the rocks in newspaper and carry them home in your rucksack. You can clean them up and display them in drawers or boxes at a later date. Iron pyrites tends to crumble when exposed to the air for any length of time and it is best coated with clear varnish, but the other rocks and minerals need no special attention. You can polish pebbles in a tumble polisher to enhance their beauty, but this does not enhance their value in the collection.

You Will Need

A sturdy hammer
Chisel
Rucksack
Adhesive tape
Old newspapers

Dendritic Manganese
Looking like delicate ferns, it consists of crystals of manganese dioxide spreading over the surfaces of other rocks.

Amethyst
This mineral consists of quartz crystals which are stained with violet-coloured impurities.

Granite
Granite is a very hard igneous rock (see text) which consists of quartz crystals, black mica (biotite), and feldspar.

Gneiss
A gneiss is a metamorphosed granite in which the various minerals have been re-arranged by pressure into irregular bands.

Flint
This is a hard, glassy mineral usually found in chalk rocks.

Schist
A schist is a metamorphic rock (see text) in which the minerals have been re-arranged into parallel flaky layers.

Pisolite
This is a form of limestone made of pea-sized grains which originally rolled around on the sea bed.

Iron Pyrites
Iron pyrites is a shiny yellow mineral, sometimes called fool's gold. Streaks of it often occur in coal.

Quartz
Quartz is one of the hardest minerals and it is the main constituent of sand. In its pure form, it makes clear, rocket-shaped crystals.

Quartzite
A metamorphic rock formed by the cooking of sandstone. Many beach pebbles are of quartzite, and you can often polish them to a beautiful shine.

Calcite
Calcite is an extremely common mineral which is the basis of chalk and limestone, but in its purest form, seen here, it forms white crystals.

Agate
Agate pebbles consist of concentric bands of a greyish form of quartz called chalcedony. Sliced pebbles are in great demand for jewellery.

Galena
Galena, which is the main ore of lead, is a soft mineral; it is cubic in form.

Conglomerate
Conglomerate is a sedimentary rock (see text) in which rounded pebbles are embedded in a natural cement of sandstone or limestone.

COLLECTING FOSSILS

Where to seek out these fascinating remains of ancient plants and animals

Fossils are the remains of animals and plants that lived on the surface of the earth in times gone past. They are usually the hard parts of organisms that have fallen to the bed of the sea or a lake or a river and have been buried by the sediment accumulating there. As that sediment turned to stone over the vast span of geological time the organic remains have become entombed and altered in some way so that their shapes, at least, have been preserved even if, as is usually the case, the original matter has long since disappeared.

The best place to look for fossils is in an exposure of sedimentary rock. Thinly bedded limestones and shales are usually good places to look since, if nothing is visible on the surface, these can be broken and split easily to reveal fresh rock faces. A heavily weathered outcrop can also be a good place to look as sometimes the rock has rotted away leaving the more durable fossil protruding from it. In these situations the fossil can be easily removed.

Once a good fossil site has been found, go over it carefully and remove from it the specimens you wish to take home. Always take enough notes to remind you of where and how the specimens were found – important details can be so easily forgotten in the excitement of setting up a collection. A photograph of the exposed fossil is also useful.

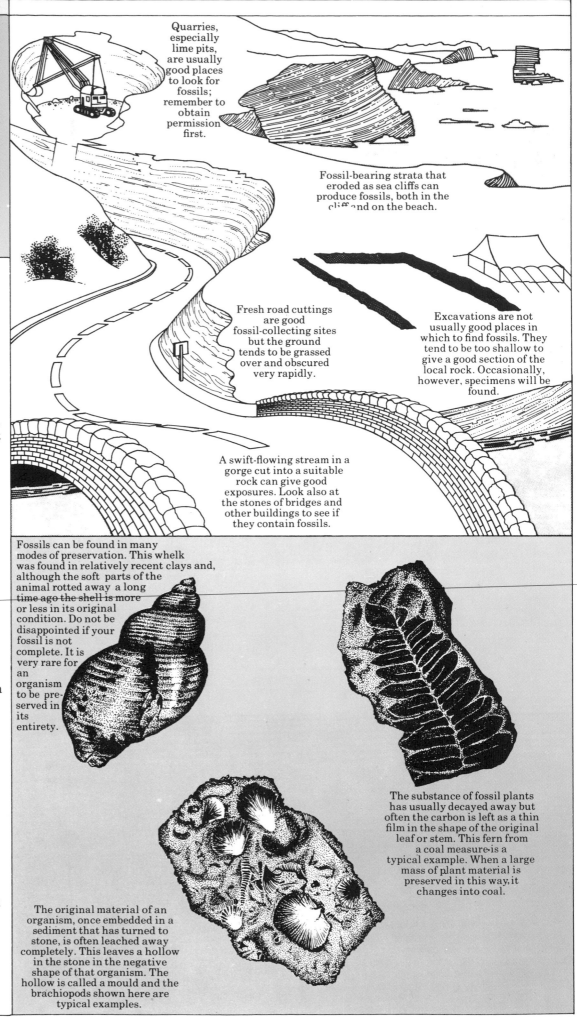

Quarries, especially lime pits, are usually good places to look for fossils; remember to obtain permission first.

Fossil-bearing strata that eroded as sea cliffs can produce fossils, both in the cliff and on the beach.

Fresh road cuttings are good fossil-collecting sites but the ground tends to be grassed over and obscured very rapidly.

Excavations are not usually good places in which to find fossils. They tend to be too shallow to give a good section of the local rock. Occasionally, however, specimens will be found.

A swift-flowing stream in a gorge cut into a suitable rock can give good exposures. Look also at the stones of bridges and other buildings to see if they contain fossils.

Fossils can be found in many modes of preservation. This whelk was found in relatively recent clays and, although the soft parts of the animal rotted away a long time ago the shell is more or less in its original condition. Do not be disappointed if your fossil is not complete. It is very rare for an organism to be preserved in its entirety.

The substance of fossil plants has usually decayed away but often the carbon is left as a thin film in the shape of the original leaf or stem. This fern from a coal measure is a typical example. When a large mass of plant material is preserved in this way, it changes into coal.

The original material of an organism, once embedded in a sediment that has turned to stone, is often leached away completely. This leaves a hollow in the stone in the negative shape of that organism. The hollow is called a mould and the brachiopods shown here are typical examples.

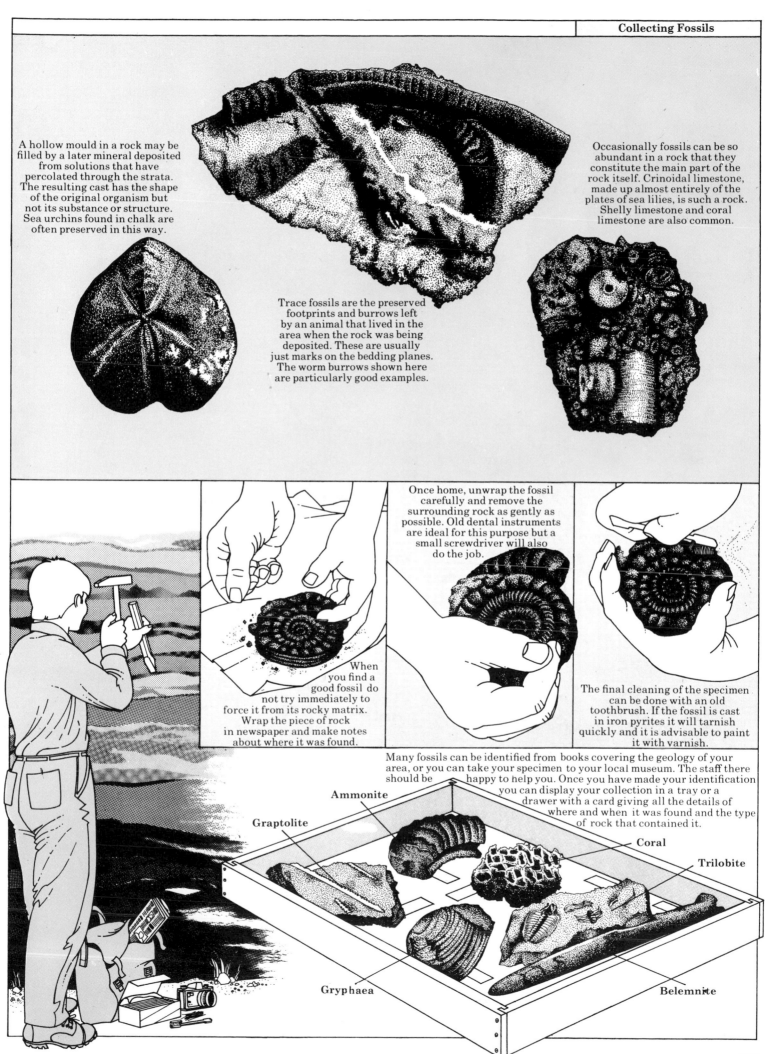

A hollow mould in a rock may be filled by a later mineral deposited from solutions that have percolated through the strata. The resulting cast has the shape of the original organism but not its substance or structure. Sea urchins found in chalk are often preserved in this way.

Occasionally fossils can be so abundant in a rock that they constitute the main part of the rock itself. Crinoidal limestone, made up almost entirely of the plates of sea lilies, is such a rock. Shelly limestone and coral limestone are also common.

Trace fossils are the preserved footprints and burrows left by an animal that lived in the area when the rock was being deposited. These are usually just marks on the bedding planes. The worm burrows shown here are particularly good examples.

Once home, unwrap the fossil carefully and remove the surrounding rock as gently as possible. Old dental instruments are ideal for this purpose but a small screwdriver will also do the job.

When you find a good fossil do not try immediately to force it from its rocky matrix. Wrap the piece of rock in newspaper and make notes about where it was found.

The final cleaning of the specimen can be done with an old toothbrush. If the fossil is cast in iron pyrites it will tarnish quickly and it is advisable to paint it with varnish.

Many fossils can be identified from books covering the geology of your area, or you can take your specimen to your local museum. The staff there should be happy to help you. Once you have made your identification you can display your collection in a tray or a drawer with a card giving all the details of where and when it was found and the type of rock that contained it.

Graptolite

Ammonite

Coral

Trilobite

Gryphaea

Belemnite

CLUES TO THE PAST

Looking at rock features to see how a piece of landscape was formed

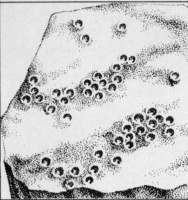

Unconformities

An unconformity is a break in the normal sequence of rocks. It usually occurs when a sequence is first deposited and solidified and then raised above sea level, where it is eroded. Eventually the area may sink below sea level once more, and later rocks are laid down upon them. The beds above and below an unconformity are usually of different types of rock and lie at different angles, and so the feature is easy to recognize.

tratigraphy – the study of the changing conditions at the earth's surface – is another fascinating pursuit that does not necessarily call for any great prior knowledge. By noting the features and characteristics of a piece of rocky landscape – the shapes and compositions of the included fragments, the fossils entombed in it and the sedimentary structures – you will be able to form an idea of the nature of the rock and how it has changed.

Some of the evidence can be easily seen. Limestone, for example, is only formed at the bottom of the sea, while shale, being solidified mud, was laid down in muddy water. Sandstone, on the other hand, may have been formed on or near a beach, on a river bed or in a desert. A closer look is needed to determine which, and the sedimentary structures can be one way of telling.

The bedding planes that make up the rock may not be flat but may have a distinctly rippled surface similar to the ripple marks formed on sandy beaches. Alternatively, a cross-section through the rock may show the bedding planes twisted up with one another in S-shapes. This is caused by the building out of a delta at a river mouth where the current deposits each layer down the curving slope of the delta front. Desert sand dunes are formed in a similar way – except that winds are are the driving force.

Ripple marks that form when sand is deposited below a few inches of water can often be preserved in the bedding planes of a sandstone.

When a muddy pool dries out, the mud can shrink to produce a series of cracks that split the surface mud into polygonal blocks. These can be found in sandstone.

Rain pits form where an area of dry mud has been subjected to a rain shower and has then been covered by another deposit of mud.

Current Bedding

Current bedding is one of the most common and significant sedimentary structures to form a sandstone. When a delta builds itself out at a river mouth, each new deposit of sand is tipped down the end of the last one as the current slackens on reaching deeper water. The result is a horizontal series of very fine S-shaped beds. The delta environment is very unstable and so the sea level can change fairly rapidly. If the new deposit sinks, the sea floods in and the delta starts building out again from its original starting point. When this happens the new currents wash away the top part of the old bed, leaving only the bottom halves of the S-shapes before building out a new bed on top of it.

Current bedding is usually found on a very small scale but there are some huge examples that were formed, not by deltas, but by sand dunes. A sequence of sand dunes forms in the same way as a delta front: the sand particles are blown by the wind up the windward face and dropped down the lee face where they are deposited. Large-scale bedding caused by sand dunes is found most often in rocks dating from Devonian times – 400 million years ago – and the Permian and Triassic periods – between 280 and 190 million years ago. At these times Europe and North America lay in desert belts and many thousands of feet of red desert sands were deposited.

CHAPTER 9

TECHNICAL SECTION

Useful equipment for the
adventurous naturalist, with
suggestions on which types to buy
to suit your needs

WILDLIFE SOUND RECORDING

Using a cassette recorder in the field

If yours is one of the many families that own a cassette recorder, you will be able to spend some very rewarding hours using it to record birds and other animals in the wild. You will not, of course, be able to make top-quality recordings with simple equipment, but by following a few simple rules you will be able to make some very presentable recordings, and you will find a great deal of pleasure in listening to them later – perhaps even setting your friends some fascinating puzzles by asking them to name the animals they hear.

Any cassette recorder can be used, but one with a manual recording-level control is best, because you can adjust this yourself according to the volume of the sound you are recording. Most cassette recorders have an automatic volume control, but this can be a disadvantage for wild-life recording because wild-life sounds often come in sudden bursts and do not give the automatic system a chance to adjust itself. It is a very good idea to use headphones or an ear-piece plugged into the recorder so that you can hear exactly what the microphone is picking up. If you are using an open-reel recorder, use the highest possible speed, for this gives the best quality. Make or buy a good carrying case and strap for taking the recorder into the field.

The pencil-shaped microphones that generally come with the cassette recorders are satisfactory, but you can improve the quality of your recordings with a more expensive microphone. Be sure to get what is known as a low-impedance microphone, as this will allow you to use a long lead, and so get the recorder and yourself well away from what you are trying to record. Always try to avoid holding the microphone in your hand, as the slightest movement of your fingers can be picked up. One way to overcome this problem is to fix the microphone to a long stick as shown in the illustration.

A naked stick microphone is often satisfactory only if you can get it very close to the source of the sound, as it can pick up only a small proportion of the sound waves. A parabolic reflector is a very good investment if you plan to do much recording. This type of reflector is very carefully shaped to catch additional sound waves and focus them on the microphone mounted in the centre (see illustrations).

Noise is always a problem when you are out in the countryside, and it is often worse than you think because the human ear can cut out some unimportant sounds, but the microphone picks them all up. Wind is the worst problem, but you can overcome this to some extent by putting some light-weight cloth over the microphone, as shown opposite, to create a zone of still air immediately around it. Try to put your body in between the microphone and any other troublesome noise, such as the rustling of leaves in the trees, and get the microphone as close to the animal as possible.

If you are intent on recording birds, watch them for a while and see where their song posts are situated. Get a concealed microphone as near as possible and wait for results: the birds will fly off initially but very soon will return to the song post. Place yourself and the recorder as far away as you can, and keep still and quiet. Do not wear brightly coloured clothes. It is also

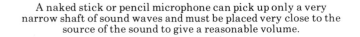

A naked stick or pencil microphone can pick up only a very narrow shaft of sound waves and must be placed very close to the source of the sound to give a reasonable volume.

Clip the microphone to a short stick and 'plant' it among the flowers. Observe which insects arrive, so that you can annotate your recording.

Hang your microphone over a cage of grasshoppers, the latter being illuminated by a fairly strong lamp. The bright light and the warmth will make the males sing.

well worthwhile putting the microphone by a bird table feeder (see page 52) to pick up the sounds of the feeding birds, and if you have a spare microphone you could fix it into an artificial nesting box (see page 54) before the breeding season. Connect it up to your recorder for a few minutes each day to hear what goes on.

As soon as you have made each recording, it is essential that you add a short commentary so that you can identify each part of the tape. The commentary should include at least the date and place of the recording and the weather conditions; some animals perform only under certain conditions, and your tapes will be of much greater value if you give full information.

You might not want to keep all you record, and it is a good plan to make master tapes. To do this you will need another tape recorder. Perhaps a friend will lend you one. Use the machine on which you recorded the sounds to play them back, and re-record them on the second machine. Introduce each item with a few words, pointing out the essential features of the recording – the name of the animal (even if you yourself know perfectly well what it is), the time of year, the habitat, and so on. A well-made tape can be very instructive for young naturalists who are not yet familiar with the sounds of the countryside. Used in conjunction with an ear-piece, the cassette can even be used as a guide to your own nature trail (see page 22).

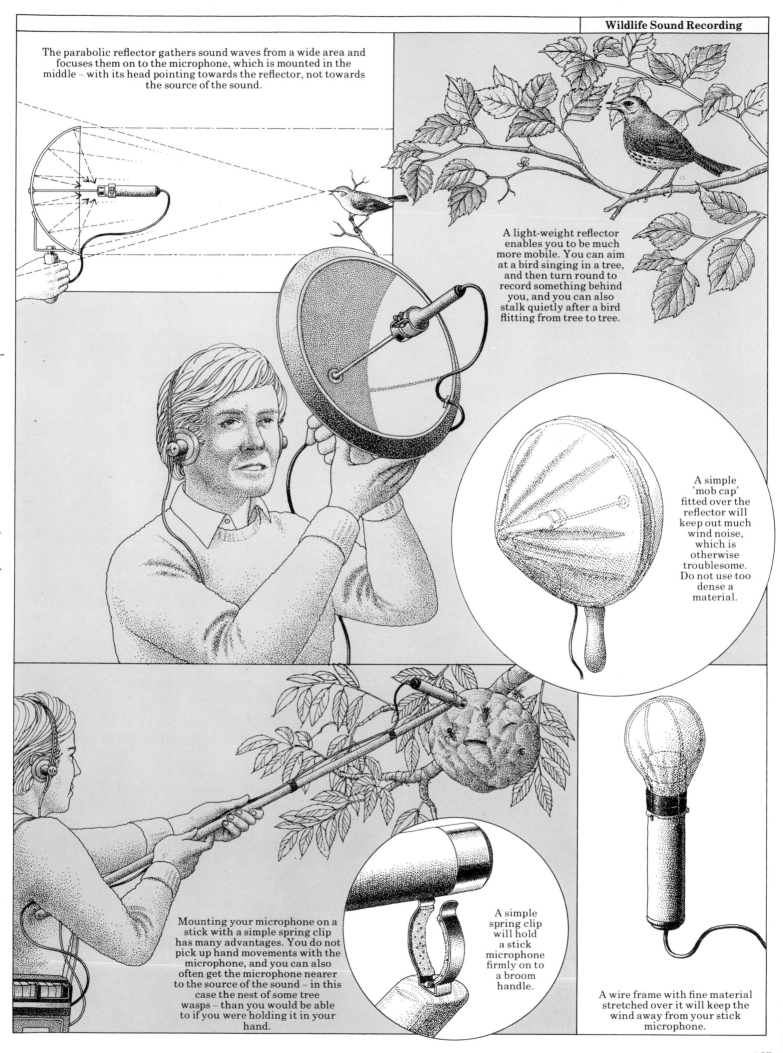

The parabolic reflector gathers sound waves from a wide area and focuses them on to the microphone, which is mounted in the middle – with its head pointing towards the reflector, not towards the source of the sound.

A light-weight reflector enables you to be much more mobile. You can aim at a bird singing in a tree, and then turn round to record something behind you, and you can also stalk quietly after a bird flitting from tree to tree.

A simple 'mob cap' fitted over the reflector will keep out much wind noise, which is otherwise troublesome. Do not use too dense a material.

Mounting your microphone on a stick with a simple spring clip has many advantages. You do not pick up hand movements with the microphone, and you can also often get the microphone nearer to the source of the sound – in this case the nest of some tree wasps – than you would be able to if you were holding it in your hand.

A simple spring clip will hold a stick microphone firmly on to a broom handle.

A wire frame with fine material stretched over it will keep the wind away from your stick microphone.

165

CHOOSING BINOCULARS

How to select the most suitable binoculars for your favourite natural history pursuit

he naturalist, particularly one who is interested mainly in birds, will not take long to decide that he or she needs a pair of binoculars. The range of equipment is enormous and perhaps bewildering to the novice, and the information given here is designed to help amateurs choose the best type for their particular needs. Binoculars that are ideal for one purpose are rarely ideal for another.

Binoculars are essentially designed to magnify distant objects so that you can see them more clearly and identify them without having to get too close. You might think, therefore, that you ought to get the most powerful ones that you can, but this is a mistake. For a start, just take a look at the most powerful binoculars in the shop: they are the biggest ones and they are very heavy. You would soon get tired of walking with those hanging round your neck. In addition, the most powerful binoculars cannot focus on anything nearer than perhaps 10 metres (33 ft). This means that you could not use them to look at birds close-up, or at an insect sitting just out of reach – on a water-lily leaf on a pond, for example. The only people who really need these powerful binoculars are coastguards and sailors, aircraft spotters, and those ornithologists who are concerned only with sea birds. The ordinary naturalist needs something much less powerful.

If you look at a pair of binoculars you will normally see two figures engraved on the body. 8 × 30 is a typical example that you might see, but there are several other combinations, such as 7 × 50, 9 × 40, and so on. The first figure of the pair indicates the magnifying power of the binoculars, and the second figure is the diameter of the objective lens (see diagram below). Both figures are important when you are choosing your binoculars.

Do not choose any with a magnification below × 6, for these will not enable you to identify the smaller birds from any distance. Magnifications of × 7, × 8, and × 9 are the most useful, and then you must decide on the size of the objective lens. The larger lenses let in more light, and are thus more suitable if you intend to use your binoculars much at night; at the same time, though, the magnifying power also affects the amount of light passing through the glasses. Divide the objective diameter by the magnification and you will get a figure known as the *exit pupil diameter*. The higher this figure, the better the light-gathering power of the binoculars and the better they are for use in dim light. A pair of 7 × 50 binoculars (exit pupil diameter 7.14) is thus better for night use than an 8 × 30 pair (exit pupil diameter 3.75). The chart at the bottom of the next page shows which binoculars are the most useful for various types of natural history activity, and also indicates that the best all-purpose binoculars are 9 × 40 or, if you want them for night use as well, 7 × 50.

Having decided which size you require, you must then select a model to fit both you and your pocket. Prices vary a great deal and, in general, you should buy the most expensive that you can afford. The higher price usually indicates better manufacture and better lens quality. Test the binoculars thoroughly before buying them. Do they feel comfortable in your hands and up at your eyes? Is the focusing control smooth? Reject any pair in which the focusing knob is hard to turn, and also any in which it is so slack that it turns with the slightest jolt. Most binoculars have an independent focusing device for one of the eye-pieces so that you can correct for any variation between your two eyes.

Test the field of view of the binoculars by looking at a brick wall and counting the number of bricks that you can see across the middle of the field. Glasses with the same magnification normally have the same field of view, but some of the better ones are designed to give a wider field. Other things being equal, choose the pair which shows you the most bricks on the wall. A wide field of view is very useful for scanning a habitat for signs of life. You should also test the binoculars to make sure that the lenses are free from distortion. Take the binoculars to the shop doorway and focus on a lamp-post or some other straight object. Test each side to make sure that there is no bulge in the centre of the image. A slight blurring at the edges is always present, but the central part should be perfectly sharp.

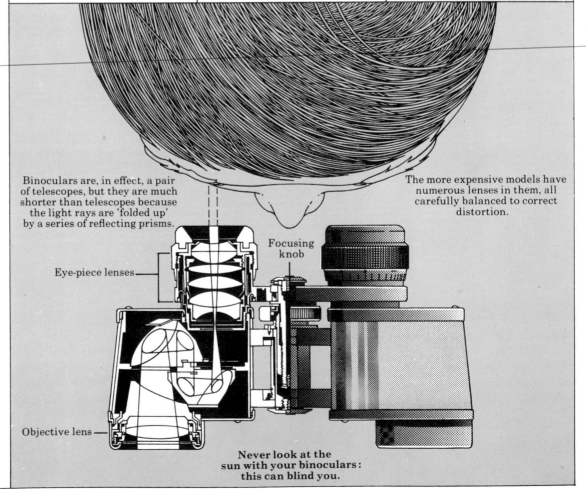

Binoculars are, in effect, a pair of telescopes, but they are much shorter than telescopes because the light rays are 'folded up' by a series of reflecting prisms.

The more expensive models have numerous lenses in them, all carefully balanced to correct distortion.

Eye-piece lenses

Focusing knob

Objective lens

Never look at the sun with your binoculars: this can blind you.

Caring for your Binoculars

When they are not in use your binoculars should be in their case, where they cannot get covered with dust. In humid climates it is a good idea to put a little sachet of silica gel into the case to absorb moisture. When you are using your binoculars you should always keep the strap round your neck to prevent accidents – particularly if you are bird-watching from a boat. It is worth insuring a good pair of binoculars against loss or damage.

You will not want to be continually putting on and taking off the lens caps that come with your binoculars, because you could miss an exciting bird while removing the caps, but it is important to keep your lenses clean. The illustration at the bottom of the page shows one simple way of protecting the eye-piece lenses, which are the more vulnerable because they point upwards. Glue the caps to a piece of leather or other material in such a position that they fit neatly over the lenses,

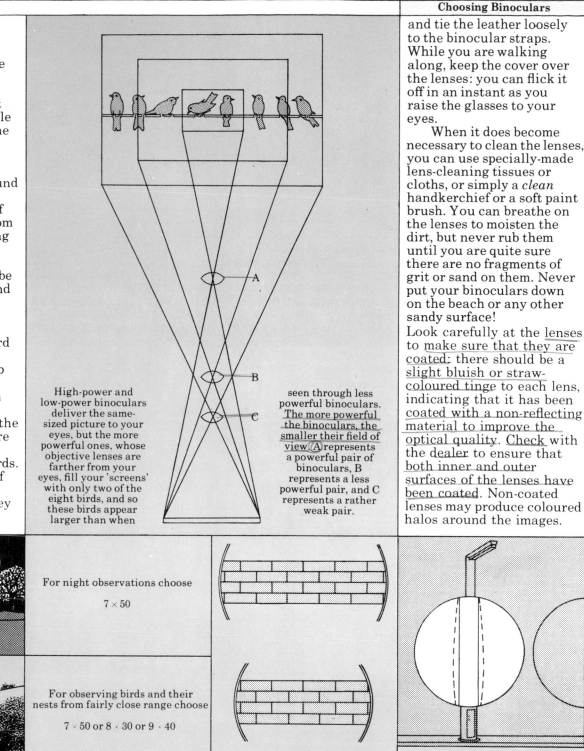

High-power and low-power binoculars deliver the same-sized picture to your eyes, but the more powerful ones, whose objective lenses are farther from your eyes, fill your 'screens' with only two of the eight birds, and so these birds appear larger than when seen through less powerful binoculars. The more powerful the binoculars, the smaller their field of view. A represents a powerful pair of binoculars, B represents a less powerful pair, and C represents a rather weak pair.

and tie the leather loosely to the binocular straps. While you are walking along, keep the cover over the lenses: you can flick it off in an instant as you raise the glasses to your eyes.

When it does become necessary to clean the lenses, you can use specially-made lens-cleaning tissues or cloths, or simply a *clean* handkerchief or a soft paint brush. You can breathe on the lenses to moisten the dirt, but never rub them until you are quite sure there are no fragments of grit or sand on them. Never put your binoculars down on the beach or any other sandy surface!

Look carefully at the lenses to make sure that they are coated: there should be a slight bluish or straw-coloured tinge to each lens, indicating that it has been coated with a non-reflecting material to improve the optical quality. Check with the dealer to ensure that both inner and outer surfaces of the lenses have been coated. Non-coated lenses may produce coloured halos around the images.

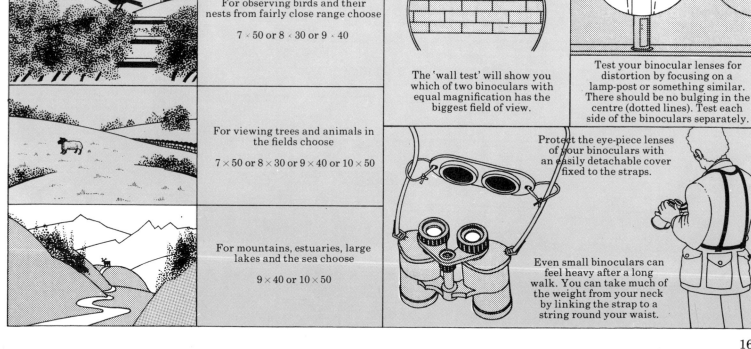

For night observations choose

7 × 50

For observing birds and their nests from fairly close range choose

7 × 50 or 8 × 30 or 9 × 40

For viewing trees and animals in the fields choose

7 × 50 or 8 × 30 or 9 × 40 or 10 × 50

For mountains, estuaries, large lakes and the sea choose

9 × 40 or 10 × 50

The 'wall test' will show you which of two binoculars with equal magnification has the biggest field of view.

Test your binocular lenses for distortion by focusing on a lamp-post or something similar. There should be no bulging in the centre (dotted lines). Test each side of the binoculars separately.

Protect the eye-piece lenses of your binoculars with an easily detachable cover fixed to the straps.

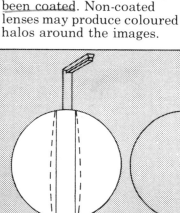

Even small binoculars can feel heavy after a long walk. You can take much of the weight from your neck by linking the strap to a string round your waist.

A FAMILY MICROSCOPE

Discover some of nature's miniature beauties with the aid of a microscope

A microscope is not an inexpensive piece of equipment, and is not an essential requirement for the naturalist, but there is no denying that a whole new world opens up when you look at small creatures through even a low-powered instrument.

The variety of microscopes available is immense, but they fall into two very distinct groups: monocular microscopes and binocular microscopes. If we leave out the models at the upper end of the price range – and these can be very expensive indeed – it is generally true that the monocular models, with a single eye-piece, provide higher magnifications ($\times 100$ or more) than the twin-eye-piece binocular types ($\times 15$–$\times 50$ or so). The two have rather different uses, and you must decide what you want to do with your microscope before deciding on which model to buy. If you want to study the detailed cellular structure of plants you will obviously need a fairly high-powered instrument, and a monocular type is indicated. For help with identification of insects, and for simply looking at the beauty of little plants and animals in close-up, you need a binocular microscope.

The monocular microscope, such as that shown on this page, can be used only with very small objects, which must be mounted on thin glass slides placed on the stage. The objects must also be very thin and translucent if you want to see their internal structures, because the light comes via the mirror underneath the stage and up through the object. Thin slices of plants prepared as shown on the opposite page make excellent subjects for study. They need to be stained if you are to see everything to its best advantage, and two of the most useful stains are safranin and spirit blue. Safranin is a red stain and it affects the woody tissues in a plant – the water-carrying tubes and associated fibres – while the spirit blue stains only the softer tissues. Using them, you can see in detail how a plant is constructed. The stained sections can be made into permanent microscope slides if you wish, but they need a good deal of preparation, the details of which are outside the scope of this book.

Small insects can be examined with the monocular microscope, but for best results their bodies should be 'cleared'. This involves putting them into a dilute solution of potassium hydroxide for a while to 'digest' away most of the soft tissues. The light then comes through quite clearly. The insects, such as lice, fleas, aphids, and small flies, can be made into permanent slide specimens by washing them free of potassium hydroxide and mounting them in a drop of gum chloral on a slide (see opposite).

If you buy a few specially made cavity slides, which have a shallow 'pool' in the middle, you can use them to look at the fascinating microscopic life of a pond. Using an eyedropper, put a small drop of not-too-muddy pond water into the cavity of the slide and cover it with a cover-slip. Have a look at the water through the microscope, and you will be amazed at the number of tiny creatures rushing to and fro. Most of them will belong to the group known as protozoans – animals whose bodies consist of just a single cell.

The simpler forms of binocular microscopes come with magnifications of between perhaps $\times 15$ and $\times 30$. This is by no means a high magnification, but it is high enough for you to be able to examine the structure of insects' feet and eyes. There is also a good working distance between the objective lens at the bottom of the microscope body and the object, allowing you to manipulate the object as required, and there is a fairly good depth of field. You can get binocular microscopes on conventional stands, as shown in the centre of the opposite page, but the general naturalist might prefer one on an adjustable stand, as shown at the bottom of the page. This is extremely useful if you want to examine the minerals or fossils in a large lump of rock: you can raise the horizontal arm to place the rock underneath, and you can also swivel the microscope body into the horizontal position to examine part of an even larger object. Remember that good lighting is necessary for all microscope work, and the greater the magnification, the more light you need.

Photography with your Microscope

You can take some good photographs, known as photomicrographs, by coupling your camera to your microscope. The normal procedure is to remove the camera lens and, using a special attachment, clip the camera directly over the eye-piece of the microscope. You need a single-lens reflex camera for this, so that you can focus properly, and the only way to work out the correct exposure times is by trial and error, unless you have a built-in meter.

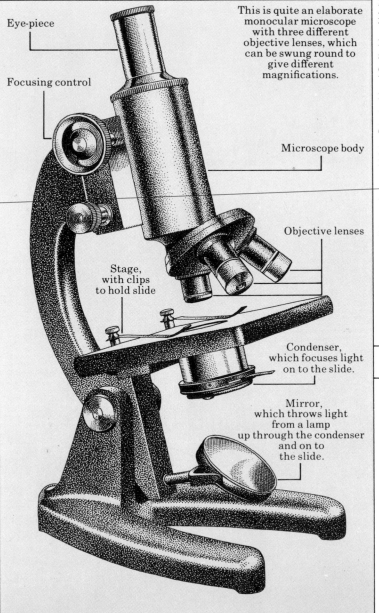

This is quite an elaborate monocular microscope with three different objective lenses, which can be swung round to give different magnifications.

Eye-piece

Focusing control

Microscope body

Objective lenses

Stage, with clips to hold slide

Condenser, which focuses light on to the slide.

Mirror, which throws light from a lamp up through the condenser and on to the slide.

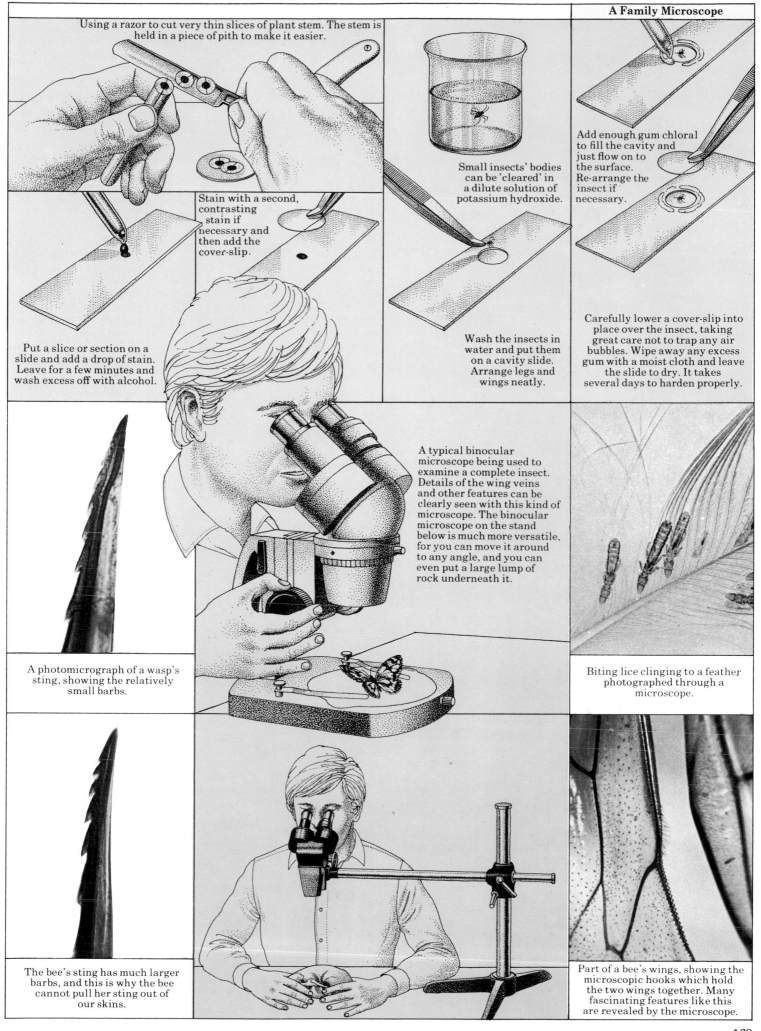

Using a razor to cut very thin slices of plant stem. The stem is held in a piece of pith to make it easier.

Small insects' bodies can be 'cleared' in a dilute solution of potassium hydroxide.

Add enough gum chloral to fill the cavity and just flow on to the surface. Re-arrange the insect if necessary.

Stain with a second, contrasting stain if necessary and then add the cover-slip.

Put a slice or section on a slide and add a drop of stain. Leave for a few minutes and wash excess off with alcohol.

Wash the insects in water and put them on a cavity slide. Arrange legs and wings neatly.

Carefully lower a cover-slip into place over the insect, taking great care not to trap any air bubbles. Wipe away any excess gum with a moist cloth and leave the slide to dry. It takes several days to harden properly.

A typical binocular microscope being used to examine a complete insect. Details of the wing veins and other features can be clearly seen with this kind of microscope. The binocular microscope on the stand below is much more versatile, for you can move it around to any angle, and you can even put a large lump of rock underneath it.

A photomicrograph of a wasp's sting, showing the relatively small barbs.

Biting lice clinging to a feather photographed through a microscope.

The bee's sting has much larger barbs, and this is why the bee cannot pull her sting out of our skins.

Part of a bee's wings, showing the microscopic hooks which hold the two wings together. Many fascinating features like this are revealed by the microscope.

WILDLIFE PHOTO-GRAPHY

How to take good photographs of flowers, insects, birds, and other wildlife subjects

Some very fine wildlife photographs have been taken with the simplest box camera, but a box camera does have its limitations. It can perform well only if the light is good and the subject is fairly close and fairly large. For successful wildlife photography, you must have a camera which will perform under a wide variety of conditions, one which can cope with close-up work as well as distant subjects, and which can capture a fast-moving subject as easily as a sedate daisy growing on the grass. A single-lens reflex camera with a detachable lens is the choice of most photographers, for it fulfils all the above requirements. The reflex system, involving a mirror and reflecting prisms, allows you to see *exactly* what the lens sees, right up to the instant you press the button, while the detachable lens allows you to add extension tubes for close-up work or to replace it with a telephoto lens for distant shots.

The range of cameras is immense, and so is the range of prices, and you must be guided largely by the depth of your pocket. A camera with through-the-lens (TTL) metering is very useful because it will give you the correct exposure very easily, no matter what lens or attachment you are using. A separate exposure meter works perfectly well, and has some advantages over the built-in type, but if you are using bellows or extension tubes (see below)

you will have to do a little arithmetic to arrive at the right exposure. Correct exposure is important in all photography, but especially so if you are using colour film.

Single-lens reflex cameras come in two standard sizes – 35 mm and $2\frac{1}{4}$ in square. There is no denying that the larger size produces better-quality enlargements, but the cost of the larger cameras and the films to go in them are also much higher. The amateur will generally go for the 35-mm size.

The standard lens fitted to the 35-mm camera will be adequate for general photography of habitats, clumps of flowers, shrubs, and so on. It is also very good when used in conjunction with extension tubes or bellows for close-up work. The tubes or bellows are inserted between the camera body and the lens, allowing you to focus on very near objects and to produce larger-than-life photographs of very small creatures (see illustrations on right).

The naturalist photographer will, however, soon feel the need for a telephoto lens, which makes it possible to obtain reasonable-sized images of distant animals. The most useful telephoto lenses for general purposes have focal lengths of 135 mm or perhaps 200 mm. These will allow

you to take good pictures of small birds two or three metres away, whereas the standard lens would reveal them as not much more than small blobs on the negative. Telephoto lenses are also useful for photographing insects that you cannot approach too closely – dragonflies, for example. The technique is to use the telephoto lens in conjunction with an extension tube, thus allowing you to get nearer than you could with the telephoto lens alone.

Lighting is extremely important. Natural lighting is obviously the best, but there are many situations in which some form of artificial lighting is needed. The most useful form of lighting is undoubtedly the electronic flash, which has a short duration and which can therefore 'freeze' all but the fastest movements.

Do not use the flash-gun mounted directly on to the camera for close-up work. This will not adequately light up a very close subject, and it may throw unpleasant shadows on to the background. Use the flash on an extension lead, so that you can position it at the right angle (see illustrations on right).

Real wildlife photography is always done in the field, but it is accepted practice to bring insects and some other small animals indoors and to photograph them under

controlled conditions. The wind problem is avoided by doing this, and if you provide some natural-looking backgrounds your photographs will obviously reflect this, but don't try to pass them off as photographs taken in the wild.

Always release the animals again in their natural habitat as soon as possible.

Do not pick wild flowers for studio photography unless they are very common; use a wind-shield to keep the wind off while you photograph them in the wild. A plain green or blue background paper placed just behind the flowers may help to show them up better.

For close-up photography of plants and insects in the wild, camera and flash are best mounted on a single bracket which allows you to angle the flash in the right direction. Set the required distance on your camera, and slowly move in until everything is in focus. Two simple studio set-ups are shown on the right.

The Photographer's Code of Conduct

Naturalists and photographers have combined to produce a list of very sensible rules for the wildlife photographer. The first rule, which beautifully sums up the whole code, is that the welfare of the subject is always more important than the photograph. You should make yourself familiar with the natural history and behaviour of wild animals before attempting to photograph them. Pay careful attention to the laws relating to wild plants and animals; remember to obtain permission before you photograph rare birds, also that it is an offence to disturb almost any wild bird at its nest. Do not do anything which would draw the attention of predators (including humans!) to the subject of your photograph. Distinct tracks and trampled areas of grass readily give away the position of rare plants or nesting birds. Do the minimum of 'gardening' around a plant: you can gently bend back intrusive grasses, but do not pull them up. Always restore the habitat to its natural condition after taking your photograph, and do not disclose the sites of rarities to all and sundry. Remember to ask permission before entering private land for the purpose of taking photographs.

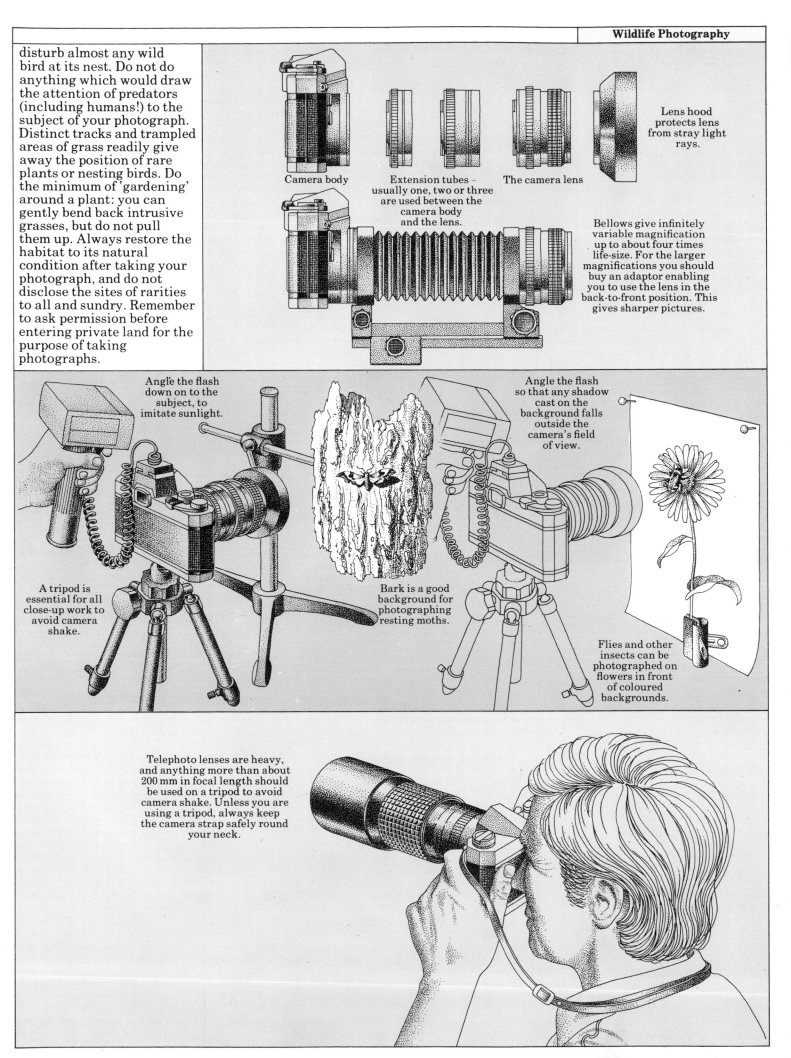

Camera body

Extension tubes – usually one, two or three are used between the camera body and the lens.

The camera lens

Lens hood protects lens from stray light rays.

Bellows give infinitely variable magnification up to about four times life-size. For the larger magnifications you should buy an adaptor enabling you to use the lens in the back-to-front position. This gives sharper pictures.

Angle the flash down on to the subject, to imitate sunlight.

Angle the flash so that any shadow cast on the background falls outside the camera's field of view.

A tripod is essential for all close-up work to avoid camera shake.

Bark is a good background for photographing resting moths.

Flies and other insects can be photographed on flowers in front of coloured backgrounds.

Telephoto lenses are heavy, and anything more than about 200 mm in focal length should be used on a tripod to avoid camera shake. Unless you are using a tripod, always keep the camera strap safely round your neck.

A telephoto lens and very accurate focusing
were necessary to get this shot of a female gannet
and her chick on a rocky cliff. A wide aperture
has thrown the background out of focus,
making the birds very clear.

These mute swans standing in a line going away from the camera called for the smallest possible aperture in order to get them all in focus. Strong
natural lighting helped here by allowing a very short exposure, thus 'freezing' the birds' movements.

A very short exposure was necessary to capture this picture of a swan taking off from the water, but even so the fast-moving wing-tips are blurred.

This beautiful picture of beech trees in the autumn illustrates the artistic side of photography – the importance of composing the picture and choosing the right viewpoint. When you get great contrast of light and shade, you will always have to compromise with your exposures: some parts will be 'washed out' and others too dark, but the overall effect is very pleasing.

173

A wide aperture was used to throw the background snowdrops out of focus and make the foreground ones stand out more clearly. A smaller aperture, bringing more flowers into focus, would have produced a rather muddled picture.

Study the behaviour of your subject before photographing it. Try to find out whether the animal follows a regular pathway through its habitat. If so, select the best possible viewpoint with the best background, as was done for this fine photograph of a fallow deer.

Making 'Photographs' Without a Camera

If you have access to a photographic enlarger you can make some very beautiful 'photographs' without using a camera at all. Instead of using a photographic negative in the enlarger, you put some delicate biological material between two pieces of thin and very clean glass and use that as your negative. Small feathers, insect wings with clear veins, feathery seeds and fruits, and microscopic sections of plant stems (see page 168) can all be used. First making sure that the red filter is in place on the enlarger, put some photographic paper on the baseboard and focus the image on to it. Remove the red filter, expose the paper for the right amount of time (trial and error will tell you this), and develop it in the normal way to produce attractive white-on-black pictures. You can make prints of larger objects, such as grasses (*see below*), by simply laying them on the photographic paper.

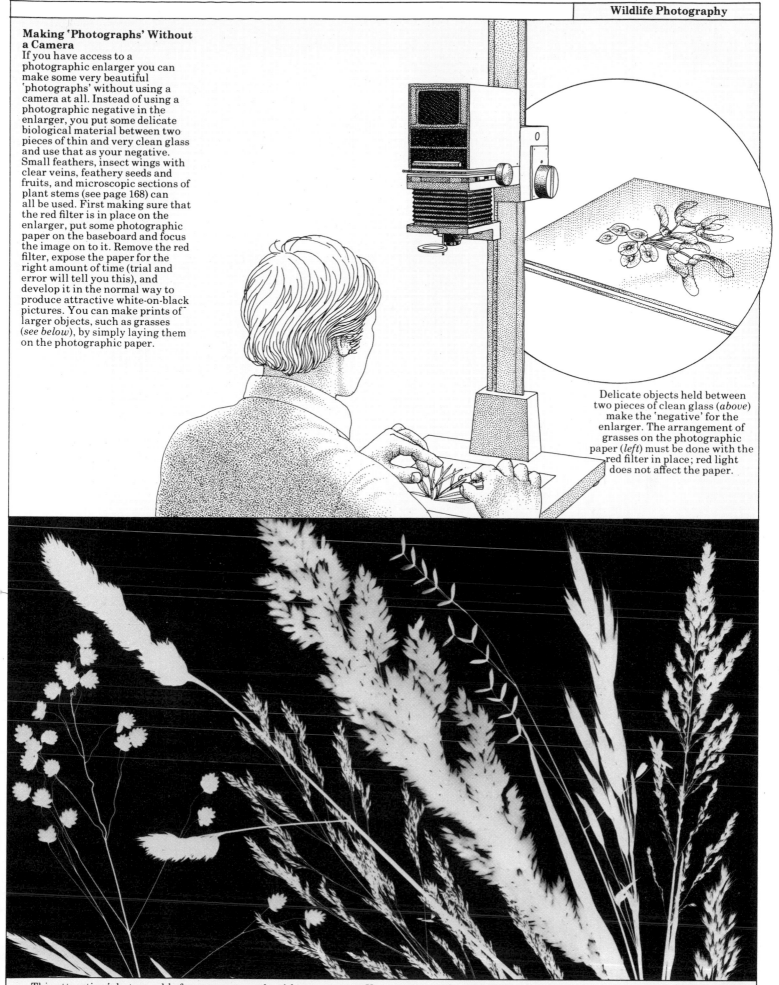

Delicate objects held between two pieces of clean glass (*above*) make the 'negative' for the enlarger. The arrangement of grasses on the photographic paper (*left*) must be done with the red filter in place; red light does not affect the paper.

This attractive 'photograph' of grasses was made without a camera. You can even make such pictures without an enlarger. Arrange the grasses on photographic paper in red light – that from the bars of an electric fire will do – and then shine white light on to them for one second. Develop the paper in the normal way: those parts covered by the grasses will come out white.

Artificial Sea Water

To make 10 litres of sea water equivalent, you will need:
300 gm sodium chloride (common salt)
5 gm potassium chloride
32 gm magnesium chloride
6 gm sodium bromide
14 gm calcium sulphate
24 gm magnesium sulphate
1 gm calcium carbonate.
(There are 28 grams in one ounce.) Dissolve all the the above materials in distilled water and make the total volume up to 10 litres (about 17½ pints). Sea water varies in composition from place to place and you may come across other formulae, but the above mixture should keep most marine animals happy in an aquarium.

Berlese's Fluid

This material is also known as gum chloral and it is a very useful gum in which to mount small insects and other animals when making microscope slides. You can buy it ready-made, but generally only in rather large quantities. Make up your own according to the following recipe.

Dissolve 15 grams of gum arabic (powdered) in 20 ml of distilled water. Add 10 ml of glucose syrup then add 150 grams or more of chloral hydrate until the solution will dissolve no more. Add 5 ml glacial acetic acid, and store the fluid in a well-sealed bottle. The mixture is poisonous.

Agar Jellies for growing Fungi and Bacteria

Agar is a gelatine-like material that is obtained from seaweeds. In combination with other materials, it makes an excellent medium on which to grow moulds and other fungi and bacteria. You can buy the agar in pellet form from biological supply companies, and you then dissolve it in water to make up the various media according to their particular recipes. After making up the media, you must sterilize them before use by immersing their containers in boiling water for half an hour. This should kill most of the fungal and bacterial spores present in the mixture. The fungi and bacteria that you want to grow are best grown in little glass dishes called petri dishes or in small conical flasks. One very interesting, perhaps even alarming, experiment is to press your finger tips lightly on to the surface of some potato agar in a petri dish and leave it covered in a warm place for a few days. It is surprising how many bacteria (germs) will grow where you touched the previously sterile agar.

Malt Agar

Dissolve 7·5 grams of agar in water and filter the solution through a filter paper or clean blotting paper in a funnel. Dissolve 10 grams of malt extract in a little hot water and add it to the agar. Make up to 500 ml with water and use it for growing a variety of fungi by merely scattering the spores on to the jelly when it is set.

Potato Agar

Chop up 500 gm (about 1 pound) of clean potatoes and boil them in water for about half an hour. Strain the liquid into another container and make it up to one litre with distilled water. Add 15 gm agar and boil the mixture thoroughly. This jelly is good for both bacteria and fungi.

Dung Agar

Soak about 1 kilogram of dung (just under 2 pounds, but the quantities are not critical) in cold water for a few days. Strain off the liquid and add distilled water to it until it becomes pale yellow in colour. Add 25 grams of agar to each litre of liquid and boil well. Use it for growing fungi.

USEFUL FORMULAE

Recipes for materials that the naturalist is likely to need

CHAPTER 10

INFORMATION GUIDE

Edited by Barbara Neill,
Senior Instructor,
The Alexander M. White Center
American
Museum of Natural History,
New York

THE LIVING LANDSCAPE

A traveller's view of farm crops, trees and animals

In a land as varied and as vast as the United States it is necessary to generalize about what can be seen and so only the highlights of the innumerable kinds of trees, farm crops and animals will be described and identified.

From the super-highways that run in long, straight lines bypassing the towns and through the countryside, most travellers in the East observe little more than a blur of trees, in the Central states grain fields and in the Southwest stretches of desert. You must exit from these speedways and take older roads linking towns and farms to get a more detailed view of the countryside.

The entire Northeast was once heavily forested and even now woods are most commonly seen just beyond the grassy borders of the main highways. The trees, usually second growth, may be the edge of an extended woodland, or they may be a narrow strip hiding farms, towns or stumps of cut-over forest. Pines, spruces, hemlocks and birches are prominent here along with various oaks and maples. Maples give the region its brightest colours in the fall when their leaves turn shades of red and yellow.

In summer woodchucks are often seen eating grass alongside the highway, and occasionally a cottontail rabbit is seen; crows are the roadside scavengers; white-tailed deer are sometimes glimpsed in the woods and at night skunks, raccoons and opossums cross the road.

There are few really large farms here with the exception of those in the potato-growing area in Aroostook County, Maine. And there are good-sized dairy farms and apple orchards in New York and Pennsylvania. A great variety of crops is grown throughout the Northeast. From the secondary roads in southern New Jersey you can see truck farms with their tomatoes, lettuce, asparagus, strawberries, sweet corn and other market crops. In Lancaster, Pennsylvania, home of the 'Pennsylvania Dutch' and one of the few places where farm horses are still used, crops of corn, winter wheat, potatoes, tobacco and hay are raised. Both dairy and beef cattle will be seen here and elsewhere in the Northeast. Isolated, unusual crops may be found, for example the cranberries on Cape Cod, which are harvested from flooded fields; and the Sumatra tobacco for cigar wrappers grown in the Connecticut valley under cheesecloth.

Travelling southward, you will see a great deal of cigarette tobacco, this being one of the main crops in the Southern states. North Carolina is the largest producer. Cotton is seen throughout the Deep South, especially in Mississippi, though more cotton is grown now in Texas than any other state. Peanuts and peaches are big crops in Georgia. Large horse farms can be seen in Kentucky. Rice is grown on low, flat lands in Arkansas, Louisiana and Texas. Flax is also raised in the Gulf states. Besides these main crops there are countless others, for example, pecans, sweet potatoes, corn, wheat, soybeans, and sorghum. Cattle, sheep, goats and pigs will be seen.

Down in Florida huge groves of citrus fruits are seen, also many acres of truck farms. Beef cattle are raised, Brahmans being one of the unusual but well-established breeds there.

The phrase 'Southern pines' is apt since, especially in North Carolina, Georgia and Alabama, there are extensive pine forests. Longleaf pine with needles up to 46 cm (18 in) long is most distinctive; it is a source of turpentine as well as lumber. Live oaks are prominent and picturesque when festooned with Spanish moss. Bald cypress favours low, boggy places; native palmettos are seen from the Carolinas southward.

Animals native to the Northeast are also seen here, but turkey vultures, scarce in the North, are the most abundant scavengers in the South where they are usually called buzzards. More snakes and turtles are seen beside the road than in the North. In the Deep South armadillos are seen.

Travelling across Texas you are well and truly among the famed 'widely open spaces'. A great deal of this land is now irrigated. Fruits and vegetables, as well as cotton, are big crops in Texas.

Grain, hay and cattle are seen on large ranches, the average size of which is over 600 acres. In the sparsely populated western part of the state and in the neighbouring Southwestern states sheep and goats are raised, often in the same flock; the goats are apt to be Angora, which provide mohair.

Despite the dryness of the Southwest, beef cattle are seen everywhere, even in Nevada which has the least rainfall of any state. Ranches are large since grazing is sparse. But in some places irrigation makes possible such wonders as lush green fields of alfalfa where the surrounding land grows only sagebrush.

The land in the West is rugged, young-looking; mountains rise abruptly from great stretches of empty, flat land; rivers cut deep, rocky arroyos, dry much of the year. This contrasts sharply with the smooth, forested hills and valleys of the East. The lack of woods in the West gives a long, unobstructed view. One can see mule deer half a mile away. Coyotes and gophers are seen on the plains. In some areas pronghorns can be seen. Desert dwellers include lizards, badgers and roadrunners. Besides the many kinds of cactus in the desert there are joshua trees, juniper and mesquite to be seen the year around. Early in the year after the winter rains, the desert is said to 'bloom' when millions of blossoms burst forth on plants only an inch or two high.

Southern California continues the desert landscape. One of the unusual crops here are the dates from the groves of date palms planted long ago around Indio. In the central valleys between the mountains of the Coastal Range and the Sierra Nevadas there are miles of truck farms raising everything from melons to celery. Cotton is raised here too.

Northern California is the land of big trees; both the coastal redwood and the giant sequoia are native here and parks have been set aside for them. Farther up into the Northwestern states of Washington, Oregon and Idaho there are large forested areas. Ponderosa pine, lodgepole pine, and western hemlock are abundant, with Douglas fir probably the best known

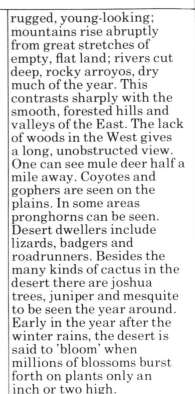

In the Willamette Valley, Oregon, which is well over 100 miles long, an equable climate and good soil have helped produce a great variety of fruit such as cherries, strawberries, raspberries, loganberries, apples, plums and blackberries. Other crops are filberts, hops, potatoes, cabbage and hay. Dairying is important also. Among the interesting sights in the Puget Sound area of Washington are the large fields of daffodils and other flowering bulbs grown for the nursery and greenhouse trade. Washington has huge apple orchards and produces many other fruits.

Idaho is rightly famous for its potatoes but it also grows great numbers of sugar beets. Wyoming is a big cattle-producing state, but sheep are also seen on the huge grassy plains in the east and in Colorado. In Montana and in North and South Dakota, where winters are severe, varieties of spring wheat are planted.

Kansas is the largest wheat-growing state. Here you can see literally miles of nothing but wheat. This will be winter wheat, planted in the fall. Much sorghum is raised in Kansas as well as Oklahoma. In Iowa, Illinois and Indiana hundreds of acres of corn may be seen on one spread. Soybeans are a big crop in Illinois and in other parts of the Midwest. They not only provide animal food but oil which is used in linoleum, paint, soap, etc. Many other crops are seen: oats, barley, rye, buck-wheat, and alfalfa, and animals such as beef cattle, hogs, turkeys in Minnesota, and dairy cows in Wisconsin, and everywhere there is corn, by far the most abundant crop in the United States. Not surprisingly, Iowa, the leader in corn growing, is also the leading hog producer. Corn is not only fed to livestock; it is used to make oil, syrup, starch, whiskey and other products. Small patches of shorter-growing corn close to a house are sure to be sweet corn, a separate variety yielding corn-on-the-cob and other delicacies.

THE COUNTRY CODE

Some important dos and don'ts for visitors to the countryside

The countryside is a very important safety valve for many people, particularly those living in the cities, for it enables them to get away from the hustle and bustle of modern life and to enjoy peace and quiet and the beauty of plants and animals.

The countryside is no less important to country-dwellers, for they enjoy the peace and beauty just as much as the visitor from the city, and many of them owe their livelihoods to the countryside. Look around you in the country and see how much of the land is under some form of cultivation. The farmlands are of vital importance to city-dwellers, as well as to the farmers, and it is important to remember that much of our timber and water supplies come from the countryside.

When visiting the countryside, remember that it has these important roles to play, and respect it so that it can continue to play them. People nowadays are more conscious of environmental problems, and naturalists of many lands have drawn up codes of conduct to be followed by all visitors to the countryside (a Code to Protect Wildlife appears on page 13). Mostly the rules of such codes are based on common sense, but the following general points are worth stressing:

1 **Leave No Litter**
2 **Guard Against Fire**
3 **Fasten All Gates**
4 **Keep to Paths on Farmland**
5 **Keep Dogs Under Proper Control**
6 **Avoid Damaging Fences, Hedges and Walls**
7 **Safeguard Water Supplies**
8 **Drive Carefully on Country Roads**
9 **Protect Wildlife**
10 **Respect the Life of the Countryside.**

Leave No Litter
Litter is unsightly for those who follow you and it can kill farm animals if they eat it. Pick up your rubbish and leave the countryside as you found it.

Guard Against Fire
A carelessly dropped match or cigarette butt can destroy huge tracts of land within minutes, yet it would take decades for the wildlife to recolonize the area.

Protect Wildlife
Do not pick large bunches of wild flowers or break branches from the trees. Do not uproot plants other than on your own land or with the owner's permission. Never interfere with any bird's nest.

LOOKING AT FARM ANIMALS

Pictures to help you identify some of the many breeds of livestock you may see while travelling through the countryside

lthough there are thousands of registered pure-bred farm animals in the United States, most of the livestock you will see will be of mixed breeding. However, many can be recognized as being of predominantly one or two breeds.

The three major breeds of beef cattle, Hereford, Angus and Shorthorn, are easy to identify. And the Brahman and Charolais are unmistakeable. Beef cattle may be seen grazing on big ranches in the West; they may be kept in small feed lots to be fattened, and in the East you may see them in rich, grassy pastures like dairy cows.

There are a great many different breeds of hogs, the Hampshire and Duroc breeds being the most popular. By cross-breeding older breeds, new breeds have become established which are less easy to recognize. Generally, hogs are from the Midwestern states.

Except in a few Western states, large herds of sheep are not common. In the East farmers may raise a few sheep for their meat. Sheep in the West are raised primarily for their wool, although lambs are often sent to market.

Horses are raised nearly everywhere but some of the finest horse farms will be seen in Kentucky, the traditional home of the Thoroughbred and Saddlebred. Ranch horses are much in evidence in the West and Southwest; these are mostly Quarter horses.

Quarter Horse
Named for its great speed over a quarter of a mile, this breed is the most numerous in the United States. Typically a rather short, heavily-muscled but refined-looking horse. Large Quarter horses with Thoroughbred blood may be trained as hunters.

Thoroughbred
Originally developed in England by crossing Arabian stallions with European mares. Most Thoroughbreds are bred for the race track but many become hunters and jumpers. They are tall horses with great refinement, usually dark brown or chestnut, occasionally grey.

Standardbred
Much like Thoroughbreds but in general smaller and longer-bodied. These are the racing trotters and pacers driven in sulkeys at the harness tracks. Ex-racers are popular as driving horses with the Amish in Pennsylvania since their religion forbids cars.

Morgan
A medium-sized, pretty, rather chunky horse with a heavy mane and tail. Nearly always a shade of brown with little or no white. Seen mostly in the East.

Arab
These handsome riding horses, raised originally in and around Arabia and noted for their intelligence, grace and speed, carry themselves proudly. They have attractive wedge-shaped heads and high-set tails. Especially popular in California. May be chestnut, bay or grey.

American Paint Horse or Paint
This breed is identical to the Quarter horse but is spotted. Strong and sturdy, they are popular as riding horses, especially in Texas.

Appaloosa
A medium-sized, general-purpose riding horse developed in the West, with startling colour patterns. Appaloosas may be solid-coloured except for a white 'blanket' over the hips which may contain dark spots, or the horse may be white but splashed with round or raindrop-shaped spots.

American Saddle Horse or Saddler
These are primarily show horses. They are tall, impressive, upstanding horses, very smooth-bodied. Usually solid-coloured with a white trim. Seen especially in the South and Midwest.

Hampshire
Black with a white belt over the shoulders and down the front legs. A little smaller and shorter-legged than most breeds but very active; Hampshires do well on pasture.

Yorkshire
Large white hogs with erect ears. Very long-bodied. Once considered the best bacon type, it is now equalled by other breeds.

Chester White
White hog with drooping ears, nearly equal in size to the Yorkshire. The sows produce large litters which gain weight rapidly.

Duroc
Red-brown in colour, Durocs may be very light or quite dark. They are large hogs and except in colour are very similar to the Poland China.

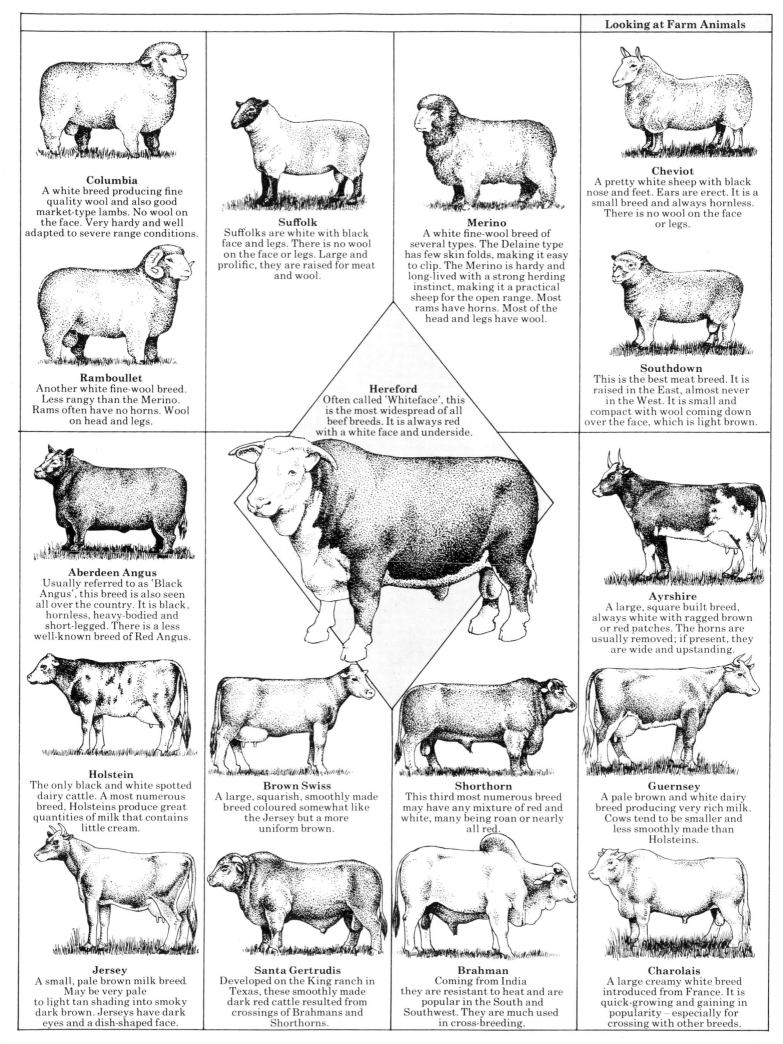

Columbia
A white breed producing fine quality wool and also good market-type lambs. No wool on the face. Very hardy and well adapted to severe range conditions.

Ramboullet
Another white fine-wool breed. Less rangy than the Merino. Rams often have no horns. Wool on head and legs.

Suffolk
Suffolks are white with black face and legs. There is no wool on the face or legs. Large and prolific, they are raised for meat and wool.

Merino
A white fine-wool breed of several types. The Delaine type has few skin folds, making it easy to clip. The Merino is hardy and long-lived with a strong herding instinct, making it a practical sheep for the open range. Most rams have horns. Most of the head and legs have wool.

Cheviot
A pretty white sheep with black nose and feet. Ears are erect. It is a small breed and always hornless. There is no wool on the face or legs.

Southdown
This is the best meat breed. It is raised in the East, almost never in the West. It is small and compact with wool coming down over the face, which is light brown.

Hereford
Often called 'Whiteface', this is the most widespread of all beef breeds. It is always red with a white face and underside.

Aberdeen Angus
Usually referred to as 'Black Angus', this breed is also seen all over the country. It is black, hornless, heavy-bodied and short-legged. There is a less well-known breed of Red Angus.

Holstein
The only black and white spotted dairy cattle. A most numerous breed, Holsteins produce great quantities of milk that contains little cream.

Jersey
A small, pale brown milk breed. May be very pale to light tan shading into smoky dark brown. Jerseys have dark eyes and a dish-shaped face.

Brown Swiss
A large, squarish, smoothly made breed coloured somewhat like the Jersey but a more uniform brown.

Santa Gertrudis
Developed on the King ranch in Texas, these smoothly made dark red cattle resulted from crossings of Brahmans and Shorthorns.

Shorthorn
This third most numerous breed may have any mixture of red and white, many being roan or nearly all red.

Brahman
Coming from India they are resistant to heat and are popular in the South and Southwest. They are much used in cross-breeding.

Ayrshire
A large, square built breed, always white with ragged brown or red patches. The horns are usually removed; if present, they are wide and upstanding.

Guernsey
A pale brown and white dairy breed producing very rich milk. Cows tend to be smaller and less smoothly made than Holsteins.

Charolais
A large creamy white breed introduced from France. It is quick-growing and gaining in popularity – especially for crossing with other breeds.

LOOKING AT FARM CROPS

Pictures to help you identify the crops you see growing in the fields

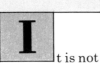t is not always easy to identify the crops in their early stages – grains, for example, all look just like grass when they are young – but the ripe crops are usually easy to recognize, even from a distance, because the fields take on very characteristic colours and appearances. Some of the more common field crops are shown on these pages.

You will often see fields containing nothing but waving grass and perhaps some clover in early summer. These are, of course, the hay fields ready to be cut. The grass is usually cut in June, and it may be dried to make the traditional hay or it may be taken straight off to be made into silage. A field full of clover or alfalfa may also be cut for hay.

Cotton
Cotton is an upstanding, shrubby plant, 1–1½ m (3–5 ft) tall. When mature, the fluffy white cotton balls are much in evidence. Sometimes, before machine harvesting, all the leaves are removed chemically. Young plants produce pinkish blossoms.

Flax
Flax in blossom is a pretty sight; flowers are blue or white and about 12 mm (½ in) across. The plant is slender-stemmed with narrow leaves. Flax is grown for the seeds which provide linseed oil, and linseed meal which is fed to livestock.

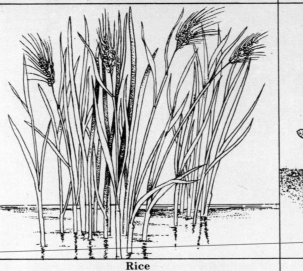

Rice
Rice most closely resembles oats but the seed head is smaller and tighter, Although there are upland varieties of rice which do not need flooded land, rice typically starts its growth under water. All processes of rice-growing are mechanized.

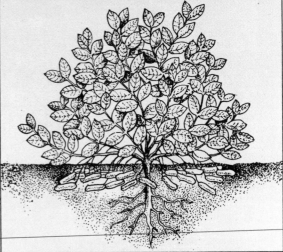

Peanuts
Peanuts are legumes growing 30–60 cm (1–2 ft) high; the plant tends to sprawl and spread. Peanuts develop their pods underground and are dug by machine. Two main types are the large Virginia peanut and the smaller, red-skinned Spanish peanut.

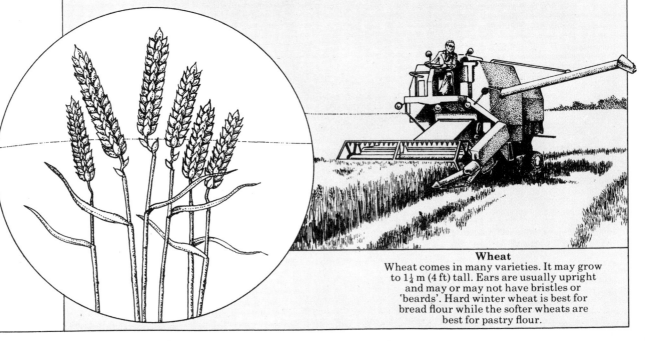

Wheat
Wheat comes in many varieties. It may grow to 1¼ m (4 ft) tall. Ears are usually upright and may or may not have bristles or 'beards'. Hard winter wheat is best for bread flour while the softer wheats are best for pastry flour.

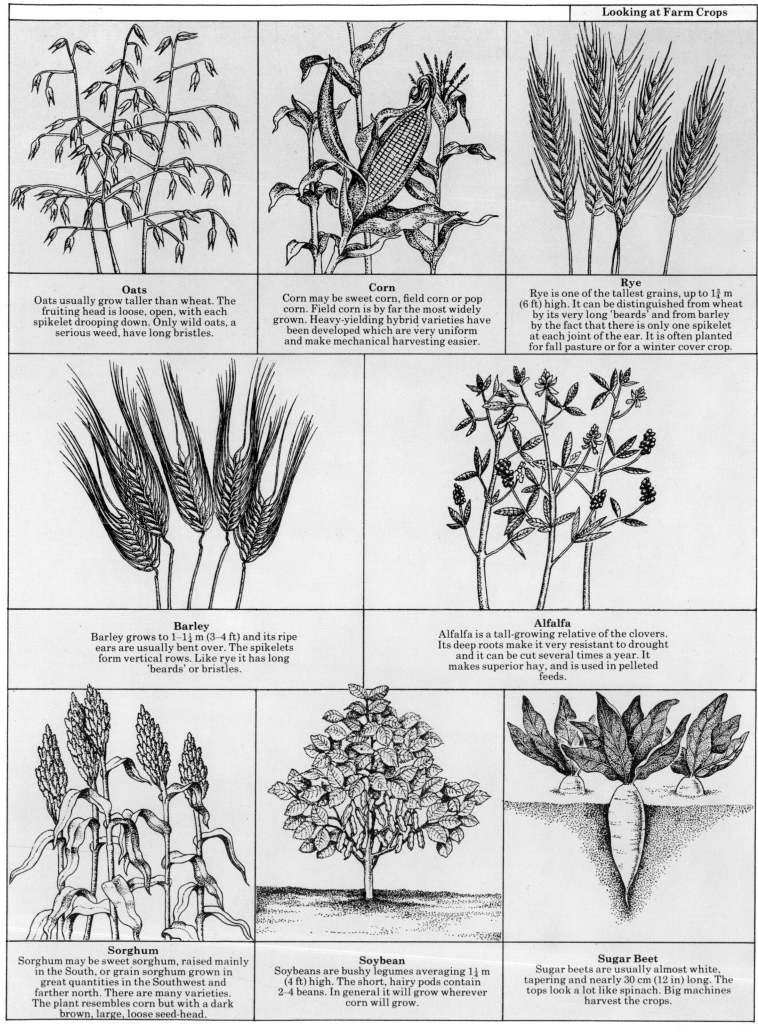

Oats
Oats usually grow taller than wheat. The fruiting head is loose, open, with each spikelet drooping down. Only wild oats, a serious weed, have long bristles.

Corn
Corn may be sweet corn, field corn or pop corn. Field corn is by far the most widely grown. Heavy-yielding hybrid varieties have been developed which are very uniform and make mechanical harvesting easier.

Rye
Rye is one of the tallest grains, up to 1¾ m (6 ft) high. It can be distinguished from wheat by its very long 'beards' and from barley by the fact that there is only one spikelet at each joint of the ear. It is often planted for fall pasture or for a winter cover crop.

Barley
Barley grows to 1–1¼ m (3–4 ft) and its ripe ears are usually bent over. The spikelets form vertical rows. Like rye it has long 'beards' or bristles.

Alfalfa
Alfalfa is a tall-growing relative of the clovers. Its deep roots make it very resistant to drought and it can be cut several times a year. It makes superior hay, and is used in pelleted feeds.

Sorghum
Sorghum may be sweet sorghum, raised mainly in the South, or grain sorghum grown in great quantities in the Southwest and farther north. There are many varieties. The plant resembles corn but with a dark brown, large, loose seed-head.

Soybean
Soybeans are bushy legumes averaging 1¼ m (4 ft) high. The short, hairy pods contain 2–4 beans. In general it will grow wherever corn will grow.

Sugar Beet
Sugar beets are usually almost white, tapering and nearly 30 cm (12 in) long. The tops look a lot like spinach. Big machines harvest the crops.

COUNTRY MENUS

Enjoyable food and drink that you can collect from the woods and fields

Everyone who knows the countryside will be able to recognize the common blackberry and the wild strawberry as delicious and nourishing fodder for hungry stomachs on a country walk. A few more adventurous people will diligently search for edible fungi such as the common mushroom and the delicious chanterelle. But these are only a very small proportion of the many edible and very nutritious plants that you can gather freely in the countryside. From among the flowering plants, you can gather fruits, leaves and stems to eat raw or cooked. The flowers of some plants can also be used for making tasty drinks, but go sparingly on this, for over-picking can cause damage to the flora. Many seaweeds are also edible when collected in a fresh condition; be careful to wash types such as oarweed thoroughly to get rid of the salt and sand.

Among the non-flowering plants, the fungi are bountiful producers of food in the autumn, but beware of the poisonous species (see page 186). Never collect any unless you are absolutely sure that they are edible. Five good species are shown on this page. There are so many species of mushrooms and so many 'look-alikes' between poisonous and non-poisonous species that it takes much studying to become an expert. At first make yourself thoroughly familiar with just one or two of the common types.

Many nuts and berries are good to eat, but never put any plants in your mouth unless you are absolutely sure that they are harmless. Some of the more brightly coloured berries are very dangerous (see page 186).

Prickly Pear

There are both Eastern and Western species of this cactus. The fruits are somewhat pear-shaped, 2·5–5 cm (1–2 in) long, and a rosy red colour. The pulp is juicy and thirst-quenching. The only problem is removing the short bristles on the skin. This is best done by rubbing the fruit against a rough cloth. It is said that in earlier days prickly pear saved the lives of many thirsty desert travellers.

Shaggy Mane Mushroom

This grows at the edges of woods and in fields in summer and autumn. Gather the fungi while they are still in the elongated egg stage (right-hand specimen), scrape the caps gently, remove the stems, and fry the sliced-up caps with bacon and egg. Cook them until they start to brown, otherwise they are rather watery and tasteless. The shaggy mane is also good in stews, but you must cook it soon after picking, otherwise the gills become black and inky.

Boletus Edulis

Found worldwide, this is a highly prized species in Europe. It has a smooth brown cap much like a toasted bun, and pale yellowish round pores, rather than gills, underneath it. A similar species, one to be avoided, has red pores and yellow flesh which turns blue when cut; this one, *Boletus luridus*, is poisonous, and is illustrated on page 186.

Chanterelle

One of the most sought-after fungi, the chanterelle is found in woodlands, especially beech woods, in summer and autumn, and it is easy to recognize by its deep yellow colour and slight smell of apricots. Stew chanterelles in milk and add them to omelettes, or else fry them in the normal way. The false chanterelle, which is edible but not exciting, has a much more orange cap and no apricot smell.

Chickweed
This can be gathered in armfuls from
neglected gardens and from the edges of
fields. Cook it with a little butter and
chopped onion for a tasty dish of greens.

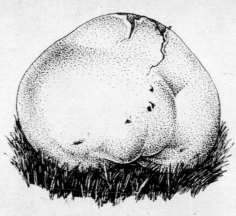

Puffballs
These fungi are round and stemless, or
nearly stemless. The giant puffball is huge,
and often weighs several pounds. They
should be eaten while the flesh is firm and
white. As puffballs age, the interior becomes
yellow, then brown. One of the puffballs
(*Scleroderma*) is not edible; its flesh is
greenish-yellow even when young.

Meadow Mushroom
The common meadow mushroom grows
in fields in late summer and autumn. The
gills are pink at first, and then become brown.

Nettle
Stinging nettle leaves have many uses.
Washed well and cooked in a little butter,
they make a pleasant dish of vegetables.
You can also make soup with them. Use only
the young shoots and leaves.

Common Milkweed
Young shoots of this plant can be eaten
early in the spring. It should be boiled in
several waters to remove all trace of the
bitter milky juice. Young seedpods can
be cooked the same way in the autumn.

Dandelion
Dandelion leaves can be used in sandwiches
and in salads, where their slightly bitter
taste is much appreciated. Select the
youngest leaves for eating raw, but you can
cook older leaves like spinach. The flowers
make a pleasant wine, while the root can
be dried and ground up to make a type of
coffee.

Staghorn Sumac
This shrub or small tree has long leaves with
11–29 leaflets. The leaflets have pointed tips
and saw-toothed edges. The fruit is an
upright, fuzzy-looking red cluster of small
berries, each covered with red hairs.
When the berries are soaked in water the
resulting drink makes a good substitute
for lemonade.

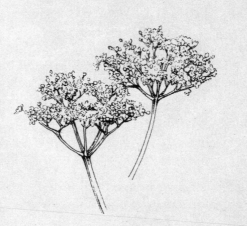

Elderberry
Elderberry wine is a well-known drink, but
you can also make a delicious drink from
the flowers. Put about half a dozen
freshly gathered flower heads in a large
stone jar with 4½ litres (1 gallon) of water
and about 500 gm (1¼ lb) of sugar. Add two
tablespoonfuls of white wine vinegar.
Stir well to dissolve the sugar, cover and
leave for a day or two. Strain off the liquid
and bottle it. Drink it any time after two
weeks. It tastes far better than it smells.

Burdock
Burdock, which is best known for its strongly
hooked seed-heads or burrs, is a large bushy
plant of waste ground and roadsides. Its
huge leaves are rather like those of rhubarb,
except that they are furry. The young leaf
stalks can be used in salads in the summer.
Cut them into short lengths and strip off
the skins to leave yourself with the crisp
core. Its pleasant taste is also a welcome
addition to soups and stews.

FORBIDDEN FRUIT

A brief guide to some poisonous plants of the countryside

Many of our woodland and roadside plants produce brightly coloured fruits. These fruits attract birds, which eat the fleshy parts and scatter the seeds. The bright colours and juicy nature of these fruits attract young children too, and it is important that children are taught that many of them are very poisonous. There is no simple guide as to whether a fruit is poisonous or edible, and you certainly cannot rely on the birds to help you: the birds' digestive systems are not the same as our own and they can deal quite happily with fruits that are deadly to us. The safest thing is to learn to recognize all the poisonous plants individually. Alternatively, you can learn to recognize the few really good edible fruits and leave all the rest severely alone.

Berries are the most likely cause of trouble with young children, but they are by no means the only dangers in the countryside. Quite a few of our common flowers, including all the buttercups, contain poisonous substances, and then there are, of course, the fungi. By far the most deadly in this respect is the death-cap, whose pale cap is not too different from that of the common edible mushroom. The most sinister thing about the death-cap is the fact that it does not produce any symptoms until several hours after it has been eaten, by which time it is too late.

About 90 per cent of all deaths caused by fungus eating have been due to eating the death-cap or its close relatives. But it is really very easy to distinguish the death-cap from the edible meadow mushroom: the death-cap has white gills, compared with the pink or brown gills of the meadow mushroom, and it always has a cup at the bottom of the stalk (it might be hidden in the grass or leaves) and a frilly ring just below the cap. The meadow mushroom may have a ring, but it never has a cup. There is no easy way of separating poisonous from non-poisonous species, but the beginner would be well advised to avoid all mushrooms with cups at the base.

The pictures here show only a selection of poisonous plants. Do not assume that a plant is harmless just because it does not appear here. Never put *any* fungus or other plant into your mouth unless you are absolutely sure that it is harmless.

And finally there should be a warning about those plants that are poisonous to touch: poison ivy, poison oak, poison sumac, and the Florida poisontree.

Poison sumac grows in damp or swampy places and is not usually common. It has fewer leaflets than the non-poisonous staghorn sumac. Poison sumac has white berries which droop rather than the upstanding red fruit of other sumacs.

The poisontree with its thin, mottled, red-brown bark grows only in southern Florida. It is a shrub or small tree, and its leaves are composed of 3–5 and sometimes 7 oval, smooth-edged leaflets.

Several types of poison ivy are common in the East and poison oak is common in the West. Either may be a ground-hugging, slender vine, or a low, dense shrub, or a huge, thick vine climbing 10 metres (33 ft) up a tree.

Just remember the old jingle, 'Leaflets three, let it be.' Poison ivy leaflets are usually shiny and smooth-edged (occasionally somewhat jagged) while poison oak usually has notched or lobed edges. Both have white berries.

Boletus Luridus
This poisonous fungus is found in deciduous woods in summer and autumn. It has a greenish-grey cap and pores instead of gills. The pores are blood-red; the flesh is yellow and turns blue when cut. There is a network of red lines on the stem.

Fly Amanita
This plant is found in pine and birch woods in autumn. It can be recognized by its bright red cap, which usually has white patches. Deadly.

Death-cap
The death-cap is found in deciduous woods in summer and autumn. The cap is yellowish-green or almost white, the gills and stalk white. It has a prominent cup and ring. It is deadly. The related destroying angel is pure white with a scaly stalk, and is also deadly.

Poison Ivy
Commonly found in the East. There are low-growing vine types, tall climbers and dense shrubs. Leaflets are usually shiny, and the plant bears white berries.

Oleander

A decorative shrub or small tree commonly grown in the South and West. Sometimes it is seen as a house plant in the East. All parts are poisonous.

Climbing Nightshade

This is a climbing or trailing plant found in fields and waste ground. The flowers are purple, and the berries turn from green to red. Very poisonous.

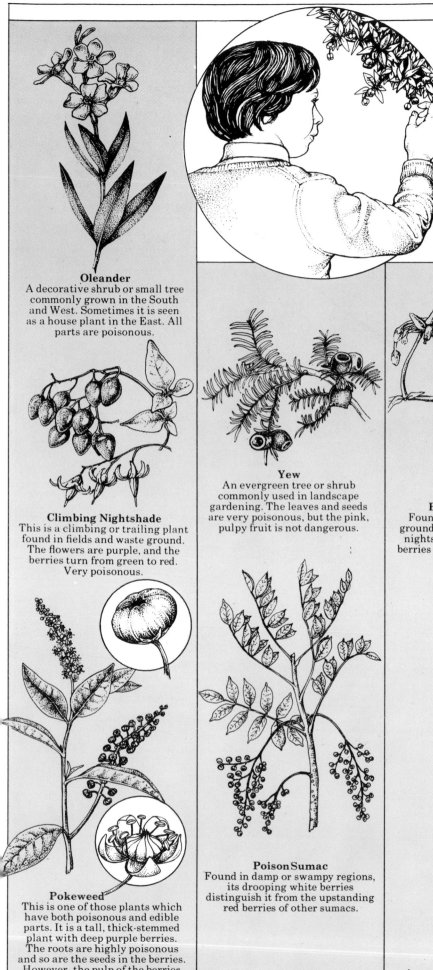

Pokeweed

This is one of those plants which have both poisonous and edible parts. It is a tall, thick-stemmed plant with deep purple berries. The roots are highly poisonous and so are the seeds in the berries. However, the pulp of the berries is edible. In springtime young shoots of the plant are boiled as substitutes for asparagus.

Never eat any wild fruit, fungus, or other plant unless you are completely sure that it is harmless. Seek medical advice immediately for anyone you suspect has eaten a poisonous plant.

Yew

An evergreen tree or shrub commonly used in landscape gardening. The leaves and seeds are very poisonous, but the pink, pulpy fruit is not dangerous.

Poison Sumac

Found in damp or swampy regions, its drooping white berries distinguish it from the upstanding red berries of other sumacs.

Black Nightshade

Found in gardens and waste ground, the flowers of the black nightshade are white, and the berries turn from green to black. Very poisonous.

Foxglove

A common garden flower. The whole plant contains dangerous poisons.

Privet

A shrub commonly used for hedges, with sickly-smelling cream flowers and small black berries. All parts of the plant are poisonous.

Water Hemlock and Poison Hemlock

Both usually grow in damp places. All parts of the plants are poisonous. Poison hemlock can be recognized by the purple blotches on the stem but water hemlock does not always have them. Both resemble parsley but poison hemlock has finer, almost fern-like foliage. The safest thing is to avoid all wild plants which look like parsley.

Jimson-weed or Thornapple

An introduced plant that crops up on farmland and waste ground in the West and especially in the South. The trumpet-shaped white flowers and the strange spiky fruits attract a lot of interest, but all parts of the plant are very poisonous.

187

REFERENCE SECTION

Places to visit organizations and suppliers to write to, and books for further reading

Many large areas in the United States are set aside for national parks or monuments, wildlife refuges, and national forests. These are favourite spots for camping, hiking or other outdoor activities. Many of these areas have spectacular scenery. National monuments are similar to parks but always contain some special feature, either natural or historical, with the landscape. For example, the Dinosaur National Monument in Utah and Colorado contains numerous fossils in its 200,000 acres; in Arizona the Saguaro National Monument preserves the giant Saguaro cactus, and the Devil's Tower in Wyoming features a tremendous rock of volcanic origin that is 266 metres (865 ft) high. There are more than 75 national monuments, but some of the historical monuments contain only a few acres.

There are less than half as many national parks, but all have substantial acreage. Some are famous, among them the Grand Canyon, Yosemite, Mount Rainier, Carlsbad Caverns, and the Everglades. The Yellowstone, established in 1872, was the first national park to be created. They are administered by the National Park Service. Since both parks and monuments were established to preserve everything within their boundaries, nothing, not even stones or leaves, is to be removed. This is an important rule because millions of people visit these places each year.

On national forest land, hunting and fishing is permitted and even logging is allowed in some areas. The US Department of Agriculture administers about 182 million acres of national forest in 39 states. Some national forests contain refuge areas: in the Sespe Wildlife Area of the Los Padres National Forest in California, for example, the condor lives in a protected environment. Each wildlife refuge was set aside for a particular species of plant or animal. In Florida the Corkscrew Swamp Sanctuary preserves ancient cypress trees, some of them more than 40 metres (130 ft) tall. Red Rock Lakes Refuge in Montana saved the trumpeter swan from possible extinction, and Jackson Hole in Wyoming preserves an elk population. Biological research is carried on at some Refuges, and these may not be accessible to the public.

Lists of pamphlets about the parks and other areas may be obtained by writing to the Superintendent of Documents, U.S. Government Printing Office, Washington, D.C. 20402.

List of National Parks
(total areas in acres given in parentheses)
Acadia, founded in 1919, Maine Coast (41,642). Includes the sea-encircled Mount Desert Island, highest point on the Atlantic Coast.
Arches, 1971, Southeastern Utah (73,234). Has the world's largest concentration of stone arches, 88 altogether, and pinnacles and pedestals eroded from the desert sandstone.
Big Bend, 1935, Southwestern Texas (708,221). A vast region of wild mountains and desert.
Bryce Canyon, 1924, Southwestern Utah (36,010). Natural canyons containing many eroded pinnacles of bright colouring.
Canyonlands, 1964, Southeastern Utah (337,258). A series of multi-coloured eroded pinnacles and mesas at the junction of the Colorado and Green Rivers.
Capitol Reef, 1971, South Central Utah (241,671). A 20-mile cliff, 1,000 ft high, with colourful sandstone formations, narrow gorges, and the Waterpocket Fold – of special interest to geologists.
Carlsbad Caverns, 1930, Southeastern New Mexico (46,753). A chain of linking limestone caverns, probably the world's largest.
Crater Lake, 1902, Southwestern Oregon (160,290). A bright blue, clear lake situated in a great crater and surrounded by tall lava cliffs and forests.
Everglades, 1947, Southern Florida (1,400,533). A vast network of waterways set in dense mangrove forest; the subtropical climate has populated the Everglades with interesting plants, animals and marine life.
Glacier, 1910, Northwestern Montana (1,013,129). Part of the Waterton-Glacier International Peace Park, it contains huge precipices, peaks, forests, waterfalls, numerous lakes and 60 small glaciers.
Grand Canyon, 1919, Northwestern Arizona (673,575). A famous and spectacular gorge, one mile deep, formed by the Colorado River.
Grand Teton, 1929, Northwestern Wyoming (310,350). Focal point of the Teton range of mountains, formed by glaciers.
Great Smoky Mountains, 1934, Western North Carolina-Eastern Tennessee (516,626). A large mountain range and hardwood forest; the name derives from the smoke-like mist that rises from the forest.
Guadalupe Mountains, 1966 Texas (82,279). Special features of the mountain range include Guadalupe Peak and McKittrick Canyon.
Haleakala, 1960 Hawaii (27,283). Situated on the island of Maui, this is a volcanic area with one of the world's largest craters.
Hawaii Volcanoes, 1916 Hawaii (220,345). A large volcanic region on the island of Hawaii, including two of the world's most active craters.
Hot Springs, 1921, Central Arkansas (3,535). A forested mountain area containing 47 natural hot springs, water from which is piped to public bathhouses for hydrotherapy treatments.
Isle Royale, 1931, Michigan Coast (539,341). A wild archipelago in Lake Superior that supports a varied and unusual animal and plant population.
Kings Canyon, 1940, Middle Eastern California (460,331). A wilderness region that includes two canyons of Kings River, the high peaks of the Sierra Nevada, and a rich forest of giant sequoia trees.
Lassen Volcanic, 1916, Northern California (106,934). The volcano here was recently active, there are interesting lava formations for the geologist, and hot springs.
Mammoth Cave, 1941, Southwestern Kentucky (51,354). A series of caverns with a river flowing 360 ft below ground level.
Mesa Verde, 1906, Southwestern Colorado (52,074). Best known for its finely preserved prehistoric cliff dwellings.
Mount McKinley, 1917, South Central Alaska (1,939,493). At 20,320 ft the highest mountain in North America, Mount McKinley Park also contains large north-flowing glaciers of the Alaska Range.
Mount Rainier, 1899, West Central Washington (241,781). The mountain is a dormant volcano with many glaciers.
North Cascades, 1968, Northwestern Washington (505,000). Glaciers and lakes occur frequently throughout this mountainous area.
Olympic, 1938, Northwestern Washington (896,599). A large, densely forested region with many mountains and glaciers, and abundant wildlife.
Petrified Forest, 1962, Eastern Arizona (94,189). This Park features petrified conifers, one of which makes a natural bridge, and also includes part of the Painted Desert.
Platt, 1906, South Central Oklahoma (912). A hilly region with wooded valleys, best known for its mineral springs.
Redwood, 1968, Northwestern California (57,094). A forested part of the Pacific coastline containing some of the world's tallest and oldest trees (see page 109).
Rocky Mountain, 1915, North Central Colorado (262,324). This section of the Rocky Mountains includes 107 peaks more than 10,000 ft high.
Sequoia, 1890, Middle Eastern California (386,863). The world's largest tree, the General Sherman, stands in this Park of giant sequoias (see page 109).
Shenandoah, 1935, Northwestern Virginia (193,539). A spectacular part of the Blue Ridge Mountains, with large hardwood forests and a varied population of wild flowers.
Virgin Islands, 1956, US Virgin Islands (15,150). Islands with white sandy beaches and coral gardens, also remains of prehistoric Carib Indian cultures.
Voyageurs, 1971, North Central Minnesota (219,431). Northern lakes and forests; interesting geological structures and fine scenery.
Wind Cave, 1903, Southwestern South Dakota (28,059). Prairie grasslands and limestone caves with calcite crystal formations; home of the bison, elk, and pronghorn.
Yellowstone, Southwestern Wyoming-Southwestern Montana-Eastern Idaho (2,221,773). The first National Park, it features geysers and hot springs, brightly coloured canyons, and a wildlife refuge.
Yosemite, 1890, Middle California (761,320). An especially rich and varied area, with forests, canyons, granite domes, giant sequoia trees, alpine meadows and snowfields.
Zion, 1919, Southwestern Utah (147,035). A series of narrow canyons surrounded by brightly coloured sandstone cliffs.

National Monuments of the United States – a Select List of Larger Monuments of Interest to Naturalists
(total areas in acres given in parentheses)
Badlands, founded in 1939, South Dakota (244,067). A region of irregular ravines, ridges, and cliffs formed by weathering and erosion, containing remains of prehistoric animals.
Biscayne, 1968, Florida (96,300). A living coral reef in the Upper Florida Keys.
Canyon de Chelly, 1931, Arizona (83,840). Canyons with prehistoric cliff dwellings.
Craters of the Moon, 1924, Idaho (53,545). A range of volcanic phenomena, including fissure eruptions, cinder cones, craters, and lava flows.
Death Valley, 1933, California-Nevada (1,907,760). A desert region incorporating the lowest point in the United States, 113 m (282 ft) below sea level.
Dinosaur, 1915, Utah-Colorado (206,234). This monument contains many fossil remains of large prehistoric animals.
Glacier Bay, 1925, Alaska (2,803,840). A wild region best known for its glaciers and rare wildlife.
Grand Canyon, 1932, Arizona (198,280). Part of the Grand Canyon of the Colorado River, affording an unusual view of the inner gorge.
Great Sand Dunes, 1932, Colorado (36,740). A large expanse of the highest-piled sand dunes in the United States.
Joshua Tree, 1936, California (558,184). Rich in desert plants, the region is especially known for its cholla cactus and examples of the rare Joshua tree.
Katmai, 1918, Alaska (2,792,137). A coastal region of bays and lagoons, with glaciers and a dying volcanic area.
Lava Beds, 1925, California (46,239). Numerous lava caves and tunnels.
Organ Pipe Cactus, 1937, Arizona (330,874). Includes many species of desert animals and plants, notably the organ pipe cacti.
Saguaro, 1933, Arizona (78,644). A cactus forest, rich in giant saguaros.
White Sands, 1933, New Mexico (146,535). A region of extraordinary, glistening sands of wind-blown gypsum, and a unique plant and animal life.
Wupatki, 1924, Arizona (35,233). Contains some 800 prehistoric Indian dwellings.

National Wildlife Refuges
There are more than 300 national wildlife refuges and they are supervised by the Bureau of Sport Fisheries and Wildlife in the Department of the Interior. Only a few of the refuges have facilities for camping that are

comparable to the national parks, but about half have resident personnel and there are leaflets available with information about the wildlife to be seen. Sightseeing, bird-watching, swimming and fishing are all enjoyed in the refuges. Even restricted hunting is allowed in certain areas of the largest. Leaflets and bird and mammal lists may be obtained from the regional directors, as follows: Below are a few of the best-known refuges:

Region 1,
Federal Building,
730 N.E. Pacific Street,
Box 3737, Portland,
Oregon 97208.
Region 2,
Federal Office Building,
400 Gold. S.W.,
Box 1306, Albuquerque,
New Mexico 87103.
Region 3,
1006 W. Lake Street,
Minneapolis,
Minnesota 55408.
Region 4,
809 Peachtree, Seventh Building,
Atlanta, Georgia 30323.
Region 5,
U.S. Post Office Building and Courthouse,
Boston, Massachusetts 02109.
Brigantine National Wildlife Refuge, near Atlantic City, N.J. (18,100 acres). Heavily used, especially by bird watchers. Much of the area is saltwater marshes and tidal bays. Waterfowl and shore birds are abundant. Some hunting is permitted.
Bombay Hook NWR, near Dover, Delaware (16,300). Waterfowl are plentiful here and there are observation towers. Picnicking is permitted and there are lunch tables.
Okefenokee NWR, Southeast Georgia, near Florida border (341,000). Guided tours are available for viewing herons, ibises, kites, otters, alligators, and other animals.
J.N. 'Ding' Darling NWR, Lee County, Florida (3,000). Located on the tropical island of Sanibel, a resort area. Roseate spoonbills and other waterfowl are seen here.
Wichita Mountains NWR, Comanche County, Oklahoma (59,000). Contains buffalo, elk, and wild turkey. There are public camping areas.
Santa Ana NWR, south of Alamo, Texas (2,000). Features birds that are hardly seen anywhere else. Mexican species such as chachalacas and green jays make this a favourite with bird watchers. There are photography blinds.
Aransas NWR, Gulf Coast of Texas (47,250). Well known for its whooping cranes. Including marsh, tidal flats and some sandy areas and fresh water. There is limited camping.
Desert NWR, Clark and Lincoln Counties, Nevada (1,500,000). The largest refuge in continental USA, it has mountains, desert, and plains. Bighorn and mule deer are found here. There is a recreation area at Cold Creek.
Charles M. Russell NWR, along the Missouri River, Montana (951,000). Recreation areas are maintained by the US Army Corps of Engineers. Sharp-tailed grouse, pronghorn, bighorn sheep, elk, and waterfowl live here.
Minidoka NWR, near Rupert, Idaho (25,630). It is on a reservoir where whistling swans can be seen. Sage grouse live in the uplands. Fishing, boating and camping are allowed.
Tule Lake NWR, Modoc and Siskiyou Counties, California (37,000). Millions of birds, including Snow Geese, Canada and Ross Geese and species of ducks, come to this sanctuary. There is limited camping.

Organizations Concerned with Natural History
For a complete list of conservation organizations, the National Wildlife Federation has a 'Conservation Directory', which you will find in your local public library.

Friends of the Earth,
529 Commercial St.,
San Francisco,
California 94111

National Audubon Soc., Inc.,
950 Third Avenue,
New York, N.Y. 10022

The Fund for Animals,
140 W. 57th St.,
New York, N.Y. 10019

Defenders of Wildlife,
1244 19th St. N.W.,
Washington D.C. 20036

National Wildlife Federation,
1412 16th St. N.W.,
Washington D.C. 20036

Sierra Club,
1050 Mills Tower,
San Francisco,
California 94104

Izaak Walton League of America,
1800 N. Kent St.,
Suite 806,
Arlington, Virginia 22209

Nature Conservancy,
1800 N. Kent St.,
Suite 800,
Arlington, Virginia 22209

Wilderness Society,
1909 Penn. Avenue N.W.,
Washington D.C. 20006

Biological Supply Companies
For specialist materials that you are unable to obtain through a pet shop, druggist or nursery, write to a biological supply house. The largest are listed below.

Carolina Biological Supply Co.,
2700 York Road,
Burlington, NC 27215

Their Western address is:
PO Box 7,
Gladstone,
Oregon 97027

Ward's Natural Science Establishment Inc.,
PO Box 1712,
Rochester, NY 14603

Their Western address is:
PO Box 1749,
Monterey,
California 93940

Fisher Scientific Co.,
52 Fadem Rd.,
Springfield, NJ 07081

Turtox/Cambosco,
Macmillan Science Co., Inc.,
8200 S. Hoyne Ave.,
Chicago, Ill. 60620

Traps for small mammals (see page 62) exist in several versions, but if you have any difficulty write to the makers of the Longworth trap mentioned in the text.
They are:
Penlon Ltd,
Radley Road,
Abingdon,
Oxfordshire, OX14 3PH
England

Bird Rings
If you find a dead bird with a metal ring on it, remove the ring and, if it bears no other return address, send it, with details of where you found it, to:
US Fish and Wildlife Service,
Washington, DC.
This information helps ornithologists to keep a track of bird movements.

Useful Books

General and Regional Guides
Borland, Hal, *Beyond Your Doorstep: A Handbook to the Country,* New York, Knopf, 1962.
Butcher, Devereaux, *Exploring Our National Parks and Monuments,* New York, Houghton Mifflin, 1969 (6th edition).
Davids, Richard C., *How to Talk to Birds & Other Uncommon Ways of Enjoying Nature the Year Round,* New York, Knopf, 1972.
Dennis, Eve, *Everyman's Nature Reserve: Ideas for Action,* Newton Abbott, David & Charles, 1973.
Frome, Michael, and Freeman, Orville, *National Forests of America,* New York, G. P. Putnam's, 1968.
Gibbons, Euell, *Euell Gibbons' Beachcombers Handbook,* New York, McKay, 1967.
Gross, Phyllis, and Railton, Esther P., *Teaching Science in an Outdoor Environment: Handbook for Students, Parents, Teachers, and Camp Leaders,* University of California Press, 1972.
Leopold, Aldo, *Sand County Almanac: With Other Essays on Conservation from Round River,* New York, Oxford University Press, 1966.
Murphy, Robert, *Wild Sanctuaries,* New York, E. P. Dutton, 1968.
Ormond, Clyde, *Complete Book of Outdoor Lore,* New York, Times Mirror, 1964.
Palmer, El. Laurence, *Fieldbook of Natural History,* New York, McGraw Hill, 1975 (2nd edition).
Teale, Edwin W., *Autumn Across America,* Dodd, 1956.
—*Lost Woods, Adventures of a Naturalist,* Dodd, 1961.
Vosburgh, John, *Living With Your Land,* New York, Scribner, 1972.
White, C. Langdon, and Foscue, Edwin J., *Regional Geography of Anglo-America,* Englewood Cliffs, N.J., Prentice-Hall, 1974 (4th edition).

Aquariums
Atz, James W., *Aquarium Fishes: Their Beauty, History and Care,* New York, Viking Press, 1971.
Axelrod, Herbert R., *Axelrod's Tropical Fish Book,* New York, Arco, 1972.
—*Tropical Fish as a Hobby,* New York, McGraw-Hill, 1969 (revised edition).
Innes, William T., *Exotic Aquarium Fishes,* New York, E. P. Dutton, 19th edition.
Jackman, L. A., *Sea Water Aquaria,* A. S. Barnes, 1975.
Miller, Agnes D., *Sand Designs for Aquariums and Terrariums,* Neptune, N. J., T. F. H. Publications, 1975.

O'Connell, *Aquarium Plants and Decorations,* New York, Scribner.
Payson, Karl, *Guide to Aquarium Fish,* New York, Quadrangle, 1975.
Schiotz, Arne, *A Guide to Aquarium Fishes and Plants,* Philadelphia, Lippincott, 1972.
Straughan, Robert P., *The Salt Water Aquarium in the Home,* A. S. Barnes, 1976 (4th revised edition).

Farm Animals
Bundy, Clarence E., and Higgins, Ronald V., *Livestock and Poultry Production,* Englewood Cliffs, N.J., Prentice-Hall, 1968 (3rd edition).

Photography
Angel, Heather, *Nature Photography: Its Art and Techniques,* New York, Scribner, 1974.
Hosking, Eric, and Gooders, John, *Wildlife Photography: A Field Guide,* New York, Praeger, 1974.
Kinne, Russ, *The Complete Book of Nature Photography,* Garden City, N.Y., Amphoto, 1971 (2nd edition).
Maye, Patricia, ed., *Fieldbook of Nature Photography,* San Francisco, Sierra, 1974.

Plants
Britton, Nathaniel L., and Brown, Addison, *Illustrated Flora of the Northern United States, Canada and the British Possessions,* 3 vols, New York, Dover, 1970.
Gibbons, Euell, *Stalking the Wild Asparagus,* New York, McKay, 1962.
Golden Nature Guides, *Non-Flowering Plants,* also *Trees of North America,* New York, Golden Press.
Golden Regional Guides of America (all titles in series recommended), New York, Golden Press.
Medsger, Oliver Perry, *Edible Wild Plants,* New York, Macmillan Co., 1959.
Muenscher, W.C., *Poisonous Plants of the United States,* New York, Macmillan Co., 1939.
Russell, Helen Ross, *Foraging for Dinner,* New York, Thomas Nelson, 1975.
Rydberg, Per A., *Flora of the Prairies and Plains of Central North America,* New York, Dover, 1971.

Taxidermy
Grantz, Gerald J., *Home Book of Taxidermy and Tanning,* Harrisburg, Pa, Stackpole, 1970.
Labrie, Jean, *The Amateur Taxidermist,* Hart, 1972.

INDEX

Page numbers in italics refer to illustrations

Index

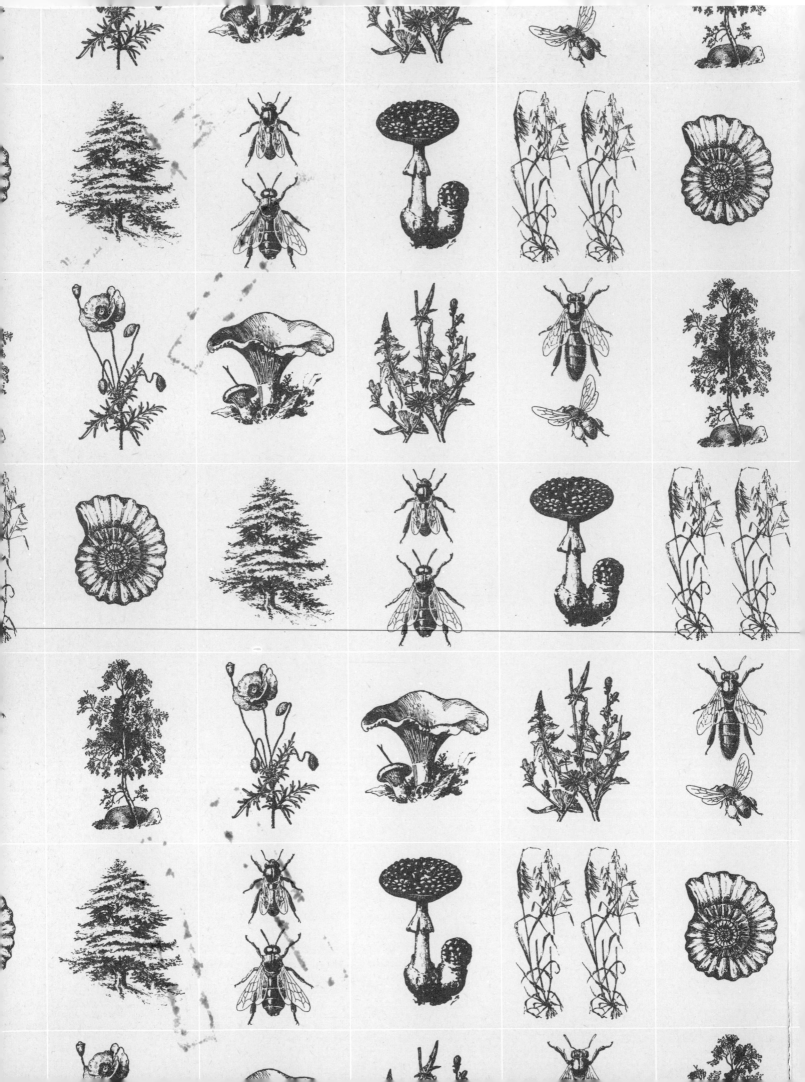